THE ABUSE OF POWER

THE ABUSE OF POWER

THE PERMANENT GOVERNMENT AND THE FALL OF NEW YORK

JACK NEWFIELD
PAUL DU BRUL

PHOTOGRAPHS BY JANIE EISENBERG

THE VIKING PRESS NEW YORK

First published in 1977 by The Viking Press
625 Madison Avenue, New York, N.Y. 10022
Published simultaneously in Canada by
The Macmillan Company of Canada Limited

LIBRARY OF CONGRESS CATALOGING IN PUBLICATION DATA
Newfield, Jack.
   The abuse of power.
   Includes index.
   1. New York (City)—Politics and government—1951–
2. New York (City)—Economic conditions.
3. New York (City)—Social conditions.
I. Du Brul, Paul A., joint author. II.   Title.
JS1230 1977.N48   309.1′747′104   76–30706
ISBN 0–670–10204–0

Printed in the United States of America
Set in Linotype Caledonia

Grateful acknowledgment is made to the following for permission to reprint:

Fortune Magazine: From an article by Wyndham Robertson, August 1975, and from an article by Sanford Rose, December 1975.

David Muchnick: From his article that appeared in the Winter 1976 issue of *Dissent.*

The Village Voice: From an article by Adam Walinsky, March 1, 1973. Copyright © The Village Voice, Inc., 1973. Reprinted by permission.

The Wall Street Journal: From "New York City's Fiscal Ills . . . ," October 21, 1970. © Dow Jones & Company, Inc., 1970. All rights reserved. Reprinted by permission.

FOR JANIE, ANITA, AND SASCHA

AUTHORS' NOTE

We began work on this book in February 1973. In the course of research and writing, we interviewed more than 250 people. We have also relied on our own personal experiences for anecdotes and observations.

This book was written as an act of gratitude and loyalty to New York City by two native sons. The only bias we admit to is a love for this city, and particularly for its neighborhoods. We were born here. We grew up in working-class families in neighborhoods called Bedford Stuyvesant and Elmhurst. The only reason we both have college educations is that the City University was free in 1956. We come from a tradition that believes in paying your debts. Our way of repaying New York City for our free college education is to try and tell the truth about what is happening now to our city.

This book was born, four years ago, in our mutual recognition that something was profoundly wrong with New York and that the condition was worsening, despite decades of talk about "reform." The knowledge and the anger in these pages were nourished by day-to-day involvement with the city's small agonies. Welfare mothers with lead-poisoned children. Working-class Polish and Italian families losing their homes of a lifetime for someone else's profit. The unspeakable suffering, and the unspeakable corruption, in the nursing-home industry. A brave and difficult rent strike waged by 50,000 people in Co-op City.

These are the people for whom we wrote this book, although many of them will perhaps never read it. We hope, though, that by describing the reality, by naming the names, and by proposing some remedies, we are offering a tool for others to use in liberating New York City in the future. This is the repayment of our debt.

JACK NEWFIELD
PAUL A. DU BRUL

ACKNOWLEDGMENTS

We wish to thank: Nicholas Pileggi, for letting us pick his brains and use his files; Alexander Cockburn, for his economic insights and for finding us the perfect quotation from Marx; Pete Hamill, for being so generous with his ideas and so infectious with his passion for New York; Ron Shiffman, for sharing his planning and housing expertise with us; Jack Bigel, for giving us access to his storeroom of data and charts even though he disagreed with us most of the time; Wayne Barrett, for getting us the day-care leases and other documents; and Robert Caro, for the debt we owe to his book *The Power Broker*.

CONTENTS

ILLUSTRATIONS

THE ABUSE OF POWER

HOW DOES A CITY DIE?

How does a city die?

What does its death-rattle sound like? What are the terminal symptoms?

More than a million citizens on welfare. A $13 billion paper debt. A decline in population of more than three hundred thousand in four years. The loss of 450,000 manufacturing jobs in six years. Thirty thousand apartment units abandoned every year.

How does a city die?

Ten per cent unemployment—40 per cent among black teen-agers. Default under another name. The loss of democratic sovereignty to an unelected consortium of bankers, brokers, and businessmen. An upsurge in drug use, pornography, alcoholism, and gambling—all escapes from an unbearable reality.

What is killing New York City?

Pretty red opium poppies in Turkey, Mexico, and Indochina. Ribbons of highways, strangling the city and making gigantic suburbs possible. The Vietnam war, and the billions of our national treasure squandered there. A private group decision in March

1975 made by wealthy and privileged bankers and bond under-writers—with little-known names like Labrecque, Kezer, Smeal, Palmer, Brittain, Page, Berkeley, and Butcher—not to sell any more notes or bonds for the city of New York. A secret decision made by New York bankers even earlier to dump billions of dollars of city securities.

A century of racism in the American South that exiled hundreds of thousands of rural, uneducated blacks to New York on buses from Meridian in Mississippi, Waycross in Georgia, Jacksonville in Florida, and Bessemer in Alabama.

What else is killing New York City?

National priorities that diverted our tax dollars to defense contractors, interstate highways, and agribusiness in the "Sunbelt" from Atlanta to San Diego, and threatened to make the whole Northeast quadrant a slum belt.

Moral obligation bonds, a paper scam that John Mitchell huckstered to Nelson Rockefeller.

A man with a .22-caliber gun in a dirty kitchen pantry in the Ambassador Hotel in Los Angeles.

A national plague of unemployment and inflation.

A generation of municipal politicians who could not tell the truth.

A walker in New York today can see many symbols and omens of its doom.

In a single police precinct in Brooklyn—the 77th—seven people are murdered during one hot summer weekend. At the South Bronx Neighborhood Youth Corps Center, a thousand teenagers line up by midnight for a chance at fifty summer jobs when the doors open the next morning at 7:30.

In East Harlem, a fourteen-year-old boy is dead of a heroin overdose. It doesn't even make the papers; in 1970, a twelve-year-old named Walter Vandermeer died of an OD, so it is not "news" any more.

At 122nd Street in East Harlem, a $45-million apartment development called Taino Towers stands vacant and vandalized. There is no money to complete the thirty-five-story buildings, which were intended for poor and middle-income families. Most of the windows are broken, and even the large, outdoor lighting fixtures have been stolen. The city fathers say that the architecturally distinctive project is 90 per cent completed.

In the Bronx, 435 families, mostly working-class Italian, have been evicted to make way for a "new Fordham Hospital." The city has spent $6 million on site acquisition and relocation, and another $1.5 million for architectural design, but the money has run out. No new hospital has been built. The money has been wasted. The families have been evicted for nothing. Where their homes once stood, there are today three blocks of rubble, garbage, beer cans, broken bottles, and dead trees.

In Brooklyn, the Lindsay Park housing development is falling apart nine years after it was opened at a gala ceremony. It is a $47-million middle-income cooperative development. But large shards of plaster are falling down from the ceilings of 3000 apartments. The roofs of all seven of the project's high-rise buildings leak seriously.

In Times Square, a blind man is mugged and his seeing-eye dog stolen by junkies. On Fox Street, a nine-year-old girl is raped and thrown off a rooftop. On 111th Street, parents are begging money on the street to pay for the funeral of their baby, who fell out of a tenement window. In Harlem, two men freeze to death in a slum building owned by a landlord named Gold, who lives in Miami.

In the Bronx, Hans Kabel, seventy-eight years old, and his wife Emma, seventy-six, commit suicide together after being robbed and terrorized in their own small apartment. They leave a suicide note behind that says, "We don't want to live in fear any more."

The slums of the Mott Haven community in the Bronx have bred a new strain of "super-rat" that is immune to poison. Super-rats eat warfarin and other "anticoagulants" with no ill effect. The new rat mutations, often sixteen or eighteen inches long, have survived the Bureau of Pest Control's costly extermination campaigns. When the city fired more and more sanitation workers, more and more garbage accumulated in the South Bronx, and more and more super-rats bred and passed immunity on to their offspring. By the summer of 1976 the Bureau of Pest Control had discovered that almost 15 per cent of the city's estimated 9 million rats could eat ten times the normally lethal dose of poison without dying. The Bureau of Pest Control has had to fire almost 500 employees during the last two years, as part of a budget cutback. But this will mean more children bitten by rats, and more disease spread by rats and rat droppings.

At 116th Street and Eighth Avenue, there is an open, outdoor heroin supermarket. At any time on any day at least a hundred buyers and sellers are milling around on the corner. This awful street, called the Pit, with the Royal Flush Bar, the Shelton Hotel, and a candy store, is the end of the heroin trail that begins in the Golden Triangle of Southeast Asia. The dealers sell their heroin under brand names like "Jaws," "Malcolm's Gold," "Good Pussy," and "Death Wish." On the same crowded street, other men and women sell rubber hoses and syringes. The dealers use fourteen-year-olds as messengers and money carriers. If they are arrested, they are under Family Court jurisdiction and likely to receive only a few months in a juvenile facility. These fourteen-year-old money-carriers have been seen shooting baskets for $100 a hoop in a schoolyard two blocks from the Pit. Lieutenant Stephen Herrer, district commander of the Harlem narcotics division, says of the heroin supermarket, "It's there because it always was."

Almost two years ago, newspaper stories publicized the heroin supermarket. Films were shown on television news programs. A few "buy and bust" arrests were made. But the main effect, according to Sterling Johnson, the city's special narcotics prosecutor, was that "the dealers moved from one side of the street to the other, that's all." Meanwhile, budget cuts have destroyed Johnson's effectiveness. His office budget was slashed from $2.4 million in fiscal 1974–75 to $1.1 million for 1976–77, and in one year his staff was reduced from 122 to 76. The Police Department's narcotics squad has been cut by 33 per cent since 1975.

At the same time, Turkey has increased its cultivation of opium poppies to 135,000 acres.

All over Harlem, people ask: If a twelve-year-old kid can find a pusher, why can't the police? And some of us remember the campaign promises of 1973, repeated from a hundred platforms, that Abraham Beame, if elected mayor, would add 3000 policemen to the force.

By the early 1970s, the South Bronx was perhaps the most wretched urban slum in America—its only rival Brooklyn's Brownsville. The infant mortality rate there was 29 per 1000 births. In 1970, the average median family income in the South Bronx was $5,200, compared to the city-wide average of $9,682. The South Bronx has a quarter of all New York's reported cases of malnutrition and 16 per cent of all its cases of venereal disease. In 1972 less than 6 per cent of the public-school pupils could read at grade level. Three out of every four housing units were below standard and in violation of housing and health codes. There were 6000 abandoned buildings. Residents ran wires from an abandoned building with electricity to an inhabited one with none. Street gangs were armed with automatic weapons, and packs of wild dogs lived in the abandoned buildings.

Engine Company 82—immortalized in the book by Dennis Smith—responded to twenty alarms a night. The firemen were often ambushed and pelted with bricks and glass by teenagers.

Starting in the summer of 1975 a new factor began to make the South Bronx an even worse hell, an even more grotesque symbol for the fall of New York. Arson. Organized, systematic burning. Thirteen thousand fires broke out in the 12 square miles of the South Bronx in 1975. Forty people were killed, including three firemen. More than half the fires were reported as "cause unknown." Block after block today is in ruins, with only occasional charred halves of tenements standing.

An assistant district attorney in the Bronx told us that many of the fires were set by "teams of teenagers working very professionally. One kid would hack slits into the baseboards to free the way for the air and flames to come up from the floor below. A second kid would spread the gasoline all over the place. A third kid would actually toss the match in. And then a couple more would begin stripping the plumbing fixtures and metals before the ashes got cold. And it's hard to prove that any of the separate acts is a crime. And since the kids are thirteen or fourteen, even if they were caught and prosecuted they wouldn't do any time. It's a smart system. Somebody is paying the kids $100 a night." Bronx District Attorney Mario Merola believes that most of the torching is instigated by landlords in order to collect fire insurance. Insurance on a four-story tenement can be more than $10,000. One landlord who was indicted for arson in the South Bronx owned six buildings and had filed $125,000 in insurance claims. Robert Kirschenbaum of the New York Property Insurance Underwriting Association says that $10 million was paid to landlords in the South Bronx for 1975.

It is estimated that between 10,000 and 20,000 of the city's poorest people have been made homeless refugees by these arson-for-insurance fires. Families have been burned-out three and four times. Many of the victims now have to live in welfare hotels around the city, and large families have been broken up. Some of the arson victims have applied for public housing. But in the summer of 1976,

150,000 families were on the waiting list for public housing in New York City. The Housing Authority says it will take fifteen years to exhaust that current list.

How does a city die? How many ways can it die? Can a city commit suicide?

In Vietnam, an army commander said of the village of Ben Tre: "We had to destroy it in order to save it." That same deranged logic was applied to New York City. In 1976, under a three-year financial plan and debt moratorium, the banks were saved and the city was condemned. Under pressure from the Ford administration, Treasury Secretary William Simon, and the city's own moneyed and propertied class, the city budget was cut in ways that accelerated the city's decline.

For complex reasons, the decisions of the budget technocrats were self-defeating.

Dozens of young, honest undercover narcotics cops were fired. This meant more heroin, more crime, more fear, and more middle-class families moving out of the city. And in the Police Department as a whole, as of October 1, 1976, 6058 cops had been lost. All the cuts were made on the strict, rigid basis of seniority, with no allowance for performance or dedication. This meant that young, aggressive cops who could run a few blocks were let go, and the old, cynical, and more highly paid ones remained. So today the Police Department has 469 bosses in brass who earn $50,000 a year or more, including pensions. Its personnel bureau still has 525 cops, supervised by 52 bosses, even though there is a freeze on all new hiring. Not one of the Department's 76 deputy inspectors, with salaries above $50,000 including pensions, has been dismissed. That two cops must go together in every patrol car remains the Department's antiproductive policy, because of the police union.

Out-patient health clinics were closed. So poor people got sicker and went into municipal hospitals, and the city had to pay out more in Medicaid.

Day-care centers were closed. So working mothers quit their jobs and went on welfare, and the city, in the end, ruined some lives but saved no money.

Thousands of the lowest-paid city employees were fired, instead of more highly paid bureaucratic paper-pushers with clubhouse friends. Many of these dismissed city workers—disproportionately black and female—also swelled the welfare rolls.

The subway fare went from 35 to 50 cents. Morrisania and Fordham Hospitals closed. And after 129 years, the policy of free higher education in New York City died on June 1, 1976. The passage of upward mobility out of the slums—the dream that sustained each immigrant generation—was annulled in the bicentennial year.

There are many reasons for New York City to exist and endure as an entity in history. We are a great port and center of transport. We are an incubator of ideas and culture. We are a mecca for tourists. One reason for our existence should be the quality of life in this busy metropolis. Free higher education, adequate police protection, and good health care are among the many reasons for people to live in New York City. But families and businesses have moved out of New York because of crime, bad schools, lack of housing, loss of amenities. Each senseless, selfish budget cut has insured more crime, worse schools, less housing, fewer amenities. And more white flight. And a smaller tax base.

Those in power have tried to blur and conceal accountability for these suicidal decisions. When the subway fare was raised by 43 per cent without a public hearing, the directors of the Municipal Assistance Corporation (MAC) blamed Mayor Beame. Mayor Beame blamed the federal government and the appointed members of the Metropolitan Transportation Authority (MTA). The MTA directors, who were appointed by Governor Nelson Rockefeller, blamed Governor Hugh Carey. Governor Carey blamed "the bond market" in public and Mayor Beame in private.

The same cynical ping-ponging of responsibility occurred over the death of free tuition at the City University. Mayor Beame and Governor Carey had pledged their commitment to the principle that all students, of all classes, should receive free, public higher education if their high-school grades were good enough. But Beame and Carey, and the city's new money managers, wanted free tuition ended to balance the budget. Yet they didn't want to be held accountable by history. So they tried to force the appointed, almost anonymous members of the Board of Higher Education quietly to accept public responsibility for the dirty deed, shielding those really making the decision. The BHE's chairman, Alfred Giardino, quit in protest rather than needlessly end the policy that had permitted him, like so many others, to rise out of the working class, gain a college education, and become a lawyer. Four of his colleagues on the BHE also resigned rather than be stooges for the bankers and politicians.

The next day, Mayor Beame appointed a new chairman and three new members, certain that they would vote to terminate free higher education. The new BHE chairman appointed by Beame was Harold Jacobs, sixty-three, an affable, respected, and rich man. Ignoring the formal screening committee for the first time in history, Beame also appointed Albert Maniscalco, a politician and director of several banks; Loretta Conway, a lawyer; and Nicholas Figueroa, a former prosecutor in the Bronx DA's office. After studying the problem for seventy-two hours, the three new members voted almost without asking any questions, to end a policy and a tradition that had begun 129 years earlier.

Harold Jacobs, by pushing through the tuition vote, gave Beame, Carey, and the power brokers as much cover as the press would allow. Jacobs is a rather typical member of the permanent government that rules New York with concentrated, concealed power. And his credentials as a member of the city's unelected, bipartisan, governing elite are worth noting. He is chairman of Precision Equities, a mortgage-financing company he founded. He is a generous campaign contributor. He was appointed to the city's Youth Board by a Republican mayor, John Lindsay. His son, Joseph Jacobs, was appointed a city marshal by Lindsay in 1971. In 1972 Harold Jacobs was a coordinator of Democrats for Nixon. His daughter is married to Daniel Chill, the former counsel to Speaker of the New York State Assembly Stanley Steingut. Jacobs and Steingut are both directors of a company called Modular Cities, Inc., which made a quick killing on a land deal in Staten Island. Jacobs is past president of the Brooklyn Jewish Community Council and current chairman of the Union of Orthodox Congregations. And he is one of Mayor Beame's oldest and closest friends.

The ideal last-minute executioner of free tuition, the company man whom the establishment could trust to annul hope and protect power.

Each day, as we compose our book, this wounded Paris, this hemorrhaging Athens, dies a block at a time, a family at a time.

In Queens, an alcoholism-treatment program closes and an old man goes to the bars again. A forty-five-year-old fireman has a fatal heart attack trying to fight a fire on his second overtime shift in two days. An after-school tutoring program closes in Bedford-Stuyvesant, and a chance for college dies. A mugger goes free because the cop who arrested him has since been laid off, and doesn't show up in criminal court to testify. A day-care center is "defunded" and an eighteen-year-old mother has to quit high school and go on welfare.

At the same time, Consolidated Edison, New York's mammoth electric utility company, declares the largest quarterly dividend in its history for its stockholders. The clubhouse hacks are still larding the municipal payroll. The Port Authority of New York and New Jersey still has a huge surplus in its bank account and portfolio. The profits at Citicorp are at record levels, and Salomon Brothers reports that profits for the year ending September 30, 1976, jumped a record 50 per cent.

When Robert Kennedy spoke against the Vietnam war, he often quoted what Tacitus said of Rome: "They made a desert, and called it peace." In our city, they are making a desert and calling it a balanced budget.

THE TRUE HISTORY OF THE FISCAL CRISIS

The indebtedness of the state was in the direct interest of that fraction of the bourgeoisie which ruled and legislated in parliament. The state deficit was, in fact, the actual object of its speculation and its main source of enrichment. At the end of each new year a new deficit. After four or five years a new loan. And every new loan gave the financial aristocracy a fresh opportunity to swindle the state, which was artificially kept hovering on the edge of bankruptcy and was forced to do business with the bankers on the most unfavorable terms. Every new loan provided yet another opportunity to plunder that section of the public which invested its money in government securities by means of maneuvers on the Bourse [the Paris stock exchange], into the secrets of which the government and the parliamentary majority were initiated.

In general, the uncertain position of government bonds and the bankers' possession of state secrets put them and their associates in parliament and on the throne in a position to create sudden, unusual fluctuations in the price of government securities, which invariably resulted in the ruin of a mass of smaller capitalists and in the fabulously speedy enrichment of the big gamblers. The fact that the state deficit served the direct interest of the ruling fraction of the bourgeoisie explains why the extraordinary state expenditure in the last years of Louis Philippe's reign was more than double the extraordinary state expenditure under Napoleon. The enormous sums of money which thus flowed through the hands of the state gave rise, moreover, to crooked delivery contracts, bribery, embezzlement and roguery of all kinds. The wholesale swindling of the state through loans was repeated on a retail basis in public works. The relationship between parliament and government was reproduced in the relationship between individual administrative departments and individual entrepreneurs. . . .

. . . The July monarchy was nothing more than a joint-stock company for the exploitation of France's national wealth.

— KARL MARX
The Class Struggles in France: 1848 to 1850

The depression of 1974–75, the worst worldwide economic collapse since the Great Depression, hit rock bottom in March 1975. Ten million American workers were officially "unemployed" while millions of others, especially young blacks, weren't even counted in the statistics since they had never been able to hold *any* job. While every other economic indicator was plummeting, the cost-of-living index pushed to record levels. The inflation rate for the whole year of 1974 was 12 per cent and food prices pelted ahead at an even faster pace. Real wages for those lucky enough to have jobs dropped below those of 1973. Pollsters found the people angry and depressed, distrustful of government, business, and the banks.

This was the last month that New York City was allowed to borrow "normally" in the nation's credit markets. A month before, Nelson Rockefeller's favorite erector set, the New York State Urban Development Corporation, had defaulted on its short-term debt to investors. (The agency, in deep trouble since 1972, was actually scheduled to default five months earlier, at the height of the state election campaign, but it was bailed out by the major banks in a last-ditch attempt to aid the faltering attempts of Republican Governor Malcolm Wilson to fend off his Democratic challenger, Hugh Carey. The bankers lent $150 million of their depositors' money to an agency which they knew was losing $1 million a day.)

Vast subterranean economic pressures, built up over decades, were shaking the foundations of the postwar economy and threatened to topple the nation's biggest banks, the securities markets, giant corporations, and government agencies that stood at the pinnacle of an almost incalculable base of debt. The tremors had been felt since Richard Nixon's sudden devaluation of the dollar in 1971, and now they broke through at the system's most vulnerable point, New York City, the financial capital of the world.

Since then the city, and all of urban America, has been wracked by a series of aftershocks. In San Francisco and New York municipal workers have struck in impotent rage against massive layoffs. Unemployment, despite a fragile economic "recovery," remains at heartbreaking levels. Urban crime has reached a new peak and the overcrowded prisons are in open revolt. Bands of young Nazis roam the fringes of Chicago's white neighborhoods preaching racial Armaggedon. Detroit has been forced to rehire hundreds of laid-off policemen to impose a state of martial law. The nightmares forecast for our cities in the 1960s are fast becoming the day-to-day realities of the 1970s.

Millions of words have already been written about New York City's fiscal collapse. For months it dominated the news, and the spasms of other major cities were treated as a footnote to the story. The agony of the cities has now merged into the permanent scenery of the American spectacle. Like floods, hurricanes, and other natural disasters, it is taken for granted. As it continues to unfold on our front pages and television screens, the majority of the nation sits back, saddened for the victims, but relieved that this unavoidable disaster is happening to someone else.

We reject this fatalism about the cities. What happened to New York was neither inevitable nor inescapable. New York and the rest of our cities *can* be saved, but we must first understand how the current crisis emerged. In this and the next chapter we shall counterpose what we call "the true history of the fiscal crisis" to what has become the "official" history written by the press and academic commentators. It is this official history which has become the greatest barrier to achieving the many fundamental changes necessary to rescue our cities.

Abe Beame was wrong when he said, in late 1975, that "the dilemma of our city really has no villains, only victims." There *are* villains in New York's collapse, men who saw what was happening, could have prevented it, and profited from the agony of millions. But few of these villains are to be found in the ranks of journalists who reported on the fall of New York. Their sins were for the most part sins of omission. Reporters failed to dig deep enough, trusted sources who lied to protect themselves, allowed the "tunnel vision" that afflicts any reporter on a story to block out the simple truth that New York's problems had deep-rooted causes outside the city and its government. In the rush to judgment that is the bane of writing for daily deadlines, they accepted the "easy" villains they were fed: a bookkeeper-mayor and his acolytes who had financed with mirrors; municipal unions that had used their putative political muscle to extract massive pension settlements from an impoverished government; politicos who had a lust for cutting ribbons on new programs without caring where the money came from to finance them.

Inevitably the idea of these surface villains, and this deadline punditry about the urban crisis, created a myth: New York was different from other cities; it had tried to do too much for its citizens; now it must be punished. The hero in this trite little morality play then became that small band of professional money-men who had supposedly unmasked the city's Ponzi scheme at the last moment, before it destroyed the widows and orphans who had bought its worthless paper in innocent trust. A short term in the fiscal slammer would reform the culprit and everybody could then go on about their business as before.

An excellent synopsis of this "official" version of the New York crisis was given by Wyndham Robertson in the August 1975 issue of *Fortune:*

As the nation's largest city struggles to extricate itself from the financial quicksand that has been threatening to drag it under, Americans watching the suspenseful spectacle have begun to wonder whether other large cities are headed for the same kind of trouble. The answer is fairly reassuring: New York is a special case.

New York is different because it has had a credit card that enabled it to live beyond its means. For years its elected officials have had the sort of license that politicians dream about, but that only those at the Federal level were presumed to enjoy—namely the opportunity to spend without the concomitant necessity to tax. . . .

With that credit card available, city politicians seldom had to bring themselves to say no to anybody—whether union leaders making extravagant demands at contract time or citizens seeking benefits for themselves or others. If the city government had been forced to match expenditures more closely with cash revenues, hard choices would have been unavoidable. But the borrowing power, coupled with enormous political pressures from a citizenry both accustomed to costly services and suffering from some of the highest taxes in the U.S., led city officials to ignore fiscal realities. As a result, New York got committed to do more things than it could afford.

It was this concept of New York as a "special case" which eventually did the most harm. No longer just a sleazy con man hiding behind a fancy front, New York became the Typhoid Mary of cities, as the crisis deepened and threatened to spread to the nation's financial structure. If New York alone was the victim of this fiscal malady, it must be quarantined.

Few people did more to legitimize the idea that the only responsible solution to the fiscal crisis was massive layoffs and service cuts than Steven R. Weisman, who reported the crisis on a daily basis for *The New York Times*. Subtly, and often merely by omission, Weisman slanted his "objective" reporting to echo the latest thinking of the bankers and Felix Rohatyn, the critically important member of all the emergency committees set up to rescue New York. Weisman used the imagery of the city as a fiscal "junkie" whose only possible cure was to kick the habit "cold turkey." He made few comments about the profits, motives, or obligations of the pushers who addicted the junkie, however.

Weisman later became notorious among colleagues in the press for the "victory" jig he danced with Rohatyn, chairman of MAC, to celebrate the fact that the United Federation of Teachers' chief, Albert Shanker, had been forced to capitulate and buy additional MAC bonds for his union's pension fund. As one reporter from another daily paper recounted the event to us: "I've never seen anything like it on any other story I've covered. I started to take a punch at him but somebody grabbed my arm. No wonder anybody who reads the *Times* doesn't know what's really going on."*

---

* When Alexander Cockburn reported in his "Press Clips" column in the *Village Voice* that Rohatyn and Weisman had been seen "embracing and tickling each other after Shanker gave in," an indignant Weisman protested what he felt were homosexual innuendoes in the piece. That was hardly the implication, or the point, of what Cockburn had written. He was doubting Weisman's objectivity, not his manliness.

Weisman did something far worse in October 1976. On behalf of Chase Manhattan, he undercut an investigative piece by his colleague Martin Tolchin which confirmed for the first time that the big New York banks, led by Chase, had "dumped" billions in city securities, thereby causing a panic, and New York's exclusion from the bond market. A Chase vice-president crowed to us that "the Bank" had gotten Tolchin's piece buried, literally, on the obituary page. When we pursued this claim, we found that Weisman had challenged the Tolchin story with the desk and managed to get it rewritten and buried. For more details see our article in the November 22, 1976, *Village Voice*.

Timothy Crouse, whose *The Boys on the Bus* is the best modern book on the American press, has a marvelous scene in which he describes our top political reporters comparing the leads they have written on presidential campaign stories to determine the consensus view that they will send to their editors. This kind of "pack journalism" now afflicted New York; the cardinal sin was to say something different from what everyone else was saying.

And so the myth grew, nourished by repetition. As a result, those who actually provoked the city's crisis—the banks—were effectively absolved of all guilt until subsequent investigations bared their machinations. An easily frightened national money market in desperate need of reform became the hero, not the villain, of the piece. A national administration that had heaped responsibility after responsibility on the tottering city not only escaped its share of blame for the crisis, but had a field day flagellating New York for collapsing under this unfair burden. All this was bad enough, but the greatest irony of all was that the city was cut off from the only thing that could solve its real problems: massive infusions of new money to restore its dwindling economy and provide stable jobs for the growing ranks of the welfare poor.

As with all myths, of course, the myth about New York City grew around a kernel of truth. As we will show, the city's finances *were* in an incredible mess; its debt *had* accelerated at an unsustainable pace; bookkeeping gimmicks *were* used to mask actual budget deficits. Some of the pensions won by municipal labor unions *were* excessive; some fringe benefits (such as giving cops two days off every time they donated a pint of blood) *were* bizarre and unnecessary. But none of these things, alone or together, caused the fall of New York. If we were to abolish all of them, lay off thousands more in addition to the tens of thousands of city workers already fired, close every city hospital, and destroy even more programs, we could never restore the city to fiscal health.

In fact, the current "recovery" program has significantly accelerated the city's decline. New York's budget won't be balanced in three years, and even with massive federal assistance the job may only be accomplished in a decade. In the meantime, more businesses and jobs leave the city as police and fire protection are cut back, the mass transit system becomes unworkable, and the banks refuse capital for expansion. The city itself has been forced to abandon the construction of piers, markets, industrial parks, and shopping centers that would have created 22,000 private jobs.

It is important, therefore, to understand what really happened in those years and months before the banks slammed the credit windows shut on the city's outstretched fingers; to see why the federal administration jubilantly sought to "cut the city off and float it out to sea"; and to discern the larger implications behind the financial community's eagerness to force all the cities and states of America to reduce their demands on the nation's capital supply— and how it used New York's battered corpse to accomplish this goal. This is the "real history" we shall now seek to unravel.

The headline on the *Wall Street Journal* story was:

NEW YORK CITY'S FISCAL ILLS BOOST ITS COST BY $7.4 MILLION AT $233.8 MILLION BOND SALE

NEW YORK—This city's shaky budget condition resulted in a sharply higher interest cost on $233.8 million of various purpose bonds it auctioned yesterday, market analysts said.

The article then explained how an 0.3701 increase in the interest rate would actually mean an added cost to taxpayers of $7.4 million over the eight-and-a-half-year life of the bonds.

The city's steeper cost was linked primarily to its well-publicized financial crisis. . . . [The mayor] recently estimated that New York's annual revenue had declined between $100 million and $150 million as a result of the nationwide economic slowdown, and he warned that city employees could be subjected to "payless paydays, pay cuts and layoffs."

The city's controller described the city's budgetary woes as only "one of several factors" responsible for yesterday's higher rate. He also cited a current supply logjam in the tax-exempt market, which is attempting to absorb a staggering $568 million of new state and city bonds this week alone.

The date on that story was October 21, 1970.

Anyone dipping into New York City's history in the last decade can find dozens of almost identical reports. We chose this one simply because it exemplifies so perfectly the coverage that preceded the city's fiscal collapse in the spring of 1975. All the elements of the final downfall are there: maximum interest being extorted from a city already in economic trouble, a national economic decline reducing tax revenues while at the same time forcing greater expenditures on a shaky municipal budget, a credit market unable to absorb the growing demands placed on it. And the two leading city officials trying to outdo each other in explaining away the mess. (For those with short memories, the mayor's name was John Lindsay and the controller was Abraham Beame.)

The deepest historical roots of New York City's fiscal crisis go back to Robert Moses and the creation of public authorities in 1934. The authorities meant the end of accountability. Moses and his successors, like Edward Logue and William Ronan, were able to spend money and make mistakes without democratic restraint. As Robert Caro has pointed out in *The Power Broker*, during a fifteen-year period Robert Moses was able to spend $4.5 billion on public works, while the mayors and members of the Board of Estimate spent a total of less than $3.8 billion on public works. The authorities also became the device used to destroy neighborhoods and dispossess tens of thousands of families. Caro quotes one study that says between 1946 and 1956 alone Moses evicted 320,000 people from their homes.

So the people of the city began to lose control over their democratic destiny in 1934; but a dangerous new element was added to this anti-democratic drift in 1960: moral obligation bonds. A series of historic meetings were occurring in New York City between two men who were to play significant roles in New York's history and in the history of the nation: Nelson Rockefeller and John Mitchell.

Nelson Rockefeller became governor of New York State in January 1959. One of the first problems to gain his attention was the increasing deterioration of the state's major cities, especially New York City. At the core of this problem was the flight of white, middle-class families to the burgeoning suburbs. The postwar suburban housing boom, fueled by Veterans Administration and Federal Housing Authority mortgages and by federal and state funding for a vast new highway program that provided automobile access to jobs in the downtown business districts, was in full swing. While the feds were busily subsidizing these new communities of single-family homes, however, they were doing nothing to provide new housing at moderate rentals in the cities. As young families grew, therefore, the only suitable housing offered them was outside the neighborhoods and cities where they had grown up and married.

New York had recognized this problem in 1955 when it adopted the Mitchell-Lama middle-income housing program. But not much new urban housing had actually been constructed because of the requirement imposed by the state constitution that all new debt be approved by the voters at a general referendum. There was little enthusiasm among upstate and suburban voters for housing debt, which was seen primarily as a benefit for New York City. Besides, property values in these areas would continue to rise only as long as the suburbs grew and more home buyers could be attracted from the big cities. Small housing bond issues passed, but by narrower and narrower margins. As the population balance between city and suburb continued to tip, they were fated for defeat.

Rockefeller now looked to the financing mechanisms pioneered by the state's public authorities. These agencies issued bonds outside the state's publicly approved debt limit. They were "revenue" bonds, paid off through the collection of user fees, e.g., bridge tolls or admission charges at state parks, as opposed to the "full faith and credit" bonds of the state, which were backed by state tax collections. The projects financed by "revenue" bonds were said to be "self-liquidating" or "self-sufficient."

He therefore had the legislature create a Housing Finance Agency (HFA) which, using the state's superior credit rating and the lure of tax-exempt income, would issue bonds and then lend low-interest funds to private developers for the construction of middle-income housing. The bonds would be liquidated over their term by rental payments.

James Gaynor, Rockefeller's Commissioner of Housing, had called in John Mitchell, one of the nation's leading bond lawyers and later Nixon's attorney general, to help draft the HFA legislation. Mitchell questioned the revenue bond approach. As he later testified to the state commission investigating the collapse of the Urban Development Corporation, he told Rockefeller that issuers of mortgage-participation certificates and other real-estate obligations had defaulted in great numbers during the 1930s and the "investment community was pretty sour on that type of obligation." Investors would therefore exact a very high interest rate on the new bonds, which in turn would significantly raise rents and discourage tenancy.

Mitchell then proposed that "something more" be added to sweeten the pot: He suggested that the bonds include a "legislative intent" to provide appropriations from general revenues to back any shortfalls in the rentals necessary to pay off the bonds. This meant that the state would have a "moral obligation" to back its paper; but since the bonds were the debt of the agency and not the state and there would be no "legal" obligation for the legislature to appropriate money to assure repayment, the requirement for a public referendum was avoided.

While Mitchell went around peddling the new concept to the private rating agencies that appraise public offerings and the underwriters who buy bonds and resell them to institutions and wealthy investors, Rockefeller did his characteristic hard sell with the reluctant legislature, hammering away at the "self-liquidating" nature of the new debt. Robert Moses had long ago taught the legislators that public authorities could be a major patronage trough. The concept was adopted.

The reception accorded the first issue of HFA bonds in 1961 exceeded even Mitchell's enthusiastic projections. They received a high rating from Standard and Poor's, a leading rating agency, and as a result were sold at a low interest rate. Of equal importance, the U.S. Controller of the Currency ruled that the "moral obligation" allowed the bonds to be considered as general obligations of the state, and therefore suitable for investment by the nation's commercial banks. The banks, anxious to reduce federal and state tax obligations, gobbled up the new tax-exempt securities. The only cloud on the horizon was the negative reaction of the state's Democratic Comptroller, Arthur Levitt, who objected to circumventing the constitutional limits on borrowing and warned major bankers in several meetings in the early 1960s that the state's credit was being "distorted" by the new form of debt.

John Mitchell had given Nelson Rockefeller another Aladdin's lamp when he created "moral obligation" financing for the authorities. All the governor had to do was rub it and out poured even more massive building projects, jobs, and profits for banks, builders, architects, lawyers, developers, and dozens of related professionals. Running for re-election in 1962, Rockefeller promised to turn a handful of seedy teachers colleges into a full-fledged State University. The State University Construction Fund was established under the aegis of HFA and subsequently spent $1.7 billion planting campuses across the state—as much to meet the needs of local Republican politicians as to meet those of higher education. The bonds were to be repaid with the tuition fees of students—which is one of the reasons why Rockefeller perennially attempted to impose tuition on the separate and free City University system, whose tuition-free competition made him look bad and created pressure to keep the lid on tuition at the state schools.

Four years later, another election year, HFA was assigned the task of providing funds for a massive nursing-home program for the elderly. Eventually the agency would provide financing for public and private hospitals, neighborhood clinics, mental-health facilities, housing for the elderly, offices, and libraries. Its total debt in October 1975 equaled $5.29 billion.

HFA was only one, albeit the largest, of the 230-odd authorities which flourished under Rockefeller. Admittedly, a vast authority superstructure had long been in existence in New York State as the private empire of Robert Moses. But Rockefeller proved an incredibly eager pupil. During his term of office, the number of authorities was doubled. While Moses had actually created a shadow government standing separate and apart, Nelson Rockefeller extended that shadow until it overwhelmed and engulfed the formal state government apparatus. The authorities ultimately encompassed the universe of public concerns, stretching alphabetically from the Atomic and Space Development Authority to the United Nations' Development Corporation. Unnoticed by most, Nelson Rockefeller had created his own U.S. government in miniature. (New York even has its own Navy.) But then he had always warned us that he was practicing to be President.

Even this pyramid of vast wealth and power did not circumscribe Rockefeller's experiments with "creative financing." He also developed a series of complicated lease-purchase agreements involving the credit of the state's cities and counties. The most notorious of these was the development of the gargantuan Albany Mall (officially the Empire State Plaza) office-construction project, initially estimated to cost $250 million but ultimately consuming almost $1 billion in construction funding. Rockefeller induced Albany County to undertake the project by committing the state to lease office space on a flexible schedule that covers debt service and allows for all inflationary costs in building. In effect, this means that the state's taxpayers will absorb the entire cost of the project through annual rent payments in the state's operating budget for decades to come.

This private empire of authorities, always yoked with his own vast personal wealth, became the real foundation of Rockefeller's political power. He had learned well the lesson taught by another Hudson River Valley patrician, Franklin D. Roosevelt: "Spend, spend, spend; elect, elect, elect." The steady generation of construction jobs allowed him to buy the fealty of the powerful and nominally Democratic building trade unions, with at least 200,000 members in the state. (At the same time, he was successfully buying the support of state and city civil servants, especially the police and firemen, first by making pension agreements a subject for col-

lective bargaining and then by consistently increasing the percentage of pension contributions to be paid by the state. This forced the
city into a costly game of leapfrog with public employee pensions.)
The constant flow of new bonds and new projects also guaranteed
him a constant source of munificent campaign contributions from
grateful bankers, builders, and developers; these supplemented the
vast resources of his own family. Few commentators grasped the
full irony of their own words when they wrote of Rockefeller's
ability to "cement" together disparate coalitions.

The men he appointed to run these satrapies were generally
skilled but low-key administrators, and he assured their loyalty
with personal gifts and loans to supplement their lavish public
salaries. Primary among them was William J. Ronan, ironically a
trenchant critic of the independent power of the authorities when
he directed a study for the legislature in 1956 as dean of the New
York University School of Public Administration. Ronan became a
rapid convert to the benefits of authorities, first as Rockefeller's
secretary and subsequently as chairman of the Metropolitan Transportation Authority, which runs all public transit in New York City
and the region's crucial commuter railroads.

Disclosures extracted during Rockefeller's confirmation hearings
for the vice-presidency showed that he showered Ronan with
$625,000 in gifts and loans, money which Ronan used, among other
things, to speculate in suburban real estate. Despite Rockefeller's
"retirement" from politics, Ronan remains as one of his more dubious contributions to public life, continuing to exercise decisive
power over mass transit in the region as chairman of the New York-
New Jersey Port Authority—the oldest major public authority in
the United States and a prime target of his 1956 study.

But even the best administrators that money could buy couldn't
keep Rockefeller's financial bubble from bursting eventually. Paul
Bellica was Ronan's counterpart at the HFA. A self-effacing Swiss,
Bellica ran his growing agency with all the conservative care befitting a Zurich banker. He took the concept of "self-sufficiency"
seriously and took great pains to choose, in consultation with his
colleagues at the Department of Housing and Community Renewal,
only those projects that would produce revenues adequate to pay
back the bondholders, first and foremost, and then meet their own
operating costs. These studies took a great deal of time. Moreover,
Bellica applied the same standards as the banks that bought his
bonds. He refused to invest in changing neighborhoods; not only
did the banks redline vast areas of the state, but so did the state's

major housing agency. As he complained in a memo to Department of Housing and Community Renewal Commissioner Charles Urstadt, "The program [HFA] has never been intended to satisfy the need of the lowest income group and to supplement the public housing system."

But there was no longer a growing public housing system. Federal appropriations had been reduced to a trickle during the escalation of the Vietnam War, and Richard Nixon soon shut off the faucet entirely. Between 1962 and 1965, five propositions for state-financed public housing had been soundly defeated at the polls. Yet the overwhelming demand of the cities was for decent housing to replace almost a million units of decaying, dilapidated apartments in low-income neighborhoods. The immense revenues that HFA was originally given the power to raise for housing had been diverted to other, politically more sexy projects.

Now the galloping inflation produced by the seemingly endless war in Southeast Asia meant that even those limited funds invested in housing built less and less at a higher and higher price. Ghetto riots over slum conditions were erupting with alarming frequency. Rockefeller was again gearing up for another shot at the presidency in 1968, having been so bitterly denied the nomination by the suicidal Goldwater legions in 1964. John Lindsay, New York's matinee-idol mayor, challenged him for the title of the nation's leading Republican liberal, and Lindsay was capturing the limelight as the man who had effectively "cooled" the most explosive ghettoes in America. The governor felt boxed in.

Rockefeller's answer to any problem had become reflexive: He would create yet another authority—bigger, more daring, almost all-inclusive—a super-authority. Actually he now combined two new authorities that his staff had designed, one to provide jobs for the urban unemployed, the other to provide housing in areas abandoned by private investment and the HFA, and he called the new entity the Urban Development Corporation.

On January 17, 1968, Rockefeller asked Edward J. Logue to review the proposal he was preparing to send to the legislature. Logue was at the peak of his career as a "master builder," a man with a national reputation for erecting large-scale projects without being stymied by the political squabbles or community resistance that condemned so many other urban-renewal projects to remain elegant cardboard models on display in the anterooms of mayors and governors. He had started by rebuilding downtown New Haven and then moved on to the Boston Redevelopment Authority. John

Lindsay had gotten Logue to make the plans for New York City's Housing and Development Administration, but Logue had refused to take the top job in this new agency because the powers he sought over planning, design, and development had been whittled down by city officials, concerned that he wanted not only the title of "housing czar" but the powers that such a title implied. He and the multimillionaire governor shared the view that opposition constituted obstruction. But many city housing and planning officials and community groups saw him as a "young Robert Moses," and they hadn't recovered from the old one yet.

Logue submitted a long memorandum on the draft proposal to Rockefeller on February 21, and the bill that was actually submitted to the legislature on February 27 contained his basic recommendations. The new agency would have the powers to override local zoning laws and often outdated and unnecessarily expensive building codes. It would be allowed to use the "fast track" method of construction—that is, to carry on through the primary stages of site selection, design, and the preparation of final plans and specifications before having a final mortgage commitment. The bonds and notes that would finance the agency would be based on "the full faith and credit of the corporation"; in other words, rather than being amortized by the income of specific projects, the basis of HFA financing, bonds would be repaid from the total income stream of UDC from all its projects.

The state legislature hesitated, perhaps fearing that UDC's mandate to build in "substandard, blighted areas" might finally put to the test their willingness to back up the "moral obligation" with hard tax dollars if the agency experienced a series of project difficulties. Suburban legislators were fearful of the provision that allowed UDC to override local zoning; they saw it as an opening wedge for building low-income (read minority) projects in previously middle-class (read white) areas. (Most planners by now accepted the premise that "white flight" from the central cities was inevitable; they now simply held that it was necessary to provide blacks with the option of leaving the cities as well, thereby providing them access to suburban job opportunities and slowing the trend toward black-majority cities surrounded by a "white noose" of suburbs.)

For a while the bill languished in Albany; then history intervened. Martin Luther King, Jr., probably the most important black leader in American history, was assassinated in Memphis on April 4, 1968. Black outrage exploded in devastating riots all over America's cities. The following morning Rockefeller, never a man to miss an opportunity, sent a "message of necessity" to the legislature reducing the amount of time permitted to elapse before a vote could be taken on the UDC bill. On April 8, he flew to Atlanta to attend Dr. King's funeral with the rest of the nation's elite. The bill was rushed through the state Senate as King's funeral was in progress, but the Assembly voted it down that same afternoon, a minority rejecting the governor's move as "opportunistic" and "cynical"; the opposition to the zoning-override provision held firm, and a handful of liberals presciently charged that the proposed new authority would not provide meaningful housing aid for the poor.

Rockefeller quickly flew back from Atlanta and pulled out all the stops. His top aides and housing officials went scurrying down the corridors of the legislature—issuing threats, calling in old debts, and making promises. Early the next morning, the pummeled Assembly, terrified as much by radio reports of growing black violence as by Rockefeller's ham-handed lobbying, reconvened and passed the bill by the same margin by which it had defeated it the previous afternoon.

George Woods, former head of the World Bank and a director and former chairman of the First Boston Corporation, a major investment banking firm, was Rockefeller's first choice as chief executive officer of UDC. Someone who could reassure the banking fraternity—in addition to Rockefeller himself, of course—was needed to raise massive amounts of cash for the new agency. Woods explained that he had no experience in real-estate financing or development, and declined. But Rockefeller continued to press, and Woods finally agreed to become chairman of the board on the condition that First Boston would become the senior managing underwriter for all UDC offerings. (The senior underwriter receives the lion's share of the profits in the syndicates formed to buy public offerings and then resell them to the public. The profits derive from the spread between the interest rate that government must pay, say 8½ per cent, and the rate that is paid to secondary purchasers such as banks or wealthy individuals, say 7½ per cent. Comptroller Levitt subsequently revealed that the seven underwriters, among them Citibank, Chase Manhattan, Morgan Guaranty, and Salomon Brothers, had earned profits of $3.9 million on the initial UDC offering of $250 million.)

The writer Mary Perot Nichols subsequently revealed in *The New Republic* that Woods also demanded protection from any charges of conflict of interest. He received a secret letter from State Attorney General Louis Lefkowitz, always a willing Rockefeller ally, absolving him of any conflict as long as he refrained from voting at board meetings on matters affecting the business of First Boston. (Lefkowitz's son Stephen would become general counsel for UDC.) This was a complete charade, since Woods remained the dominant financial voice at UDC, and the other members of the board subsequently testified to the state commission that they had no expertise in the bond markets and "depended on Woods's judgment in these matters." Woods's role in these financial decisions did not become a public issue until after the UDC collapse, however.

On April 27, 1968, Logue was appointed president and chief executive officer of the new corporation (he received $200,000 in "gifts and loans" from Rockefeller during his tenure) and began to carry out what he later called "a directive to go out and build, build, build." And he did. By December 31, 1970, UDC had in construction or planning 45,438 units of housing with an estimated cost of $1.9 billion, as well as commercial and industrial developments around the state. (He actually completed less than 30,000 housing units.) For a brief time, Logue became the right man in the right place at the right time.

Shortly after the creation of the UDC, Congress had passed the capstone of the Great Society, the Housing and Urban Development Act of 1968, which contained direct subsidies (Section 236 monies, they were called) that reduced the interest charges on approved projects to only 1 per cent. On paper, at least, these subsidies made many projects viable that would otherwise be unrentable. Logue had really the only agency in the nation geared up to absorb the new subsidies on a large scale, and the Rockefeller-Logue combination had an open door with the new Republican administration which came to office in 1969. As a result, Logue snatched 66 per cent of all Section 236 monies available for the entire country before Nixon impounded the program in January 1973.

Logue had been so sure of federal funding that he had 58 projects in process that required Section 236 subsidy when Nixon dropped his bombshell—but he had never bothered to ask for formal federal commitments. UDC would have collapsed on the spot then and there, but Nelson Rockefeller scuttled to Washington and got Nixon's domestic chief, John Ehrlichman, to suspend the moratorium for Logue's projects.

The overwhelming irony is that Logue finally built very little housing for the poor in either the cities or the suburbs. Despite the legislation's clear mandate that the new housing should be for "persons or families of low income," the UDC unilaterally established its own formula, which stipulated that 70 per cent of the housing on any site would be for middle- and moderate-income families, 20 per cent for low-income families, and 10 per cent for the aged.

The concept of publicly subsidized "moderate"-income housing was actually a UDC creation. In effect, it meant, after applying the complex formulas of various state housing programs, that families earning up to $65,000 a year fell into this category. "Middle-income," originally defined by statute to mean those earning between $8,000 and $12,000 a year, in practice came to mean those earning between $18,000 and $25,000 a year. The rents in Logue's projects came in so high that they never effectively competed with the better deal which most families could still get by moving to the federally subsidized suburbs.

When Comptroller Levitt released a report on the "Financial Viability of Completed Projects" on October 29, 1974, he disclosed that an apartment then renting at $159 in Coney Island required an 84.9 per cent rent increase simply to meet its mortgage costs, exclusive of escalating operating costs. A Yonkers apartment renting for $190 would have to be raised to $365, a 92.1 per cent increase. The smallest rent increase projected by Levitt was 29 per cent.

Logue actually tried to introduce a very modest housing program for the minority poor into the suburbs, but Rockefeller caved in to the demands of Republican legislators from suburban Westchester County (this was known as the Nine Towns controversy), and the provision allowing UDC to override local restrictions was repealed on June 5, 1973. Logue received an additional $500 million in bonding authority as a consolation.

As a result of the fantastic escalation in building costs and the failure to fill existing projects, the money kept going out faster than it could be repaid. Attempts were made to get Logue to cap the building program or at least to slow it down until income and outgo achieved some sort of balance. A typical Logue response was given in an internal memorandum in late 1971: "We are going to build as much as we can. . . . When, having prudently managed our affairs, we have gone as far as we can go, and we can't borrow any more, that is another day." That day would not come for another two years and only after UDC had borrowed $2 billion.

UDC was hit with a series of body blows in 1973. Nixon's moratorium was the first. Then the UDC accountant refused to certify its 1972 financial statement, provoking uncomfortable disclosures, and on October 5, Moody's lowered the UDC's bond rating to Baa, the lowest possible level at which many banks and institutions could still invest in its bonds. Then, on December 12, Nelson Rockefeller resigned as governor in order to allow Lieutenant-Governor Malcolm Wilson, his perennial second fiddle and enforcer in the party's conservative wing, to accede to the top post in preparation for a run at a full four-year term the following November.

During his fifteen-year reign, Rockefeller had increased the state's debt from $1.97 billion in 1961 to $13.37 billion in his final budget year—a seven-fold increase. With the imposition of "moral obligation" debt, he had radically altered the shape of the nation's credit markets (many other states had followed in New York's footsteps), had provided a bonanza in profits and tax-exempt income for banks and wealthy individuals, and had actively stoked the forced-draught economic expansion that a few months later would collapse, plunging the nation into its second worst depression in history. As Hugh Carey, his successor, who always showed restraint when dealing with Rockefeller's excesses, later blurted out: ". . . in New York State, we haven't found only back-door financing. We got side-door financing and New York's borrowing over the years—through the state government, its authorities and agencies and UDC and MTA—we got money going out the doors, the windows, and the portholes."

It was UDC that finally caused this multi-billion-dollar house of cards to collapse. Morgan Guaranty pulled out as an underwriter soon after Rockefeller's departure. In May 1974, UDC had to withdraw a $100-million short-term note sale because the interest rates asked by the nervous banks were prohibitive. By the end of the summer, the major underwriters, led by the Chase Manhattan Bank, were in fact running the agency and provided funds adequate to keep UDC from collapsing under Wilson's election campaign.

After Wilson's defeat in the fall of 1974, the credit dried up. Carey attempted to win a $178-million appropriation from the state legislature to cover UDC's immediate cash needs, but he failed, and on February 25, 1975, UDC defaulted on $104.5 million in short-term notes that had fallen due. It was the biggest collapse of a government agency since the Depression. The state investigating commission subsequently estimated that it would require "a total of $240 to $320 million of State funds" to complete UDC projects in construction when the collapse came, and much much more "if projects don't meet the required level of income"—almost an inevitability. The bubble had burst.

Two months later, New York City found itself facing the specter of default for the first time.

Whatever else one may say about Nelson Rockefeller, he was magnanimous with his opponents. As Democratic Mayor Robert Ferdinand Wagner, Jr. came to the end of his twelve years in office in 1965, he had a problem. His budget didn't balance, and he needed $255.8 million. He proposed to borrow the money needed to cover the deficit, and he needed the approval of the state legislature to do so. While Republican legislators responded to this proposal with cries of outrage, Nelson Rockefeller shrugged and said "Why not?" After all, "creative financing" had worked for him; maybe the city deserved a taste of the good life.

The two master politicians then went about constructing a complicated compromise. Rockefeller received the Democratic votes he needed to institute a state sales tax, and Wagner received the Republican votes he needed for an increase in the city sales tax and a new borrowing formula that allowed the city for the first time to borrow against *estimated* revenues. In the past the city had been allowed to issue "Revenue Anticipation Notes" (RANs) against state and federal aid and uncollected taxes and fees, but there were strict limitations: All the uncollected funds had to be due in the same fiscal year in which the loan was made, and the amount of state and federal aid borrowed against could not exceed the amount that had actually been received in the prior fiscal year. Under the new formula the mayor would be limited no longer to prior-year collections but to what he said the collections should be. The taxes and fees owed need no longer be payable in the fiscal year in which the loan was made—minor changes actually, but then so is a pin-sized hole in a dike.

John Lindsay, then the Republican-Liberal candidate for mayor, denounced Wagner's "credit-card" budgeting. Abraham Beame, Wagner's controller and the Democratic mayoral aspirant, squeaked that the Wagner plan was an "unsound proposal, which threatens the credit and financial standing of the city." Wagner, a man who genuinely despises conflict, answered with one of his classic evasions: ". . . a good loan is better than a bad tax." Since any tax is a bad tax to politicians, who never know whose support they may someday have to seek, this aphorism hardly closed the debate.

Almost invariably, the "official" commentators have named

Wagner's borrowing scheme as the "original sin" in New York City's long decline to perdition. Frankly, this is unfair. Wagner was certainly no great problem-solver, but he kept a fairly tight rein on city finances and worked hard and competently to increase the city's niggardly share of state and federal aid. Many of the real innovations of the subsequent federal War on Poverty were pioneered in New York. Wagner granted the unions collective-bargaining rights, a long-overdue inevitability, but he proved a masterful and tight-fisted bargainer and frequently gave labor little more than his ready smile. It was John Lindsay, with his anti-union bluster and Ivy League aides, who ended up granting a succession of union benefits which the city treasury simply couldn't support. Lindsay was the one who avidly joined the pension competition with Rocke-feller, and went along with larcenous gimmicks such as using out-dated mortality tables to understate the actual costs of the pension settlements he had negotiated.

Yes, Wagner opened the door to the astronomical increases in city borrowing that took place under his successors, but he didn't push them through it; they went of their own accord.

In reality the major effect of that Wagner-Rockefeller deal lay not so much in the fact that it allowed city borrowing to increase, as in the fact that it removed pressures on city officials to collect the funds necessary to support that borrowing. The point may seem subtle, but it was crucial in setting the city's budget adrift on the churning currents of urban politics. It is part of the hidden history of the fiscal crisis that we would now like to examine in detail.

For many years we have heard the refrain that New York has been doing "too much" for its citizens, that its taxes were too high and its tax base was shrinking as a result, that only massive retrench-ment—layoffs, salary freezes, program slashes—would restore a balanced budget. The rhetoric has recently become more hyperbolic; the writer Ken Auletta has even suggested that the basic flaw lay in the city's attempt under Lindsay to create "local socialism," a per-ception of urban policy that would no doubt come as a profound shock to the residents of Harlem and the brokers of Wall Street.

And while there may be differences of opinion among editorial writers and politicians as to where cuts should be made, or how many layoffs would actually do the job, only one set of "solutions" has ever received serious consideration: to reduce expenditures. One of the many problems with this prescription is that it ignores a basic lesson taught to all freshman accounting students: that there are two sides to every budget—income and expenditures. If you have exhausted all sources of income, then obviously you limit expenditures to achieve a balanced budget. But only then.

Astoundingly, New York City hasn't done this. In 1976 alone, more than $1 billion in taxes, fees, and fines went uncollected. If the amounts uncollected just since 1970 were added to this sum, a figure between $2 and $3 billion would accumulate—a substantial portion of the short-term debt that the city found itself incapable of "rolling over." In addition, New York City has been systematically bilked, through welfare and Medicaid frauds, of hundreds of millions of dollars. Another serious drain has resulted from borrowing costs occasioned by the painfully slow transmittal of aid funds owed by the state and federal governments. Put these figures together, and a radically altered picture of the city budget emerges; in fact, it almost balances—without meat-ax layoffs, without transit-fare increases and service reductions that simply create greater future deficits, without the destruction of a free university, without elimination of those services to the poor which offered the only meaningful hope of trading a welfare check for a payroll check.

What were the sources of this fantastic money hemorrhage?

First and foremost are cumulative unpaid arrears in city real-estate taxes amounting to $570.8 million as of June 30, 1976. (Interestingly, the nonpayment of real-estate taxes, and Tammany's nonchalant response to it, was a major factor in the first bankers' "takeover" of city government during the 1930s Depression.) The issue has been a political hot potato for at least a decade. A handful of liberals have fought to change the state law governing the collection of these taxes, but they have never received the support of city administrators, who would have benefited most from up-to-date collections. While the City Council recently moved unilaterally to reduce the allowed delinquency period to one year, it is doubtful that their action is legal, and it simply promises a long court fight with the landlords. We present the real-estate tax delinquencies as an interesting case study of how one special interest has been protected by a succession of city administrations, which in turn depended heavily on campaign contributions from the same group of people.

Landlords in New York City are not required to pay real-estate taxes for three years. (Until a few years ago, it was four.) While they must pay interest charges on arrears, the interest has always been lower than that charged for loans by commercial banks. In effect, then, the city has been making low-interest loans to property owners, among them some of the largest commercial landlords in New York, during a period when it was forced to borrow at extortionate rates in the municipal market.

After the three-year period has expired, the city may move in court to take the property "in rem" (in place of) the taxes it is owed. Several studies have shown that at this point three out of four landlords will make a payment sufficient to forestall foreclosure, although never the full amount owed. And then the cycle begins all over again. (Those buildings actually seized by the city—buildings now freed of excessive mortgage payments—can provide operating profits equal to the previous taxes.)

The landlords have always successfully argued that they are unable to keep current with their taxes because of the strictures of New York City's rent-control system. But 43 per cent of the arrearages occur in tax payments for uncontrolled commercial properties (office buildings, hotels, and stores) and 23 per cent for single-family homes. The remaining third are arrears in tax payments for multiple dwellings, where rent controls have been seriously relaxed in recent years. As rent rolls have risen, however, so have tax delinquencies. One dead-beat landlord candidly admitted that the taxes weren't paid simply because they were "the cheapest loan in town." Pressed on this issue at the height of the fiscal crisis, Mayor Beame kept promising to advocate state legislation to reduce the allowable length of delinquency, but at the end of the legislative session of 1976, no bill had even been introduced.

New York City is not the only culprit in the tax-evasion boondoggle. In recent years the state has become responsible for collecting the city sales tax. According to one source, the city is losing $200 million a year in taxes collected by merchants but never turned over to the tax collector. The state itself loses $300 million a year from uncollected sales taxes; combined, this is a cool half-billion dollars. The sales-tax collection system is a fantastic giveaway for retailers even if they don't cheat. The taxes, collected with each purchase, are required to be turned in only every three months. The bank interest earned by the retailer in this period is his "reward" for serving as a tax agent. In the meantime, the state and city must borrow to cover their own weekly operating costs. Out-of-state merchants collect city and state sales taxes but rarely turn back anywhere near the amount collected. They are never audited.

In May 1976, City Controller Harrison Goldin privately distributed to the top officers of the city an audit of one tiny part of the city's sales-tax collection system for an eight-month period that ended on February 29, 1976. This audit showed that "the city's sales tax collecting unit issued assessments of $7.5 million, while incurring operating costs of $359,000." This works out to $20 of sales-tax assessments for every $1 the city spends to fund the unit. A 20-to-1 ratio would seem a wise investment for a bankrupt city. But the collection unit has not been expanded.

Withholding taxes, taken from the wages of employees to cover state and city income taxes, also have a strange habit of disappearing before they ever enter the public treasury. Comptroller Levitt found in a 1972 audit (not published until 1975) that employers simply kept $36 million in these taxes owed to the state. It may be assumed that these companies did the same with the smaller wage taxes owed the city, for a combined amount of $50 million. There have been no audits published for succeeding years, but it should be remembered that 1972 was an artificial "boom" year, created with a massive increase in the money supply by a friendly Federal Reserve Bank to insure Nixon's re-election. In the following recession years, it can be conservatively assumed that this amount doubled—a loss somewhere in the range of $400 million to both levels of government. Levitt found that little of this money was ever recovered because the statute of limitations for prosecution frequently ran out before state tax auditors discovered the delinquency.

The list goes on. Of the twenty-two separate taxes levied by New York City, not one can be certified as fully collected. The state, with more than twice the number of residents, has an equally depressing record. The problem is hardly restricted to New York, however. One congressional staffer estimated in an article in *Washington Monthly* that as much as half of all state taxes go unpaid. Two years ago, officials of the Multistate Tax Commission, a confederation of state tax agencies trying to stem the problem, told us off the record that the annual state tax shortfall, exclusive of property taxes, was then $12 billion. But New York, unlike California (an effective tax collector), has never even bothered to join the MTC in order to benefit from jointly conducted sales tax audits of the biggest national companies.

Medicaid frauds cost New York City at least $300 million a year, according to a U.S. Senate study. As Robert Sternberg, chief auditor for medical payments of the city Department of Social Services, told *The New York Times:* "We don't have enough help to process the paper, let alone audit the providers." He said that a staff of only three auditors, working with a computer, had detected duplicate payments of $2.5 million to Medicaid "mills" in 1975. "If we had six people, we would have collected $5 million."

Nine per cent of the city's million welfare recipients were "ineligible" in 1976. If they had been expunged from the rolls, the city would have saved an additional $100 million.

Landlords who received city loans to rehabilitate vacant buildings through the scandal-plagued municipal loan program owed $107 million. Tenants in city-owned buildings owed $10.4 million, a 68 per cent increase in a one-year period. Ironically, many of these tenants are welfare recipients; apparently one city department isn't even capable of collecting from another.

An audit of the Parks Department revealed that $2 million was owed by concessionaires, including Good Humor ice cream and the Circle Line Sightseeing Boats (whose chairman, Francis Barry, is a Bronx Democratic wheelhorse and a member of the Municipal Assistance Corporation set up to issue city debt and supervise the revision of the city's accounting practices).

Obviously not every last cent owed to New York City was collectible, but a good part of it was. No one tried—and billions were irretrievably lost. The master managers who were swept into power with the formation of MAC and the Emergency Financial Control Board in 1975 have shown no more interest in collecting delinquent revenues than the hacks they replaced, who could always shrug off a tax shortfall with another loan. Apparently stringent collection policies don't fit in with the new "pro-business" image that is being cultivated by both City Hall and Albany. It is now more than two years since the fiscal crisis became official; an army of auditors has been poring over the city's books and issuing one damning report after another. But there should be another army of auditors poring over the books of landlords, department stores, manufacturers, proprietary and voluntary hospitals, Medicaid mills, and the dozens of other institutions that have been milking the city for at least a decade. That army doesn't exist, and there is little likelihood it will be formed. In fact, some of the city and state auditing personnel have been cut back in the budget crunch—to "save money," of course.

As we found when we were both involved in investigating the putrid nursing-home scandals in 1974, auditors are the key to efficient management of all government programs. Any auditor is worth at least ten times his annual salary in the money he will recover.

Just the knowledge that someone is looking over their shoulders is enough to deter many of the predators who have made large fortunes ripping-off government programs. In the long run, it is the legitimate businessman and the honest taxpayer who are the victims of the tax deadbeats and thieves. They must carry a larger burden when the unscrupulous are allowed to run free without paying.

The list still goes on and on: $4 million owed in mortgage payments by private landlords, $3.5 million in uncollected water bills (for several years the city had been sending the water bill for a luxury high-rise apartment house to a neighboring city park). It is a portrait of almost mind-boggling incompetence and mismanagement. Yet consistently, the politicians who run the city have been excoriated by the press and the business community for borrowing too much, rarely for collecting too little. Why?

The answer is inescapable. There is an unspoken, conservative bias in the efforts to restructure the city government, which holds that the poor and the powerless must now pay the price for decades of economic and political misgovernment.

The city's crisis is a reflection of a much larger national and international crisis affecting the entire capitalist system. And while New York is always *sui generis,* it is important to recognize that the "solutions" imposed nationwide by the Nixon-Ford administration— massive unemployment, reduction in government services, a general decline in the standard of living—are the same as those being prescribed for the city. At the center of this strategy is a vast, complex struggle over who will control the limited capital resources of mankind in the decades to come.

In the next chapter, we shall analyze in greater detail this struggle between corporate priorities and democratic priorities, the conflict between investing for profit and investing for the needs of people. An awareness of this struggle is critical to any understanding of the city's turbulent present and its uncertain, ominous future.

Right now it is important to keep that broader perspective in mind as we consider another crucial element in the real history of New York's fiscal collapse: the role of the banks in the final withdrawal of credit. There is no element of New York's recent history that has been so poorly reported or badly misunderstood. As we shall show, the generally accepted perception that the banks were hoodwinked by the city's politicians is pure myth.

Instead it was the bankers who did the hoodwinking—lying to thousands of hapless investors, to the press, and even to the City

Hall sharpies who were left holding the bag after a fullfledged market panic had commenced. The true story has taken almost three years to emerge: New York didn't jump; it was pushed.

In early 1973, UDC was already deeply in trouble and First Boston and the other underwriters, including Chase, Citibank, and Morgan Guaranty, knew it. Logue, in his usual blunt fashion, told them that UDC "would not be self-supporting" for some time and proposed that they continue selling bonds so that he might "roll over" current debts as they came due—borrowing to pay off earlier borrowing. They acceded, but as the state investigating commission reported: "They also realized that UDC would probably at some future date be the first test of the state's legislative intent to honor its 'moral obligation' to make up a deficiency in a debt service reserve fund." And if the legislature reneged—down would come the whole house of cards.

The report continued:

It was clear to the underwriters that, at best, the Legislature was not aware of UDC's financial condition and, at worst, as a result of the Nine Towns controversy, was antagonistic to UDC. Significantly, the uncertainty over future legislative backing for UDC did not depreciate the viability of the moral obligation in the eyes of the managers, because they were assured that UDC had an excellent relationship with the Governor. Given Mr. Rockefeller's preeminent position in the political power structure of the State, this was no small assurance.

And there you have it. The banks didn't give a damn about the soundness of paper that the state, or the city for that matter, had been churning out, for as long as Nelson Rockefeller held the reins of power, they felt protected. It was Nelson's "moral obligation" that motivated them, not the legislature's, and his assurance that he would always place their interests first in any subsequent crisis. He would keep the legislature in line, as he had so often in the past, using his personal wealth, the patronage powers of his office, and his entrée at the White House to see that whatever happened the banks would be protected.

And then Rockefeller resigned. It was a thunderclap for the banks. As the state investigators noted in their classicly understated prose, "His long tenure in Albany had created expectations on the part of the financial community, and Malcolm Wilson's succession cast doubt on those expectations."

The banks were already being buffeted on all sides. Defaults on real estate investment trusts, the Yom Kippur war, and the Arab oil boycott had all occurred only a few months before, throwing money markets into chaos and auguring a major change in international power relationships. There was talk of war coming from Henry Kissinger and the White House, and this was not simply an attempt to get Richard Nixon off the Watergate hook. Even without the unsettled oil situation, the United States had begun its slide into the recession long forecast for 1974. With inflation raging as never before, it was clear that not even the Chairman of the Federal Reserve, Arthur Burns, could bail the banks out as he had after the 1970–71 nightmare. And now Rockefeller was gone, perhaps to await the call to lead the nation that had never come in more stable times, but perhaps not.

The time had come for the bankers to take a careful look at all that New York state and city paper with which their vaults were stuffed. They didn't like what they found. It was at this point, in February 1974, that Morgan Guaranty dropped out as an underwriter for UDC. This should have served as a signal—to the legislature, the financial press, the editorial writers, the financial markets, even the bevy of Rockefeller watchers, always sensitive to even the slightest movements around the throne. With everything else in such a state of flux, however, the Morgan action passed almost unnoticed.

While the banks kept a stiff upper lip in public, a note of panic was seeping into internal memorandums. Consider this statement from hitherto secret minutes of Chase Manhattan's municipal credit portfolio review committee in mid-March 1974—exactly a year before the banks shut off the city's credit:

New York City is a different problem. In terms of the credit quality the City's rating has been wobbling between a— and baa+ for over a decade. In recent months the City's financial situation has deteriorated, partly because reality began to catch up with past budget gimmickry and partly because of the re-emergence of a growing gap between receipts and expenditures. Although New York City's economic base is enormous and a financial collapse is difficult to imagine, we view the City as being saddled with fundamentally adverse financial trends. . . .

New York City obligations present a special problem because of the City's disappointing financial performance. Although a final assessment of the City's credit should await completion of the new study currently in progress, our present impression is that the market's evaluation of the New York City name once again could begin to slip. In view of this assessment, our judgment is that the portfolio's New York City bond holdings are somewhat heavier than desirable, particularly since sizeable additional New York City obligations are held in the short-term note account.

Within the framework of overall Bank objectives regarding loss taking, holdings of New York City bonds should be reduced while New York State and energy-related issues should not be increased.

By August 1, the minutes of Chase's portfolio strategy committee listed as its first priority in tax-exempt bonds: "Look for opportunity to sell about $50 M [million] of intermediate New York City's [bonds] taking small loss if possible." By November 20, the bank's dealer strategy committee noted that it was "continuing to sell NYC obligations at every opportunity." The panic was on.

As subsequent investigations by the federal Securities and Exchange Commission and the state's Office of Legislative Oversight and Analysis would show, the big New York City banks, as well as other major banks across the nation, quietly dumped approximately $2.3 billion in New York City securities on the market between the summer of 1974 and March 1975 when that market finally collapsed. Many of these sales were made without charging commissions, a symbol of the extent of the banks' panic. During the same period, many of these same banks were underwriters for the billions in new debt issues which New York required to meet its daily needs and stave off default.

This pattern of using "inside" information as a basis for dumping doubtful securities was chillingly familiar to those who knew how the big banks had bailed out just before the Penn Central collapse in 1970.* History was repeating itself.

---

* The following brief account of that episode and the accompanying chart on page 39 are from Christopher Elias's *The Dollar Barons* (New York, 1973):
   "Between May 15, 1970, and June 19, 1970, the Chase Manhattan Bank, the Morgan Guaranty Trust Company, and the Continental Illinois National Bank and Trust Company bailed out of a dying Penn Central, as any prudent investor might. But the banks, as well as half a dozen other financial institutions, were not acting so much as prudent investors as insiders privy to information that was not public. That was the claim, at least, of the Subcommittee on Domestic Finance, a part of the House Banking and Currency Committee. On May 21, 1970, for example, the commercial lending side of the Chase Manhattan Bank learned that a $100 million debenture offer planned by the Penn Central was being canceled, meaning the Penn Central might be without badly needed capital. The next day, on May 22, the Chase Manhattan Bank's

In private meetings, the bankers who were members of Controller Goldin's technical debt committee—Thomas G. Labrecque, the 39-year-old executive vice-president of Chase Manhattan; Rich-

NUMBER OF SHARES SOLD OFF

DATE	Chase Manhattan Bank	Morgan Guaranty Trust Co.	Continental Illinois Bank & Trust
May 21	2,000	200	0
22	134,300	0	0
23	—	—	—
24	—	—	—
25	53,200	0	500
26	32,100	0	0
27	31,700	0	9,500
28	35,300	0	10,000
29	0	44,900	0
30	—	—	—
31	—	—	—
June 1	12,100	28,500	0
2	0	25,900	0
3	0	24,200	0
4	3,000	40,600	0
5	100	31,000	0
6	—	—	—
7	—	—	—
8	0	0	0
9	0	96,500	0
10	0	44,100	500
11	0	8,400	0
12	90,700	0	108,950
13	—	—	—
14	—	—	—
15	0	0	56,100
16	0	0	37,700
17	500	0	44,200
18	1,500	11,600	24,600
19	1,800	1,100	19,400

SOURCE: House of Representatives Banking and Currency Committee. Cited from Christopher Elias, *The Dollar Barons* (New York, 1973).

---

investment trust department sold 134,200 shares and continued selling stock all week long. When it let up, the Morgan Guaranty Trust started selling, then, in turn, the Continental Illinois National Bank. It was a sale of great coincidence, perhaps clairvoyance, commented Wright Patman, chairman of the House Banking and Currency Committee, when the banks denied any collusion, or even access to inside information. The wall between their trust departments and the commercial side of their banks could not be breached, they said. Thus when the commercial side learned of the debenture cancellation, a week before the public announcement, or just the length of time of the Chase Manhattan bail-out, it did not tell the trust department."

ard F. Kezer, senior vice-president of Citibank; and Frank P. Smeal, executive vice-president of Morgan Guaranty—meantime warned that the interest rates which Beame and Goldin had jointly denounced as "unfair, unwarranted and outrageously high" would be going even higher in order to attract buyers in a "glutted" market. Goldin had clear indications that the banks might be "bailing out," because his staff had presented him with Federal Reserve reports early in 1975 which showed that the banks were heavy sellers of municipal obligations for their own accounts. These figures did not reflect what the bank trust departments, which manage large aggregations of money left in their care by institutions and wealthy individuals, were selling, but as the Penn Central situation showed, the "Chinese Wall" which is supposed to exist between separate divisions of a bank is often full of gaping holes.

In an interview with us in September 1976, Goldin, with a mournful bust of Abraham Lincoln peering over his shoulder in his cavernous office in the Municipal Building, admitted that he had "suspicions" as early as the summer of 1974. He muted his statements to the press, however, because the information presented him was not "dispositive," a lawyer's word for conclusive. "I don't know to this day that they did" dump the city's obligations, he said.

Goldin, however, did present his suspicions to the Board of Estimate, in some of the "crisis" meetings that were to become an almost daily occurrence as the situation worsened. The Board is a unique feature of New York government, a hangover from the days when each county Democratic machine wanted to make sure it was getting its fair slice of the pie. On it sit the mayor, controller, City Council president, and the borough presidents of each of the five boroughs, or counties, that make up the city. In the past, the borough presidents sat as surrogates for their county leaders. This situation has changed only slightly in recent years, with the minor inroads of the city's reform Democrats. Until the Emergency Financial Control Board (EFCB) was created by the state, the Board of Estimate had vast powers, far greater than the almost irrelevant City Council, and it still must pass on all major city contracts as well as the capital budget submitted by the mayor. It was the real locus of power in city government until September 1975, although in effect a creature of the mayor since most of its members are allied with the mayor through the county Democratic organizations. (The Board of Estimate was a bone in Lindsay's throat until he made peace with the Democratic machines after his re-election in 1969.) If there was to be a counterattack against the banks' undermining of the securities markets, this was where it must be generated. City Council President Paul O'Dwyer, a perennial candidate for higher office even though he was then in his late sixties, at least tried. On several occasions he denounced the banks for attempting to decide the city's social priorities. A few other Board members mumbled similar populist sentiments and were quickly jumped on by the establishment.

No one dared to mention that it was the banks themselves that had overloaded the market. So as everyone rushed for the exits, the city's leading politicians sat with their hands folded and said nothing, lest they cause a "panic." This left the banks in an awkward position. After they had decided to stop peddling the now worthless city paper, it was important to let everyone know that the panic had already taken place. To solve this problem, Jac Friedgut, a vice-president of Citibank, held a session in Washington with the city's congressional delegation in mid-March 1975, and told them that his bank would no longer buy city notes because the city had lost the confidence of the market. Beame was in Washington the same day and rejoined, "If he made that statement it's outrageous. The top officials of that bank owe the city an explanation." Poor Abe. No one had told him the show was over because the theater had burned down.

William Haddad, an award-winning investigative reporter who had been one of the first to notice that Robert Moses had clay feet back in the 1950s, was one of the first people poking around in the ashes. After more than a decade in private business, Haddad had returned to public service as director of the Office of Legislative Oversight and Analysis in the state Assembly, a sort of inspector-general for the Democratic majority in the lower house. He intuitively figured out what the banks had been up to, although he at first thought it an elaborate scam to drive up interest rates when in fact the banks were more than grateful simply to escape with a whole skin.

Haddad wanted the Assembly to hold hearings immediately, but he was shot down by his nervous employers. (When he asked for crucial documents, the banks threatened that his investigation might cripple the state's delicate refinancing arrangements with them; similar threats were made to SEC staffers during the initial stages of their investigation.) He kept on plugging away, as can be seen by the following confidential memorandum he sent to George Cincotta, chairman of the Assembly Banking Committee on July 7, 1976:

... As you may recall, the premise of our inquiry was based on the following chronology.

(1) The political changes in Albany (Rockefeller's departure and Wilson's inability to win the election) caused the banks to review their portfolios. The UDC crisis was on the horizon already and with their protection in Albany removed, they were exposed.

(2) They began to rapidly and quietly (and, perhaps improperly and illegally) unload their New York City bonds *and thus saturated the market* [italics in original]. You recall, they claim the market was saturated and hence they could not sell their bonds. This seems to be untrue. In fact, it appears that Chase unloaded two billion dollars' worth of bonds in a very short time!

... Here is where the situation gets sticky for the banks. They had knowledge of the problems ahead, but they kept this knowledge to themselves while unloading their portfolios to others. They created the panic by their heavy sales. There are many examples of poor, little people being crushed by this fraud (one a blind woman, several who had moved to Florida for a year while testing out the climate there and investing their money in "safe" municipal bonds, etc.).

In short, Chase alone unloaded two billion dollars of paper they knew was going bad without telling their customers. They not only created the panic, but profited from it.

(3) When the banks saturated the market with their own paper [i.e. city bonds originally purchased for their own accounts], they turned to the State and the City and shouted "Help." The market was flooded and they could not sell their bonds. This, in turn, led to us bailing them out, and to higher interest rates for every municipality in the country. It led to the EFCB and a substantial portion of the enormous debt service we are now carrying.

If I do nothing else with this office, this is a case we need to prove. We now have the SEC as our ally, at least at the team level here (top-flight lawyers). And we were right last year when we said all this and everyone smiled at us.

By the time this was written, no one was smiling—least of all the banks. The City of New York brought suit in August 1976 to stop the SEC investigation, claiming the agency lacked jurisdiction over municipal securities sales.

There can be little doubt that had the press reported, and the public fully understood, how the New York City crisis had been artificially fostered by the bank panic, New York's immediate history would have been quite different. Even someone as obtuse as

Gerald Ford or wearing the ideological blinders of an Arthur Burns or a William Simon would have been hard pressed to pillory the city for a crisis for which it was only partly responsible. The impact on the banks, already reeling under the disclosure of failing loans to the real-estate investment trusts, to builders of giant oil tankers that would never be used, to overextended corporations and shaky foreign dictators, would have been profound. As it was, eleven insolvent banks were forced to close their doors in 1975, the highest number since the country emerged from the Depression in 1942. Disclosure of bank manipulation of the municipal-securities markets might have doomed some of the biggest on the list of almost 300 "trouble" banks maintained by the Federal Deposit Insurance Corporation—and Chase Manhattan would have been among the first to go.

When Tom Labrecque approved the order to sell the more than $1 billion Chase held in city securities, he entered the ranks of the nation's all-time high rollers. He wasn't playing only for the solvency of his own institution; the stability of the international banking community rode on his decision. And he won, because no one—city officials, the state legislature, federal banking regulators, or the City Hall press corps, which at least heard rumors about what was going on—bothered to tell the people.* The big loser of course was the city and its people. But everyone in the nation lost as well. Michael C. Jensen, writing in *The New York Times* of October 19, 1975, estimated that *all* states and municipalities ended up paying an additional $3 billion in inflated borrowing costs as a result of the

---

* Fred Ferretti, another City Hall reporter for *The New York Times* during the fiscal crisis, subsequently wrote a book called *The Year the Big Apple Went Bust.* In it Ferretti treats the banks' "bailout" as a throwaway line in his first chapter. Writing of the summer before the crisis year, he says: "During this period too the banks began to toy with unloading their own stacks of city notes, and later they were to sell off great chunks." That's all.

Reviewing Ferretti's book in the June 21, 1976, *Village Voice,* the political writer Geoffrey Stokes quoted a line in the book, "What is the purpose of a government—to care for its citizens or make heroes of its accountants?" and went on shrewdly to observe: "New Yorkers have asked that question in a dozen different languages and one hundred different accents over the past eighteen months. For us—and for Ferretti—the answer is obvious: The real question is why it wasn't equally obvious to the powers in Washington and on Wall Street. One reason is that they'd been reading *The New York Times,* in which the passion that informs Ferretti's book has been conspicuously lacking. Indeed, the tone of his book is an implied indictment of Ferretti's own daily reporting. . . . Ferretti, who concludes his book with an impassioned defense of the city's efforts to make life as decent as possible for its inhabitants, has been systematically turning out daily reporting that counteracts the book's angry thrust."

New York crisis. Jensen figured, "That amounts to $14 for each man, woman, and child in the United States." A high price to pay for protecting the good name of the banks.

Before we move on to a consideration of the federal government's participation in the city's crisis, there is one final item, also obscured or ignored by the "official" chroniclers of the crisis, that demands our attention. This is the long-term breakdown of the municipal credit markets—no small contributor to the current mess. After all, New York City accounted for only 5 per cent of the country's total municipal debt before it collapsed, although it issued 29 per cent of the short-term debt.

As Sanford Rose noted in the December 1975 issue of *Fortune:*

> The effects of New York's troubles have cast a pall over the entire municipal market. Yet it would be a gross overstatement to say that the current crisis in the market is solely, or even primarily, a consequence of New York's situation. Actually, the crisis started before that city's difficulties became well known in the market place, and is likely to continue long after its problems are resolved. . . .
>
> . . . The municipal market is going through a crisis—one of the worst in its history. It is a crisis that could well lead to a thorough revamping of the market's structure.

The reasons for that crisis aren't hard to find. As Rose explains, "State and local governments are expanding borrowings at a rapid pace just when traditional holders of tax-exempt bonds are cutting back on their purchases."

The municipal bond market caters exclusively to banks, corporations, and wealthy individuals seeking to protect their income from federal, state, and local taxes. Constitutionally, one level of government is banned from taxing the financial instruments of another. This means that the federal government cannot tax the income from a New York State bond, for instance. New York State and the city also treat income on their bonds as tax exempt. For individuals and corporations in high tax brackets this is a major boon. For someone in the 50-per-cent tax bracket, an interest rate of 8 per cent on a tax-free bond is equal to an interest rate of 16 per cent on a taxable corporate bond. Since taxable bonds rarely pay such high rates, at least not bonds from corporations with any prospect of remaining in business long enough to pay back the original investment in the bond, municipals have been good deals for the wealthy and even the not-so-wealthy. With municipals today paying interest that is about 80 per cent of that paid by corporates, even people in the 30-per-cent bracket—$15–$20,000 a year—can make a tidy profit from the offerings of government agencies. The same goes for smaller corporations.

Tax-free institutions (a major portion of the national capital pool) such as pension funds, foundations, churches, colleges, and mutual savings banks gain no benefits from this tax exemption, however, and when they buy municipal bonds it is only as a safety hedge against the mercurial nature of the stock market.

Until recently, the largest purchasers of municipals have been commercial banks and, to a lesser degree, the casualty insurance companies. Wealthy individuals constitute the third largest component of the market. But in the last few years the banks have developed so many other tax loopholes that they have significantly cut back on new purchases of municipals. They still account, however, for about half of municipal-bond holdings.

Banks pay almost no federal taxes and minuscule state taxes. For instance, in 1974 the ten largest bank holding companies in America paid an average of only 2 per cent in federal taxes on worldwide earnings of $2 billion.* All of the large banks, those with $500 million or more in deposits, paid only 11 per cent in taxes, while medium-sized banks, those with deposits between $100 million and $500 million, paid only 12 per cent. In contrast, a worker earning $8,000 in 1974 paid 20 per cent in federal taxes.

Aside from the purchase of municipals, the banks' tax writeoffs have come from two gaping loopholes. In recent years, almost half the profits of the big banks are coming from operations in foreign countries. But the taxes paid to those countries—a cost of doing business abroad—are treated as if they were paid to the U.S. Treasury. That is, the banks can deduct foreign taxes from U.S. tax liabilities on a dollar-for dollar basis. Besides seriously depleting the Treasury and shifting the tax burden to those least able to pay, this

---

* The ten were: BankAmerica, Citicorp, Chase Manhattan, J. P. Morgan, Manufacturers Hanover, Chemical New York, Bankers Trust New York, Continental Illinois, Security Pacific and Wells Fargo. Chase Manhattan, with profits worldwide of $235.5 million, and Chemical, with $97 million, actually shared tax rebates from the federal government amounting to $21.6 million because of the laxity of the tax laws. The statutory tax rate for all corporations is 48 per cent, and after standard deductions and investment credits, the average effective corporate tax is 30 per cent.

loophole constitutes a major inducement to export American wealth and jobs abroad, frequently to dictatorships like Iran, Brazil, and Korea, where the rate of profits is high because workers can be shot for striking for higher wages.

The second loophole is a product of the bank holding company laws first passed in the 1960s. This allows banks to use their capital to buy other businesses. As a result, banks have taken to leasing high-cost machinery like computers to industry and taking the depreciation and investment tax credits allowed by Congress as an inducement for capital spending. The banks are in fact only middle-men, but they take the lion's share of these benefits.

Purely and simply, the banks have found these new writeoffs more profitable than municipal bonds. In addition, the banks are beginning to worry that the public may be waking up to the full amounts of tax ripoffs they are allowed. In order to keep things quiet, they must pay at least token taxes, and, with the embarrass-ment of options now available to them, municipals are losing their allure.

As for the casualty insurers, also major purchasers of municipals, they have had no profits to protect from taxes since they took such a bad bath in the stock market in 1975 and since the costs of re-placement parts for cars, for instance, have been driven through the roof by the giant auto monopolies. This situation is now changing because lax state insurance regulators have allowed astronomical rate increases for drivers, and insurance company profits are due for a sharp rebound; but this hardly spells salvation for the municipal market.

In fact, it is interesting to note that the market is particularly hard hit by the roller-coaster ride the economy has been taking. Demand for municipals falls at the very time when economic de-cline places the greatest pressure on state and local spending. The market is increasingly dependent, therefore, on wealthy individuals. This entails a number of problems. First, the rich have other more profitable income-protection schemes available, despite all the blather about tax reform. Second, to avoid the ravages of inflation, a lot of their wealth is increasingly invested in property rather than paper. Third, the rich lie a lot, and put their money in Swiss banks.

All of this leaves too narrow a market to support government borrowing needs, and it leads to constantly increasing interest rates. The fastest way to expand the market would be to offer municipal bonds to the many moderate- and middle-income investors who would jump at the chance to buy them. However, these bonds are offered exclusively in such large denominations ($25,000, $10,000, and occasionally $5,000) that ordinary people can't invest; one bond might equal their total savings. There have been continued demands from city officials to reduce these amounts—offering, for example, $100, $500, or $1,000 bonds. But even at the height of New York's crisis, this alternative was rejected by the banks and other municipal sellers, who claimed it would increase administrative costs for the city. But since this increase would be balanced by lower interest costs from a broader market, the argument doesn't hold water. The real reason for the hostility is much simpler: Financial institutions don't want to lose the vast amounts they now hold in small savings accounts at federally prescribed low interest rates. This is especially true of the savings banks that systematically ship large amounts of capital from the Northeast to other parts of the country—a drain that is responsible for a severe capital shortage in the very areas that generate most of America's capital.

(Small investors have been given a break in the Tax Reform Act of 1976, which allows mutual funds to invest in municipals for the first time. Now an investor can buy a share in a block of high-priced bonds and still receive the tax exemption on his portion of the interest.)

In addition, the municipal market has been overwhelmed by a glut of spurious new "municipals" that are in fact simply private borrowings hiding behind a government fig leaf. These are the "pollution-control" and "industrial-development" bonds. Many localities also issue general-obligation bonds to subsidize everything from private colleges and hospitals to commercial baseball and football teams.

As *The Wall Street Journal* revealed on July 21, 1976, the basic problem with industrial-development bonds is that they often go sour. For instance, Burns Flats, Oklahoma, issued industrial-development bonds to build a factory for the Western States Plastics Company. The company, not the town, was liable for repayment of both the face value of the bonds and the interest; it quickly went under and investors were left holding the bag. The SEC and the Oklahoma Securities Commission have been investigating the case for fraud—a frequent charge in many of these issues. As the *Journal* noted: "In many cases, government investigators' preliminary findings on suspected fraudulent issues seem to implicate not only the recipients of the bond money but also the sponsors who helped bring the issues to the public."

Similarly, in the case of "pollution-control" bonds, everyone seems to lose but the company that is having its equipment financed. As Rose explained in *Fortune:*

Federal law premits state and local agencies to issue tax-exempt bonds in order to finance pollution-control equipment for the benefit of private corporations. Typically, the equipment is leased to the corporations, with the lease payments structured to meet the debt service on the bonds.

The pollution-control bond gives the corporations a triple or, in some cases, a quadruple subsidy. The company gets the benefit of the state's lower borrowing costs. It can also treat the pollution facility as its own property, and so depreciate it on an accelerated basis, and, under certain conditions, it may even be able to deduct a part of the lease payments as business expenses. As if that were not enough, in most states, pollution-control facilities are exempt from local property taxes.

Rose cites one federal source as estimating that $4–$7 billion is now tied up in this kind of financing.

Many solutions to these problems have been bandied about for years. Rose and others, among them Senator Edward Kennedy, favor the issuance of taxable municipals underwritten by direct federal interest subsidies. Since the federal government now loses about $1.40 in taxes for every $1 saved by municipal borrowers, they feel that the subsidy would save money for both the Treasury and lower levels of government. While taxable bonds would have to pay higher yields, they would open the market to the tax-free institutions, and this significantly increased demand should keep a reasonable lid on yields. At the same time, by reducing the supply of tax-exempt bonds, yields for those exclusively interested in the tax exemption would fall and prices would rise. This would both stabilize and broaden the market, they argue.

Opposition to these proposals comes primarily from municipalities who fear dependency on a federal subsidy that might be withdrawn by some future Congress. The investment bankers are also opposed, because a simpler market might put them out of business.

Many large cities are hesitant about the taxable bonds, but they certainly want to see Congress act to restrict the proliferation of new types of bonds, such as the industrial-development and pollution-control issues. They think the feds should subsidize these activities through direct investment tax credits.

We'll have more to say about this when we make some recommendations for salvaging the cities at the end of the book. Right now we would simply observe that it is fascinating that an administration which went berserk dreaming up tax writeoffs for utilities, defense contractors, and giant corporations left the municipalities and a major securities market to twist in the wind. Treasury Secretary Simon was at great pains to reassure Congress that no reforms in the municipal markets were necessary—after New York had been excluded. Almost every other observer feels that our outdated, inadequate municipal markets are long overdue for a complete restructuring.

NIXON WAS THE ONE

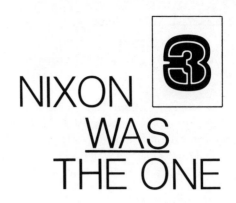

In early 1973, Robert Lekachman, the most incisive of our popular economists, wrote, "President Nixon ... is celebrating his second term with the most coherent conservative program of redistribution of income, wealth, public services and political power from poor to rich that has been offered by any major American politician in living memory." The major victim of the Nixon counter-revolution was America's cities, especially the aging cities of the Northeast and Midwest.

Only a few short years after the trauma of Watergate, it is hard to remember just how powerful Richard Nixon was in the wake of his landslide victory over George McGovern. It was the height of the Imperial Presidency. Congress was impotent, despite its over-whelming Democratic majority. If it passed legislation that Nixon disapproved, Nixon would veto it. If it overrode his vetoes, he would impound the monies it appropriated. If it sued to set aside his im-poundments, the issue would wend its way through the courts, even to a Supreme Court whose conservative majority he had shaped. To all intents and purposes, Richard Nixon was *the* American government.

Yet Nixon seemed immune to the nourishing mystique of the presidency. Although a cunning politician, as a president he was lacking in self-confidence and driven by insecurities, paranoia, and petty venality. He probably did not burn the White House tapes out of fear of losing certain tax advantages. He seemed to doubt his own legitimacy to rule. As JFK once said, he "had no class." He brooded over minor resentments and past slights. In the twisted mire of the Nixon mind, he resented—among so many things— America's large cities, with all their unruly minorities and non-conformists.

He signaled his intentions in a now-famous postelection interview with *The Washington Star* when he vowed to stop "throwing dollars at problems." Whether carefully rehearsed or spontaneous, this was a brilliant phrase, and its echoes can still be heard—not only from Republicans but from a whole new generation of Democrats with their admonitions to "lower our expectations." Nixon captured in that one phrase all the frustrations of the many hard-working, tax-paying Americans who saw government—all government—as an alien bureaucracy demanding an ever greater share of their paychecks in order to lavish new benefits on blacks and other minority groups; pot-smoking, foulmouthed college students; and insolent, "unproductive" public employees.

The reality of course was quite different. The Great Society had never been even minimally financed to deal with the true scope of the problems it vowed to eradicate. Seventy per cent of the increase in social spending during the late 1960s and early 1970s had been for Social Security and Medicare, and the rest was mostly window dressing. Meanwhile, progressive taxes on businesses and wealthy individuals had been cut by $25 billion between 1969 and 1974 while regressive payroll taxes on workers had been raised by $20 billion.

No matter, at the heart of Nixon's re-election campaign had been a promise to punish all of the groups in our society that had raised their voices against exclusion and oppression. Now Nixon read the election returns as a mandate to repeal not only the modest social experiments of the Great Society years but the profound accomplishments of the New Deal as well. His first postelection budget was a blueprint for vengeance, an "enemies list" that included the majority of the American people.

Nixon proposed to eliminate or sharply reduce no less than 101 programs that had developed over almost four decades. Lekachman has cited a few of the outstanding examples:

The Nixon body count includes reductions in housing for lower-income families, rural electrification, public service employment, special programs in mental health, model cities, urban renewal, manpower training, some aids for education, student loans, support for libraries, improvements and extensions in the national parks, research and development on mass transportation, and training programs in medical and biological research. Just for good measure, the White House has also impounded half the money Congress appropriated for pollution control, disbanded the Office of Economic Opportunity and placed in limbo its generally acclaimed legal services program, and interred the Family Assistance Plan, a year or two ago hailed by the President as the center-piece of his New American Revolution.

A quick glance shows that most of these programs had as their principal purpose the improvement of conditions in the large cities.

All of this would be done in the holy name of fighting inflation and reining in the "runaway" federal budget. Not that Nixon actually intended to reduce spending: Even while slashing social and antipollution programs by $14 billion, he projected an $18-billion overall increase to cover increased debt service costs, Social Security hikes necessitated by inflation, and a $5 billion expansion of the Pentagon budget for new weapons and old wars—including the continuing conflict in Vietnam. He skillfully danced around the fact that 54 cents of every dollar in the national budget would go for military spending. It still does.

In Nixon's view, a view shared by conservatives in both parties, gorging the Pentagon was "necessary spending"; spending for education, housing, health care, or clean rivers and lakes was "wasteful spending."

Actually, the Congressional liberals lent Nixon a great deal of unwitting support in his program against social spending and the cities. This was the year when the long crusade for "revenue sharing" finally bore fruit—and revenue sharing was predominantly a liberal program. Although first introduced by Republican Congressman (later Defense Secretary) Melvin R. Laird in 1958, the idea had been rapidly adopted by John Kennedy's staff, especially by Walter Heller, his chairman of the Council of Economic Advisers. As Milwaukee Democratic Congressman Henry Reuss described the idea in his 1970 book, *Revenue Sharing:*

In the main, state and local governments must still look after our great domestic needs—education, public safety, public health, the environment, welfare, the future of our cities. But demands for public services are fast outstripping local financial resources.

The problem is exacerbated because state and local governments rely mainly on property and sales taxes that fall especially hard on the person of modest income. The Federal government relies heavily on the progressive income tax, based generally on ability to pay. Moreover, Federal revenues grow with the economy much more rapidly than do state-local revenues. Increasingly, therefore, the federal government will have the revenues, and state and local governments will have the problems.

Reuss and other liberals supporting revenue sharing foresaw a massive "peace dividend" at the end of the Vietnam war. They wanted to take these monies and share them with state and local governments to redress the imbalance in the tax bases. At the same time, they felt that the Washington bureaucracy was too rigid in its administration of social programs, and too remote from the groups being served.

Behind these arguments lay another purpose, however. The proliferation of categorical grant programs, especially the War on Poverty designed under Kennedy and enacted by Johnson, tended to weaken the power of state and local Democratic machines. More and more, the feds were dealing directly with new neighborhood groups and nonprofit agencies, and even the funds flowing through elected administrations or establishment institutions required "citizen participation" and oversight by local community people. This reduced the potential for old-fashioned patronage and weakened the power bases of incumbents, who wanted to be able to go to Washington with the assurance that everything would remain quiet on the home front. Revenue sharing with local governments would return the control over social spending to the traditional machines.

When revenue sharing was finally enacted, the Vietnam war still was dragging on. (As usual the liberals had underestimated the power of the military-industrial complex: even after the war ended, there was no "peace dividend." Instead, the money went into the maw of the Pentagon to develop new weapons, to reassure our frightened allies that we had not gone "soft" in the face of defeat, and to finance that other brainchild of misguided liberals—a volunteer army.) Instead of surplus revenue in 1973, Congress was faced with a budget where the cost of everything had been driven up by war-induced inflation. In Nixon's hands, revenue sharing therefore became a tool for severely cutting, not increasing, social spending.

Let's take a look at just one area to get some idea of the program's effects. The Community Development Revenue Sharing program, introduced by Nixon in March 1973 and signed by Ford thirteen days after he came into office, lumps together a series of pre-existing programs such as model cities, rehabilitation, code enforcement, and demolition; and it establishes a yearly funding that the cities can then allocate to their needs as they see fit.

The federal Office of Management and Budget and Department of Housing and Urban Development arbitrarily established a first-year funding level of $2.3 billion—as opposed to a real need estimated by the U.S. Conference of Mayors and by an independent survey of 200 cities at $5.5 billion. New York would receive an allocation of $101 million against a spending need of $240 million.

In addition to serious underfunding for the major cities, the program, through a bureaucratically established national formula, actually shifted money away from the areas of greatest need to the suburbs and growing cities of the Sunbelt. New York and Chicago, for example, remain frozen at prior spending levels, while other major cities fare even worse, as David Muchnick explained in the Winter 1976 issue of _Dissent:_

> The next seventeen biggest central cities in the North and the East eventually will lose an estimated $168 million yearly, compared to their combined average yearly receipts between 1968 and 1972 under previous programs. From a five-year average of $378 million, their funding will be sliced almost in half, to $210 million yearly in fiscal 1980. Philadelphia, Detroit, Baltimore, Washington, D.C., Boston, and Cincinnati will lose over $97 million annually among them. By contrast, Houston, Dallas, Memphis, New Orleans, Phoenix, Jacksonville, Fort Worth, Miami, El Paso, and Birmingham will gain over $71 million annually. . . .
>
> To finish the illustration, Massachusetts' 14 central cities will lose $6 million annually by fiscal 1980, while aid for its suburbs and rural areas will increase by $15 million and $1 million respectively—a net annual statewide loss of $30 million. Alabama's 18 central cities will gain $5.4 million annually, while funding for its suburbs and rural areas will increase by $23 million and $6 million respectively—a net annual statewide increase of $34 million. Nationwide, central cities will lose $276 million annually by 1980, while Federal investment in suburbs and rural areas will increase by $757 million and $291 million respectively. . . .

Local officials of these older central cities argue that the consequences of universal entitlement on the basis of population results in the loss of dollars by cities with declining populations, in the provision of scarce funds to wealthy communities with no poor and no overcrowding, and in the financial, administrative, and political reinforcement of those suburbs that deny residential and occupational opportunities to low-income workers, poor people, and minorities.

In other words, the federal government takes from the poor and gives to the rich, a Nixon-Ford twist on the old Robin Hood legend.

The revenue-sharing fiasco was only one of the nasty surprises that Nixon had in store for American cities. As we have noted, he suspended the subsidized housing programs in January 1973, even before he was sworn in for a second term. Now he enunciated a new program that concentrated almost all federal housing dollars in the Sunbelt and left the cities with a "trickle-down" rent subsidy program that virtually ended the production of new housing for the poor and middle classes.

Traditionally, American housing policy has overwhelmingly favored the construction of single-family private homes. The federal government does this in a number of ways: Mortgage interest payments are exempt from taxation; FHA and VA insurance is structured to induce builders to construct this type of housing; and the government often underwrites the capital costs of providing the sewage treatment plants and street networks needed for new subdivisions. Private-home subsidies accounted for two-thirds of the $15.3 billion in federal housing support and tax preferences in 1972. Nixon vowed to intensify this approach.

In that same year, two out of every three new private homes in the country were already being built in the South and the West, and the South and Southwest accounted for more than half of all federally insured mortgages on new homes, according to Muchnick's figures. "The southern and southwestern real estate industry's contribution to GNP reached more than $41.6 billion in 1971, providing nearly 2 million jobs in the nonagricultural sector," he notes.

In the rest of the nation, new construction and building employment remained at a standstill:

In the North and East [Muchnick continues], this policy will continue to provide subsidies for suburban homeowners and secure transfers of ownership in the existing stock of private homes. More than nine out of ten federally insured mortgages in the Northeast in 1972 covered such transactions, compared to 75% nationally. In that year, New England, New York, New Jersey and Pennsylvania accounted for only 5% of the FHA new homes. Only on the fringes of metropolitan areas are new federally insured units likely to be built. Elsewhere in the metropolis, the higher costs of land, construction and financing have pushed prices of new single-family dwellings to the limits of federal insurance ceilings, and, more important, beyond the financial reach of more than four out of five American families.

Since the Depression, the federal government had recognized the refusal of the private market to finance housing for the urban poor. Although public housing began as a program to put unemployed construction workers back on the job, a variant of WPA, it continued as the only way in which decent housing could be created at reasonable rents for the many city-dwellers whose only other option was festering slums. As we have seen, private housing construction for anyone except the very rich would have been at a standstill in New York had it not been for city, state, and federal housing construction programs in the 1960s and early 1970s. Much the same was true in other older northern cities.

Now Nixon brought new construction in the cities to a wrenching halt. As a substitute he offered rent subsidies to the poor, especially the aged poor, under a program known as the Section 8 program. Instead of providing for the construction of new housing, Section 8 forced the eligible poor to shop on the *free market* for available housing. If government housing agencies approved the new dwelling, a subsidy would be paid to the landlord, in addition to a quarter of the tenants' income, to meet the rent cost. The logic was that with these new dollars floating around, private landlords would independently build new housing to attract subsidized tenants.

In most aging cities, that plan is a cruel hoax. First of all, banks won't invest in new urban construction, preferring instead to meet the highly profitable demands for their scarce funds coming from the booming, federally subsidized Sunbelt. One part of the federal program therefore cancels out the other. Second, the plan ignores racial segregation, a fundamental component of the urban housing problem. Landlords in all-white areas are afraid to rent to non-whites lest they set off a panic that the neighborhood is "going" and thereby reduce the resale value of their buildings. Speculators might in fact participate in the Section 8 program, but this is a prescription for rapid housing decline, not improvement. Besides, most speculators operate only in minority neighborhoods; they lack the capital to buy buildings in stable, white neighborhoods. Third, landlords traditionally seek maximum occupancy in existing buildings. It would be counterproductive for them to construct new housing, even in tight rental markets like New York's. When a housing shortage occurs, they will subdivide existing apartments rather than build new ones. This, of course, means a further decline in the quality of the housing stock. This Nixon program, like so many others, is built on the rhetoric of the free market, not the reality of the existing capitalist system.

Realistically, the Section 8 subsidy will only achieve a further inflation of rents in existing low-income neighborhoods. While some families will perhaps move into marginally better housing, the net effect will be negative, the more so because the program provides the illusion of hope where none exists. It is a program for slumlords, not tenants.

In one after another problem area, the pattern is the same. In the 1960s, cities, and especially New York, had rushed to establish programs that would be eligible for federal support. They often created job opportunities for unemployed or underemployed minority group members. (Mayor Beame told a congressional committee that employees in federally aided programs in New York had increased 37 per cent while cops, firemen, etc. had declined 4 per cent in the last decade.) People became dependent on the services—such as welfare mothers who could find jobs because of the availability of day care for their children. Then the federal government sharply reduced its support or ended it entirely. The problems didn't disappear, nor did the demand for the services, which had so obviously improved people's lives. The cities attempted to absorb the costs and continue the programs, and stumbled deeper into debt.*

Here are just two brief examples: Head Start was one of the clear, identifiable successes of the Great Society. It confirmed the long-held belief of educators that children's learning capacities should be engaged at a much earlier age than the customary kindergarten or first-grade starting time for public school. Middle-class

---

* Another outrage, in our view, is the fact that many of the scarce millions of public funds intended for the poor were siphoned into the machines of ghetto hustlers who became not only politically very powerful but rich. See below, Chapter 8, for our discussion of Ramon Velez in the South Bronx and Samuel Wright in central Brooklyn, both of whom became city councilmen and almost became congressmen through poverty program ripoffs.

parents now deem preschool education a must for their children. When the poor were given an opportunity for the same advantage, thanks to Head Start, their children matched the achievement levels of other children in the first few years of formal schooling. Then the glaring inadequacies of ghetto schools began to take their toll, and the children fell behind again as they grew older. The obvious solution was to continue improving and enriching the higher grades in these schools; but the Nixon-Ford response was to freeze funding for Head Start so that it could not be expanded, and the cities were forced to absorb the costs of existing programs as the inflationary spiral continued. Head Start, the brightest hope for true educational equality, today has become minuscule, with only a minor effect on schools in low-income areas, which each year fall farther behind nationally accepted norms.

As a result, the public-school system in our cities is deserted by parents who have the resources to send their children to private schools. The disastrous inadequacy of the public schools is often the determining factor in the decision of moderate-income families— both white and, increasingly, black—to move to the suburbs. Racial apartheid in the cities is the inevitable result.

Neighborhood health centers, first sponsored by the federal Office for Economic Opportunity, and subsequently by the Department of Health, Education and Welfare, were the replacement for the family doctors who deserted inner-city neighborhoods in droves during the 1950s and early 1960s. The centers provided good medical care for the sick and instituted screening programs, especially for children, to identify diseases in their early, curable stages. The major beneficiaries were families of the working poor who earned too much to qualify for welfare medical benefits but too little to pay the costs of traditional health care. When the Nixon-Ford administration suddenly ordered these centers to become "self-supporting," it was the working poor who were turned away. In New York, with its network of municipal hospitals, the burden of caring for these people was then dumped on an already seriously underfinanced system. The results were growing deficits for the city and a continuing deterioration in the quality of health care.

When aides to President Ford denounced the Great Society during the 1976 presidential campaign for having "raised the hopes of the poor and then dashed them," it was an exercise in political chicanery. Even Daniel Patrick Moynihan, now New York's junior senator, who provided Nixon and Ford with much of their more sophisticated rhetoric against the Great Society, admitted that it had been "underfinanced and oversold." The inescapable fact is that the anticity policies of Nixon and Ford "dashed the hopes of the poor" and hastened the bankruptcy of our cities in the process.

On Thursday, June 26, 1975, in Washington, D.C., promptly at 9:45 A.M. the Commerce, Consumer and Monetary Affairs Subcommittee of the House of Representatives convened in Room 2247 of the Rayburn House Office Building. Ben Rosenthal, a deceptively meek-looking congressman from a Jewish middle-class district in the heart of Queens, was in the chair. Sitting before him at the witness table, his hair so sleekly brilliantined that it reflected the overhead lights, was William Simon, erstwhile Wall Street bond peddler, currently the Secretary of the Treasury.

The subcommittee had scheduled three days of hearings to find out what help the federal government could provide to New York, as its inability to borrow in the open market brought it closer to default with each passing day. Rosenthal said he also wanted to examine the role of the banks in the collapse, and the performance of the three federal entities that are supposed to regulate them.

Mayor Beame had been the first witness when the hearing opened on June 23, and he mumbled his usual litany of excuses for the city's situation. He danced around the issue of whether or not the banks had dumped city securities, hinting broadly that he found the sudden cash boycott "puzzling." So much for Abe Beame as populist whistle-blower.

George Mitchell, vice-chairman of the Board of Governors of the Federal Reserve System, had appeared next, a stand-in for the sacrosanct Arthur Burns. Mitchell admitted that the Reserve system had the power to make loans to the city, but he denied that the city met its criteria. Primarily, he doubted New York's ability to solve its problems on a short-term basis, and he rejected the idea that its bankruptcy "would have a significant detrimental economic and financial impact on the surrounding area, the region, or the nation." Mitchell said, "Access to a source of temporary credit . . . may tend to defer or prevent the remedial actions that are necessary, difficult as they may be." In other words, we intend to hold your feet to the fire until you do exactly what we tell you. He did have other interesting things to say, too. Under sharp questioning by Rosenthal, he left the distinct impression that every large bank in New York except Morgan Guaranty was in a shaky position, but he was emphatic that their weaknesses didn't stem from the amount of New York City bonds they held—by now reduced to only $1.26 billion.

Now, on the second day of the hearings, Bill Simon appeared as a uniquely qualified "expert" witness. From January 1964 until December 1972 he had directed the municipal and government bond departments at Salomon Brothers, one of the biggest operations on Wall Street. He had been a key member of the small band of men—no more than twenty-five—who "make" the market for municipal bonds. And business had been good.

He had also served as a member of Controller Beame's technical debt management committee and had sat across the table from him at a meeting on April 20, 1971, when Beame ranted about a Virginia bank that had called New York "a potential Penn Central." Simon had sold more than $1 billion of the short-term loans floated in 1971 and 1972. If anybody knew New York's finances, it was Bill Simon.

Now, of course, he wore a different hat. *Business Week* had called him "Washington's No. 1 Capital Gap Crusader," a misnomer since the title actually belonged to Federal Reserve chairman Arthur Burns and Simon was simply Burns's front man. He was, instead, "Washington's No. 1 Capital Gap Salesman."

What is a "capital gap"? The phrase had begun to appear with amazing regularity. Chase Manhattan had been the primary popularizer of the concept, taking full-page ads in major publications with bold headlines like "OUCH!" and "SCREAM!" The basic message was simple: American corporations and individuals weren't saving enough of their incomes to provide for the massive investment in new sources of energy, industrial modernization, and foreign expansion that would be needed in the next decade. As a result, we would fall behind in competition with other nations and no longer be Number One among the world's powers.

The major villain in the Chase scenario was government. It collected too much in taxes (apparently Chase wasn't satisfied with the multimillion-dollar tax rebate it had gotten from the feds in 1974) and thereby blunted the profit incentive; it borrowed too much in the capital markets, "elbowing" out the corporations; it pumped too much money back into the economy and therefore caused "runaway" inflation. The answer to these evils was simple enough: The federal government should reduce taxes on corporations and wealthy individuals and underwrite risky new corporate investments. It should sharply reduce its costly social spending. It should balance its budget and reduce its finance market competition with industry for the savings of the nation. If these admittedly profound changes were accomplished, American capitalists could then go on to build the future for which they had already drafted blueprints: carpet the nation with nuclear power plants, develop a trillion-dollar synthetic fuel complex, fully automate basic industry, and accelerate the corporate penetration of developing Third World economies.

The realities behind this scare campaign were rather more complex. The rate of profit was inexorably falling in mature industries and advanced nations. Unemployment, which had always been used to cow labor's wage demands, could do so no longer since workers had fought for and won benefits that would sustain an acceptable standard of living even during layoffs. Capitalism had exhausted the profit potential in the radical changes in life-style, such as suburbs, superhighways and shopping centers, that had accompanied the growth and development of the automotive age. Natural resources were rapidly and tangibly disappearing. The specter of a static and therefore profitless economic system was haunting the boardrooms. It threatened to usher in an age of democratic planning and income redistribution such as the world had never seen. Government had been manipulated to create every Golden Age of profit in the past. Government funds had underwritten the construction of the canals and railroads, the permanent war economy, the leap into space, and America's expansion into war-torn Europe and the underdeveloped world. Now government must underwrite the costly investments necessary to pump new blood through the aged and cracking arteries of capitalism.

This was really just an echo of what Nixon had been saying all along. Inflation, not unemployment and poverty, was the nation's "real" enemy and inflation was caused by government spending, which in turn produced the dual evils of full employment and high wages. (The conservative economists around Nixon and Ford simply shrugged away the paradox that prices were rising at record rates during the second worst economic downturn in modern history. Democratic claims that monopoly control of the leading industries led to "administered prices," and that this was the real source of inflation, were dismissed as "anticorporate propaganda.")

So Simon would now appear to give the House subcommittee another lesson in "fighting inflation" and the evils of spending tax dollars on people rather than corporations. As is often the case in hearings of this sort, the chairman invited him to summarize his

written statement, and Simon then gave the standard recitation of
conservative plaints about the city: New York spent more per capita
on its citizens than other American cities; its pensions were too
generous; and it had more employees per thousand residents than
other cities. (He happily noted that Baltimore, New York's close
runner-up in this last category, had just been forced to lay off 20
per cent of its payroll.) It had a tuition-free university, too many
ineligibles on welfare, too many municipal hospital beds. It had
borrowed to meet deficits, and as its borrowings accelerated, the
market got leery and finally closed down. He was at great pains to
emphasize that the anonymous "market," not the all too identifiable
banks, was the source of New York's calamity.

He then briefly ran through the decision-making process that
had led the Ford administration six weeks before to reject aid to
New York City after the by-now famous May 13 meeting between
Beame and Carey and Ford/Rockefeller/Simon *et al.;* and he went
on to say that the creation of the Municipal Assistance Corporation
had made things better (this was soon to change precipitously,
MAC debt becoming as suspect as the city's, and as unsalable) and
to cite parallels between New York and the federal government
itself. He concluded with the admonition, "Whether we can prevent the nation from falling into the same plight as our greatest city
is now the central issue before us." He spent the rest of the morning in hostile but vague bantering with the subcommittee members
for the benefit of the assembled press corps. He reiterated his view
that New York's collapse would occasion a "moderate, short-lived
disruption." He did let it slip that meetings between his staff and
the city's fiscal people had uncovered the fact that New York
had been shortchanged by $90 million in welfare reimbursement,
but he dismissed this as petty cash. Otherwise, no one laid a glove
on him.

The press and the committee ignored Simon's written statement.
This should be a cardinal sin in Washington, as I. F. Stone has
proved by decades of the best Washington journalism that has ever
appeared. Stone, almost completely deaf for most of the years he
spent digging out federal secrets, was forced to read written statements and reports instead of listening to the press-conference and
official babble that suffices for most journalists, and he got some
of his biggest scoops from these public documents. We bothered to
read Simon's statement. It contains a chillingly frank dissection of
President Ford's decision to refuse aid to New York City, and leaves
the inescapable impression that this policy was based on the as-

sumption that New York would default, and that this outcome was to be heartily applauded. New York's default had become crucial for Ford's economic plan to deal with inflation by putting the nation's cities through the wringer. It also provided him with a convenient blood sacrifice to offer up to the implacable gods of Republican conservatism in his bitter contest with Ronald Reagan for the party's nomination.

We quote this section of Simon's testimony in its entirety:

In the course of numerous meetings at all levels, we stressed this disturbing set of facts to City officials. And we were not alone. From *The New York Times*, from the New York Clearing House, from the Citizens Budget Commission, the same message was repeated again and again: get your spending into line with your ability to pay.

How did the City respond? Speaking bluntly, I think they thought we were all a bit naive. You could fight crime, you could fight pollution, you could fight poverty and ignorance, but—in New York—you could not underestimate the powerful forces for spending being brought to bear on the City's elected officials, driving the City into the slow and painful death of bankruptcy.

Now I know enough about New York to know that Mayor Beame and his colleagues would be in the fight of their lives the moment they touched their scalpel to the growing layer of fiscal fat which is strangling the City. One only has to look at that incredible pamphlet off-duty policemen, firemen and others were handing out to tourists earlier this month to appreciate the kind of problem the Mayor was dealing with. But we make a tragic mistake when we resolve questions solely on the basis of which side is more threatening or more unscrupulous.

But as of early May, when I, and then the President, met with the Mayor and the Governor, no resolution of the problem was in sight. The issue as then presented was plain and simple: give us the money to get us through the immediate crisis, then we'll begin to worry about a solution.

As I have indicated, it had become clear that the only real solution lay in a responsible program of fiscal reform. Such a program would reopen the market and avert the possibility of a default by New York City. But because no such program had even been suggested by City officials, it was our responsibility to evaluate the constant suggestions that a default by New York would have a devastating impact on the capital markets, the banking system and the national economy as a whole.

It was quickly apparent that the principal adverse effects would be based on psychological factors, not objective ones. To be sure, many parts of the economy—especially in New York City—would suffer severe harm. On the whole, however, our markets, our banking system and our economy are large and diversified enough to withstand the temporary inability of even an entity the size of New York City to meet its obligations.

But I have been around markets long enough to know that one ignores psychology at his own peril. Accordingly, before reaching a decision, we asked ourselves three more questions about the psychological effects of a default:

First, what impact would a default have on the securities markets, particularly the municipal markets?

Second, would a default influence the condition of the major banks?

And third, what impact would a default have on public confidence nationally?

With respect to impact on the market, it is fair to say that there were differences of opinion. Certain market professionals from the private sector did tell us the effect could be devastating. But my staff and the Federal Reserve Bank of New York, which as you know serves as the focal point for our public securities markets, advised me that whatever impact did occur would be temporary, and even so confined, would be negligible.

Three factors produced this judgment. First, it was uniformly believed that any default would be shortlived and that there was enough underlying value in New York City to assure that all holders would eventually be paid 100 cents on the dollar. Second, the municipal market had recently experienced the prospect of a major tax-exempt issuer default—New York State's U.D.C.—and had weathered it well. Third, New York's problems had been public knowledge since at least November and the market, at least in large part, had reflected this risk by discounting the prices of New York City and other weaker issues. This last judgment was confirmed by the strong rally in the municipal market when "Big Mac" was established.

We found the banking system even better equipped to handle whatever shock might occur. The New York City holdings of the major New York banks, while large in absolute terms, were only a fraction of one percent of the total assets of these institutions. The sophisticated investors, whose large deposits were in question, were aware of this fact, and were also aware that, upon a default, this portion of the banks' holding of New York securities would hardly become worthless.

This lack of a realistic basis for fearing large withdrawals was coupled with a recognition that the system was designed to handle such an event, if it did occur. A primary reason for establishing the Federal Reserve System was to correct temporary imbalances of liquidity in our banking structure. And the System clearly would have been able to handle any imbalance which might have occurred in these circumstances.

Finally, working with Chairman [Alan] Greenspan of the Council of Economic Advisers and senior economists at the Federal Reserve, we looked at potential consumer and business reaction. In view of the general knowledge of New York's situation and an awareness that at least many of the underlying problems were of the City's own making, we saw little risk that a default would be viewed as an indication of more widespread economic malaise.

Concluding that a default would not have precipitated an economic crisis did not mean that a default should not be avoided at virtually any cost. But when we reviewed our analysis of what other cities have done and are doing to meet the economic challenges of these times, another barrier to special treatment for New York became apparent. Many of our leading cities are having troubles these days, troubles largely attributable to the recession and unemployment levels, and to the impact of these phenomena on municipal revenues. But as I discussed earlier, and as confirmed by a recent Joint Economic Committee staff study, virtually all these jurisdictions have met their problems head on recognizing that meaningful cuts in spending levels were a critical part of any solution. As we in this town are altogether too aware, spending cuts do not come easy for any elected official, especially when a direct impact on one's own constituents can be identified. But throughout the country, brave local leaders have literally put their political futures on the line by insisting that all questions, however painful, be addressed and that the problems be solved in a responsible manner.

Under our system of government, it is not, and should not be, the job of the Federal government to manage the finances of State and Local government. That function must be handled locally, by government's duly elected leaders. But we do have a responsibility to those leaders not to undermine their efforts. And if we had provided funds to New York, what would we have said, for example, to the Mayor of Detroit or to the Mayor of Cleveland, each of whom has incurred the wrath of major political forces in his own city by taking steps to see that they pay their own way. No, if our system is to continue to function, it was clear we had to protect the credibility of local leaders. And aid to the one major city which had not taken action to meet its fiscal responsibilities would have destroyed that credibility overnight.

These were the elements of our decision-making process. As you can see, the decision was not made hastily, lightly, or without complete attention to all relevant considerations. It was not an easy decision, but I think events to date have shown it was the right one. With the Federal avenue closed off, so to speak, all parties could again turn their full attention to developing a solution at the appropriate government level.

About the only question that wasn't asked was: What would be the effect of default on the 7½ million Americans who lived in New York? The answer was, however, clearly understood.

Simon, although tightly wrapping himself in a cloak of "economic realism," had laid out a political, not an economic, plan. As he acknowledged, all of America's big cities were in serious trouble. In his own words, "by comparison to other cities, New York was not a particularly hard-hit victim of the recession or the so-called urban crisis." While that judgment is, of course, relative, it was accurate as far as it went. The rest of urban America was coming apart at the seams. And most cities had been forced to resort to suicidal layoffs of public employees that accelerated their decline. If New York were able to avoid drinking the hemlock pressed on it by the administration, they would all seek a reprieve.

Unwittingly, Simon was taking a page out of another country's history. Henri Christophe had the unfortunate habit of occasionally shooting the last of his soldiers to climb over a mountain. "Pour encourager les autres," he would explain. Now Simon, at the behest of Burns and Ford, was issuing a death warrant for New York—"to encourage the others."

As the situation worsened from month to month, and the financial community and Congress became more restive about the fallout from a federally induced default by New York City, the "capital gap" gang around the vacuous Gerald Ford drafted stronger and stronger denunciations for him to issue against the beleaguered city. In August, for instance, he went out of his way to berate New York to a puzzled Zivorad Kovacevic, mayor of Belgrade, who welcomed the president and his attendant phalanx of correspondents in Yugoslavia. Ford had managed to give New York a karate chop from 6000 miles across the globe. In mid-October, he vowed: "I can tell you—and tell you now—that I am prepared to veto any bill that has as its purpose a federal bailout of New York City to prevent default."

On October 29, he made a nationally televised speech to the

National Press Club in Washington outlining his proposals for placing the city in bankruptcy after what then seemed its imminent default. Like a Mafia don, he would send the biggest wreath to his enemy's funeral.

From the beginning, Ford, Burns, Simon, and a frustration-poisoned Nelson Rockefeller had sought one goal. All the speeches, and leaks, and meaningless meetings with city and state officials had only one purpose. It was left to the inimitable *Daily News* headline writers to compose the perfect epitaph. When the early-bird edition hit the stands the evening of Ford's October 29 speech, the front page said it all:

FORD TO CITY:
DROP DEAD

In the end, though, it was Gerald Ford or, more accurately, Arthur Burns who "blinked" in this colossal but ridiculous stare-down. On October 17, the city had almost gone down until Albert Shanker of the United Federation of Teachers was finally bullied late in the afternoon into buying more MAC bonds with his union's pension funds. But this latest episode in the city's "perils of Pauline" had given a foretaste of what might have come from an actual default. The stock market had plummeted and the bond market, corporate and municipal, was motionless, seemingly frozen in terror. The international currency markets also held their breath; gold prices soared. (In August, *U.S. News and World Report* had estimated that holders of *all* municipal bonds had experienced a loss of $12 billion in the value of their holdings since the crisis began the previous March.) On October 18, the Holy Trinity of New York's big banks, Citibank's Wriston, Chase's Rockefeller, and Morgan Guaranty's Patterson, issued a joint statement to the Senate Banking Committee warning that "the recent decline in the value of the dollar, which followed a period of strength, is probably an indication of anxiety about New York City and the consequences of default." What a flair for understatement! The rest of the capitalist world thought Ford was crazy. Foreign bankers attending the American Bankers Association convention in New York in November said in unmistakable terms that if New York went under, there would be a massive run by foreign depositors on the city's banks, period.

Also in November, the Federal Reserve published a report showing that 546 banks in 26 states held $4.178 billion in New York City, state, and state agency bonds. (By now, everyone assumed that the three were so intertwined that they would all go down together.) It also showed that 179 banks in 24 states had at least half of their capital in New York bonds; 367 banks in 26 states had between 20 and 50 per cent in these obligations. The report was actually seriously understated, but it moved Arthur Burns to observe ponderously that while he still didn't believe the city merited federal assistance, "I am closer to such a conclusion than I have been in the past." The White House stated, "The President has not changed his position one iota."

Less than two months later, after the president had changed his position 180 degrees under pressure from the bankers and an increasingly nervous Arthur Burns, the Federal Reserve issued a second report with the real facts. This one, released on New Year's Eve so that few people would read it the next day, admitted that 954 banks in 33 states actually held $6.491 billion in paper issued by the city, the state, and its agencies. If they went under, 234 banks in 29 states might have seen half of their capital wiped out and 718 banks in 33 states would have lost between 20 and 50 per cent of their capital. Was this what Simon meant by "no more than a moderate and short-lived disruption"?

Early in November, Hugh Carey, who had said he would be "willing to have egg on my face, to have stones thrown at me, and to walk on nails in order to prevent a default," now proceeded to prove that he wasn't kidding. He called a special session of the state legislature. At his request, they voted additional taxes, appropriated funds to keep New York City's northern neighbor Yonkers from defaulting, put up the money to bail out the now-bankrupt state HFA, forced city workers to contribute more to their pensions, and, finally, gave Ford his last pound of flesh by enacting a moratorium on the payment of $1.6 billion in the city's outstanding notes. Noteholders would be paid interest, but not the principal, on their investment. They could exchange the notes for long-term higher-interest MAC bonds or hope that they could cash in the original short-term notes at the end of the city's three-year "recovery" period in 1978. Technically, New York had defaulted. In return, Ford agreed that the federal government would make "seasonal" loans of $2.3 billion to the city to finance its day-to-day needs until quarterly taxes and erratically spaced government aid payments were made. An interest rate 1 per cent higher than the rate paid by the federal government for these funds would be exacted. New York would be allowed to survive—crippled, degraded, perhaps mortally weakened—but it would live. Until the next crisis.

The "capital gap" crusaders had won a victory beyond their fondest hopes. Two months later, Brenton Harries, president of the Standard & Poor's bond rating agency, stated that "the bond market will remain closed to New York for the next 20 years" as a result of the federally enforced default. New York City accounted for about 5 per cent of total state and municipal indebtedness, but 29 per cent of the short-term loans. New York State and its agencies would also find themselves severely restricted in any future borrowings. Every city and state, even in the federally subsidized Sunbelt, would face higher rates and a constricted market for their obligations. This meant a shift of tens of billions of investment dollars to the corporate market and lower prices for the giant utilities, manufacturers, and multinationals seeking to expand with borrowed funds.

Perhaps even more importantly, the new repressive social policy that is a must for continued corporate profitability was imposed in the stronghold of liberalism—and there was no revolt. The municipal unions, a new force that was viewed by the conservative elite very much as the CIO had been in the late 1930s, had been emasculated. Wages were frozen, 30,000 workers were axed, future pension benefits were reduced, and the unions' pension funds themselves—not the banks—became the major source of emergency city financing. Hospitals were closed. Transit fares—a crucial cost-of-living item in a city where 89 per cent of the population uses trains and buses to get to work—were increased by 43 per cent. A free university education—the traditional passport between poverty and the middle class—would soon be abolished. If New Yorkers could be forced to accept these reductions in the quality of life, then they could be imposed anywhere. In many cities, they already have been.

In the face of these attacks, the cities and the unions proved politically powerless. The Democrats, with overwhelming majorities in both houses of Congress, were gearing up to unseat an unelected Republican president who presided over the worst depression in forty years and was perceived by the average American as a simpleton. The Democrats were supposed to be the party of the cities and the unions. In the event, they proved helplessly divided, allowing the conservative rural and Southern tail to wag the urban-industrial dog. "After all," the conservatives said, "everyone hates New York. New York is different from Philadelphia, Detroit, Chicago, Cleveland, Baltimore, Milwaukee, St. Louis, Seattle, and San Francisco. New Yorkers are snotty, they talk too damn fast, they think they know it all. I'm not going out on a limb for those bastards." The traveling circus of liberal presidential hopefuls told New Yorkers what they thought we wanted to hear because they wanted New York votes and New York money. They did nothing in Congress. Candidates on the right openly abused the city. Jimmy Carter treated the city as if it had VD (until the general election, when New York became the key to his narrow victory). Henry Jackson said in a nationally televised debate that "the tenth floor of an apartment house is no place to live or try to raise a family."

Much more than an attitude was involved, however. There were very real sectional advantages at stake. In the midst of a depression, everyone, especially near neighbors like economically depressed New Jersey and Connecticut, wanted the industries that were fleeing New York. The large Chicago banks wouldn't mind pre-empting the big banks in New York. On a far larger scale, the Sunbelt had been sucking the blood of the Northeast for decades. First the southern and western states had lured away labor-intensive industries like textiles, clothing, and furniture with the promise of low wages and no unions. Now they were siphoning off hundreds of billions in federal taxes and investment dollars through the political power they had accumulated in both parties over the years. New York City became a pawn in this mammoth national struggle for economic primacy.

Recognition of these regional contests dawned slowly on the big industrial states. Like the cuckolded husband, we have been the last to know. In 1975, Kirkpatrick Sale conveyed the full scope of the regional struggle in his good if slightly overdrawn book, *Power Shift*. Then *The New York Times* got the message and published a series of articles on the same issue in early 1976.

The economist Richard Morris has developed the most up-to-date figures on how this giant ripoff of the Northeast works. As he points out, New York is again the biggest single victim. "The fifteen states from Maine to Minnesota pay $44 billion more in Federal taxes than they receive in Federal aid and expenditures. Their fifteen counterparts reaching from Virginia to California along the southern rim get $32 billion more than they give. For every dollar the Northeast sends to Washington, it gets 78 cents back. For each dollar the South pays in taxes, it reaps $1.35 in federal spending," he calculates.

The Northeast loses 7.5 per cent of its personal income to Washington every year, while the Sunbelt states reap a bonus equivalent to 7.1 per cent of their personal income. New York State, the biggest dollar loser, pays $14 billion more to Washington each year than it gets back—a deficit greater than the *total* indebtedness of New York City.

The explanation for this disparity is simple and at least superficially rational. New Yorkers earn more on the average than their counterparts in other states and are therefore taxed at a higher rate. What the tax laws ignore, however, is that the cost of living here is much higher than anywhere else. A New Yorker must earn $25,470 to buy exactly as much as an Atlantan earning $18,825. Similar differentials exist for people living in other large cities in the North. If cost-of-living adjustments are made, then the ten largest metropolitan areas in the Northeast have a per-capita personal income 2.8 per cent lower than their opposite numbers in the Sunbelt, yet they pay 22 per cent more per capita in federal taxes. In other words, the government is bleeding 44 per cent of its population so that another 38 per cent can enjoy relative prosperity. In an earlier day, this situation would have provoked a second civil war.

The major instrument of this regressive form of wealth redistribution has been the military budget. Half of America's military expenditures in the continental U.S. are made in the Sunbelt. California alone gets 17 per cent of the total military budget, especially those fat research and development contracts. In many states— Georgia, Louisiana, Mississippi, Tennessee, and New Mexico, for example—the defense industry is the largest employer. Seymour Melman, chairman of the Columbia University department of industrial and management engineering, has explained how this allocation took place as the "permanent war economy" became the cornerstone of American capitalism in the last three decades:

Members of Congress from the Southern States have sought out positions on the armed services committees in the House of Representatives and in the Senate and have obviously used their positions as points of leverage for funneling military installations (read *payrolls*) into their districts and states in a prodigal fashion. As this has proceeded, these states, in turn, became centers of support for military oriented policies of the United States around the world. Thus, the states of this region were the last hold-outs of major support for the Vietnam War.

Despite the experience of Vietnam and the constant fear that nuclear war is a very real possibility in an insanely over-armed

FEDERAL TAXES VS. FEDERAL EXPENDITURES, 1975
(in millions of dollars)

The Northeast

State	Taxes Paid	Expenditures Received	
Maine	760	1,277	
Vermont	319	641	
New Hampshire	714	1,145	
Massachusetts	7,622	8,474	
Rhode Island	1,204	1,243	
Connecticut	5,946	5,137	
New York	39,007	24,269	
New Jersey	11,083	8,395	
Pennsylvania	17,697	14,462	
Ohio	17,194	10,822	
Indiana	6,860	5,412	
Illinois	21,774	13,462	
Michigan	14,778	9,095	
Minnesota	6,150	4,497	
Wisconsin	5,422	4,443	
NORTHEAST TOTAL	156,530	112,774	NET OUTFLOW: $43,756

The Sunbelt

State	Taxes Paid	Expenditures Received	
Virginia	5,035	8,906	
North Carolina	5,996	6,100	
South Carolina	1,875	3,485	
Georgia	4,784	6,786	
Florida	7,787	11,512	
Tennessee	3,511	5,425	
Alabama	2,684	4,816	
Mississippi	1,167	3,740	
Louisiana	3,287	4,596	
Arkansas	1,241	2,544	
Texas	16,048	15,806	
Oklahoma	3,361	3,871	
Arizona	1,789	3,646	
New Mexico	708	2,264	
California	28,510	35,838	
SUNBELT TOTAL	87,783	119,335	NET INFLOW: $31,552

SOURCES FOR FEDERAL TAXES: 1975 Annual Report of Internal Revenue Service.

SOURCES FOR FEDERAL EXPENDITURES: *Federal Outlays In Summary,* Community Services Administration, December 1975, with the following adjustments: public debt interest, foreign aid payments, international organization subsidies, TVA bonds, and civil service life insurance deducted because geographic data was misleading.

world, the 1976–77 military budget was the largest in American history. It may be suicidal, but for the moment it's very good business for the most economically buoyant area in the nation.

New York City's plight is merely part of a much larger world economic crisis. Nations, as England's recent experiences have shown, as well as regions and cities are being torn apart in the scramble to rule in the new era of scarcity. Right now those who have always ruled—the rich, the powerful, and the ruthless—are successfully shaping the future that we and our children will have to endure. It is, by any measure, bleak and hostile. At the end of this book, we shall discuss some of the alternative solutions that we feel could improve New York's, and other cities' chances for survival. But narrow, local answers are impossible in a world as concentrated and overcrowded as ours.

If any of us are to survive in dignity, all of us must. This will require a profound restructuring of political and economic power and the creation of a whole new set of democratic institutions. One of the basic theses of this book is that New York is ruled by a small group of unelected power brokers. We call them the permanent government. Yet there is a "permanent government" in Washington, as there is certainly a "permanent government" in Peking and Moscow; there is one in every major city and every small town in America. Perhaps the simplest way we can outline the political goal of this book is to say that it is our objective to make the rule of all these "permanent governments" as temporary as possible.

THE PERMANENT GOVERNMENT

By the powerful we mean, of course, those who are able to realize their will, even if others resist it. No one, accordingly, can be truly powerful unless he has access to the command of major institutions, for it is over these institutional means of power that the truly powerful are, in the first instance, powerful.

> — C. WRIGHT MILLS
> *The Power Elite*

Ultimate power over public policy in New York is invisible and unelected. It is exercised by a loose confederation of bankers, bond underwriters, members of public authorities, the big insurance companies, political fund-raisers, publishers, law firms, builders, judges, backroom politicians, and some union leaders.

The power of this interlocking network of elites is based on the control of institutions, money, property, and the law-making process. It endures no matter who the voters elect as mayor, governor, or president. Its collective power, when organized, is greater than the elected, representative government.

This permanent government is not an invincible conspiracy. It is only the creative self-interest of the rich. It sometimes can be beaten, as when 50,000 residents of Co-op City waged a thirteen-month rent strike in 1975–76 that successfully conquered a rent increase. Or when neighborhood activists stopped the Lower Manhattan Expressway in 1967.

The permanent government is not as monolithic now as it was a decade ago, when Nelson Rockefeller and the men around him controlled public and private power to a terrifying extent.

The balance of power within this elite group shifts. A few years ago the real-estate developers and construction unions had more influence than they do now. But with the onset of the recession, foreclosures, and the fiscal crisis, the banks and financial institutions that control lines of credit, bonds, venture capital, and mortgages became much more important. But our point is this: Whenever an assemblyman casts a vote, or when a public-works project is begun, or when a developer gets a zoning variance to build a highrise, or when federal funds come into a district, or when a decision is made to raise the interest rates that the banks charge the city—in all these situations, the real decision-makers are usually off stage, and unknown to the public. This means the average citizen does not know who is controlling his or her life. This is, fundamentally, a book about the abuse of power.

A few more qualifying statements.

Power in New York is less centralized than in other places. There is no one political boss like the late Richard Daley of Chicago. There is no single controlling financial family, like the Mellons in Pittsburg, or the Duponts in Delaware. New York is so big that even the Rockefellers have to share power with the Vanderbilts, Astors, Whitneys, Schiffs, Loebs, and Lehmans.

There are occasionally titanic conflicts within the power elite. One famous example was when the Rockefeller brothers finally ended the 44-year public career of Robert Moses in February 1968. Another was Mayor Wagner's turning against Carmine DeSapio, Charles Buckley, and the Democratic machine in 1961.

Elections can make a difference. They can change the balance of power between rival elites. If Richard Nixon had lost the presidency in 1968 it would have had a great beneficial effect on New York. If Herman Badillo had won the Democratic primary for mayor in 1973 it would have made a significant difference. Lindsay's defeat of Beame in 1965, Wagner's defeat of Levitt in 1961, and Rocke-feller's defeat of Harriman in 1958 did alter various power alignments.

In 1974, a preponderance of the monied interests backed Howard Samuels for governor in the Democratic primary. But Hugh Carey had a millionaire brother and shrewd handlers in David Garth and Alex Rose, so Carey won. Yet today the banks have more power than ever.

New York's permanent government has different components than the national power elite. The national elite is dominated by multinational corporations like ITT and conglomerates like Gulf & Western; giant oil companies like Mobil, Gulf and Exxon; the defense establishment, CIA, and military contractors like Lockheed and General Dynamics; agribusiness corporations like Tenneco; and, as ever, the banking industry. The shift of wealth and power within this structure to the Sunbelt has had a severe negative impact on New York and the entire Northeast region.

Not all the members of the permanent government represent inherited wealth. A few rose out of the working class during their own lifetimes, on their own talents: lawyer William Shea, union leader Anthony Scotto, publicist Howard Rubenstein, union pension fund consultant Jack Bigel, and political boss Meade Esposito.

But despite all these qualifying disclaimers, there *is* an unseen power establishment. New York is not like Dallas, where a dozen bankers and oilmen can assemble in one board room and settle everything. But there are about 1500 or 2000 people in New York City who have pieces of a power that is decisive, concealed, and therefore unaccountable. And over the last fifteen years, this group, plus three mayors and one governor, has been responsible for the policies and decisions that have swept New York to the lip of ruin. These 1500 or 2000 people all know each other and deal with each other as members of the same club.

Who are the people who rule New York without the consent of the governed?

The most powerful circle is composed mostly of banking and international finance:

• Walter Wriston: the tough, Tory chairman of Citibank, which has $56 billion in assets.

• Nelson and David Rockefeller: who together control not only the Chase Manhattan Bank, with $45 billion in assets, but also the Rockefeller Foundation, Rockefeller Center, the Rockefeller Brothers Fund, Rockefeller Institute, Rockefeller University, and, indirectly, the bi-state Port Authority and the state Republican Party of New York. David has been a flop at Chase, but it hasn't mattered too much.

• Felix Rohatyn: a general partner in the prestigious international investment banking firm of Lazard Frères; chairman of MAC; the dominant member of the EFCB; a director of six corporations including the infamous ITT. He is also Governor Carey's financial adviser, and a master at manipulating the press.

• Richard Shinn: president of the $33-billion Metropolitan Life Insurance Company; chairman of the Mayor's Management Advisory Board; a director of the Chase Manhattan Bank; and a director of Allied Chemical. Shinn is a Republican contributor to Nixon, Rockefeller, and Javits.

• Simon Rifkind: senior partner in the powerhouse law firm of Paul, Weiss, Rifkind, Wharton & Garrison. He is a director of the Sterling National Bank, Loews Corporation, and Revlon, and he helped to create MAC—for a legal fee of $1.2 million. He is 75, and a former federal judge.

• Other key bankers and brokers are: Peter Peterson, chairman of Lehman Brothers and formerly President Nixon's Secretary of Commerce; Ellmore Patterson, chairman of Morgan Guaranty Trust; Donald Cook, managing partner in Lazard Frères, a former chairman of the American Electric Power Corporation and former chairman of the SEC; Donald Regan, chairman of Merrill Lynch; and William Salomon, chairman of Salomon Brothers.

• Other unelected power brokers of the first rank include: Jack Bigel, the sixty-four-year-old brains behind four municipal unions— District Council 37, led by Victor Gotbaum; John DeLury's Uniformed Sanitationmen; Barry Feinstein's Teamsters Local 237; and Matthew Guinan's Transport Workers. A radical organizer of municipal workers in the 1940s, Bigel is now consultant to the civil-service unions' gigantic pension funds, and he masterminded the $3.7-million loan from the pension funds to the city which prevented formal default.

• Harold Fisher: the sixty-six-year-old Brooklyn lawyer who supported Hugh Carey for governor early in 1974. Fisher is a member of the MTA; chairman of the Dime Savings Bank of Williamsburgh; and director of American Plan, a holding company that owns two insurance companies. In the last year he's added six lawyers to his firm to handle all the new business, much of it from clients who want access to state agencies. And if you want to become a judge or an appellate judge, Fisher is a good man to know. He was chairman of the Brooklyn judicial convention in 1976.

• John J. McCloy: at 81 still powerful after all these years. McCloy is the senior partner in the law firm Milbank, Tweed, Hadley & McCloy, which numbers the Chase bank among its clients. McCloy is a former chairman of the Chase Bank, former chairman of the World Bank, and an elder statesman in the kingdoms of law and banking. He is a director of Dreyfus, Mercedes Benz of North America, Stott Capital Development, and Squibb.

• Howard Rubenstein, successor to the much less savory Sydney Baron as the proprietor of the most politically influential public-relations firm in New York City. Rubenstein's clients range from most of the major builders and landlords to McDonald's fast food chain, to the ASPCA, to the sanitation workers union, to eleven voluntary hospitals. An intimate of Mayor Beame, Rubenstein has a reputation for telling the truth, even when it hurts.

• Abraham (Bunny) Lindenbaum, lawyer and lobbyist for most of the big landlords, skillful Democratic Party fund raiser from his landlord clients (he was forced to quit the City Planning Commission in 1961 for shaking down city contractors for contributions), and one of Mayor Beame's best and oldest friends. He can drop in on the mayor any time he wants. Some of Bunny's clients are now being passed along to his son, Sandy, who collects art and zoning variances.

• William Shea: senior partner in Shea, Gould, a law firm of eighty-three lawyers; a director of five companies and trustee and general counsel of the Metropolitan Savings Bank; probably the most effective political fund raiser in New York; a lawyer whose clients range from the Catholic Archdiocese to Shoup Voting Machines, to Colonial Sand & Stone Company, to Yonkers Raceway, to nursing homes and day-care–center landlords, to the Morgan Guaranty Trust. Shea is also very smart—he thinks for the permanent government—and nice to everybody. The Queens baseball stadium was named after him in 1964. In 1976, Shea's law firm was paid a record lobbying fee of $80,830 by the Securities Industry Association to lobby for repeal of the stock transfer tax. The stock transfer tax was repealed.

• Among landlords and developers we would include: Alton Marshall of Rockefeller Center; Harry Helmsley; Richard Ravitch; Samuel Lefrak; and Lewis Rudin.

• Among lawyers: former Mayor Robert Wagner; Theodore Kheel;

Roy Cohn; Bernard Ruggieri, of William Shea's firm; Robert Douglas, a former member of the Port Authority and now executive vice president of Chase Bank; and Donald Elliot, former chairman of the City Planning Commission, and now naturally a favorite lawyer for landlords who want favors from the commission.

• Among union leaders: Anthony Scotto of the longshoremen, who makes big contributions and donates his printing presses to politicians; Albert Shanker, leader of the well-organized teachers; Harry Van Arsdale, chairman of the Central Labor Council; and Victor Gotbaum, leader of the largest municipal employees union.

• Also: Charles Luce, chairman of Con Edison; William Ronan, chairman of the Port Authority; Rupert Murdoch, publisher of the *New York Post, Village Voice, National Star,* and *New York* magazine; Michael O'Neill, the editor of the *Daily News;* and "Punch" Sulzberger, publisher of *The New York Times.* Sulzberger's inherited and unaccountable power was clearly displayed in September 1976, when the *Times* editorial-page editor, John Oakes, and the majority of the *Times* editorial board members were strongly opposed to the candidacy of Daniel P. Moynihan for the Democratic Party nomination for senator, but Sulzberger imposed an editorial endorsement of him anyway. Moynihan defeated Congresswoman Bella Abzug by less than 1 per cent of the vote, and the Sulzberger editorial was probably the deciding factor.

• Backroom clubhouse power, once dominated by Carmine De-Sapio, is now dispersed among Meade Esposito and Stanley Steingut of Brooklyn; Patrick Cunningham of the Bronx; Donald Manes of Queens; Percy Sutton, who speaks for the blacks; and Vincent Albano, the Manhattan Republican boss with many business interests from banking to public relations.

This is the permanent power structure. With individual exceptions, these are the institutions that controlled the decisions which helped New York City decline and go broke: to invest billions of dollars in a World's Fair and a World Trade Center; to bulldoze and redline neighborhoods in New York City; to build highrise luxury housing rather than to restore and renovate existing housing for moderate-income families; to make large profits on selling the city's notes and bonds and then close the market; to accept the concept of moral obligation bonds and create an Urban Development Corporation that would go bankrupt; to keep the Port Authority's surplus funds from being used to subsidize mass transit; to loot and ruin the Mitchell-Lama housing program that should have kept the middle class in New York City; and to help Abraham D. Beame become New York's 104th mayor.

The permanent government is essentially bipartisan. Above a certain level of wealth, above a certain level of power, there are no Democrats and there are no Republicans. Except perhaps on Election Day.

Alton Marshall, the Republican president of Rockefeller Center, sits on the board of directors of the City Title Insurance Company with Stanley Steingut, the Democratic Speaker of the Assembly. The board of directors of Madison Square Garden includes Leonard Hall, the former Republican national chairman, and Milton Gould, who is Bill Shea's law partner. Shea was appointed to the MTA by Nelson Rockefeller, but he also raised money for Beame and Carey.

When the influential Republican party leaders Perry Duryea was indicted for violation of the state election law, Harold Fisher was his lawyer—although Fisher had helped rewrite the law. Fisher also was appointed to the MTA by Nelson Rockefeller, and then, with his son, contributed $45,000 to Hugh Carey's campaign. One of Fisher's law partners is Syracuse Republican power broker, Gary Axenfeld.

In 1973, the Republican Rockefeller and the Liberal Alex Rose tried to draft Democrat Wagner to run again for mayor, this time as a "fusion" candidate. In 1973, David Rockefeller contributed $5000 to Democrat Beame. Among the names on the original charter for Century National Bank are Vincent Albano, the Republican boss of Manhattan, and Bernard Ruggieri, then an aide to Democratic Mayor Wagner, now a partner in the Shea, Gould law firm.

In a city as large and complex as New York, the permanent government takes great pains to control philanthropic and cultural institutions. They sit on the boards of hospitals, universities, museums. And whether Catholic, Jewish, or Protestant, they become the fund raisers, the voluntary counsels, the go-betweens with government. The same is true for the vast network of ethnic organizations in this most ethnic of cities. And, in the greatest irony of all, it is these men, frequently from the wealthiest levels of society, who control the institutions serving the poor: the settlement houses, the Community Service Society, Legal Aid, Catholic Charities, the Federation of Jewish Philanthropies. Once this was a logical arrangement since they in fact provided the lion's share of financing for such undertakings. This is no longer true. Almost all of these agencies today are dependent on government grants or broad support from the general public. But the power remains concentrated in self-perpetuating boards of the very rich.

The cornerstone of the permanent government is the Golden Triangle of politics–real estate–banking. New York has no natural resources, like oil in Texas, or tobacco in North Carolina, or coal in West Virginia. It became the nation's greatest city and center of commerce because it was the nation's pre-eminent port. Its great fortunes were built on the crazily escalating value of its land. Much of the Wall Street financial district at the tip of Manhattan was once swamp, but landfill operations to expand the amount of real estate in this choice location began before the Revolution and continues to this day. And just as the squatters' hovels of nineteenth-century "river rats" were razed to make way for expanding commerce, it remains the dream of banks and realtors to drive out the poor who cling to neighborhoods surrounding the financial district (like the Lower East Side, Little Italy and Chinatown) in order to construct a walk-to-work "golden ghetto" for the financial community. Banker Rexford Tompkins, a former chairman of the Real Estate Board who once said, "Every wealthy person in the world should live on the Island of Manhattan," told the City Council in 1970: "Easier evictions is our only hope for reviving the sagging construction industry."

It was natural, then, that political life in New York more than in any other American city came to revolve around issues of land: who owns it, what can be built on it, how much tax it will pay. Real estate is the primary generator of wealth, of jobs, of the quality of life. The value of the land, in many cases its scarcity, has shaped the life style of the city and its people. For instance, because of high land costs the vast majority of New Yorkers live in apartment houses as opposed to the private homes that predominate in most other cities. Less than 10 per cent of the city's residents own their own homes. New Yorkers aren't immune to the American dream of a "home of one's own," as the suburban exodus of white middle-class families in the postwar years clearly showed. It is simply that home ownership today, except in certain ghetto neighborhoods, is becoming less and less possible for all but the very rich.

So the vast majority of New Yorkers, some 2 million families, live under roofs that someone else owns. It is a misnomer to speak of a "housing" industry in New York, however, since this implies that the purpose and profitability of the industry lie in providing people with a fundamental necessity—a place to live. In fact, profitability in the industry involves the ability to buy and sell buildings and maximize gains despite the tangled skein of local, state and federal tax laws affecting real estate; "housing" and the people who live in "houses" are at best secondary considerations. Similar observations can be made about the commercial rental market. (Even the largest corporations rarely own their headquarters buildings, although many buildings are named, and renamed, after the largest tenants; e.g. the Uniroyal Building has just become the Simon and Schuster Building.)

The current investment in land and buildings in New York is astronomical, more than $100 billion. Almost all of this capital has come from banks, which of course make money by investing the money of their depositors. This means that the most powerful realtors and America's largest banks are perpetually trying to figure out ways to increase their profits on investments in New York real estate—a realization that might cost the average New Yorker a lot of sleep if he bothered to think about it at all.

The primary way in which the banker and real-estate magnates can accomplish this goal, next to their unstinting attempts to rape the Internal Revenue Code, is to manipulate the politics of New York city and state. They've been at it for a long time, and the relationship has proven fruitful for everyone but the people.

An amazing number of individuals can become involved in any building project in New York City: the seller of the site, the builder of the project, architects, dozens of separate construction trades, title-search insurance brokers, contractors, property insurance brokers, truckers, building inspectors, bankers (to finance the sale of the land, the cost of construction and ultimately a long-term mortgage)—and almost all of them will be accompanied by legions of lawyers, accountants, and tax experts. Real estate remains the nation's most irrational, fragmented, and arcane industry, something to make the medieval guilds blink in admiration. It is New York's $100 billion cottage industry. In turn each of these groups has its own lobbyists, string-pullers, and political godfathers operating at City Hall and the State Capitol, and each is a source of campaign contributions, favors, and political foot-soldiers for "sympathetic" politicians.

Whenever a major building project is under consideration at the Board of Estimate, City Hall looks as if it were under assault from an army of pinstripe-suited ants. The most outraged and organized community defending itself from such a project is no match for this onslaught. Ordinary people who must give up a day's pay to attend a public hearing are unlikely to do so; zoning lawyers

who earn $100 an hour are more patient, and have a longer span
of attention. Even the most honest politicians, even the ones who
refuse the massive campaign contributions, the jobs for supporters
(private patronage is as important, if not more important, than jobs
on the public payroll for the city's thriving political machines), the
implied promise of lucrative employment after public office—even
they find the permanent government irresistible in these situations.
For in the forefront of this phalanx march the "experts," the good-
government representatives who never tire of speaking of the
"trickle-down" benefits to the city's poor from each new building
project. Then come the city's own architects and planners—responsible only to the mayor—who praise the brilliance of yet another
new scheme to evade the zoning laws; followed by the private
engineers and architects, who gently tell the elected officials that
while *they* may not understand all of the intricacies of the proposal,
it has all been worked out by computer. (Some members of the
Board of Estimate, seriously burned by two recent projects—Yankee
Stadium and the Bronx Terminal Market, where former city officials
were quoted in the *Times* as bragging about how effectively they
had lied to them—contemplated putting city officials under oath
and making them subject to perjury penalties, but they discarded
the idea when the public outcry abated.)

In the last analysis, the permanent government simply over-
whelms the temporary elected government. Those officials whom it
can't buy are bludgeoned into submission, for they lack the cadre
of professionals, public-relations men, and political operatives
throughout the infrastructure of government which banks, developers, and realtors can command. The permanent government, representing an alliance of special interests, is more powerful than the
elected government, which theoretically represents the interests of
all the people.

During a period when government at all levels is in low esteem,
is this arrangement necessarily a bad thing? After all, we live in a
nation where private profit is officially perceived as the maximum
good—the engine of all progress. The permanent government is
hardly unique to New York. It has its analogue at the national level
where giant oil companies, defense contractors, and multinational
corporations have effectively defined the nation's priorities and allocated its resources through a long series of administrations that have
unswervingly agreed with Calvin Coolidge's observation that "the
business of America is business." In the early 1960s, John Kennedy
quickly learned that a president, no matter how popular, who con-

fronts the combined interests of corporate America is walking into a meat grinder. Faced with the choice between massive public works and social spending, or the "trickle-down" economics of business to cure the Eisenhower recession, he found it expedient, in the face of a carefully orchestrated corporate propaganda campaign, to opt for investment credits for industry and tax cuts that aided the wealthiest segments of society. In dealing with the nation's balance-of-payments problems, he encountered the same wall of opposition and finally observed: "It's a ridiculous situation for us to be squeezing down essential public activities in order not to touch private investment and tourist spending—but apparently that's life."

"Life" hasn't changed much in Washington, New York, or hundreds of other cities across the land as we begin the nation's third century. Corporate power still dominates public need.

There are many ways in which the permanent government is bringing about the downfall of New York. We have seen that it was the driving force behind the city's borrowing binge. It has held the large amounts of federal revenue available for basic public services hostage to its own private master plan for the city's future. It has systematically wasted the tax revenues necessary to maintain vital services like police, fire protection, schools, and health care. The irony, of course, is that the visible clowns of the elected government have been held responsible for these disasters by the press and the public, while the permanent government has been given even greater control over the life-support system of the city.

What we have outlined, and shall develop in greater detail, is simply "business as usual" in the nation's largest and most important city. Power fattens on the tragedies of the powerless. The operations of most members of the permanent government are not illegal, although as we shall suggest in Chapter 10 organized crime is an active, if silent, partner in some of the areas of city life under the hegemony of the permanent government.

Why break the law when it was drafted to serve your purposes? As long as the rich and powerful are the only source of the vast amounts of money needed to wage a successful campaign for public office, elected officials from the mayor and governor on down will court their favor and do their bidding. Why bribe a commissioner or regulator when it is perfectly legal to offer him a high-paying job instead? The example to young, honest idealists is that government service can be a profitable audition for a career with the permanent government.

Elliot Vestner, for example, was the state's regulator of banking until he quit in 1975, at the age of thirty-nine, to become senior vice-president and general counsel to Irving Trust, New York City's seventh largest commercial bank.

Vestner's predecessor as state banking superintendent was Harry W. Albright. Albright had resigned his job to become president of the Dime Savings Bank.

During the Lindsay administration there was constant traffic from that "reform" government to the executive offices of the real-estate industry. Jacquelin Robertson, a member of the City Planning Commission, quit to become vice-president of Arlen Realty and Development Corporation. Robert Rosenberg, a deputy Housing and Development administrator became general manager of Starrett City, a vast housing development owned by a subsidiary of the Kinney Corporation. Joseph Stein, Lindsay's Buildings Commissioner, resigned to become a vice-president of Tishman Realty. Albert Walsh, the city Housing and Development administrator, quit to take a $75,000-a-year job as head of the National Realty Board, an organization of landlords and real-estate investors. Kenneth Patton, Lindsay's Economic Development administrator, resigned to become president of the Real Estate Board of New York, also at $75,000 a year. Lester Schulklapper, the city's housing lobbyist in Albany, took a job with the Citizens Tax Council, a landlord lobbying group. He was interviewed for the job by two of the city's biggest landlords—Harry Helmsley and Charles Benenson. Donald Elliott, once the chairman of the City Planning Commission, is the lawyer for some of the biggest landlords and developers in the city.

And then there is the case of Edgar Fabber, the city's deputy commissioner for Economic Development. At EDA, Fabber negotiated a ninety-nine–year lease with the United States Lines for 187 acres on Staten Island, and the city then agreed to spend $71 million to build a containerport for the shipping company. The deal was severely criticized as a give-away, and a law suit was filed to stop it on the grounds that there was no competitive bidding. State Supreme Court Justice Morris Spector threw out the suit, but admitted in his decision that there was no competitive bidding. On January 31, 1976, Edgar Fabber left his $38,771-a-year job with the city and went to work at a much higher salary for Walter Kidde & Company, the conglomerate that happens to own U.S. Lines.

Almost all of the elected legislators at City Hall or in Albany are lawyers who spend a few days, or in many cases a few hours, a week doing the public's business and the rest of the time conducting their own. Public office for at least one of the partners in a law firm is considered a great draw for business. Lawyer-legislators who determine the budgets of public agencies then go on to represent clients with cases before those agencies. They propose bills that can aid a client and fight to kill those that might harm his interests—without any requirement even to show their own financial interest in the legislation before them.

(Few scandals in New York have shocked the public more than the disclosure of massive frauds perpetrated by owners of nursing homes, who maintained the sick and the elderly in concentration-camp misery while milking the federal, state, and city treasuries. Yet in the face of uniform public outrage, the Albany lawmakers steadfastly refused to ban their members from representing nursing homes, or any other private business client, before state agencies attempting to protect the public's health and tax dollars.)

The lawyer-legislators would obviously prefer to risk the public's wrath than to alter a system whose rewards are so lucrative. The oldest laws of politics is "The public has a short memory"; the second oldest is that the powerful pay only for "value received."

Why would any power broker bother with the classic "little brown envelope" filled with cash, when he can "buy" the vote of key legislators, committee chairmen, and even the top leaders of the legislature with a legal retainer or an insurance contract? Influence peddling in New York is a carefully codified business where everyone knows the rules, and anyone willing and able to pay the price can play.

There is no better single example of the overwhelming power of the permanent government than the way it has implemented its private master plan for the development of Lower Manhattan—with massive subsidies from public tax dollars.

The brainchild of David Rockefeller, this monumental twenty-year undertaking set off a speculative building boom from which the city may take decades to recover. It has undermined the financial viability of existing office buildings, not to mention their tax value; overwhelmed the human services in the downtown area, especially the mass transit network; and for almost a decade threatened to bulldoze some of the city's most stable ethnic neighborhoods in order to build yet another expressway. Hundreds of thriving small businesses have been destroyed. Ninety acres of landfill have been dumped into the already polluted Hudson River. Public revenues desperately needed for transmit improvements in two states have been sequestered to pay off bond-holders in the biggest white-elephant construction project in history—the twin towers of the World Trade Center.

For two decades, the balanced growth of the rest of the city, indeed of the entire metropolitan region, has been sacrificed to the demands of the downtown financial elite. Even after these plans were exposed by events as ludicrous pipe dreams, hundreds of millions in public monies are still tied up in projects that will never be built. More than $1 billion in federal transit funds remain earmarked for Westway a four-mile super-highway to serve Wall Street and the minuscule 3 per cent of daily commuters who would use the road, while the subway system, which serves 89 per cent of the city's workers and desperately needs these monies, is allowed literally to crumble away.

Debating which Rockefeller brother, Nelson or David, actually has the most power long ago became a parlor game at New York cocktail parties. By the mid-1950s, both were clearly on the way to the top. David had entered the family business, the Chase Manhattan Bank, and while still a vice-president was a crucial decision maker in what was then America's, and perhaps the world's, leading financial institution. From the bank's aging headquarters at 18 Pine Street, David looked out at a financial community that was stagnating. The major corporations that made their headquarters in New York seemed to be moving uptown en masse to the midtown area where new office buildings were springing up in one of the city's periodic building booms. Chase itself was planning to consolidate its various functions, which were sprinkled in a number of downtown office buildings. If Chase followed the exodus to midtown, there was a widespread fear that the other major financial institutions would follow suit, sounding the death knell for the old financial district. David decided to stay, and to reshape the Wall Street area into a citadel befitting what one of his aides called "the heart pump of the capital blood that sustains the free world."

There is still a dispute about the magnanimity of this gesture. Perhaps David had merely been infected by the "edifice complex" that afflicted his father and brother. Others suspect that he was more interested in protecting the bank's $40-million investment in downtown real estate. Whatever the real motivation, he took the plunge in classic Rockefeller style.

In 1956, he called together fifty-five of Wall Street's most powerful leaders and established the Committee for Lower Manhattan, which emerged two years later as the Downtown–Lower Manhattan Association with himself as chairman. From that time on, he called the shots in a multi-billion-dollar reconstruction of the financial district. The DLMA quickly issued a plan calling for an initial investment of $1 billion in public and private monies to be spent for office buildings, housing developments, parks, highways, and transit improvements.

David's master plan envisioned the expansion of the Wall Street district into a sort of "golden ghetto" where financial executives and junior staff would live, work, and play in a carefully controlled environment. The whole of Lower Manhattan would be cut off by a Chinese Wall expressway running across Broome Street from the Holland Tunnel to the Williamsburg and Manhattan bridges—a long-time dream of master builder Robert Moses. The area south of the expressway, encompassing the traditional communities of Little Italy, Chinatown, and the Lower East Side—economically healthy and self-regenerating—would be incorporated into the new city of finance. When David looked at these communities, he saw only an area "largely occupied by commercial slums, right next to the greatest concentration of real estate value in the city." He chose to ignore the fact that some 50,000 people had considered it their home for generations. "I don't know of any other area in the city where there's as good an opportunity to expand inexpensively," he stated.

Chase put some of its money where David's mouth was, and began construction of a $120-million headquarters building. Characteristically, the centuries-old street names adjoining the building were erased, and the new structure became 1 Chase Manhattan Plaza. But the cornerstone of the downtown renaissance was to be another Rockefeller brainstorm—a mammoth World Trade Center that would attract and consolidate a major hunk of the city's commercial renters in 9 million square feet of office space in two 110-story towers surrounded by six smaller buildings and acres of retail space, plazas, and a 2000-car garage.

The World Trade Center was to fill a totally unperceived need. New York had stumbled along as a leader of world shipping and commerce for 200 years without any demand being raised for this

kind of super-concentration under one roof. As the small businessmen and residents on the World Trade Center site charged in court,
the whole concept was simply a gimmick to give the New York-New
Jersey Port Authority an excuse to undertake the project as a "public
benefit" for the district.

David Rockefeller could not have found a more willing partner
for his enterprise. Established by New York and New Jersey in 1921
to establish order in the chaotic transfer of cargo between ships and
the region's rapacious railroads, the Port Authority had slipped the
reins and become an institution in search of a purpose. Perhaps because of its early failures, those who ran the public agency had developed a violent dislike for anything that ran on rails. During the
Depression it had built the Holland Tunnel and the George Washington Bridge to facilitate auto travel between the two states. It
subsequently took over operation of the two city-constructed air-
fields, La Guardia and Kennedy (then Idlewild). In the late 1950s
and early 1960s, there was a growing public demand that it return
to its original purpose and coordinate the collapsing rail transport
system between New York and New Jersey. But the suggestion was
anathema to the long-time guiding hand of the Authority, Austin
Tobin, who had managed to play the two states off against one
another and ran his vast empire as he saw fit.

In 1960, David asked the governors of the two states (his brother
Nelson had become governor of New York in 1959) and the mayor
of New York to have the Port Authority undertake a feasibility study
for constructing an international trade center. By 1962, both state
legislatures had given go-aheads; New Jersey exacted a promise that
the PA would continue to operate the now bankrupt Hudson and
Manhattan railroad, the only remaining rail link for the many Jersey-
ites working in New York City. The Port Authority agreed to this
compromise, but in turn demanded that it be absolved of any other
rail involvements; it incorporated this provision in the bonds it sold
for the joint project, bonds that will not be paid off until well into
the twenty-first century.

The involvement of the huge Port Authority was crucial: It could
sell tax-exempt bonds for the project, bonds that were backed by its
vast flow of revenue and would be snapped up by investors. (As an
underwriter for the bond sale, Chase of course made a bundle.) In
addition, it had the power to condemn land, avoiding both the delay
and escalation of price involved in a negotiated sale by a private
party.

The site tenants, small commercial businesses who had done

business happily and profitably at the same location for decades, resisted bitterly, but they were attacking a dinosaur with snowballs. After being moved from the site, many didn't even bother to reopen, since their customers, accustomed to coming to the same location over the years, would never know where to find them. Another problem emerged when it became obvious that the new towers would destroy television reception in a broad swath reaching into Westchester County, since signals transmitted from the top of the Empire State Building, until then the highest point in the city, would bounce off the new aluminum-sheathed monsters. The Port Authority's imperious answer: "Move your aerials."

Although still uncompleted, the Trade Center opened for tenants in the early 1970s. Long before, however, it had become apparent that the buildings could not attract enough occupants to be self-sustaining. The bright young men of Mayor Lindsay's City Planning Commission had been busily devising loopholes in the zoning law that sparked an artificial office-building boom. Manhattan was glutted with vacant office space. In the first ten years of the Downtown–Lower Manhattan Association, 14 million square feet of new offices were built in the financial district alone, compared with only 3 million in the previous decade. By the end of 1972, another 28 million had been completed. When the Trade Center was looking for tenants in early 1971, 15 million square feet of prime office space elsewhere in Manhattan was vacant, about 12 per cent of all the space that had been constructed since World War II.

When your brother is the governor of the richest state in the nation, however, being stuck with a few million feet of vacant space in your favorite project need only be a brief embarrassment. In 1969, the state's Office of Government Services had begun a crash effort to consolidate its various New York City offices under one roof. Strangely enough, that roof was the World Trade Center, where it signed forty-year leases for about a quarter of the total floor space.

Once the World Trade Center construction was assured in the mid-1960s, additional schemes for Xanadu on the Hudson could be unleashed. And new players were clamoring to join the game.

An imposing foundation is required for a project the size of the World Trade Center. Miles of earth must be excavated and, in the normal course of events, dumped someplace else. In 1966, the Port Authority and the city signed an agreement requiring that the rock and dirt excavated for the Trade Center be dumped into the Hudson River in a giant landfill adjacent to the site.

Nelson Rockefeller, running for re-election as governor, then unveiled a proposal sure to stir the lust of the politically potent construction trades. He would build 14,000 apartments, a 2200-room hotel, and two 67-story office towers on the landfill site. The brothers Rockefeller seemed intent on erecting a new Stonehenge at the mouth of the Hudson. Nelson called his segment Battery Park City.

The announcement of plans for Battery Park City set off a decade of bitter in-fighting between the city and state, the city's minority communities and the powerful building trades unions, and ultimately within the permanent government itself. The harsh street noises of the city were beginning to disrupt the placid dreamers in Wall Street's executive suites.

(David got a brief glimpse of the handwriting on the wall when the Lower Manhattan Expressway was killed by Mayor Lindsay after several vacillations in 1967. A united community, and a public increasingly disenchanted with New York's gagging air pollution, had won a stunning upset in the last round of a twenty-year fight. Most importantly, a whole new attitude about preserving and strengthening existing neighborhoods had taken root in the public consciousness—this largely through the work of Jane Jacobs, a brilliant writer and urban-planning critic who had been an important leader in the fight against the expressway and in the successful effort to preserve the adjacent West Village community from Robert Moses's bulldozers.)

Lindsay countered Rockefeller's plan for Battery Park City with a more modest version of his own. A final plan emerged in 1968, close to the Rockefeller original. Having already milked the Port Authority for the World Trade Center, the governor established a new authority to build his city within a city. The chairman of the new authority was Charles Urstadt, formerly Rockefeller's state housing commissioner. Urstadt had been the principal owner of a major real estate management firm, Douglas Elliman Co. He is best remembered for his successful gutting of New York City's rent control law in 1971 and the introduction of vacancy decontrol, which removed rent controls on apartments as their tenants moved out. This stroke of genius led to rents doubling and tripling in the city's stable middle-class communities, and managed to drive untold thousands of young white families to the suburbs at a time when the city most needed them to provide tax dollars and racial balance in its schools.

Battery Park City was conceived not only as a big office-building scheme but as a community for executives and their families. It was one of a number of ephemeral ideas for attracting back corporate staff who had fled to suburban tax havens in New Jersey and Connecticut, where large backyards and good schools were plentiful. The unstated logic was that a separate community—white, affluent, and well serviced—could be insulated from the general problem of New York City while offering all of its advantages, such as proximity to the theater, cultural institutions, and fine restaurants. The site also offered spectacular views of New York Harbor, still one of the most exciting vistas in the world.

But construction costs were escalating dizzily because of the building boom, and it soon became evident that even this community for the moderately wealthy would have to be subsidized with public monies. This threw the issue before the Board of Estimate and into the turbulence of racial politics in the late 1960s. Compromise was inevitable and, after a bitter series of public hearings and private meetings among city officials, finally emerged in 1969. The office towers, 7 million square feet of office space for Lower Manhattan, would be constructed first. The housing would be divided equally among moderate income—$100 a room per month; middle—$70; and low—$30, which would be traditional and separate brick public housing.

The Battery Park City Authority accepted the compromise grudgingly, and warned that renting would be difficult. They particularly protested a requirement that the office space be forced to subsidize the housing component. But the project moved ahead, at least on paper. In 1972, the Authority sold $200 million in "moral obligation" bonds through the Wall Street firm of Goldman, Sachs (whose president was the late Gustave Levy, a Rockefeller confidant and appointee to the board of the Port Authority). The proceeds of the bond sale were deposited with Chase Manhattan. (In 1976, the proceeds that had not been spent for administrative overhead—$110 million—were still in the hands of Chase.) The only benefit that New York City has thus far derived from Battery Park City is that its vacant expanse served as an ideal viewing stand for the Operation Sail extravaganza staged by the city on July 4, 1976, in celebration of the Bicentennial.

While Battery Park City limped forward, David Rockefeller was preparing another pyramid to optimism on lower Manhattan's eastern flank. In 1972, he and John Lindsay announced a mammoth $1.2 billion project, developed by the city government's Office of Lower Manhattan Planning, which they called Manhattan Landing. This included plans for 6 million square feet of office space; 9500 units of exclusively luxury housing; a new building for the New York

Stock Exchange; a 400-room hotel; and a permanent home for the sailing ships and restored blockfronts of the South Street Seaport; as well as a marina, an indoor sports complex, and a 1000-car garage. Lindsay—who was then in the midst of his abortive campaign for president, generously financed by builders and developers who had cashed in on his Planning Commission's largesse—called the proposal "a strong affirmation of faith in the city's future by the planners who conceived it, the financial community who will back it, and the developers who will build it."

In fact, the sponsors for the various Manhattan Landing projects were a roster of the permanent government. Twenty commercial and savings banks were to finance the private share of the construction to arise on the 113-acre landfill site. Major builders—Uris, Trump, DeMatteis, Tishman, and Arlen Realty and Development— all laid claim to parts of the package. Prominent architectural firms like Edward Barnes; Davis, Brody; and the ubiquitous Skidmore, Owings & Merrill were already busily at work.

There were a few hitches, however. First, Manhattan Landing made Battery Park City unworkable. Urstadt was willing, even anxious, to tell any listener that he couldn't rent high-income apartments in a mixed-income project if he had to compete with an all-luxury project with greater amenities only a mile away. This problem had one obvious solution—and the Lindsay planners jumped at it. They simply tore up the 1969 compromise and severely reduced the proportion of low- and middle-income housing in Battery Park City. Despite opposition from Manhattan Borough President Percy Sutton, the city's highest black elected official, and Bronx Borough President Robert Abrams, this new plan for Battery Park breezed through the Board of Estimate.

Other problems were less easily resolved. To make it marketable even for tenants earning $65,000 a year, Manhattan Landing would require massive public subsidy, including an 80 per cent tax abatement and a minimum direct investment of $100 million in public funds for construction. The city had nearly exhausted its middle-income housing funds (many public middle-income projects had already defaulted on their mortgages), and it had created yet another bonding mechanism, called the Housing Construction Fund, to pump money into programs that had been largely vitiated by the rapidly inflating building costs stimulated by the Vietnam war. Since two-thirds of the HCF monies were reserved directly for hardcore slum areas, Manhattan Landing alone would absorb the lion's share

of the remaining housing-construction monies available for most of
the city's neighborhoods.

As chief executive of the city's poorest and most troubled
borough, Bronx Borough President Robert Abrams led the opposition to Manhattan Landing. He had been a consistent critic of con-
centrating city housing subsidies in Manhattan, its wealthiest
borough:

> There is something inherently immoral in creating artificial land on
> the fringe of Manhattan's financial district at a cost of $40 a square
> foot [he wrote], while hundreds of acres of existing land stand vacant
> or undeveloped in other parts of the city and a once thriving com-
> munity like Brownsville is a square mile of rubble. . . . New construc-
> tion of low-income and middle-income housing in the boroughs outside
> Manhattan has fallen to a trickle, and we continue to lose more housing
> units each year than we build. There is obviously something desperately
> wrong with our housing and planning priorities. . . . Manhattan Landing
> is a luxury we simply cannot afford in the face of spreading neighbor-
> hood decay throughout the city. Could there be any conceivable bene-
> fit to either the business community or the community at large if this
> pleasure dome were left standing resplendently in the midst of a city
> in ruins?

When the project was brought before the Board of Estimate for
a public hearing, Abrams continued his attack, this time revealing
an internal Planning Commission report that questioned the rent-
ability of the proposed office space. "One unanticipated result of
past office construction is a substantial oversupply of office space,"
the report said. "This oversupply is not a result of the recession but
a miscalculation of the total demand and a breakdown of the financial controls on office buildings." In other words, so many new
offices and luxury housing projects would not have been approved
all at once if the Planning Commission itself had not provided
gimmicks and incentives for the builders.

One of these gimmicks is the sale of air rights over existing
buildings, which allowed builders to add floor space that an ad-
herence to the zoning laws would have forbidden. Another is the
granting of several additional floors in a building if a plaza is
provided at ground level. Caught up in the spirit of the times, one
midtown apartment-house builder, for example, had simply gone
ahead and added three extra floors to a building he was construct-

ing, and was outraged when a chairman of the neighborhood planning board happened by and counted the number of floors. This small detail had eluded city inspectors on the job. "Creative zoning," like "creative accounting," obviously has its moment of truth.

Since office space under construction in 1972 might not be fully absorbed into the market before 1978, the report went on to warn of a cut-throat price war in the rental market: "Any narrowing of the rent differential between old and new office buildings will weaken the competitive advantage of old structures. If the current surplus of office space (particularly in lower Manhattan) causes a general reduction in rental level in 'middle-aged' buildings, unmodernized pre-1920 structures will lose tenants and may go under."

Confronted with this analysis by his own staff, the Planning Commission chairman, Donald Elliott, stared at Abrams for a moment and then blithely replied, "Well, you just have to have faith in the city's future." With that bit of gallows humor ringing in its ears, the Board of Estimate proceeded to vote acceptance of Manhattan Landing.

Today there isn't even a peeling signboard left to mark the Manhattan Landing site. Battery Park City is a wind-blown wasteland. Since 1970, 132 brokerage firms in Lower Manhattan have merged or gone out of business. Others have moved across the Hudson River to New Jersey. The employment potential of the financial district is rapidly shrinking under the impact of automation. At least one source estimates that there are 30 million square feet of unrented office space in Manhattan, and a number of large, middle-aged office buildings have been placed in receivership. Many smaller office buildings have stopped paying real-estate taxes to the city, and before long we may observe the phenomenon of abandoned office buildings.

On February 29, 1976, state Comptroller Arthur Levitt, suggested that the governor consider dissolving the Battery Park City Authority and making some arrangement to pay off the $200 million in bonds that were borrowed for the project. Levitt noted that the Authority was paying its own salaries and current interest on the bonds with interest on the capital funds it has invested. He estimated that all of the money would be dissipated by 1984 unless revenue-producing facilities could be built on the site, but said there was "no indication of an early disposition" of the obstacles that had kept both housing and offices from construction.

Charles Urstadt is desperately trying to keep things afloat and, ironically for such a Republican wheelhorse, obviously hopes that a new Democratic administration may bail out his project with federally insured mortgages.

The Port Authority, now under the direction of Nelson Rockefeller's long-time aide William Ronan, is still looking for tenants for the World Trade Center. And despite a recent Supreme Court ruling that held invalid its bond provisions against involvement in mass-transit projects, it still refuses to use its vast resources to upgrade the region's collapsing rail lines.

David Rockefeller can look down from his office at Chase Manhattan Plaza at a radically altered financial district, and, if he cranes his neck a bit, he can see three of the four boroughs that were experiencing a slow death while he and his cohorts in both the elected and permanent governments concentrated the diminishing resources of the city on tinkering with "the heart pump of the capital blood that sustains the free world."

If the permanent government has any claim to legitimacy, it is that it uses its wealth, power, and prestige for what it defines as the "best interests" of New York City and its eight million people. Echoing Charles Wilson's famous dictum, "What's good for G.M. is good for the country," members of the permanent government lay claim to the support, if not the affection, of the rest of us because their various projects and businesses provide jobs for everyone from construction workers to waitresses. The facts—that much of the speculative office construction is vacant, that no one but the very wealthy can pay the rents in even publicly subsidized new housing, and that the whole infrastructure of the city, from its subways to its sewers, is collapsing because public revenues are inadequate—are conveniently ignored.

As the city teeters on the edge of ruin, the sophisticated boosterism of the permanent government has developed a hollow ring. There can be little doubt that the David Rockefellers, the Urises, and the Urstadts sincerely believe that they have done well for the people whose lives they dominate. Their problem is that the people are beginning to understand that in fact they have merely done well for themselves.

More than any other group in the permanent government, the banks are now encountering a crisis of confidence from a once unquestioning public. The word "redlining" is slowly entering the average New Yorker's vocabulary. And with it comes the growing sense of outrage and vicitimization that must befall someone who has just been robbed with his own gun.

Redlining has become the one-word definition for the growing pattern of urban disinvestment practiced not only by banks, but by insurance companies, pension funds, and other financial inter- mediaries. It is derived from the way mortgage officers once drew a red line around a section on a map and refused to make any further investments in the proscribed neighborhood. Today whole counties, some would even claim the entire city of New York, has been red- lined. But no bank loan officer would be foolish enough to commit his bias to paper. After all, this is the age of the "equal opportunity lender."

Redlining first emerged as a national urban problem in ghetto areas; then it rapidly spread to so-called "transitional" neighbor- hoods undergoing racial change. Today, any urban area that might someday undergo racial change is liable to be redlined—in other words all parts of our cities except gilt-edged communities like Man- hattan's Sutton Place or Chicago's Lake Shore Drive. But resistance to the banks' redlining habits has grown rapidly, especially in white ethnic homeowner areas in industrial cities like Chicago, Cleveland, and Buffalo. "Anti-redlining" coalitions, often consisting of white working men and middle-class blacks, have been formed to demand disclosure of bank lending policies by state legislatures and Con- gress and, more recently, to confront local banks and savings-and- loan associations directly and to withdraw savings en masse from those that refuse to plough back investment into the neighborhoods.

In New York City, the redlining issue has been slow to take hold. Embattled tenants in most neighborhoods, facing declining services and rising rents, directed their protests at landlords—not realizing that many landlords only begin seriously to "milk" a building in preparation for abandonment after they have discovered that the banks have already given up the neighborhood as lost.

As noted earlier, the only true value of a property to a landlord is its resale value. Without bank financing, resale becomes almost impossible and landlords can extract their capital only by literally destroying the building. In recent years, more and more landlords in redlined areas have put the torch to unsalable properties so as to gain the insurance money. The epidemic of arson in areas like the South Bronx is directly traceable to redlining, while no less heinous for that reason.

The bitter irony in all this is that the victims of disinvestment are the only source of deposits for the savings banks and savings-and-loan associations. The same observation can be made about the insurance companies and certainly about union pension funds. It's *our* money, but *they* spend it.

Since savings banks are the principal source of mortgage investment in the city, we shall concentrate on their role in redlining. A brief excursion into banking history is required.

Savings banks have always been the poor relations among the nation's financial institutions. In the early days of banking, the large commercial bankers dealt exclusively with business firms. They spurned the nickels and dimes of immigrant workers and small farmers, and by the time they realized that enough nickels and dimes together can be big business, a separate system of banking had grown up beneath their feet.

Many savings banks actually started as burial societies, with several employers in one area or industry getting together to accept the small deposits of their workers and then reinvesting them to provide enough incentive to keep the workers saving for a decent funeral. In 1834, a group of employers in the old Bowery meat market established the first savings bank and called it, logically enough, the Bowery Savings Bank. They kept deposits in a small leather-bound wooden chest fourteen inches wide and seven inches deep. The Bowery still preserves the chest to remind it of its humble beginnings.

The most logical, and safest, form of investment in those early days was mortgages on the homes and small businesses being erected in the rapidly growing city. Mortgages are still the safest investment next to federal bonds. In the 1974–75 economic collapse, only five mortgages in every 10,000 defaulted.

Savings banks initially were neighborhood institutions. They found it too risky to invest in areas that their officers and directors didn't know personally. Because they were local institutions, the savings banks developed a high degree of loyalty among depositors, who also were their major borrowers; this loyalty persisted long after the banks had changed their size, character, and function. But when the savings banks tried to move further afield, the commercial banks were quick to induce legislators to pass laws restricting the geographic scope of savings-bank activities and the type of services they could offer.

So the first crucial lesson that the commercial banks taught their fledgling competitors was that banking and politics go hand in hand. Savings banks soon made it a point to add prominent local politicians to their boards of directors and to court friends in Albany and at City Hall. It was a lesson that began paying big dividends. Today in New York City the boards of savings banks read like a *Who's Who* of the permanent government: William Ellinghaus, a member of the EFCB, and vice-chairman of AT&T, is a trustee of the Union Dime Savings Bank. Alton Marshall, former secretary to Governor Rockefeller and now president of Rockefeller Center, is a trustee of the Lincoln Savings Bank. Former Governor Malcolm Wilson is a trustee of the Manhattan Savings Bank.

E. Virgil Conway, a member of the Mayor's Management Advisory Board and a director of Con Edison, is president of the Seamen's Bank for Savings. Charles Urstadt, whom we met as chairman of the Battery Park City Authority, is a trustee of the New York Bank for Savings. Eugene Keogh, the former Brooklyn congressman, a director of City Title Insurance Company and of Mortgage Affiliates, is a trustee of the East New York Savings Bank.

Paul Screvane, the chairman of the Off-Track Betting Corporation, is a director of the Jamaica Savings Bank. Former Mayor Robert Wagner is a trustee of the Metropolitan Savings Bank, and so is William Shea. Harold Fisher, the peripatetic lawyer and MTA member, is chairman of the Dime Savings Bank of Williamsburgh. David Yunich, former chairman of the Metropolitan Transportation Authority, is a trustee of the East River Savings Bank. Donald Elliott, former chairman of the City Planning Commission, is a trustee of Independence Savings Bank. William Ronan, chairman of the Port Authority, is a trustee of the Metropolitan Savings Bank. And so is Vincent Caristo, who as president of the Caristo Construction Corporation gets most of the city's contracts to build schools.

Federal housing insurance, instituted in 1934, then supplemented by veterans' insurance in 1945, made a big difference for the savings banks, for it meant that they could invest in mortgages outside their immediate areas without fear of being sandbagged by local speculators out to bilk the city boys. But state laws regarding uninsured commercial loans were still highly restrictive. So were branching regulations, which allowed savings banks to open only one additional branch a year.

The savings banks conducted a war of attrition. First, they had their friends in government pass a bill allowing branching in other counties, mostly in Manhattan's central business district and later in the proliferating suburbs in Nassau and Westchester counties. Next, they won the right to make commercial loans in neighboring states. Finally, the big breakthrough came in 1966, when they won the right to make commercial loans anywhere in the United States.

Predictably, the banks' investments in New York City plunged as they began pouring their money into the burgeoning Sunbelt states of the south and west. These states were experiencing a historic housing boom but had little capital of their own to finance mortgages. The sky was the limit on mortgage rates.

A study conducted by New York University showed that multi-family properties in New York City secured by conventional savings-bank mortgages fell by 20–25 per cent in the years 1967–72. It is no accident that the number of housing units abandoned in the city leaped during the same period. The study also showed that disinvestment by savings-and-loan associations and insurance companies was increasing at an even faster rate. (The banks refuse to issue separate figures for New York City but admit that 65 per cent of their mortgages were in the state in 1955, only 41 per cent in 1967.)

The banks immediately countered that they were simply seeking more security for their depositors' money—a euphemism for their anxiety about ghetto unrest in the 1960s. But the NYU researchers found that there was no significant upward trend in either the delinquency rate (late payments) of mortgages or the foreclosure rate experienced by New York City savings banks. The banks were simply out to make more money. This is hardly a crime in the American economy—except for one crucial fact. Savings banks are mutual banks, theoretically owned by their depositors; they issue no stock, or bonds for that matter. They are, by law, *nonprofit* institutions. In other words, their only responsibility is to earn enough to pay the legally prescribed rates of interest to depositors and to cover overhead. In the depression-inflation year of 1974, when banks were offering premium interest rates of 8 per cent for monies left on deposit a minimum of six years, the actual costs of depositors' accounts was only 5.7 per cent while the banks earned a net return of 6.8 per cent, leaving them a comfortable 1.1 per cent, or approximately $600 million, to meet overhead. (In 1975, New York State savings banks had assets of $66 *billion;* about $44 billion was invested in mortgages—a little less than half of which, $21 billion, was invested out-of-state.)

In December 1976, the New York Public Interest Research Group, a Nader spinoff, published a study of bank mortgage practices in Brooklyn. One startling disclosure in this study came from data amassed by the Finance Administration, revealed by NYPIRG for the first time. Three of the biggest Brooklyn banks had admitted to the city that while the bulk of their deposits came from city residents, only a minuscule proportion of their mortgages was still given within the city limits. Dime Savings Bank had 73 per cent of its deposits from city residents, but only 17 per cent of its mortgages were on city properties. The ratio for the Greater New York Bank for Savings was 98 per cent in deposits, 15 per cent in mortgages. The Williamsburgh Savings Bank showed 81 per cent in deposits, 15 per cent in mortgages. Only the medium-sized Greenpoint Savings Bank was doing a creditable job, with 93 per cent of its deposits from city dwellers and 61 per cent of its mortgages held in the city. In calendar 1975, Greenpoint invested $25 million in Brooklyn. The Dime (four times its size) invested only $5.3 million. Five other banks in the survey invested amounts ranging from only $1 million to $3 million.

Despite New Yorkers' growing alarm at the increasing disinvestment in both the city and state, the savings banks continued to avoid effective regulation by the state superintendent of banks and began a major drive in the state legislature for greater power. In 1975, they won a bill that allowed them to open a limitless number of mini-branches with computer terminals in such locations as shopping centers, train stations, etc. In return, they bought a paltry $180 million in state securities to help bail out state agencies caught in the spinoff effects of New York City's fiscal crisis. And then they made their biggest power grab.

The key commercial banking preserve that had been denied to the savings banks was the right to offer checking accounts. In partial compensation, savings banks are allowed by federal law to pay a slightly higher interest rate on savings accounts, currently ¼ of 1 per cent more, than the commercials do. In several New England states the savings institutions are allowed to offer checking accounts, however, and the New York banks, which account for about half of all savings-banks deposits in the entire country, wanted the same power. They had consistently lost this battle in the state legislature as a result of heavy commercial-bank lobbying.

After another defeat in the state legislature in 1974, Harry W. Albright, Rockefeller's superintendent of banking, dredged up an ambiguous section of a banking law passed in 1965, and unilaterally granted savings banks the right to offer "payment order" accounts— checking accounts in all but name. While the commercial banks ran to court, the savings banks offered free checking and quickly signed up 176,000 customers for their new service. The courts uniformly ruled against Albright but refused to dissolve the new accounts and in effect threw the issue back to the legislature. (When Albright resigned he became president of Dime Savings Bank, the second largest in the state and third largest in the nation.)

The legislature refused to resolve the issue in its 1975 session because the Democrats had amended the checking-account bill to require the savings banks to establish a $3-billion mortgage pool over a ten-year period; anyone denied a mortgage by a savings bank could turn to the pool, which would have a publicly appointed board of directors, as a lender of last resort. It was hoped that this mechanism would limit the effects of redlining and encourage the banks to make more loans, since they would ultimately have to bear the risks of the same mortgages through the pool.

When insurance companies had begun redlining ghetto areas in the 1960s, the banks had supported the pool concept to provide fire insurance for all landlords. (In New York State, the mortgagee, usually a bank, receives the proceeds of any fire-insurance policy first; the landlord gets whatever is left. There is no requirement that the insurance be used to restore a partially damaged property. This arrangement actually serves as an inducement to arson.) But when the pooled-risk concept was applied to them, the savings banks fought it like a cornered tiger. They preferred to let the checking-account bill die than to be told where to spend their money—correction, *our* money.

Although originally slated as a sleeper, the checking-account bill became one of the most bitter issues of the 1976 legislative session in Albany. Urban liberal Democrats, spurred by a decision in the Court of Appeals that would force the banks to dissolve the illegal checking accounts by April 1 unless the legislature legitimated them, prepared to mount a drive for the mortgage pool. They were in for a rude shock.

First Governor Carey announced an agreement drafted by his superintendent of banking, John Heimann, and agreed to by the banks. Under this plan, the banks would publish their loans by census districts, theoretically allowing local groups to monitor bank lending policies and to publicize redliners. After reading the fine print, however, activists rejected the plan as too weak. Besides, they countered, a federal district court in Ohio had held that redlining was a crime. Would the superintendent negotiate an agreement with embezzlers, or would he put an end to their criminal behavior? Heimann then announced that he supported a "naked" checking-account bill—without the mortgage-pool requirement—a complete reversal of the position he had taken in the previous legislative session. When questioned by angry legislators, he simply announced that he had been "new," i.e. inexperienced, the previous year.

Heimann's sudden change of heart wasn't the last urban legislators would encounter. The mortgage-pool concept had been the official Democratic position throughout the prior legislative session. Now the Democrats learned from Assembly Speaker Stanley Steingut that this was no longer so. As a matter of fact, Steingut called the "antiredliners" into an angry late-night session and frankly told them that he had made a deal with Warren Anderson, Republican leader of the state Senate; the checking-account bill would pass both houses as long as the Democratic reformers in the Assembly did nothing "duplicitous," like adding the mortgage-pool amendment. George Cincotta, a wheelhorse of the Brooklyn Democratic machine and chairman of the Assembly Banking Committee, was the sponsor of this "naked" bill. Cincotta has close ties with the savings banks in Brooklyn. ("George can get anyone a mortgage in an hour," one Assembly Democrat told us.) His son is a vice-president of Citibank.

The savings banks were, of course, carrying on an unprecedented lobbying campaign. Huge billboards urging passage of a checking-account bill assaulted the legislators as they drove into Albany on the State Thruway. Full-page ads appeared in newspapers across the state, especially in New York City. As the debate heated up, the ads took on a harsher tone. The savings banks ignored the redlining issue and posed as a populist force seeking to give the people free checking accounts. (There had been no specification that the accounts would be free in Cincotta's original bill; an amendment to require this was added by the antiredliners in the floor debate.) At one point, opponents of the "naked" bill were accused of being tools of the commercial banks. Meanwhile the savings banks stimulated thousands of letters from depositors who wanted the convenience of doing all of their banking under one roof and saving a few extra bucks on their checking accounts in the bargain. Most depositors seemed oblivious to the likelihood that if the savings banks weren't forced to provide more mortgages in their neighborhoods, the banks might be the only roof left standing.

At one point, an angry group of state senators, led by Manhattan's Franz Leichter, probably the most anti-bank legislator in Albany, confronted Governor Carey on the issue. Carey said he would try to get the banks to negotiate a bill containing the mortgage pool. The anti-redliners were jubilant, but the governor's commitment evaporated like the Irish morning mist. The banks went on to offer minority legislators secret mortgage commitments for a handful of their constituents if they would vote against the mortgage-pool clause. The anti-redlining coalition was slowly reduced to a corporal's guard, which voted against the final bill. The Democratic leadership praised the bill as a victory for consumers.

As a result, things have never looked better for the savings banks. With the passage of the checking-account bill, they have become small commercial banks. The next logical step seems to be the transformation of the larger ones into stockholder-owned institutions, which will give the commercial banks a chance to acquire them on the open market or through negotiated mergers. This kind of "bank consolidation" was proposed by a special federal study group appointed by Richard Nixon, and it seems the most lucrative road for the industry. Savings banks are rapidly diversifying their investments and drawing back from their mortgage commitments, not only in the cities but throughout the entire Northeast.

Things have never looked worse for New York City housing. Savings banks not only provide the capital to maintain a market in buildings but are the source of the mortgage refinancing that allows landlords to renovate buildings. As the banks have accelerated their withdrawal from the city housing market, they have required faster repayments of financing at higher rates of interest, making it difficult for even the best landlord to upgrade profitably.

New York City, which supplies three-quarters of all the savings-bank deposits in the state, is America's largest single capital exporter —at a time when its own housing stock is literally crumbling before our eyes for lack of capital. The banks themselves have created this abandonment problem, which they then point to as the rationale for reducing investment in the city. For the sake of profit and institutional aggrandizement, they are willing to see the city die. Yet the permanent government, which controls not only many of these institutions but also the state apparatus that could force them to change lending policies overnight, allows the hemorrhage to continue unabated.

Some housing activists suspect that a Machiavellian game plan to destroy rent control lies behind these disinvestment policies. Certainly the banks have always hated rent control, but this is largely because it symbolizes the threat of adoption of controls in other communities—not because of any real economic impact in New York, where rents are actually rising faster than in the rest of America. The banks are sophisticated enough to know that rents in New York have reached their upper limits and are already absorbing an extraordinarily high degree of disposable income (often more than 35 per cent)—a much higher expenditure for housing than is found, for instance, in home-owner communities (where it may be as low as 10 per cent).

The poor pay the highest rates, both as a proportion of their income and in absolute terms, since for decades rent increases of 15 per cent every two years were allowed for new tenants, and the least desirable slum apartments had a high turnover rate. Slum buildings are abandoned for only two reasons: The tenants are in revolt and refuse to pay rent because of lack of services; or some major system, such as the heat or plumbing, has completely broken down and requires a significant capital outlay for replacement or repair. No slum building was ever abandoned because its cash flow from rents was inadequate for ordinary upkeep.

If rent control is abandoned, there will be no upsurge in institutional mortgage lending, although more private speculators might be attracted to the market. When vacancy decontrol went into effect in 1971, there was no change in the pattern of disinvestment, although rent rolls skyrocketed.

The only conclusion that we can draw is that the permanent government is unwilling to use its vast power over financial institutions to rebuild the city—at the very moment in history when they are so vociferously demanding sacrifice from everyone else in order to "save" New York. More than anything else, it is this double standard—applied to *people*, but not to *capital*—that is destroying New York City's future as a living environment.

Throughout this analysis we have shown how the permanent government operates to shape key decisions affecting all of our lives: invisibly, through its political operatives or controlled institutions, desperately anxious to conceal the hand that pulls the strings. Occasionally, however, something goes wrong and the permanent government is forced into a raw display of its power. For a brief but instructive moment, the public has a glimpse of how things really operate.

Such a moment occurred in the closing hours of the 1976 legislative session in Albany.

The Museum of Modern Art is one of the capstones of New York's cultural life and has been a favored charity of the elite, especially the Rockefellers, the Paleys, and the Whitneys. (Nelson Rockefeller is himself probably the most important collector of modern art in the world.) While its permanent exhibition is one of the true wonders of the world, its cellars are crammed with significant masterpieces which are never seen except by those anointed by its powerful board. MOMA itself is a second-rate, perhaps even a third-rate, building shoe-horned into a side-street plot on 53rd Street off Fifth Avenue. While many museums, especially the Metropolitan, have made efforts to decentralize and reach out to the general public in recent years, MOMA has remained remote, still charges a stiff admission fee, and retains the aura of a rich man's gallery rather than a cultural repository for all the people.

In recent years, problems have set in. Lavish private contributions have been falling off, as they have in many other areas of the city's cultural life. The very wealthy—men like board chairman William Paley of CBS—control the museum but are increasingly reluctant to pay the bills for their expensive hobby. (MOMA is the only museum in memory to suffer a strike by its employees.)

Expansion, more room for the collections, and greater reliance on revenues from commercial activities like the book store and restaurant suggest one way out of this dilemma. The museum owns several adjoining small buildings and can double its size by tearing them down and building an extension. Here again, however, the private fund raisers were unwilling to raise $17 million in expansion costs, although gifts to the museum are tax-deductible.

Richard Weinstein, formerly director of the City Planning Commission's Office for Lower Manhattan and a participant in the development of the Battery Park City and Manhattan Landing schemes, left city employment to become an executive of the Arlen Realty and Development Corp. Weinstein was one of the "bright young men" under Donald Elliott who fostered the 1960s building boom at the Planning Commission. In 1975 Weinstein proposed another of his innovative schemes: This one would allow the Museum of Modern Art to expand and at the same time provide Arlen with one of the choice sites for a mid-Manhattan luxury building. (Elliott, one of the few Lindsay officials to ascend to membership in the permanent government, is now counsel to MOMA as a partner—with Lindsay—in the white-shoe law firm of Webster, Sheffield.) Between them they hatched the following plan:

The museum would demolish the extra buildings it owns on 53rd Street and build a ten-story expansion to its building; above it would rise a 40-story condominium whose units would sell in the $250,000-per-apartment range. This expansion would be financed by tax-exempt bonds to be issued by a public development corporation specifically established for this purpose. The bondhold- ers would be repaid by diverting the real-estate taxes that would normally flow to the city from a project of this size to the develop- ment corporation instead.

A bill to accomplish this complex undertaking was duly filed with the legislature, brought out in the last-minute rush to adjourn- ment when special-interest bills are customarily passed with the speed of light. At another time it might have breezed through and been praised as another example of the "creative financing" that kept New York afloat on a sea of red ink for decades. This year, however, the legislators balked. Given the specter of unfinished school build- ings, apartment houses, and health centers stopped in mid- construction throughout New York City, they refused to vote for funds to build a bigger museum and a luxury apartment house that should be the responsibility of private philanthropy. The bill was defeated in the Democratic-controlled Assembly on Monday, June 28, 1976, by a vote of 72–53. (It passed easily in the Republican- dominated state Senate.)

Then, in the early morning hours of June 30, the legislature's final day, the bill *passed* the Assembly by a new vote of 86–40. In the interim, the permanent government had gotten on the phone. Mayor Beame; his deputy and former Planning Commission Chair- man John Zuccotti; former Mayor Lindsay; William Paley; Richard Rosenbaum, state Republican chairman and a long-time trusted Rockefeller aide; Alex Rose, chairman of the Liberal Party; and several county Democratic chairmen made it clear to the runaway legislators that this bill was to pass. It did. Elliott explained to the *Times:* "We can no longer go to the big contributors because the money isn't there." He failed to mention where it had gone.

The bill is expected to be approved by New York City's Board of Estimate. In a few years, the Museum of Modern Art will have a bright new building, Arlen Realty will have another luxury apart- ment house, the taxpayers who subsidized the project will continue to pay for entry into the museum, and it is likely that schools and new apartments in East Harlem will remain uncompleted.

And the permanent government will continue to preach "sacri- fice" as the road to fiscal stability for New York City.

LEGAL
GRAFT

Everybody is talkin' these days about Tammany men growin' rich on graft, but nobody thinks of drawin' the distinction between honest graft and dishonest graft. . . . Yes, many of our men have grown rich in politics. I have myself. I've made a big fortune out of the game, and I'm gettin' richer every day. But I've not gone in for dishonest graft— blackmailin' gamblers, saloon-keepers, disorderly people, etc.—and neither has any of the men who have made big fortunes in politics.

There's an honest graft, and I'm an example of how it works. I might sum up the whole thing by sayin': I seen my opportunities and I took 'em.

— GEORGE WASHINGTON PLUNKETT

Politics is business. And legal graft is the currency of the permanent government.

Legal graft is finder's fees, title insurance, city contracts. It can be interest-free deposits of government funds, zoning variances, insurance premiums, or condemnation awards. It can be campaign contributions, bond sale commissions, public relations retainers. It can be real estate leases, mortgage closings, or, most often, legal fees.

As Al Smith said one day strolling through a law school library and noticing a student absorbed in a book: "There's a young man studying how to take a bribe and call it a fee."

Legal graft is the disguised quid pro quo. I'll get you a nursing home license, and you hire my law firm. I'll get you a ninety-nine–year lease from the city, and you give my friend some insurance. I'll make you a judge, but your two brothers each have to contribute $7500 to the party by purchasing tables at our dinners. If your union contributes to my campaign, you can name the next chairman of the workman's compensation board.

Legal graft is no stranger to residents of Chicago, Boston, Cleveland, Philadelphia, Maryland, New Jersey, or the sunwashed new communities of Arizona. But in New York City it is bigger, more sophisticated, and all-pervasive.

Legal graft built the $2-billion Albany Mall. Legal graft was the oxygen of the Robert Moses empire in New York City.

The National Commercial Bank and Trust Company of Albany was chosen by Governor Nelson Rockefeller as the depository for cash proceeds of bond sales on the Albany Mall, his gigantic building program in the state capital. About $1 billion flowed through the bank as a consequence. Democratic Mayor Erastus Corning of Albany is a director of National Commercial Bank and Trust, a member of its executive committee, and a substantial stockholder.

Two other bank accounts were set up in the State Bank of Albany: one to process the state's rentals to the county, and the other to redeem the revenue bonds. Mayor Corning and his mother and father were also directors of the State Bank of Albany.

During construction of the mall, Mayor Corning was also president of Albany Associates, Inc., an insurance agency and brokerage firm which sold construction insurance policies to M. Kramer and Sons, a contractor with $12.8 million's worth of heating and plumbing jobs on the mall. The policies sold by the mayor's company covered bodily injury up to $5 million, and property damage up to the same amount.

In April 1976, state Comptroller Arthur Levitt estimated that the final total cost of the Albany Mall—including debt service—would be $2 billion. His auditors estimate the actual final cost of construction will be $985 million. When Nelson Rockefeller had first announced the mall project, he had predicted that the construction cost would be $200 million.

In his remarkable *Moby Dick* of urban biography, *The Power Broker: Robert Moses and the Fall of New York,** Robert Caro describes how three powerhouse Democratic politicians shared in the insurance business from the Triborough Bridge and Tunnel Authority—business worth $500,000 a year in premiums and $100,000 per year in commissions. The three—Carmine DeSapio, Stanley Steingut, and James Roe—even made sure that one Republican politician, a man named John Crews, the Brooklyn county leader, received some of the premiums, since he too was in the insurance business. The public, of course, had no way to know their leaders were getting this private enrichment. Steingut flatly denied it. The distributor of this bipartisan legal graft was Robert Moses.

When he controlled the World's Fair Corporation in 1964, Moses was a Santa Claus of legal graft. Thomas Deegan, the politically well-connected press agent, told the media he would publicize the Fair without compensation—"without any fees or expenses of any kind." But Moses gave Deegan an annual fee of $100,000, plus expenses that included a $1000-a-month suite at the Waldorf and a $572 monthly salary for a chauffeur. That was for Deegan individually. Thomas J. Deegan Co., Inc., received an additional $350,000 a year. All public funds. Today Deegan is on the payroll of the Battery Park City Authority at $3000 a month as a consultant.

Meanwhile, all the insurance on the World's Fair was steered to a company favored by Carmine DeSapio, the Campo & Roberts agency. The Fair's charter required all exhibitors to purchase their insurance from companies "approved by the Fair Corporation," and DeSapio and Moses made sure that Campo & Roberts was the only "approved" insurance agency. It came to $3 million in commissions. At the same time all the legal fees from the Fair Corporation went to the law firm of Samuel Rosenman, whose newest partner was Charles Preusse. Preusse had once been City Administrator, in which role he had helped to draft the legislation that exempted the Fair Corporation from the city's Code of Ethics.

Moses and Rockefeller were Pharaohs who built pyramids. They understood that "public works" was a licence to legal graft.

Other politicians followed and built office towers, highways, bus terminals, sports stadiums, shopping centers, luxury housing, via-

* From which many of the details in the following paragraphs come.

ducts, hotels. Each project fed the construction complex of banks, unions, lawyers, insurance companies, architects, bond underwriters, press agents.

And it all helped to bankrupt and destroy New York City. We have seen how the World Trade Center—conceived by David and Nelson Rockefeller—cost $1 billion and killed the commercial real-estate market. Meantime, throughout the city, debt services grew. Priorities were distorted. Services deteriorated. Neighborhoods died. Housing decayed, since so little attention was paid to rehabilitation and restoration. The area south of Canal Street has lost 50,000 jobs since 1968, many in the printing industry, a distinctive New York business. And 30,000 construction workers found themselves un-employed—as a consequence of the insupportable orgy of over-building in earlier years.

But the construction complex became swollen and fat on all the "bribes called fees." The Moses empire—the public authorities—survives. The Rockefeller empire, anchored by the Chase bank, prospers. In 1975, the city lost 30,000 construction jobs. These flesh-and-blood workers were expendable. The institutions of wealth count, and they endure.

Legal graft is apolitical. It is important to understand that above a certain level of power, at the level of permanent power, there is no party politics. There are no Democrats and no Republicans. There are only class colleagues sharing profits.

Among the vessels of legal graft are various business enter-prises that include important politicians from both parties as part-ners. Law firms, banks, PR firms. Mortage companies. Brokerage houses. Public-utility companies.

There is, for example, City Title Insurance Company. The board of directors includes: Stanley Steingut, the Democratic Speaker of the state Assembly; Willis Stephens, senior Republican on the As-sembly Ways and Means committee; Eugene Keogh, a former Democratic congressman from Brooklyn; Alton Marshall, Nelson Rockefeller's former secretary and now president of Rockefeller Cen-ter; and Arthur Quinn, chairman of The New York Bank for Savings, and a Republican Party fund-raiser. City Title has insured the title on more than $50 million's worth of state-aided moderate-income housing projects.

The Brighton Houses is such a project in Brooklyn. City Title was awarded the bulk of its title insurance. The brokerage fees on other insurance went to Grand Brokerage, in which Steingut and Brooklyn Democratic boss Meade Esposito each owned a 25-percent interest. And the legal fees on the project went to Bunny Lindenbaum, the ubiquitous clubhouse zoning lawyer and fund raiser.

On the state-aided Brooklyn Jewish Hospital staff residence, City Title got the insurance. The firm of Alfred Lama, who drafted the state law providing subsidies for moderate-income housing, received $67,000 in architectural fees. And Steingut's law firm—Halperin, Shivitz, Scholer and Steingut—got $14,710 in legal fees.

The law firm of Shea, Gould is a factory of legal graft. Shoup Voting Machines, for instance, sold $8.5 million's worth of equipment to the city shortly after retaining William Shea's powerhouse firm. It was the first time in thirty-seven years that Shoup had been able to sell the city a single voting machine. TelePromTer Corporation got a cable television franchise from the city as soon as it retained Shea's firm in 1965.

A more complex Shea deal involved the Long Island Rail Road and First National City Bank. In 1965 Shea was designated by the state legislature to be its representative in negotiations with the Pennsylvania Railroad to buy its faltering subsidiary, the Long Island Rail Road. Shea was designated through the office of the Democratic leader in the Senate, Joseph Zaretski. (Zaretski's counsel at the time was Shea's law partner, Bernard Ruggieri.) Within seven weeks Shea and Governor Rockefeller's negotiator, William Ronan, recommended that the state pay Pennsylvania $65 million for the LIRR. According to a subsequent report by Arthur Levitt, $65 million was much too much for a line that had lost $2.5 million in 1965 and would require at least $200 million to improve its commuter service. Moreover, a Levitt audit showed that the Shea-Ronan formula would really cost the taxpayers $131 million, since they had also agreed to give up 65 acres of LIRR property, air rights over yards, and about $8.4 million in station concessions.

Several years after the dubious deal went through, Ralph Nader published a study of Citibank. Nader's study showed that $60 million of the $65 million in state funds paid for the LIRR went toward repayment of a Citibank loan for which the nearly bankrupt Pennsylvania was liable, and which probably would have been defaulted without the Shea-Ronan bailout. Nader's study also showed that Eben Pyne, senior vice-president of Citibank, had earlier been a member of a special state committee looking into the LIRR, representing the "creditor's interests," i.e., his own bank.

When the Metropolitan Transportation Authority (MTA) was created, Rockefeller's first appointments in 1968 were William Ronan as chairman, and William Shea and Eben Pyne as members.*

Legal graft can take the form of an honorary title that confers legitimacy on someone who needs it. On July 31, 1925, Bronx Democratic Party boss Ed Flynn appointed Arthur Flegenheimer an "honorary deputy sheriff of Bronx County." Flegenheimer is better known as Dutch Schultz, the efficient executioner for Legs Diamond.

Legal graft can take the form of a favor bestowed without any cash, a favor on which there is an invisible mortgage. For example, Frank Costello—the Mafia's Kissinger—used his influence to make Thomas Aurelio a State Supreme Court justice in 1943. We know this because there is a famous, legally wire-tapped exchange.

COSTELLO: "When I tell you something is in the bag, you can rest assured."

JUDGE AURELIO: "Right now I want to assure you of my loyalty for all you have done. It's undying."

Since no one could prove the commission of a crime, Aurelio became a judge despite the public release of this recording by Manhattan District Attorney Frank Hogan.

Legal graft can take the form of a job bartered for a favorable policy or decision of government.

In 1973, Paul Levine was a $32,000-a-year official in the city's Economic Development Administration. He participated in the decision to tear down two blocks of homes in a working-class, Polish section of Brooklyn called Northside. The homes must be torn down, Levine said, because the S&S Corrugated Paper Machinery Company wanted to expand. Ninety-two families were evicted and watched the bulldozer demolish their homes of a lifetime in front of their tear-filled eyes. Three months later, Paul Levine went to work for S&S. He admitted he had been negotiating with S&S for his new

---

* For all you need to know about Bill Shea, read Nicholas Pileggi's seminal article in *New York,* November 11, 1974.

job even as he participated in city meetings to plan the evictions. The city's Board of Ethics ruled Levine did nothing wrong.

Legal graft is a way to get around the law without breaking the law.

Let us examine some methodologies of legal graft in New York. We will start with the story of a real-estate developer named Christopher Boomis.

In January 1971, Luis Alimena, an official in Local 707 of the Teamsters Union, approached New York City's Economic Development Administration (EDA) with an idea to build a pier and refrigerated warehouse in the Hunts Point section of the South Bronx. Alimena was accorded easy access to the right city decision-maker, Edgar Fabber, soon to become the commissioner of Ports and Terminals. Both Alimena and Fabber were good friends of dock union boss Anthony Scotto.

Fabber's recollection of the meeting was: "Alimena said he had the right guy for the deal. A guy named Chris Boomis, a developer. I had never heard of Boomis. No one I knew ever heard of Boomis. So I checked him out with George Douris [City Hall reporter with the *Long Island Press*]. Douris was supposed to be the head Greek, and Boomis was supposed to be Greek. But Douris came up empty. He said no one knew anything about Boomis. He said Boomis must be a Turk, since no Greeks ever heard his name. . . . Mostly on Alimena's word, we gave Boomis the Hunts Point deal."

"The Hunts Point deal" was two linked leases for $37 million with no competitive bidding. For the pier project Boomis would be both builder and lessee. On the warehouse, he would be contractor and tenant.

Overnight, Boomis became a force in New York City. He had the prestige of a $37-million contract with the city. The Hunts Point project was announced in May 1972 at a City Hall press conference, with a beaming Boomis seated next to Mayor John Lindsay. The Board of Estimate approved the lease unanimously—and without debate—on April 12, 1973, and the Budget Bureau promised the Board that the city would make a profit on the lease. The mayor declared that the Boomis project would "capture 65 per cent of the total meat imports to the Northeast United States. . . . This facility will create 2000 new jobs." All this—the profit and the jobs—proved to be a fiction.

Suddenly Boomis began to acquire the discretionary favors of government. He went from mystery man to insider overnight. The city gave Boomis a two-year real-estate tax exemption to build a 31-floor luxury highrise at 96th Street and Broadway. Despite strong community opposition, Boomis had no trouble evicting the commercial-site tenants. Somehow he had clout at City Hall. *The New York Times* real-estate section published a favorable profile of Boomis by Carter B. Horsley on May 12, 1974. Boomis announced plans to build five more luxury buildings around Manhattan.

Kenneth Patton, the city's EDA Administrator, told other city commissioners that Boomis was "good for the city." State Assembly Democratic leader Albert Blumenthal assured journalist Phil Tracy that Boomis was honorable and community-oriented. Shea told bankers and mortgage companies that Boomis was a sound investment—and Boomis got $20 million in credit. Meade Esposito told cronies that "Boomis is my guy." Boomis gave a fund-raiser for Patrick Cunningham in his own lavish triplex apartment. On the hot air of word-of-mouth, Chris Boomis floated to the top of a very competive real-estate market.

In the spring of 1975, we began to research the curious rise of Boomis. How did it happen? How could he build, when all the giants of the construction business in New York—Lefrak, Tishman—and the best professionals could not build? How did he get city contracts and tax abatements and quick evictions?

Here's how.

Boomis gave all his insurance business on $24 million worth of properties to Grand Brokerage, which as we have pointed out is owned by Stanley Steingut and Meade Esposito. In 1973, Boomis says, he contributed $23,000 to Abe Beame's campaign for mayor, under his own name and through four other people who were either relatives or employees. In 1974, he gave $40,000 to Hugh Carey's gubernatorial campaign, including $10,000 after Carey was elected. (To hedge all bets, Boomis also spread around $15,000 to the loser in the Democratic primary, Howard Samuels.) His wife Zaida donated $5,000 to Republican candidate Malcolm Wilson. Boomis also gave $5,000 to a legislative campaign fund under the control of Stanley Steingut.

And Boomis gave away a 25 per cent limited partnership interest in Chris Boomis Associates to Luis Alimena for a token $100. When asked to explain this sort of charity, Boomis said that Teamster leader Alimena had "promised to introduce me to an efficient trucking company."

But Boomis was not subtle. He was not patient. He was not smart.

The first person to catch on to Boomis, to begin his fall, was a career civil servant of twenty-five years named Walter Prawzinsky. Prawzinsky was the chief engineer in the office of the city's controller. His deputy, Mario Grauso, has worked for the city for twenty years. Together they figured out that Boomis was submitting padded bills to the city for $200,000.

Later Boomis was sued by his own contractors for not paying them more than $1 million. Later still the scaffolding and building skeleton on his 96th Street site collapsed from too many violations of the safe demolition code. And after that, construction stopped at Hunts Point because Boomis would not allow an inspector onto the site.

But Boomis was still a king when Walter Prawzinsky began to scrutinize his reimbursement vouchers and bills and compare them to the terms of the written lease for Hunts Point. Boomis had tried to get the city to reimburse him for such items as legal fees, accounting fees, property liability insurance, "preliminary engineering studies," and "preparation of master plan." They were not covered by the lease.

So the civil servant challenged the fat cat. "We had two face-to-face meetings with Boomis," recalls Prawzinsky. "He screamed and yelled a lot. He dropped a lot of names. He kept saying he had powerful friends. I had read in the paper that he was a big contributor, so I treated him with kid gloves. But I gave him nothing. He implied he had influence with Cunningham and Esposito. He said he could go directly to the mayor. But we insisted he was over-billing the city by at least $200,000. Then he wrote a letter to my boss [Controller Harrison Goldin] calling me a bastard and a liar. But we had him on the facts."

After this, others began to see through Boomis. Other city agencies became wary. Boomis stopped paying his insurance premiums to Grand Brokerage, and Esposito began to pass the word that Boomis was "a nut." Investigations by law-enforcement agencies began. Banks began to foreclose on mortgages. Bill Shea began to deny he even knew Boomis.

The lesson of Boomis is in the process, not the result. He was too greedy. But for three years he played the game, and he was successful. He understood that government was really a vending machine. If you put enough coins in the right slots, the goodies came out the bottom. Boomis just tried to cheat the vending machine itself, and was dropped by the permanent government when he over-reached. The city paid Boomis $2.1 million before his mask fell.

Unnecessary construction is another staple of legal graft.

Early in 1972, Mayor John Lindsay convinced the Board of Esti-mate to approve a $24-million "urban renewal expenditure" to renovate Yankee Stadium because the owners threatened to move the franchise out of New York. Skeptics, led by the *Daily News* editorial writers, questioned the reliability of the $24 million price-tag. But Lindsay insisted $24 million was all the job would cost, and he invoked "hard fiscal data based on the operations of Shea Stadium."

Lindsay also tossed in a "sweetener"—a promise of $2 million to rehabilitate the streets and shops around the stadium, a working-class residential neighborhood fighting not to become a slum.

By November 1973 the cost of the renovation had gone up to $49.9 million. The City Planning Commission approved additional funds, and so did the City Council by a vote of 27-9. Most of the negative votes were cast by conservatives of both parties like Mat-thew Troy, Frank Biondillio, Walter Ward, Thomas Manton and Edward Curry. (All the Bronx councilmen voted in the affirmative.) During the debate Troy vainly reminded his colleagues that a whole new stadium had just been built in Pittsburgh at a total cost of $45 million.

The Board of Estimate also approved the additional $15.9 mil-lion expenditure. Lindsay voted yes, and the then controller, Abe Beame, voted yes. The vote came after the EDA administrator promised (but not under oath) that the stadium renovation would benefit the city with $3.4 million in taxes, wages, and jobs. Deputy Mayor Edward Morrison said, "This is not a luxury. This is nec-essary."

On July 16, 1975, Mayor Beame disclosed that the cost of the renovation had escalated to $57 million. When questioned, Munici-pal Services Administrator John Carroll said the new money outlay was "still a bargain for the city" and a "marvelous engineering project." On October 10, he acknowledged that the cost had risen to $66 million, but quickly added, "The overall investment in the stadium is a bargain at this price."

In April 1976, the new stadium opened at a gala ceremony of pols. The total cost as of that date was $101 million and was still rising. By then the city was bankrupt. And the original $2 million for the community near the stadium was silently deleted from the 1976–77 budget. Yet in 1975, a brand-new 80,400-seat stadium had been completed in Pontiac, Michigan, for less than $60 million.

The $101 million included $22 million to Kinney Systems, Inc., to build two parking garages and remodel a third. From this arrangement Kinney also got rent, a management fee from the city, most of the fees paid for parking, and a $2-million tax exemption. The contract was awarded without competitive bidding. Steven Sallup—as counsel to EDA—negotiated the contract for the city, but by the time the stadium opened in 1976, he was working for Kinney Systems as a lawyer.

We might also mention that Kinney is a subsidiary of Warner Communications, a conglomerate that also owns the New York Cosmos soccer team, which plays about fifteen games a season in Yankee Stadium.

The $101 million included $300,000 for "equipment" for the Yankees team, including plush carpeting and toilets in the VIP boxes.

In 1973, the Democratic Party boss in the Bronx, Patrick Cunningham, became the lawyer for the Yankees, on a retainer believed to be about $100,000 a year. Cunningham says he got the job through his friend Neil Walsh, who handles the Yankees' insurance. Walsh is also one of the city's deputy commissioners for public events. Cunningham, as Bronx Democratic county leader, helped Walsh get that job, which helps Walsh make contacts for his insurance business.

The owner of the Yankees' team franchise is George Steinbrenner. In 1974, Steinbrenner pleaded guilty to making illegal corporate contributions to Richard Nixon's 1972 campaign. He also pleaded guilty to the less commonplace felony of coercing his own employees to lie to the FBI and the grand jury, as part of a cover-up. His penalty for these crimes was a fine and an eighteen-month suspension from baseball. During Steinbrenner's suspension, Patrick Cunningham was the designated owner of the Yankees, as well as their counsel.

In April 1976, when the stadium opened, Henry Gavan, the new counsel to EDA, admitted the original estimated cost of $24 million had been "picked out of the air" by the Lindsay people.

The general contractors on the stadium were Nab Construction and Tern Construction. At Cunningham's 1975 Bronx County dinner, Nab and Tern each had purchased a table for $1,000. Most of the construction unions that worked on the stadium job also bought $1,000 tables. One reason political machines have such dinners is to set up just such a turnstile for contractors.

Everyone profited, everyone skimmed the deal—everyone, that is, except the ordinary people who live in the Bronx. No one will ever call Yankee Stadium the House that Truth Built.

Another example of legal graft in the Bronx involves the same cast of characters. The Bronx Terminal Market, built in 1935, stands on thirty-one acres adjacent to Yankee Stadium. In 1971, the city was making $300,000 a year on this wholesale produce market, where it rented stall space to merchants doing business there. The merchants wanted to convert it into a cooperative, but the city administration, in the person of EDA administrator Kenneth Patton, decided instead to award a private real-estate developer named David Buntzman a ninety-nine-year lease to operate the market. The lease was given without competitive bidding and without payment by Buntzman; he had only to put up a bond.

The ninety-nine-year lease was amended in October 1973 to make it even more favorable to the landlord. The amendments gave the Yankees two of the market's thirty-one acres for a parking lot, and Buntzman received 4.2 additional acres that the city purchased from the Erie Lackawana Railroad for $790,000. In the amended lease, the city also agreed to assume more than $6.5 million of Buntzman's obligations to make improvements in the market. And Buntzman paid the city no rent at all for the first year.

The lawyer who renegotiated this lease for Buntzman was Patrick Cunningham. Although Buntzman at first denied this, Cunningham admitted to us that he had been paid $60,000 in legal fees by Buntzman for one year.

Buntzman has raised rents in the market by an average of 80 per cent. He now charges the merchants an average of *$3 per square foot*, while he is paying the city an average of *61 cents per square foot*. In three years, he has evicted sixteen commercial wholesalers from the market in his campaign to raise rents, and this has driven 700 unskilled jobs out of the South Bronx. The evictions were approved by judges who got their judgeships from Cunningham. One —Joseph Brust—has been indicted for lying to a grand jury in response to questions about his disposition of a case based on an eviction at the Bronx market.

The city's 1975–76 budget included $9 million for the Bronx Terminal Market, and the city is also paying the debt service on the cost of construction of a $4.1 million warehouse the taxpayers built there for Buntzman. So far, Buntzman has collected $3 million in rents.

When John Hess, a reporter for *The New York Times,* asked Cunningham about this whole deal, Cunningham suggested that Hess go see John Scanlon, who had been press aide at the city's EDA when the lease was negotiated. Cunningham neglected to inform Hess that Scanlon, after leaving city employment, had become a paid public relations consultant to Buntzman. When Hess found out this salient fact, he published it, and Scanlon was forced to resign his job as public relations consultant to the Municipal Assistance Corporation. (Scanlon was also a paid flack for Anthony Scotto and the nursing-home builder Albert Schwartzberg, while working for MAC.)

In 1976, it was revealed that Buntzman had made a large, unreported cash contribution to John Lindsay's 1972 presidential campaign—six weeks before the market lease was signed, and while the negotiations were still going on.

A living legend of legal graft in New York City is the Brooklyn attorney Abraham Lindenbaum, known as Bunny to everyone. Friendly, shrewd, and philanthropic, Lindenbaum is the model of the clubhouse lawyer elevated to civic statesman.

Lindenbaum became an election captain in the Madison Club in Crown Heights at the same time Abe Beame was assistant budget director of the city and Stanley Steingut was a lawyer waiting to inherit his father's seat in the Assembly. In 1960, Lindenbaum was appointed to replace Robert Moses, who was resigning to go to the World's Fair, on the City Planning Commission. But in October 1961, Lindenbaum was forced to give up his position on the Planning Commission when he was caught soliciting campaign contributions for Mayor Wagner from builders who did business with the city. More than $25,000 had been raised from forty-three builders and landlords during a luncheon at Skakele's Restaurant on Montague Street in Brooklyn.

Since then Bunny has mastered most of the techniques of legal graft. He has received an estimated $150,000 in patronage fees from the Surrogates Court, including $25,000 in 1973 alone. Lindenbaum is now the registered lobbyist for five landlord organizations, including the Real Estate Board of New York and the Rent Stabilization Association. His lobbying fees in 1976 were more than $20,000. Lindenbaum's specialty, however, is as a zoning and tax lawyer for the city's biggest property owners. Records on file with the Board of Standards and Appeals show that over a ten-year period Lindenbaum's clients have received more zoning variances, on a percentage ratio, than any other lawyer's clients in the city. Applications on file with the Tax Commission also reveal an unmatched record of success in winning lower real-estate tax assessments. The legal justification for some of these reduced assessments was effectively questioned in a series of articles by Ralph Blumenthal in the *Times* in February and March 1973. Blumenthal reported how Jerome Minskoff was awarded a $4.5 million reduction in assessed valuation on a midtown skyscraper, even though Lindenbaum supplied the Tax Commission no income or expense data on the building.

Lindenbaum has also been the attorney on many state-subsidized housing developments, where his fees have been criticized as too high, or not warranted by the amount of legal work performed. In 1973, the city Controller's office refused to pay Lindenbaum a "consulting fee" of $36,164 for work with the city-funded West Side Convention Center Corporation. Lindenbaum was unable to provide time records and work sheets to justify his fee. The convention center's full-time counsel, John McGarrahan, said at the time that Lindenbaum had been hired to draft plans for a special zoning district. But this work was actually done by the City Planning Commission.

In July 1976, Lindenbaum was awarded a mysterious $35,500 "brokerage fee" by the city in connection with the sale of Central Commercial High School to a real-estate developer named Charles Benenson, who is a client of Lindenbaum's. When asked by John Hess of *The New York Times* what service Lindenbaum performed, Benenson replied: "He arranged the deal. . . . He arranged a lower purchase price." The price for the 150-foot-wide strip of property extending from 42nd Street to 41st Street, east of Third Avenue, was $2 million. The original asking price had been $3 million, before Bunny began to peddle his influence.

Other incarnations of legal graft are patronage jobs bestowed on clubhouse and campaign cronies who would not qualify under standards of merit.

People volunteer for election campaigns generally for two reasons—commitment to issues, and hope of some personal reward. Most of the people who helped Abe Beame run for mayor wanted jobs. And after he won, they got them, regardless of qualifications.

Abe Beame saw his mission as the rebuilding of the clubhouse system—a system that nourished his whole career. The City Club, a group of businessmen, estimated in 1976 that "5000 to 7000 unnecessary patronage jobs" on the city payroll remained filled, even after 8000 cops, firemen and sanitation workers had been fired—a public subsidy of the clubhouse system which cost the taxpayers between $100 million and $150 million a year.

At the start of 1976, nineteen Bronx Democratic Party district leaders were on the public payroll, six of them as clerks at the Bronx courthouse. Seven Queens party district leaders had jobs with the Queens Borough President, Donald Manes. More than fifty members of one political clubhouse—the Madison Club in Brooklyn—had city or state jobs, including Mayor Beame, Speaker Steingut, Comptroller Levitt, and seven judges.

Here are some typical examples. Lila Yagerman is a party district leader in Brooklyn's 42nd Assembly District. She works as a confidential investigator in the Brooklyn Surrogate's Court. Her husband, Jack Yagerman, is a $14,000-a-year assistant to the commissioner of EDA. Both Yagermans are clients of Grand Brokerage.

Shirley Weiner is a party district leader in Brooklyn's 39th A.D. She also holds a $19,050 deputy county clerk job. Similarly, Herbert Lupka is a district leader in Brooklyn's 45th A.D., and is a deputy county clerk at $13,600, and Julia Cargulio, a district leader in the 86th A.D. in the Bronx, is deputy county clerk at $23,140. Evelyn Dixson is a district leader in Brooklyn's 56th A.D., and is paid $15,050 as an administrative assistant at the Taxi and Limousine Commission. Herb Spector is a Bronx district leader and the $27,000-a-year general clerk in Bronx Supreme Court. George McCracken, the powerful district leader in the 22nd A.D. in Queens, is a $17,500 assistant to the Queens borough president.

Patronage jobs, of course, are not limited to loyal officers of the party. Arlene Wolff, one of Beame's most energetic fund-raisers, is First Deputy Commissioner for Public Events, at $29,253. Defeated clubhouse pols also get taken care of: Former Manhattan City Councilman Saul Sharison is a deputy counsel in the Health Services Administration at $25,000, and former Brooklyn Assemblyman William Giordano is paid $33,000 as a deputy commissioner of transportation. Lester Futternick, who worked full time in the Beame campaign, is a $19,000-a-year assistant to Addiction Services Administration Commissioner Jerome Hornblass. When Futternick was exposed as a "Brooklyn hack" in the District 37 union newspaper, he wrote a letter saying, "I'm proud of my association with the political establishment."

Sam Berman, a member of the Madison Club, is the election district captain for 1655 Flatbush Avenue, a highrise apartment house that generates 450 Democratic primary votes. He is paid a salary of $30,000 a year as lobbyist for the Off-Track Betting Corporation. During the austerity budget cuts of 1975, OTB *gained* 115 employees, while 4,125 cops were being dismissed. Another OTB official who kept his job was Cyril Regan, at $37,500. Regan is an ex-cop who made two $25,000 loans for the Beame campaign in 1973.

None of these pols have civil-service status. None of them had to pass a competitive exam to secure their jobs. They all have provisional, exempt, or noncompetitive positions obtained through political connections.

In September 1975, Edwin Weisl resigned as New York City Parks Commissioner. A few days after he quit, we talked to Weisl, and he candidly explained to us how the patronage system works, and how it is subversive of the public interest.

When I was first hired as parks administrator I was too naive to ask whether I could choose my own staff. But soon it became clear I could not. I had to hire people based on political connections. And I had to fire the holdover people who had no clubhouse sponsorship or protection.

My first month on the job, Jerry Kay called me up. He was a personal friend of mine. Kay said he was seeking a judgeship, and it would help his chances if I would come to dinner with him and Meade Esposito. We had dinner in a private club on Macdougal Street. Esposito arrived with a typed list of existing jobs in my agency, and a typed list of the names of people he wanted me to hire. [Kay, who set up the dinner, subsequently received his judgeship.]

Meade told me to hire William Swain [an ex-football player] for a job that paid $29,000 a year.

Paul Screvane [the OTB chairman] also called me and told me to hire Swain. Cavanagh [then first deputy mayor] also called and asked me to fire Joe Davidson and give his job to Swain. Davidson was a great career professional, so I had to make a deal with Cavanagh. In order to keep Davidson as my recreation commissioner, I agreed to hire Swain as his deputy. He never did much work on the job.

Next I was told to hire Bob Fellner. Kevin McGrath [a partner in Shea's law firm] called me up and said hire Fellner because Fellner had been an advance man in Beame's campaign, and I should give him a job. I was forced to take him. Fellner was lazy and did no work. I tried to fire him, but Tom Roche [Mayor Beame's patronage dispenser] wouldn't let me fire Fellner.

Ernest Gluckman was another of those hacks I was ordered to employ. He was a friend of Irving Goldman [Beame's cultural affairs commissioner, who was later indicted]. I had to pay Gluckman, who is seventy years old, $35,000 a year as a consultant. He literally never did one day's work. After Goldman was indicted, I fired Gluckman, but the next day I was ordered to reinstate him.

There were some people I just refused to hire. That began to make me unpopular at City Hall, and they began to leak stories that I was an incompetent administrator.

One guy I refused to hire was Fred Baroni. He was a law secretary to a judge, and totally inept. Pat Cunningham called me up and asked me to hire Baroni at $40,000. I said no.

When Matty Troy was county leader of Queens he sent me the resume of Frank Mangino. Troy wanted Mangino to get a $40,000 job. Troy wanted Mangino to run the whole field force. But Mangino had no administrative experience. Cavanagh also asked me to hire Mangino, but I just would not.

By that time, the politicians began to get suspicious of me. Stanley Steingut called me up and said I should do what I was told. Then his son [Councilman Robert Steingut] came to visit me one day. Young Steingut said that I should play ball, and that I have a great future.

In March 1975, Beame himself came to see me. He told me I was being an obstructionist. He told me it was my duty to hire loyal Democratic Party workers.

Then in July 1975 came the issue of summer jobs. There are about 4500 summer jobs in the budget. They are intended for poor and minority kids. But City Hall wanted to control 800 of these jobs for the clubhouses.

Stanley Friedman [another deputy mayor] went around me. He called my payroll department directly and put relatives of politicians on the summer job payroll, including Troy's son.

By the end of the summer I was beaten. Beame and Cavanagh wanted me to cut $1 million by closing swimming pools in the South Bronx and Red Hook. They had no interest in pre-school programs for kids. They never talked to me about solving problems, or new ideas. All they ever called about was jobs for the clubhouses. They wanted useless projects. They blocked me on management reforms. I wanted to hire more foremen to improve productivity. I wanted to hire one guy to computerize the inventory. They said no. Who wouldn't be a lousy administrator with such restrictions?

Legal grafters also love do-good programs like Medicaid and day care. For years the nursing-home industry in New York has run on conflicts of interest and legal graft. Nursing-home operators like Bernard Bergman and Albert Schwartzberg hired political lawyers and political insurance companies, and in turn got favors and preferments from the government. They got licenses, they got favorable Medicaid reimbursement rates, they got personal access to the highest officials in the state. And both became multi-millionaires, philanthropists, and respected citizens.

Bergman gave his insurance business on the Towers nursing home and the Park Crescent home, to Steingut's and Esposito's Grand Brokerage. At various times, Bergman used as lawyers Stanley Lowell, a former deputy mayor; C. Daniel Chill, the legislative counsel to Stanley Steingut; Robert Douglas, former secretary to Governor Rockefeller; and John Marchi, Republican chairman of the Senate Finance Committee. (To his credit, Douglas withdrew as counsel after a few weeks when he realized Bergman was lying to him about many facts.) For example, Chill would write a letter to the State Health Department on Assembly stationery. A civil servant or health professional would assume the political clout of Steingut was behind the request. The civil servant could not know that Chill was getting paid a fee as a private lawyer for Bergman. Chill also made phone calls to and attended meetings on Bergman's behalf with both city and state health officials. His law firm even had a legal option to get a 14 per cent interest in one Bergman nursing home on Staten Island that he was pressuring the health department to approve.

Theodore Lucas, the director of the city's Bureau of Mental Retardation, testified under oath to a special Moreland Act commission created to investigate nursing-home abuses about the pressures brought upon him by Stanley Lowell in behalf of Bergman. Lowell, he said, in the course of a meeting over the conversion of a Bergman nursing home into a facility for the retarded, reminded him that he was personally close to Beame, former Mayor Lindsay, the controller, and many city councilmen. The final Moreland commission report said that if Lucas's testimony was accurate, then Lowell's conduct was "improper" and an "attempt at a power play."

In addition to representing the Bergman family interests, Lowell was also the highly paid counsel of the New York Nursing Home Association and special counsel to the New York State Health Facilities Association. (In another case he went over the head of a dedicated city official who was doing her job. In 1971 Dr. Florence Kavaler was arranging unexpected night visits by inspectors to nursing homes to check on conditions. Lowell, instead of complaining to Dr. Kavaler or to her direct superior, Health Commissioner McLaughlin, went instead to the very political Deputy Mayor Richard Aurelio to try and get these valuable visits stopped.)

Through the influence of Steingut, Lowell, and businessman Samuel Hausman, Bergman was able to get private, face-to-face meetings with Governor Rockefeller, Governor Wilson, Mayor Beame, and other important politicians. Bergman's general, odious reputation for mistreating and neglecting his elderly patients did not seem to reach these elite decision makers. And they all professed shock when Bergman was indicted and pleaded guilty to cheating Medicaid of $2.5 million.

Albert Schwartzberg, the president of Di-Com Corporation, became New York State's biggest builder of nursing homes and remained a partner in the real estate or operations of at least twenty-five of the homes he built. Schwartzberg always seemed to get his way with government agencies. Like Bergman, he seemed to have unlimited access and invincible power.

He gave his insurance business to Youngs & Linfoot, Inc., a small company in upstate Geneseo, New York, from which state Senator James Emory receives about $20,000 a year in salary and commissions. Emory was assistant majority leader of the state Senate during the Wilson and Rockefeller administrations and is now deputy minority leader. Emory admits he brought in Di-Com as his insurance company's biggest client. Between 1966 and 1975, Schwartzberg and Di-Com paid Youngs & Linfoot more than $250,000 in premiums. Emory (like Chill) did not tell the civil servants of his personal financial interest whenever he called to lobby and pressure for Schwartzberg.

Martin Ginsberg, chairman of the state Assembly's Health Committee during the Rockefeller years, also pressured the state health department in Schwartzberg's behalf—and he too was acting as a private lawyer for Schwartzberg. When he tried to make a secret investment in one of Schwartzberg's nursing homes, however, it was discovered and disallowed by the health department. In 1972 Ginsberg ran for the Family Court and was elected. He reported $12,000 in campaign contributions, of which $4,000 came from Schwartzberg. (In December 1974 Judge Ginsberg was convicted of perjury in a case unrelated to nursing homes.)

In 1975 and 1976, the state legislature refused to enact a law prohibiting members of the legislature from representing paying clients before state agencies like the health department. Insiders called this a "one-house bill": The Democrats had agreed to vote for it and pass it in the Assembly, based on the private assurance that the Republicans, who controlled the Senate, would kill it. This permitted the Democrats a public posture of rectitude, knowing it had no meaning. And it was reciprocated when the Republicans passed a bill in the Senate abolishing the city marshal system and the Democrats killed it in the Assembly by prearrangement.

The one-house bill is merely one of the many clever devices of the permanent government.

Day care is a good idea, a very good idea. It frees women to finish school, or to work, instead of going on welfare. It is beneficial to children, improving learning and ensuring that they are well fed during the day. It fosters class and ethnic integration. It offers working-class women a chance at a second life.

But New York City's day-care program has been a textbook model of how another positive government program became exploited by the parasites who see government as a business, and reform as a market.

In day care, the permanent government took its skim in leases. Between 1969 and 1971, the Lindsay administration gave 171 leases for day-care centers directly to private landlords, with no competitive bidding. This was done by Real Estate Commissioner Ira Duchan, and approved blindly by the Board of Estimate. About 275 other day-care programs operated under indirect leases, often at much less cost, in churches and schools. (The average direct-lease day-care center costs $20 per week, per child. All other centers cost an average of $6 per week, per child.) But the direct leases were especially desirable to landlords for several reasons. The city paid the rent money directly to them. The city—not the landlord—paid all the utility bills and real-estate taxes. And the leases were all uncommonly long—for fifteen or twenty years. So prized were the leases that landlords were able to show them to banks and get construction mortgages (in redlined neighborhoods) for more money than their renovations cost.

The day-care sites were selected in an ass-backwards fashion. Instead of first looking for community groups, parents' groups, or block associations, the city started the program by reaching out first for private landlords. The people who really cared about quality day care were excluded from the process. The ultimate result of this policy, of course, was that a few politically connected land-lords, lawyer-politicians, and power brokers got rich off the pro-gram. And the children got screwed.

In 1976 we analyzed who got what out of the direct-lease system.

N. Hilton Rosen, the brother of Richard Rosen, a commissioner and assistant to the mayor in the Lindsay administration, got seven direct leases worth $886,000 in annual rents. His wife was a member of the state Labor Relations Board—at $35,250 a year. The legal fees on all seven leases went to Shea, Gould. The title insurance all went to City Title, which is one of the smaller title companies in the city.

Brooklyn Assemblyman Leonard Simon was only the second Democrat to endorse John Lindsay for mayor in 1969. In a dramatic City Hall press conference, Simon had said he was risking his career by "placing principle above party" and standing with the forces of light. Then, within eighteen months, one of Simon's law clients—Getz Construction Corporation—got 22 day-care leases from Lind-say's administration, worth $1.8 million in annual rents. Getz built the centers with fast, shoddy work, and as they began to leak, chip, flood, and attract rats, Getz sold all twenty-two to other speculators. Simon had made a windfall profit in legal fees by "placing principle above party."

Brooklyn City Councilman and district leader Samuel Wright got two day-care centers. One, the Samuel D. Wright Day Care Center, was opened in the building directly next door to his club-house, at 2071 Fulton Street in Brownsville. The architect was a member of Wright's political club. And Wright's wife Josephine was appointed executive director of the center. A second day-care lease was given to a company owned by the former president of Wright's political club. On this one, Wright also collected the legal fees. The annual rent is $100,000.

Stanley Lowell, who represented Bernard Bergman, was also the lawyer on two day-care leases (including one at 510 West 145th

Street, one of the worst in the city, with so many structural deficiencies that the city stopped paying rent for several months).

If we look at the total number of direct leases, title insurance on 40 per cent was awarded to Steingut's City Title, while the Shea, Gould law firm collected legal fees on thirty-five leases and also received fees for arranging mortgage financing on a total of forty centers, through banks where Shea was either a director or counsel. Building permits disclosed that Colonial Sand & Stone was employed by fifty centers to supply cement for construction and remodeling. (Shea is a director of Colonial Sand & Stone and counsel to the $80-million-a-year construction company.)

Three day-care leases were in the name of the late Sidney Ungar. Ungar, who died in 1974, was a most notorious slumlord, first exposed by William Haddad in the *New York Post* in 1959, when Ungar was picked by Robert Moses to be a sponsor of a slum-clearance program. Ungar was also accused of discrimination against blacks in a report by the City Commission on Human Rights issued in 1971.

Ted Menas, a Queens landlord, got two day-care leases from the city. Records on file with the Board of Elections show that Menas is a campaign contributor to Queens Democratic district leader Ralph DeMarco and to former state Senator, now judge, Nicholas Ferraro. In February 1976, Menas wanted final approval for his second direct-lease center (the Marine Terrace Day Care Center at 18–40 20th Avenue in Astoria); the lease was for twenty years, at $75,384 a year. An aide to Queens Borough President Donald Manes called the chief of the housing and real estate division of the City Law Department at least three times, trying to expedite the second Menas lease. But on August 5, Menas and his partner, Anthony Nastasi, were each indicted on six counts of trying to hide from a grand jury the books and records of several corporations they control.

Late in the 1976 legislative session, a bill was introduced that would have given the Emergency Financial Control Board authority to review all 171 direct leases and renegotiate all those found to be exorbitant. The bill passed the Senate, but was killed on the last day of the session in the Assembly, after Mayor Beame telephoned his opposition to Speaker Steingut.

In August 1976 Controller Goldin released an audit of the direct-lease program. Goldin said that twenty-six of the thirty-seven folders on individual lease negotiations that he had requested from Ira

Duchan, the Commissioner of Real Estate, "were missing." These files contained correspondence about how the leases were given out and how various rentals per square foot were calculated. Nixon and ITT apparently did not have a monopoly on shredders.

Judgeships are not exempt from the subtleties of legal graft. An honest, independent judiciary is essential to democracy and the rule of law. But a political, beholden judiciary is essential to the clubhouse system, especially to disqualify opponents who want to run against the machine in primary elections, and to dispense fees and guardianships to the right lawyers.

Judicial nominating conventions and election of State Supreme Court justices are a farce. They offer the illusion of choice. State justices are chosen by party leaders in private brokered deals. Of the last 150 State Supreme Court judges elected in New York City, 126 ran with the endorsement of both the Democratic and Republican parties.

In most cases, judgeships are not bought directly with cash. That would be illegal graft. Occasionally a judgeship can be a reward to a politician for a valued vote in a legislative fight. For instance, in 1971 Manuel Ramos, a Bronx Democratic assemblyman, broke with his party to provide a decisive vote to the passage of Governor Rockefeller's tax package. The following year Rockefeller appointed Ramos to the Court of Claims. Or again, when John Walsh, a Manhattan assemblyman from 1959 till 1972, lost a tough primary to a reformer, he joined the Democrats for Nixon. Even his best friends admit that's how he became a judge the next year.

Some people get their black robes through family pull or cronyism. Three judges appointed to the Civil and Family Court in 1975 by Mayor Beame were John DeLury, James F. O'Donoghue, and Edith Hendon. DeLury is the son of the powerful leader of the Sanitation Workers Union. O'Donoghue is Pat Cunningham's brother-in-law. And Mrs. Hendon was appointed even though the Queens Bar Association found her "not qualified." She is Mary Beame's regular mahjong partner.

There is also a perfectly legal way to buy a judgeship: have a relative make a contribution to a political party, and then promise to buy a table for $1,000 every year at the party's county political dinner. A careful reading of old election records in New York City at 80 Varick Street will be instructive in this method. Let us take just one year, 1970.

In that year Irving Rader was nominated for the Civil Court bench in Brooklyn. Election records show that Rader's two sisters, Rose and Gertrude, together happened to contribute $7,500 to the Democratic Party of Kings County. Similarly Maria Tavorminia is listed as a $7,500 contributor to the Brooklyn Democrats—and her husband was nominated for the Civil Court in Brooklyn. John Monteleone ran for the Supreme Court in Brooklyn, although he had no need to campaign at all, since Meade Esposito had arranged for him to receive both the Democratic and Republican nominations. But the records show that the Brooklyn Democratic organization received $8,000 from a campaign committee organized for the election of Monteleone—who had no competition. (Monteleone has since made several rulings favorable to organized crime figures that have angered the Brooklyn district attorney.) The same transaction shows up with Frank Composto, who was elevated to the bench, the only difference being that his campaign committee, in an uncontested election, gave the county committee only $7,500.

And where do these prospective independent jurists get the money to contribute to the political party? From clubhouse lawyers, on whose cases they will pass judgment.

On the outside of the Brooklyn courthouse, inscribed in marble, are the words: EQUAL JUSTICE UNDER THE RULE OF LAW. Scrawled on the wall in the men's room is the more realistic motto: IT'S BETTER TO KNOW THE JUDGE THAN TO KNOW THE LAW.

Property owners in New York pay a tax rate of $8.17 for every $100 of assessed valuation. The City Tax Commission gives reduced real-estate tax assessments to landlords on the basis of proven "hardship." In 1975, for example, the tax commissioners overruled professional assessors and awarded 12,000 hardship reductions on buildings they never personally visited.

The problem is that there are no precise or consistent standards or guidelines for making these judgments. It is discretionary, almost impressionistic. The seven members of the Tax Commission are all appointed by the mayor and traditionally have been highly political. John Lindsay appointed Norman Levy, his campaign fund-raiser, as chairman, and Beame named Philip Lagana, who later became a

Brooklyn Supreme Court justice through the normal clubhouse channels.

Historically, landlords who have been campaign contributors to the "right" candidates and landlords who hire the "right" lawyers have found it much easier to make convincing hardship arguments before the Tax Commission. Claims of expenses which they submit are not investigated or verified. On hardship applications we have looked at, the landlord's claims of payments of real estate, water, and sewage taxes, do not conform to the city's own billing and payment records. But the Tax Commission does not even follow or apply basic rules of accountancy. We have read hardship applications where two sets of procedures—cash and accrual—are used on the same building. The commission makes no effort to reconcile these two different accounting methods.

Finally, the city gives a landlord three years to pay real-estate taxes, although a tenant has only about three months to pay rent before he or she is evicted. The law permitting nonpayment of real-estate taxes for three years not only has cost the city treasury $570 million during a time of brutal austerities but has encouraged speculation, milking of buildings, and abandonment after three tax-free years. If a landlord can make a higher profit from his rents by buying bank certificates of deposit or corporate bonds, then he can use his tax savings to speculate, pay a small penalty at the end of three years, and still come out ahead.

In 1975, the city's Tax Commission granted 80 per cent more hardship tax reductions to property owners than it did in 1974, and 1975 was the year when New York City's fiscal gimmickry and deception became a full-fledged crisis. As a result of this generosity to a few large, influential landlords, the city collected $21 million less in real-estate taxes in 1976 than it should have. Among the recipients of "hardship" real-estate tax reductions in 1975 were: the New York Stock Exchange, the Prudential Insurance Company, Con Edison, Chemical Bank, American Shipping Company, the New York Telephone Company, the Bank of New York, Citibank, and Rockefeller Center. And in 1976 the list included: Con Edison, Metropolitan Life Insurance, New York Telephone, Rockefeller Center, Bankers Trust, and Citibank; also Distrigas, which owns the liquified-natural-gas tanks on Staten Island, got a reduction in annual taxes worth $700,000. One of the lawyers for Distrigas is Patrick Cunningham.

In 1975 Local 371 of the Social Service Employees Union completed a painstaking, six-month research project into the patterns of reduced assessments by the Tax Commission. The study, whose facts have never been challenged or disproved, concentrated on the real-estate empire of the family of Lewis Rudin. Rudin is the well-publicized chairman of the Association for a Better New York, a midtown Manhattan group of landlords that uses the rhetoric of civic boosterism as a figleaf for self-interest. Rudin and his immediate family contributed $15,000 to Mayor Beame's campaign in 1973, and $10,000 to Lindsay in 1969.

The Rudins owned thirty-three buildings in Manhattan in 1975. Lew Rudin's net worth is more than $100 million. Between 1970 and 1975, Rudin Management made 209 requests for assessment reductions to the Tax Commission. Of that number 137—or 66 per cent—were granted, and the total reduced assessments given Rudin Management was $32.3 million. During that same 1970–75 time frame, people with less political clout, owning buildings on the very same blocks as Rudin's buildings, submitted a total of 1411 applications for hardship reductions, of which only 16 per cent were approved. (For example, 40 Park Avenue, owned by the Rudin family, received six consecutive tax reductions in six years; owners of other properties on the same block made sixty-four applications for tax relief, only seven of which were granted.)

The most apparent distinction between Lewis Rudin and his neighboring Park Avenue landlords, is that he is a big campaign contributor with social access to mayors and power brokers. Rudin once said to Jack Newfield during a discussion with the executive committee of the Association for a Better New York, "The trouble with you is that you don't understand power. You think I have power. You think David Rockefeller has power. You think Felix Rohatyn has power. Well, you're wrong! You know who has power in this city? I'll tell you! The crazy people who can stop a McDonald's. That's who have power in New York!"

In terms of nonpayment of real-estate taxes the champion seems to be Sol Goldman, the survivor of the notorious Goldman-Di-Lorenzo partnership in property holdings. Goldman is the largest private landlord in New York City. Operating behind a maze of shell and interlocking companies with names like Avon, Newport, and Wellington, Goldman owned more than four hundred buildings in 1976, a majority of them commercial properties. The records of the city's Finance Administration disclosed that Goldman owed the city $18.8 million in unpaid real-estate taxes on properties assessed at a total of $445 million. Yet the Goldman empire also profited from reduced assessments. Curiously, many Goldman properties declined in assessment over the years while adjacent buildings did not.*

There is some reason to suspect that the New York City Tax Commission is a vending machine for legal graft.

Lawyers are the most frequent beneficiaries of legal graft, as wise old Al Smith understood.

Between 1963 and 1976, the controller's office of New York City awarded fifty-five mortgages to developers from the city employees' pension fund. On almost every one, the lawyer who collected the closing fee was politically influential. The attorneys were appointed by the controller. The fees, negotiated between the attorneys and the builders, usually came to thousands of dollars for a few hours' routine work that required no preparation, and could be as much as 1 per cent of the total mortgage.

Closing fees on city pension-fund mortgages are a wholly unnecessary form of patronage. The work could easily be performed by the city's own Corporation Counsel staff of thirty lawyers. But out of the 40,000 lawyers in New York City the ones chosen for this extravagant patronage plum are the elite of the permanent government.

Bill Shea's law firm handled three mortgage closings worth $4.6 million. The law firm of Brooklyn Congressman and Judge Abraham Multer was attorney for $6 million in pension-fund mortgages. Congressman Bert Podell's law firm closed two mortgages totaling $7.2 million—before he was convicted of bribery in 1975. Other favored lawyers included: Joseph Slavin, chairman of the Brooklyn Demo-

---

* A building at 18–20 St. Nicholas Place, assessed at $98,000 in 1970–71, was reduced every year and assessed at $60,000 in 1976. A property at 116–124 East 124th Street, in an attractive, middle-class community, went from $375,000 in 1970 to $340,000 in 1976. Records show that nineteen of twenty-five Manhattan properties owned by Goldman's Newport Associates had lower assessments in 1976 than they did in 1970. One typical example of apparent favoritism: A Goldman building at 18–24 Clinton Street received six consecutive tax reductions between 1970 and 1975, during which time other landlords on the same block submitted fifty-one applications and had only seven granted. Another is Goldman's property at 310–318 Convent Avenue. This property won four of six requests for reduced assessments. Other property owners, on the same block, made fourteen requests, not one of which was granted, during the same five-year period. Goldman is the landlord at 4913–23 Broadway, where he received four lowered assessments in six years. The other property owners on the same block made thirty applications for reduced taxes, and only two were granted.

cratic organization's law committee, and now a judge; former presiding Justice Bernard Botein; former Bronx Assemblyman and current Judge Alexander Chananau; former Bronx Congressman and Judge Paul Fino; Bronx Congressman Mario Biaggi; John DeLury, son of the sanitation union leader, now a judge; Howard Goldfluss, now a judge; and Irving Berman, who is also now a judge. Also, two former controllers: Joseph McGoldrick closed a $1.6 million mortgage, and Lazarus Joseph closed one for $1.5 million.

In an interview with Sam Roberts of the *Daily News,* Mayor Beame defended the current system by saying only lawyers who have special expertise in closing bank mortgages are chosen, and having the Corporation Counsel's office do the job would waste the time of lawyers who work for the city. But as usual, scrutiny of documents suggests a pattern based more on political than legal expertise. In fact, even a geo-political pattern can be discerned from the records on file in the controller's office. When Mario Procaccino of the Bronx was controller, most of the fees went to Bronx lawyers like Biaggi, Chananau, and Goldfluss. When Abe Beame of Brooklyn was controller, most of the fees went to Brooklyn lawyers like Multer, Podell, and Slavin.

For years, the city's finance administrator was allowed custody over about $10 million in city funds. This was known as "political money" to be kept in non-interest-bearing accounts in a few favored banks, as a form of political patronage. It cost the public more than $1 million a year to keep these public funds in accounts that drew no interest. These deposits were like gold to the bank, which could make a 9 per cent profit on this public money.

The manipulation of interest-free accounts, it should be underscored, is hardly a mutant activity found exclusively in New York City. Jimmy Carter has recounted how the game was played by politicians in Georgia in his book *Why Not the Best? The Washington Star* has exposed interest-free deposits in Alabama, and *The Washington Post* has exposed the practice in Maryland. And five years ago, Sam Roberts revealed in the *Daily News* how it was done by Governor Rockefeller. Early in 1972, a man named James Hellmuth changed jobs, quitting as vice-president of Morgan Guaranty Trust and becoming vice-president of the Bankers Trust New York Corporation. Hellmuth was also the treasurer of the state Republican Party and a member of the Port Authority. A month later, an $11-

million interest-free account—the stock transfer fund—followed Hellmuth from Morgan to Bankers Trust. The money had been deposited by the state with the Morgan bank for several years when it was suddenly switched.

During the Lindsay administration in New York City the two banks that profited most from these illogical interest-free deposits were Century National Bank and the Central State Bank, two of the least professional, most investigated, and most political small banks in the whole state.

Century National Bank received its charter from the federal Director of the Currency on June 24, 1963. Its original incorporators were predictably bipartisan and politically connected. One was Vincent Albano, the Republican county leader of Manhattan. Another was Joseph Ruggiero, then law chairman of Albano's county organization, and later to serve a prison term for perjury. A third was Bernard Ruggieri, a former aide to Mayor Wagner, counsel to state Senate Democratic leader Joseph Zaretski, and soon to become a partner in Shea, Gould. A fourth was Lawrence Marchni, who would become Mario Biaggi's campaign treasurer in his unsuccessful 1973 bid for mayor.

In May 1964, during the first quarter the bank was open, Mayor Wagner, Controller Beame, and City Treasurer (now Judge) Hilda Schwartz approved with uncommon alacrity the new Century Bank as a depository for city monies. Within a year Century Bank had $1.2 million in interest-free city deposits. Richard Lewisohn, who later reformed the interest-free swindle in 1973, said of the Century deposits, "It was very abnormal for a new bank to get so much so soon."

While Democrat Ruggieri's connections to Democrat Wagner helped in 1965, it was the Republican chairman of the bank, Vincent Albano, who helped when Republican John Lindsay became mayor on January 1, 1966. The interest-free accounts are under the control of the finance administrator, and Lindsay's first two finance administrators, Roy Goodman and Fred Perotta, both came out of the Manhattan Republican organization and owed their jobs to Albano. By early 1967, under the beneficence of Roy Goodman, Century Bank held $1.6 million in interest-free city deposits, more than twice what any other bank of equivalent assets, capital, and public depositors had.

Century was given all this public money even though a report filed by federal bank examiners criticized Century for sloppy and inadequate records. The federal report disclosed that the auditor for the bank was not even a legitimate CPA. Stephen McDonald, a former deputy finance administrator for the city during the Lindsay years, told us: "Century was not a good bank. The work they did for the city was poor. They would lose checks. They sometimes wouldn't send us stop-payment notices on lost checks. Their records were badly kept. And I think they had some problems with embezzlement. I once suggested we take some of our money out of the bank, but nothing was ever done."

In 1970, under Fred Perotta, Century was given a total of $1.9 million in city deposits, the absolute legal maximum permitted under the city charter, and thereby became the only bank that ever reached the legal limit. This meant an extra $100,000 profit in one year to the bank, which made loans, mortgages, and investments at high interest rates with the public money placed in its custody by the Lindsay administration.

A bank's records are private, so there is no way to tell what favors Albano did in return for these public deposits. But one favor did become public knowledge. In 1972 Albano's bank made a $9,000 unsecured loan to Sid Davidoff, who had been Mayor Lindsay's assistant, so that Davidoff could go into the restaurant business. The loan was at 7½ per cent, less than the going rate at the time. Davidoff was Lindsay's personal representative on the commission that approved and monitored the banks that got interest-free deposits. The restaurant eventually went bankrupt and Davidoff was indicted for nonpayment of taxes to the state.

Central State Bank was chartered in 1925 and taken over by a group led by the brothers Al and Nathan Kevelson in 1959. On February 28, 1962, the bank was approved by the city's banking commission as a depository of city funds. By 1966 the key directors of the bank were Alfred Lama, the ranking Democrat on the Assembly banking committee (a stunning conflict of interest by itself); the late Larry Pierez, a behind-the-scenes power in Queens Democratic politics, and James Farley, Jr., the son of FDR's postmaster general. Not one professional banker in the lot. The counsel to the bank was the ubiquitous Bernard Ruggieri, and Congressman Mario Biaggi was on the bank's payroll as a "business getter," even though he never showed up at the bank, and performed no apparent work.

During 1968, Finance Administrator Roy Goodman increased the amount of interest-free deposits in Central State Bank from $300,000 to $1 million. By 1970, the city had $1.5 million in the bank in accounts that accumulated no interest—despite the fact that the bank had a general reputation as shady. (In December 1967, a group of the bank's dissident stockholders had filed a lawsuit against the Kevelsons, Farley, and Lama, charging they had made "improvident loans to cronies that went into default." This suit was dismissed in the courts.)

In 1976, Al Kevelson, Central State's former chairman, and his brother Nathan were found guilty of seeking to cheat the federal government out of more than $900,000 in taxes on personal and corporate income. The brothers had used Central State Bank to cash checks and conceal some of the income they withheld from the government.

There is also the case of the American Bank and Trust Company, which collapsed in September 1976 and was taken over by the Bank Leumi of Israel.

American Bank and Trust was one of the most political banks in New York City. Abe Beame was a director of the bank and chairman of its finance committee between 1966 and 1969. The bank's chairman, Abraham Feinberg, had contributed more than $40,000 to both his mayoralty and Carey's gubernatorial campaigns. Patrick Cunningham was indicted for not telling a grand jury that he was paid $50,000 over two years by American Bank and Trust for legal work he never performed. But Cunningham *had* pressured city and state officials to deposit interest-free government accounts in American Bank and Trust, and Meade Esposito was also paid an undisclosed annual sum to help secure those precious government deposits.

And so, on the day American Bank finally collapsed, it had $20 million of city and state deposits—more than 10 per cent of its total, and a higher percentage than any other bank in the city. Among the causes of American Bank's failure were: the disappearance of $18 million; loans long in default kept on the books as interest-bearing; loans made in excess of the legal limit; and self-dealing with companies in which various directors of the bank had financial interests.

Our point is not that Shea, or Albano, or Steingut, or Cunningham are unique individual villains. The villain is the moral structure of the system itself. People like Steingut have mastered the rules of the game because they helped write the loopholes into the rules. As long as the line between legal and illegal graft is fuzzy, as long as the difference between a felony and a windfall is a nuance, then the Steinguts and Sheas of this world will see opportunities, and take 'em.

Most people in politics have what David Burke, secretary to Governor Carey, calls "a hole in their retina." They can't see right from wrong. Millions of taxpayers' dollars are there to be skimmed in the grey area between what is generally unethical and what is precisely illegal. As long as legislators have law practices, as long as county leaders have insurance companies, as long as campaigns need contributors, there will be legal grafters.

The few insatiable ones will be caught at some crime. The vast majority will have stadiums named after them, or perhaps law schools. The Bergmans will come and go. But the permanent government's system of legal graft remains. And will continue to prosper from twenty-year leases, legal fees, title insurance, mortgage closings, interest-free government bank deposits, reduced assessments, and all the other modern technologies of legal graft, barely imagined by George Washington Plunkett a century ago.

THE TEMPORARY GOVERNMENT: Wagner Lindsay Beame

There is nothing economically or socially inevitable about either the decay of old cities or the fresh-minted decadence of the new un-urban urbanization. On the contrary, no other aspect of our economy or society has been more purposefully manipulated. . . . Extraordinary governmental financial incentives have been required to achieve this degree of monotony, sterility, and vulgarity.

— JANE JACOBS
The Death and Life of Great American Cities

In some ways Robert Ferdinand Wagner, Jr., mayor of New York City from January 1, 1954, until December 31, 1965, was not a bad mayor.

He was a decent, shy, reasonable man who did not personalize disagreements. As a result, he got along with the city's various establishments. There were no disruptive municipal-transit, teacher, or sanitation strikes under Wagner. More housing units were added to the city's stock during his twelve years than during the next twelve years of Lindsay and Beame. Except during his last year, his budgets were balanced, and free of gimmicks and fakery. He chose his police commissioners wisely—Stephen Kennedy and Francis W. H. Adams—and police corruption declined from its rampant peak during the O'Dwyer and Impellitteri administrations. Wagner was no Pericles, but he was also neither a Tweed nor a Caligula.

Wagner's fatal weaknesses were passivity and procrastination. He didn't like conflict. He thought chicken soup and schmoozing could make the problems go away. The motto he learned from his father, New York's popular senator in the 1930s and 1940s, was: "When in doubt, don't." As a result, Wagner was cautious in dealing with the basic problems of the city then congealing just beyond the horizon of everyday life. This caution, this indecision, this passivity led him to abdicate much too much of his authority to two pure avatars of the permanent government—Robert Moses and Carmine DeSapio. Wagner created a vacuum, and they lived in it.

Wagner had a bad habit: Whenever a "problem" appeared, he would appoint a "committee" to "study" it. By the end of his second term in 1961 he had appointed more than 200 separate committees by directive. Some never met. Most had no effect at all, except to invent the illusion of action for reporters who believed press releases.

While Wagner shuffled paper committees, the two great migrations began. One million poor blacks and Hispanics moved into New York City and 800,000 white middle-class families moved out. In eight years, the city's welfare population doubled.

Meanwhile DeSapio's patronage appointees from the clubhouses greased the wheels of legal graft. And Robert Moses bulldozed sound neighborhoods that were the distinctive essence of the city. In East Tremont alone, for example, Moses evicted 1530 lower-middle-class Jewish families to make way for the Cross Bronx Expressway. And he squandered millions of dollars on what historians and journalists call the Title I scandal—since it involved federal Title I housing funds—and millions more on the 1964 World's Fair.

The downward spiral of New York City was under way.

DeSapio was Robert Wagner's principal sponsor and strategist when he ran for mayor in the Democratic primary of 1953. The Democratic bosses of Brooklyn, Queens, and Staten Island supported the incumbent, Vincent Impellitteri; Bronx boss Ed Flynn was for Wagner, but he died a month before the primary. On election day, DeSapio was the only boss standing with Wagner, and Wagner won by 169,000 votes. The next year, DeSapio arranged the Democratic nomination of Averell Harriman for governor, and Harriman was elected by a margin of 11,125 votes out of 5 million cast. As a result, DeSapio became the most powerful politician in the state. He was leader of Tammany Hall. Harriman appointed him secretary of state. He became a member of the National Democratic Committee. And he controlled most city and state patronage.

Humorless, courteous, immaculately dressed, and corrupt, DeSapio used his power selfishly. He filled the city government with clubhouse hacks. He picked bad judges. He steered business to the Broadway Maintenance Corporation, which got the valuable franchise for servicing the city's street lights, parking meters, and air raid sirens in Manhattan, the Bronx, and Staten Island. The State Investigation Commission reported that the company cheated the taxpayers out of $2 million through "extensive irregularities." (These included a billing to the city for $7.90 for changing one light bulb.) The SIC report was released in the fall of 1960; on June 30, 1961, Wagner renewed the city's contract with Broadway Maintenance. (Some things never change. On August 24, 1976, Controller Harrison Goldin reported that Broadway Maintenance had over-billed the city by $195,023.86 for the first six months of 1976. Broadway Maintenance appears to have a permanent contract with the permanent government.)

In 1960, the City Club of New York issued an ambivalent assessment of Wagner's first two terms. Among other things, the thirty-five-page pamphlet observed: "Scandals, involving theft, collusion in the sale of city-owned property, excessive rentals paid by the city to favorite real estate concerns, relocation frauds and bill padding in connection with the maintenance and repair of city property, shook what used to be the Department of Real Estate."

In 1957, a taxi driver found an envelope containing $11,200 in hundred-dollar bills in his back seat, a few moments after DeSapio had left the cab to enter the Hotel Biltmore. DeSapio denied the cash was his, although only a few school children believed him. And when no other claimants appeared, the cabby kept the cash.

This episode failed to make Wagner any more skeptical of DeSapio. On May 14, 1959, he described DeSapio as "the best leader the Democratic Party has had in New York." Earlier (on April 26, 1957) Wagner said that he "had set an example of undivided allegiance to the principles of good government—of government devoted exclusively to the needs and the welfare of the people."

When Wagner finallly broke with DeSapio it was over politics, not principle or issues or ethics. They disagreed over who should get the party's Senate nomination in 1958, and over the selection of a new Manhattan borough president in 1961. In September of the latter year Wagner defeated Arthur Levitt, the hand-picked candidate of DeSapio and the other party bosses, by 160,000 votes in a bitter primary that ended DeSapio's overt power. This was the campaign where Murray Kempton observed that Wagner ran against his own record and won. Nine years later DeSapio went to federal prison after being convicted of bribery. (He was the third modern Tammany boss to serve time, the others being William Marcy Tweed and Jimmy Hines.)

The only time Robert Moses ever tried democracy and ran for office, he lost by 808,000 votes, to Herbert Lehman in 1934. But by the time Wagner was sworn in as New York City's mayor twenty years later, Moses's empire of unelected power was at mature strength. Moses was chairman of the Triborough Bridge and Tunnel Authority. Moses was a member of the City Planning Commission. Moses was City Construction Coordinator. Moses was City Parks Commissioner. And Moses served on six state boards and commissions. Even though Moses had publicly supported Impellitteri in the Democratic primary, Wagner did not remove him from any of his three city jobs. Wagner wanted to fire him. Wagner talked about firing him. Wagner intended to fire him as Planning Commissioner. Here there was a clear conflict of interest. As Construction Coordinator Moses proposed public works projects and as Planning Commissioner he sat as judge of their merit.

In his 1967 book, *What Have You Done for Me Lately?*, Wagner's former aide Warren Moscow described how Moses bullied the new mayor:

[Moses] staged the scene differently in the crowded reception room of City Hall on January 1, 1954, as Mayor Robert F. Wagner and other members of the incoming administration were being sworn into office. Moses was a key participant because three of the many jobs he held at the moment required new oaths of office administered by a new Mayor. Wagner was willing, in fact happy, to reappoint Moses as Parks Commissioner and City Construction Coordinator, but he was listening to those in the Establishment who felt Moses should not be appointed to the City Planning Commission. . . .

When Moses asked Wagner where the third oath of office was, the latter, anxious as always to avoid a scene, stalled Moses by saying that the clerks had not yet prepared it. Moses acted with characteristic aplomb. He strode back into the clerk's office, seized a blank oath of office, sat down at a typewriter and filled in the blanks for his own reappointment to the planning post. He brought it back triumphantly to the new Mayor. Wagner, his bluff exposed, had no option but to swear Moses in for this third job.

Under the outgoing Mayor Impellitteri, Moses rather than the Mayor had dominated the administration. Wagner had been determined that would not happen in his. But at the facedown just narrated, Wagner lost his battle on the day he took office. Moses increased the dimensions of his victory by relating the story of his hand-typed oath to only 50 or so of his most intimate friends, all in city government.

Four days later Moses wrote to Wagner requesting authority to "represent" the city in negotiations with state and federal governments, as part of a redefinition of his role as City Construction Coordinator. "Certainly," Wagner wrote back. And so, for fifteen more years, Moses shaped the face of the city.

The 1950s was the decade of the bulldozer, of grand designs to end slums for all time. Experts and planners called this "urban renewal," but social workers called it "Negro removal." Federal Title I funds were available—but so was cynicism. In New York City the money and the plans for tearing down slums were under the custody of Robert Moses; among his many titles was chairman of the Slum Clearance Committee.

The Title I housing scandal was the result of the alliance between Moses and DeSapio.

The Title I scandal was peeled away like a rotten onion over several years by Fred Cook and Gene Gleason, writing in *The World Telegram,* and Bill Haddad and Joe Kahn, writing in the *New York Post*—four antiestablishment journalists who shared their information, although working for competing afternoon papers. When the revelations began on July 30, 1956, Moses was a natural target. DeSapio's friend Percy Gale was a member of the Slum Clearance Committee, and the vice-chairman was Thomas Shanahan, chairman of the Federation Bank and Trust Company, a DeSapio man who was Tammany's fund raiser (and therefore Wagner's in 1953) and Moses's banker. In 1948, the Triborough Bridge and Tunnel Authority, on Moses's order, had deposited $15 million in Shanahan's bank, all in interest-free accounts; at the time, the *total* deposits of the bank were $35 million. On the board of directors of Shanahan's Federation Bank was George Spargo. Spargo was also secretary, at $40,000 a year, of the Triborough Bridge and Tunnel Authority, and personal assistant to Moses in Moses's capacity as chairman of the Slum Clearance Committee. Thus the interlocking power of Robert Moses and Carmine DeSapio was cemented by institutions—a bank, and a public authority—whose books and records were secret.

The Slum Clearance Committee evicted and relocated an estimated 170,000 tenants across New York City. Many of these powerless tenants were dumped into Brownsville, the Brooklyn neighborhood that had produced the generation of gangsters known as Murder, Inc. Sites were condemned, and then landlords called "sponsors" were chosen by Moses and DeSapio-through-Shanahan. (Shanahan was vice-chairman of the committee that picked the landlord/sponsors.) The sponsors all had clubhouse ties, and they were all customers of Shanahan's fast-growing little bank.

Each of the eleven sites were milked and skimmed by lawyers, architects, insurance companies, banks, sponsors, stockholders, contractors, rental and managing agents, and private relocation companies. There was little heat or hot water for the tenants. Some tenants were relocated two and three times. It was a textbook case of how to make slums with a committee called Slum Clearance. And enrich a few insiders in the process.

One of the eleven Title I sites was called Manhattantown, on the Upper West Side, and its sponsor was Sam Caspert, a DeSapio crony from the clubhouses. Moses turned over to Caspert 338 apartment houses and tenements. Earlier Caspert had been given title to six blocks of property, worth $15 million, for a fee of $1 million. And Caspert collected all the slum rentals he could from these tenements.

Moses appointed a landlord named Sidney Ungar as the lucrative sponsor of Riverside-Amsterdam urban renewal site in Manhattan. Post reporter Haddad then exposed Ungar's other properties as wretched slums where children suffered rat bites, and pointed out that Ungar was a campaign contributor to Wagner and other politicians.

Robert Caro has described how the insurance on one slum clearance site was handled by a Democratic district leader, Robert Blaikie, an Impellitteri loyalist. As soon as Wagner won the primary,

"Blaikie lost the insurance account—to a broker associated with DeSapio."

Cook and Gleason disclosed in the *Telegram,* on April 24, 1957, that while favored sponsors and developers had made "fortunes" on the Title I properties, they had not even bothered to pay the required real-estate taxes to the city. "The city is holding the bag . . . to the tune of nearly $1 million in delinquent taxes and interest," they wrote. Haddad and Kahn revealed in the *Post* that DeSapio's personal publicist, Sydney J. Baron, was being paid $1500 a month by an "association" of Title I landlords. And Fred Cook documented how the Soundview project in the Bronx generated "a clear $500,000 windfall to political insiders."

While all this was going on, the *Times* was largely ignoring the unfolding scandal and still trying to depict Moses as a planning statesman above party politics. On June 25, 1959, a *Times* editorial commented: "Our confidence in Mr. Moses as an honest, incomparably able public servant is unshaken. His resignation from office would be an irreparable loss. Where is his equal?"

(The frequent misjudgments of the *Times* editorial board have been a major contribution to New York City's agony. In addition to treating Moses as a sacred cow, the *Times* also endorsed the villain of villains, Nelson Rockefeller, for re-election as governor in 1970, over Democrat-Liberal Arthur Goldberg. In a brilliant analysis of *Times* editorial policy, Christopher Norwood wrote in the November 3, 1975, issue of *New York:* "In both 1971 and 1973, the paper swallowed its own environmentalism to support transportation bond issues that still included massive highway money, on the basis of Nelson Rockefeller's debatable claim that otherwise the subway fare would immediately jump to 60 cents. The *Times* regularly quotes Lewis Mumford on 'humanizing' the city, but has backed a parade of massive undertakings that make urban humanists weep, including tracts of public housing, giant urban renewal projects, Lincoln Center, and the World Trade Center, which it greeted as 'a miracle of organization and order.' . . . For saviors, the *Times* has served up Moses, Rockefeller and Lindsay. . . .")

No one will ever know for sure how many millions of dollars of public money were wasted and grafted out of the Title I program. No one will ever know how many low-rent apartments it knocked down, how many vital neighborhoods it spoiled, how many anonymous lives it broke and stunted.

What we do know is that, during the 1950s, the people and the

institutions that launched the disintegration of New York City were
Moses and his authorities; Shanahan and his bank; Baron and his
PR firm; and DeSapio and his Democratic Party structure.

And Robert Wagner, a decent man, let them do it.

The 1964–65 World's Fair was one of those great big concepts
that everyone with power likes. It was like the Albany Mall, or the
World Trade Center, or the recurring plan to build a convention
center in Manhattan. Everyone was behind the idea of a World's
Fair in New York City—the banks, the Rockefellers, Wagner, Moses,
the construction unions, the business elite, and all the political insiders who would collect fees, commissions, and retainers.

In the summer of 1960, Robert Moses resigned his jobs as Planning Commission member, Parks Commissioner, City Construction
Coordinator, chairman of the Slum Clearance Committee, and member of the City Youth Board, to accept appointment as president of
the World's Fair Corporation for seven years. (He retained his jobs
as chairman of the Triborough Authority, chairman of the State
Power Authority, and president of the Long Island State Park Commission—all state, not city, appointments.)

Further demonstrating that real power is usually invisible power,
Moses arranged for his fawning disciple, Newbold Morris, to replace him as Parks Commissioner. Through the bumbling, deferen-
tial Morris, Moses kept control of the Parks Department payroll
and budget, and actually made all major decisions himself.

According to Robert Caro's estimate, the total New York City
expenditure to the private Fair Corporation was more than $60
million, although the exact figure is unknowable because of various
budget deceits. In addition, New York State and the federal government each spent $12 million on the Fair. And that's just the public
money. A consortium of banks held $23 million in notes from the
Fair Corporation and made millions more in loans directly to individual pavilions.

The New York City Council and Board of Estimate voted for a
$24 million appropriation to the Fair, on the promise the money
would earn the city a profit on its investment. Mayor Wagner, Controller Beame, and City Council President Paul Screvane all voted
for this $24-million "loan."

In the end, more than a billion dollars passed through the Fair's
bank accounts. And in the end, the Fair lost money for the tax-

payers. The Fair even defaulted on its notes to the banks, repaying only $10 million of $23 million. The city never got back its $24 million. When the Fair closed on October 17, 1965, it had a $10-million deficit.

Where did all the money go? Moses used the Fair, as he had used the Triborough Authority and the Slum Clearance Committee, to create a blue-ribbon pad for the permanent government of his day. The Moses pad was not like a grubby police pad with a $100 bill in an envelope. It was an imperial pad—legal, and in the millions of dollars. And it was the public's money, not some bookmaker's or madam's.

Allied Maintenance Corporation, well connected politically, got the Fair's exclusive contract for cleaning, disposal, and private garbage collection. In one year, this private carter with a monopoly franchise collected more than $10 million from exhibitors at the Fair. And the only insurance company approved by the Fair's corporate board was Campo & Roberts, DeSapio's favorite company (another sign of DeSapio's enduring covert power and relationship with Moses, even *after* his defeat in the 1961 primary election); its commissions on Fair insurance came to more than $3 million.

Further, the Fair hired the politically influential firm of Thomas J. Deegan to handle publicity. Deegan had told the press, "I . . . expect to continue to serve without any fees or expenses of any kind," but as we have seen, he received an annual fee of $100,000, plus an additional $350,000 for his company, plus a $1000-a-month suite at the Waldorf, plus a chauffeur. On top of this, the firm owned by William Donoghue, who had been Mayor William O'Dwyer's publicist, got a $400,000-a-year retainer from the Fair. The Fair also hired dozens of popular former newspapermen to make the old city-room network sympathetic: official expenses for "public relations" for the Fair's first year were $2,772,542.49.

The Fair's vast legal fees went to the firm of Moses's favorite lawyer, Samuel Rosenman, who had been close to FDR. One of the engineering contracts went to Blauvelt Engineering, a company with a new partner—George Spargo, who had been an aide to Moses for thirty-five years. And the contract for the Fair's souvenir program went to Henry Luce's Time, Inc. Both *Time* and *Life* magazines, owned by Luce, published favorable cover stories on the World's Fair and Moses; the *Life* story was called, "Everything Coming Up Moses." None of these contracts involved competitive bidding.

In retrospect, one can only imagine what might have happened if the estimated $60 million of public treasure which the city poured

into the Fair had gone instead to renovate existing housing, or upgrade the public schools, or restore the docks and port facilities; in
some way to improve the quality of life, create jobs, and thus keep
the middle class living in New York City. But Moses's genius as an
empire builder, and Wagner's passive nature, unfortunately set other
priorities.

John Lindsay gave good intentions a bad name.

John Lindsay was a vessel for a lot of expectations and a lot of
dreams. He wanted to do good, but he didn't know how.

His reform campaign in 1965, as the Fusion and Republican
candidate against Democrat Abraham Beame, was an exciting echo
of John Kennedy's 1960 bid for the presidency. The campaign poster
on every subway platform in the city showed a smiling, long-strid-
ing, lean Lindsay in shirtsleeves on a city street, and over it a quotation from the columnist Murray Kempton: HE IS FRESH AND
EVERYONE ELSE IS TIRED.

Lindsay's campaign attracted 10,000 volunteers and was able to
open up one hundred twenty storefronts to battle the clubhouses
across the city. We both voted for Lindsay.

On election night, in November 1965, the grand ballroom of the
Hotel Roosevelt was rush-hour jammed with 6000 campaign workers
—mostly the Yale-Princeton young and fashionably dressed, but also
more than a few blacks. A band played swing and Dixieland jazz as
the seesaw vote totals came in all evening. Finally, at 2 A.M., Lindsay sprinted 100,000 votes ahead on the ballots of middle-class Jews
from districts reporting from Flatbush in Brooklyn. Someone tossed
from a balcony copies of the last edition of the *Herald Tribune*, the
front page declaring Lindsay the winner. The campaign workers
ripped up the papers and joyfully tossed the instant confetti into
the electrified, smoky air.

Suddenly, a deep-throated animal roar went up, starting at the
entrance on the right, and sweeping across the mass in the ballroom.
John Lindsay was coming to the podium behind a wedge of cops
to claim his victory. He was forty-three and movie-idol handsome.
The people in the ballroom embraced, screamed, and a few wept for
joy. John Kennedy was dead. But they had a new liberal hope.

Lindsay turned out to be a disappointment, almost a tragedy, as
mayor, given his potential and the hopes invested in him.

He had been a superb advocate as a congressman, and he would have made a fine senator or Ambassador to the United Nations. But he had few talents as an executive. Lindsay dramatized the role of mayor, but he couldn't *do* it. He was the mayor of America, but not of Queens. From St. Paul's School and Yale, he lived in the bubble of Manhattan culture. He was a WASP running the greatest ethnic city on earth, and he did not understand the ordinary lives of ordinary people in the four other boroughs. Lindsay was an activist with poor judgment. Lindsay was an actor with no self-knowledge.

Lindsay's weaknesses fed each other. A poor judge of character, he was malleable in the hands of a few people. Like Augie March, his character was his fate. He always seemed to be pushed by others into his major political decisions. His brother David got him to join the Manhattan Republican Club in 1949. Former Attorney General Herbert Brownell convinced him to run for Congress in 1958. Robert Price, the clever, cynical man who managed his congressional campaigns, took him on a walk through the city in the spring of 1965 and badgered him into running for mayor. And late in 1971, Deputy Mayor Richard Aurelio and chief of staff Jay Kriegel convinced him to run in the primaries for president only a few months after he had joined the Democratic Party. Lindsay seemed to lack an inner originality about his own life.

Lindsay was always preoccupied with the appearance rather than the reality of things. As late as the summer of 1976 he could say to one of his former assistants: "You know, Beame still doesn't understand that this whole fiscal crisis is really just a PR problem, a question of restoring public confidence." And as mayor, Lindsay saw most things as a "PR problem." He made sanitation the highest priority of his second administration because it was the most visible of city services. If garbage wasn't collected or snow removed, everyone noticed. As a result, diminishing resources were directed away from more fundamental problems—housing, heroin, jobs, education —because actual progress in those areas was not so easy to dramatize to the media.

Lindsay often asked his aides, when making a decision, how will it be played by the *Times?* How will it look on the six o'clock news? The image of things dominated Lindsay's mind to a fault. He was a successful candidate because he understood the power of television, but he was a failure as mayor because he could not see the limits of television as a surrogate for reality.

Lindsay frequently named the popular mayor of New York, Fiorello La Guardia, as his hero, and he once told Newfield that was the reason he had originally registered as a Republican. But in some respects Lindsay as mayor was more like La Guardia's opposite, Jimmy Walker. Like Walker, Lindsay was a great actor who was star-struck and loved show biz. Like Walker, he was a sexy celebrity, a *Zeitgeist,* a devastating campaigner. And like Walker, Lindsay had terrible judgment in choosing his deputies and lacked the attention span to be an efficient administrator.

Lindsay's objectives were sound. Let us examine several ways he gave good intentions a bad name. He wanted to decentralize the city's bureaucratic school system. But he foolishly chose three black and Hispanic neighborhoods for the locations of the three experimental decentralized school districts. (The main influence on Lindsay's decision was McGeorge Bundy, president of the Ford Foundation.) A shrewder executive would have picked at least two white, middle-class areas, to defuse fear and criticism. A consequence was that the teachers' union president, Albert Shanker, was able to convert the decentralization debate into a bitter racial issue—black parents versus Jewish teachers. The two basic liberal constituencies of New York City were put at each other's throat by this stupidity.

Lindsay had deep and genuine empathy with the city's blacks. But he felt little empathy with the city's ethnic middle and working classes. He went on highly visible walking tours of Harlem and Bed-Stuy, but the citizens of Howard Beach, Corona, Woodside, Bay Ridge, Greenpoint, Inwood, and Belmont never saw him on their streets, although they did see Lindsay's regular visits to the black sections on television every summer. The result was a feeling of alienation in white working- and middle-class neighborhoods, already hurting from inflation and crime. They didn't vote for Lindsay. And so Lindsay resented them even more.

In 1966, Lindsay's rigidity and inability to negotiate forced a city-wide referendum on the creation of a civilian complaint review board to monitor allegations of police brutality. The concept was useful, although too symbolic to justify a costly, polarizing referendum.

Manhattan liberals and civil libertarians loved the idea of a review board. But Lindsay appeared to be handcuffing the police at the very moment crime and street violence were increasing. The review board lost, 63 per cent to 37 per cent. It went down to defeat even in some black neighborhoods, where the fear of street crime was the biggest concern of all, although Lindsay did not recognize it at the time.

One result of this avoidable confrontation was the explosive demoralization of the Police Department, a demoralization that

Lindsay and his aide Jay Kriegel would later invoke as the reason they could not move swiftly when Frank Serpico brought them evidence of widespread police corruption in April 1967.

Lindsay said he wanted to hire the best and brightest people in the country to manage New York City. He dispatched talent scouts to other cities; he talked to his friends in Congress and in the academic-foundation elite. And then he named a string of mediocrities to be his aides. Two of Lindsay's commissioners went to prison for bribery: James Marcus of Water Resources, and the late Theodore Gross of Youth Services. There were scandals in the Police Department and in the municipal loan program. Among the most obvious incompetents whom Lindsay appointed were: Arnold Fraiman as Investigations Commissioner; Howard Leary as Police Commissioner; Jason Nathan and then Albert Walsh as back-to-back Housing and Development administrators; Joseph English as president of the Health and Hospitals Corporation; George McGrath as Corrections Commissioner; and Norman Levy as Tax Commissioner.

What went wrong? A former Lindsay aide says: "John just got fooled by resumés with formal credentials.... Some of the people just didn't know New York City. Leary came from Philadelphia, Joe English from Washington, McGrath from Boston. Marcus had all these social connections with the Lodge family. Kriegel and Goldmark had the right schools on their resumés."

Lindsay wanted the bureaucracy to function better, a fine goal. So he turned to the technocrats, to the systems analysts and management experts at RAND and McKinsey and Company. Between 1968 and 1971, Lindsay spent $10 million of public funds on outside consultant contracts. Most of the studies were worthless, written in trendy jargon about minor problems.

Lindsay recruited a staff of forty-five program planners for the budget bureau, forty-one of them from Ivy League colleges. They tried to construct a rational system for an irrational environment, to quantify the unquantifiable. And Lindsay, because he saw the flow charts, thought what was on paper was reality. But it was no more the whole picture than the body counts and kill ratios were in Vietnam. The Program Planning Budgeting Systems approach created only a mirage of coherence and progress. Yet Lindsay swore by it, and preached the gospel of scientific management wherever he went. He became an admirer of McNamara and Bundy, despite his strong, early opposition to the Vietnam war.

This is what a former aide in Lindsay's budget bureau told us: "The mayor was just snowed, taken in. Lindsay was tired of hearing he was a lousy administrator. And then these bright Ivy League guys from RAND and McKinsey came to him and said they knew how to rationalize city government. Lindsay really believed they were *supermen*. Their use of statistics and charts just dazzled him. The statistics made him feel the city was controllable with expertise. So the mayor was converted without really understanding what it was all about. He was convinced that RAND had a skill that was really a *science*. I remember that I once wrote a speech for Lindsay and he made me use the phrase 'new budget science' three times in it. And I'm convinced he didn't know what the words actually meant."

John Lindsay was a mass transit man, a critic of the automobile. His first good intention as mayor was that he wanted to remove Robert Moses as chairman of the Triborough Authority.

Between Lindsay's election and inauguration he met privately with Moses at the Hotel Roosevelt. If Lindsay was naive as an assessor of men, Moses was profound. After the first meeting, Moses, then seventy-seven, prophetically told his staff: "If you elect a matinee idol mayor, you're going to get a musical comedy administration."

During his second week in office, Lindsay announced legislation creating a new, centralized transportation authority that would merge the Triborough Authority with the Transit Authority, and empower the mayor to name the chairman of the new agency.* This would also allow Lindsay to use Triborough's existing cash surplus on behalf of New York's subways, which were badly in need of renovation. Thus the young Mayor thought he would cleverly and quickly end Robert Moses's public career. Lindsay told reporters he was confident that his merger plan would be approved by the legislature in Albany, and that Moses himself appeared to be amenable to his own political execution.

A week later, the resourceful Moses blocked Lindsay's thrust with one deft maneuver. He released a "memorandum of opposition," citing his binding legal covenant, his "independent contractual obligations" with the holders of the Triborough Authority's bonds. Moses (and his lawyer Sam Rosenman) asserted that any attempt to alter the lawful covenant with the bondholders "would contravene" the New York State Constitution, and Article I, Section 10 of the United States Constitution, which forbids any state to "pass

---

* Again, we acknowledge our debt to Robert Caro, *The Power Broker*, the source of many of these facts.

any . . . law impairing the obligation of contracts." None of Lindsay's Harvard and Yale staff, fresh from Law Review honors and clerking for the right federal judges, had anticipated this argument. When the issue came before the state legislature, Lindsay and his young aides thought they were actually winning the confrontation, although all the real decision-makers were laughing at them behind their backs.

At a joint public hearing of the state Senate and Assembly rules committees on March 11, 1966, Lindsay's envoy to the legislature, Richard Rosen, arranged for only one speaker (besides Lindsay) for his side—the city's assistant corporation counsel, Norman Redlich, just hired from the faculty of the NYU Law School. He didn't pay much attention to the line-up of men speaking on behalf of Moses until a few minutes before the public hearing began. Then he saw the list. Two former governors headed it: Thomas E. Dewey and Charles Poletti. It included: former Mayor Wagner; Peter Brennan, the leader of New York's construction unions; a representative of the Chase Manhattan Bank; several investment bankers; a spokesman for the city's biggest stock brokerage firm; several respected bond lawyers; and Moses himself.

Two days after the hearing, the Chase Bank announced that if the legislature should happen to adopt the Lindsay merger plan, then Chase, as trustee of $379.3 million's worth of Triborough bonds, would file a law suit to invalidate the legislation. And Assembly Speaker Anthony Travia told a few reporters that the Lindsay plan should never have been sent up to Albany in the first place, since it did not even have the legally required home-rule message from the City Council, without which the legislature could not even consider it.

On his first day as mayor, Lindsay, with Puritan rectitude, had denounced the "power brokers" who rule the city. "They know who they are," Lindsay had said in ominous tones. But his inept losing fight to remove Moses showed that Lindsay himself had no understanding of who they were or how they operated.

Two years later Robert Moses was finally removed from power. Four able and ruthless men ganged up on the old man and forced him to accept a merger with the Metropolitan Transportation Authority and resign as chairman of the Triborough Authority. The four men whose combined guile and leverage it took to topple the unelected Moses were: Governor Nelson Rockefeller; David Rockefeller, chairman of the bank that was trustee of the Triborough Authority's bonds; former Governor Dewey, lawyer for the Chase bank; and William Ronan, Nelson Rockefeller's trusted advisor and retainer. The Rockefellers installed their own man, Ronan, as chairman of the MTA, and then the governor broke his promise to Moses—that if he went along quietly with the merger, he would be appointed as a full voting member of the new MTA—and instead Moses became a "consultant" to the now subsidiary Triborough Authority, an honorary position of no power.

The MTA members were the next generation of power brokers: lawyer Bill Shea; Eben Pyne of Citibank; William Butcher of the County Trust Company of White Plains; and Leonard Braun, president of Newport Petroleum.

At one golden moment in recent history the spiral of disintegration might have been stopped. That came with John Lindsay's re-election as mayor in November 1969. Lindsay was re-elected without the support of either major political party. He was re-elected as the Liberal Party candidate with 42 per cent of the vote, defeating Democrat Mario Procaccino and Republican John Marchi.

Lindsay began his second term liberated from many of the city's vested interests, particularly the Democratic clubhouse system. He owed his election to Alex Rose, the benign boss of the Liberal Party; to blacks, who gave him 80 per cent of all their votes; to David Garth, his brilliant media consultant; and to the fat cats who contributed more than $2 million to his campaign. He owed no other obligations.

Lindsay could have begun to make the unpopular changes that were necessary. He could have begun to annul the sweetheart deals and special favors every organized group had at the expense of the public interest. He could have pared the budget of waste. He could have reduced the city's short-term debt.

Instead of using the gift of liberation to make difficult decisions, Lindsay's staff, and then Lindsay himself, became seized with the ambition to run him for president in 1972. This ambition propelled Lindsay into voluntary dependency on the power brokers he had once derided. He needed to consolidate his local base to run nationally. So he used the lines in the capital budget and the expense budget as bribes to this group or that group to stop criticizing and let him run for president as the man who prevented riots, or as the man who had no strikes. He made deals with Democratic Party bosses for jobs and contracts, even though they had supported Procaccino against him. Boondoggles—like the twenty-year, no-bid day-care leases to landlords, the $101-million renovation of Yankee Stadium, and the 99-year lease to one landlord of the Bronx Terminal Market—were foisted upon the taxpayers, because the pols would get the gravy. Short-term borrowing from banks was increased to finance quick-fix programs designed to inflate the mayor's popularity quickly. Excessive pension settlements were made with municipal unions to improve his image as a negotiator—by averting strikes. Bunny Lindenbaum had as much mysterious influence over zoning variances during Lindsay's second term as he had during Wagner's third.

The golden moment passed. Re-elected as an independent, Lindsay had become a volunteer cuckold of the permanent government. And in the end, Lindsay was screwed by the political bosses he tried to sell out to. Meade Esposito of Brooklyn struck the crucial, disloyal blow against Lindsay's presidential campaign in 1972, suggesting, after Lindsay lost the early Florida primary: "Come home, little Sheba." This remark made the front page of *The New York Times*, and it finished Lindsay's presidential campaign.

Lindsay had violated one of the most sensible axioms in politics: Do your job well and the future will take care of itself. Plain, cold ambition ruined Lindsay's second chance.

One failure of Lindsay's administration in New York City deserves special notice. It had nothing to do with the hidden power of some elite interest. It was not an area where Lindsay's intentions were of high purpose. It was a failure that Lindsay chose of his own free will, because of his own human frailties. And it had a terrible consequence for the city. It was the failure, for three years, to do anything about police corruption, and to respond only when it became a PR problem.

Over the last fifteen years there have been few genuine heroes in the history of government in New York. Two of them are named Frank Serpico and David Durk. They were honest cops.

On the last Sunday in April 1967 Serpico and Durk came on a confidential mission to the City Hall basement office of Jay Kriegel, to tell him about police corruption. Kriegel was Lindsay's staff man assigned to liaison with the Police Department. Sergeant Durk was

Kriegel's friend, and he had helped draft Lindsay's White Paper on crime during the 1965 campaign. Serpico was a plainclothes cop who had refused to go on the pad.

Serpico had already tried, through the byzantine, military channels of the Police Department, to report corruption, but he had not been successful. He had come to the mayor's office—outside normal channels—at the urging of his friend Durk, who himself was not a witness of corruption.

Serpico talked for two hours. "I poured out my guts," he later said. Serpico told Kriegel that every plainclothesman in the South Bronx 7th Division, except himself, was taking graft. He said he had reason to believe that men at the level of the borough command were corrupt. He asked Kriegel to organize a full-scale investigation, using undercover men, cameras, electronic surveillance, all the technology the Police Department had in its arsenal. Kriegel said he would tell the mayor about the whole problem.

A few yeeks later Durk realized nothing would come of the meeting with Kriegel. Durk told us: "Jay fucked us. He decided that if he started a real investigation into police corruption, it would disrupt the department, and that might lead to riots. Lindsay's political image depended on [having] no riots in the ghettoes. . . . They told us they would investigate after the long, hot summer of 1968. Then they told us they would investigate as soon as Lindsay was re-elected in 1969. They always had some new date in the future. In October 1969 I even took Kriegel up to Pleasant Avenue in East Harlem to show him police corruption involving heroin. Not gambling, or vice, but heroin. It had no effect."

After Kriegel, Serpico and Durk went to the city's Investigations Commissioner, Arnold Fraiman, also during 1967. Kriegel was merely a staff man, a twenty-six-year-old with many other responsibilities besides police corruption. But Fraiman's only job was to investigate official misconduct. Serpico told his story to Fraiman— the story of refusing to accept $300 from a crooked cop, of his frustrating attempts to tell his superior officers about the organized pad, of the threats and pressure he felt to join it, of his growing paranoia that no one in the whole city was honest.

Fraiman suggested that Serpico wear a concealed recorder to collect evidence, but Serpico protested that this would only catch men at "the patrolman level," and that a massive investigation was required to expose the higher-ups—the sergeants, captains, and inspectors—"where the real problem was." Later Durk saw Fraiman alone and asked whether he would now begin such an investigation, but Fraiman told him that Serpico struck him as sort of a "psycho." As Durk kept pleading, the Investigations Commissioner of the City of New York turned his back on him, picked up a pair of binoculars, and stared at the ships in the harbor below his window. It was the perfect symbolic gesture of the city's attitude toward police corruption.

Desperation led Serpico and Durk to the press. On February 12, 1970, they met with reporters and editors of *The New York Times*. Accompanying Serpico and Durk, backing up their allegations, giving them credibility, was Paul Delise, a full inspector, who risked his police career of twenty years to do it. Serpico and Durk then gave the *Times* a week of secret interviews.

As soon as Lindsay learned that a *Times* story was in the works, he decided to respond, to pre-empt the criticism, to beat the *Times* to the punch, to treat the whole problem as one of aggressive public relations. On April 23, 1970, almost three years to the day since Serpico and Durk had first gone to Kriegel's office, Lindsay announced the appointment of a "special committee" to investigate police corruption. The committee included Lindsay's corporation counsel, J. Lee Rankin; district attorneys Frank Hogan and Burton Roberts; Robert Ruskin, whom Lindsay appointed to succeed Fraiman as Investigations Commissioner; and, incredibly, Police Commissioner Howard Leary, the man who had been presiding over the Police Department since 1966. It was if Richard Nixon had appointed John Mitchell and Richard Kleindienst to investigate Watergate.

In announcing the formation of the committee, Lindsay said with a stern, straight face: "This government must root out corruption and wrong-doing with every means at its command."

Two days later, on April 25, 1970, the *Times* published its exposé on police corruption on the front page under the headline:
GRAFT PAID TO POLICE HERE
SAID TO RUN INTO MILLIONS
Four days later Police Commissioner Leary was claiming that it was all part of an irresponsible smear campaign. "McCarthyism all over again," he said, alleging that the *Times* story had been based on the word of "prostitutes, narcotics addicts and gamblers, and disgruntled policemen."

The rest is history. The firestorm reaction to the *Times* story, and the backlash against Leary's comments, forced Lindsay to scrap his PR defense and appoint a commission to conduct the long-delayed probe of police corruption in New York City. Wall Street lawyer Whitman Knapp was named chairman, and its members were independent of the Lindsay administration. On July 21, the City Council appropriated $325,000 to the Knapp Commission for six months. In November the Commission received a grant of $215,-000 from the federal government's Law Enforcement Assistance Administration. On Christmas Eve the Commission's life was extended for six months by the City Council (over the bitter opposition of Matthew Troy).

The final 264-page report of the Knapp Commission, released on December 27, 1972, concluded that corruption was "an extensive, department-wide phenomenon," and that the Lindsay administration had failed to respond appropriately to the evidence brought to its attention by Serpico and Durk. But, the Commission said, it was unable to pinpoint the culpability of Lindsay personally because of unresolved contradictions in the public and private testimony of Jay Kriegel.

In his original executive session testimony, Kriegel said that he had told Lindsay about Serpico's and Durk's allegations of corruption and had reported to his boss that the two cops were dissatisfied with the way the allegations were being handled by their superiors in the department. But in his later public testimony, Kriegel claimed that Serpico and Durk had complained only about the existence of graft, not about the conduct of their superiors in the department or about the lack of departmental investigations. Then the Knapp Commission's chief counsel, Michael Armstrong—at the public hearing—asked Kriegel: "And did you also report to him [Lindsay] that the police officers [Serpico and Durk] were dissatisfied with the pace of the investigation?"

"No, I did not," Kriegel responded.

Armstrong then confronted Kriegel with his private testimony under oath that he had indeed told the mayor that both Serpico and Durk were "not satisfied" with the Police Department's response to Serpico's charges. Kriegel replied, after studying the transcript of his executive session testimony, that he "talked at some length to the mayor about that incident. And I am now clear that following the meeting with Frank and David, I did not report to him that allegation."

Lindsay was never subpoenaed to testify at a public hearing about Kriegel's two conflicting versions of what happened. At a panel discussion at the New School in 1974, Jack Newfield asked Whitman Knapp why this had never been done. "How can you investigate the man who appointed you?" Knapp replied, by then a federal judge.

The Knapp Commission report also passed this final judgment: "Although Walsh [John Walsh, first deputy police commissioner], Kriegel, and Fraiman all acknowledged the extreme seriousness of the charges, and the unique opportunity provided by the fact that a police officer was making them, none of them took any action. . . . No serious investigation was undertaken. . . ." About Arnold Fraiman, who by then was a state Supreme Court justice thanks to Lindsay, it said, "Fraiman failed to take the action that was clearly called for in a situation which seemed to involve one of the most serious kinds of corruption ever to come to the attention of his office, and which seemed to be precisely the sort of case his office was set up to handle."

Police conduct which the Knapp Commission report described as "typical" and "numerous" included:

—cops selling heroin;

cops selling information to dealers and accepting heroin in payment;

—cops protecting heroin dealers by registering them as informants;

—cops financing heroin transactions;

—cops selling the identity of police informants to the Mafia;

—cops kidnapping important witnesses to prevent them from testifying at the trials of heroin dealers;

—cops providing protection ("riding-shotgun") for heroin dealers;

—cops providing "hit men" to kill potential witnesses.

Five weeks after the Knapp report was released, before most of us could digest its mass of narrative details, the news broke that $73 million worth of pure heroin and cocaine (398 pounds) had been stolen by cops from the Police Department's own property clerk's office, between March 1969 and late 1972. The biggest single supplier of heroin in New York City turned out to be the Police Department itself.

During the last five years, city, state, and federal prosecutors have indicted more than 300 police officers in New York City on criminal charges of corruption. More than 120 have been convicted, with many cases still pending. An additional 60 crooked cops have been forced to resign from the department as a result of disciplinary proceedings.

The Knapp Commission report had one moral hole. It did not make a connection between the failure of Fraiman, Kriegel, and Walsh, and the heroin tide that became an epidemic between 1967 and 1970, the years when the Lindsay administration looked away from police corruption. It was left to Adam Walinsky, a lawyer and a former aide to Robert Kennedy, to draw this connecting thread in a moving article in the March 1, 1973, issue of the *Village Voice:*

> The issue, the unspoken story of the [Knapp] report, is the slow destruction of a generation in the ghettoes of Harlem and Bedford-Stuyvesant and the South Bronx, their minds and bodies ravaged by heroin, everything that makes a life thrown back at them from a perverted funhouse mirror. Junkies for fathers, whores for mothers, a daily fix the only routine of their days, and how many thousands cut down in the indiscribable shooting galleries of the ghetto. The Mayor, the Police Commissioner and the Attorney General, the District Attorneys and Judges pursued their routines, their ambitions, and their careers, made speeches and accepted human-relations awards. Under their blind benevolent gaze, the children died, and they continue to die today.
>
> All this the Commission does not mention. Nor does it draw the final conclusion: We have, in fact, no laws against the selling of heroin. We have a system whereby, for the appropriate license fees to the proper authorities, certain people obtain a protected monopoly franchise to sell heroin, at least to certain classes of people. Not for nothing did the police refer to Harlem, so poor in everything else, as the "Gold Coast" where the real money was to be made. . . .
>
> A few months ago, long after the facts of this report were known, John Lindsay intones that the murder of Professor Wolfgang Friedman was "the worst outrage" to afflict the city in all his term as Mayor. Not a word for the cab drivers, the little shopkeepers, the eighty-five-year-old grandmothers killed for the price of a fix. Not a word of all the years his police force sold heroin to the children of the city, while we slipped into our daily hell, our triple-locked doors and empty night streets, our life-in-death.

There was one other realm where Lindsay's motives were not good—his manipulations of the budget, his dramatic increase of the city's short-term debt, and his concealment of deficits.

During his first month as mayor, Lindsay went on television to inform the public that his predecessor had spent the city "into very serious difficulty," and he criticized Wagner for balancing the budget by borrowing. This new mayor, Lindsay promised, would not repeat the mistake.

It was not until his 1971 budget that Lindsay borrowed $360 million to balance the budget. But during his eight years as mayor, New York City's short-term debt multiplied by almost five times. This is how the short-term debt expanded, year by year:

1965–66	$1.6 billion	1970–71	$6.5
1966–67	$2.0	1971–72	$5.2
1967–68	$2.4	1972–73	$4.0
1968–69	$3.2	1973–74	$7.3
1969–70	$4.4		

And most of the increase after 1971 was the selling of Revenue Anticipation Notes and Tax Anticipation Notes to finance existing debt service. It was is if the city was an individual going to a garment-center loanshark to pay off a waterfront loanshark, at even higher interest rates.

In the October 27, 1975, issue of *New York* magazine, Ken Auletta compiled a list of twenty key decisions taken between June 1944 and February 1975 "that broke New York City," and he sensibly included Lindsay's 1973–74 expense budget. Lindsay and Controller Beame both called the document a "balanced budget," but it was balanced with gimmicks and fictions. Among the gimmicks were: listing $564 million in expense items in the city's capital budget; a rollover of $308 million in budget notes issued to cover the 1970–71 budget deficit; the inclusion of a $211 deficit and an invitation to the state to close it; the arbitrary postponing of the statutory repayment of $96 million to the "rainy day" fund. And it all papered over the biggest one-year increase in short-term debt in the city's history.

The cost of Lindsay's deceptions and promiscuous short-term borrowing was a glutted market and higher interest rates, thus more borrowing, thus more reliance on accounting tricks. In June 1975, Steven Clifford, an aide to Controller Harrison Goldin, completed a memorandum for him analyzing the recent history of budget gimmicks. Clifford estimated that *$1.5 billion* of the city's current short-term debt had been caused by "gimmicks" to create an illusion of a balanced budget. (One such gimmick was the change in the date of the city's billings. To gain additional revenue in 1973, Lindsay altered the date for water billings so that eighteen months of billings were credited to the 1973–74 fiscal year ending June 30, 1974. The immediate benefit was a quick $56 million in revenue. But because the receipt of water charges was subsequently delayed until July and August, the city had to borrow an average of $60 million to cover the delay—a borrowing that will recur every year. And the taxpayers must pay the interest on a paper illusion.)

The fiscal philosophy of the Lindsay years was inadvertently summed up in two comments that his last budget director, David Grossman, made to journalists. "You get a million dollars here and a million dollars there," Grossman once told a reporter, "and before you know it you've got some real money." On another occasion he observed that "a reasonably honest" budget was one that was really only $50 million out of balance.

When Lindsay left office he claimed that all his budgets had been balanced as mandated by law. When a thorough audit was conducted by the state and MAC accountants in August 1975, it was verified that Lindsay had left behind him a concealed deficit of about $1.5 *billion*.

Abraham Beame was Controller of New York City from 1961 to 1965 and again from 1969 to 1973. That was like being the look-out on the *Titanic*.

He was the city's chief fiscal officer when all the budget tricks started, all the estimates of revenues that did not exist, all the roll-overs, all the hidden deficits, all the raids on "rainy-day" funds, and all the trips to the money market for short-term fixes of RANs and TANs. Beame knew the truth. He sold the notes and bonds to the investment syndicates. He saw the books and ledgers. He had all the private meetings with the bankers and securities brokers. He was a CPA. He had to know.

Yet on November 1, 1970, Controller Beame released his 587-page annual report for fiscal 1969–70. New York City's debt, Beame certified, was "well within its debt-incurring power" and the city's fiscal condition was "sound and healthy." On November 1, 1973, he issued another optimistic annual report, this one 556 pages long. In it, he said the city's fiscal health was continuing to improve and again praised the city's debt-incurring power and credit rating.

Beame ran for mayor in 1973 as the quiet, prudent man who "knew the buck." He knew the real facts, the real numbers, and he promised the voters a new world. But he did not level, he did not tell us the truth—that the money was running out, that cash flow was becoming a problem, that the debt was breaking our backs. Beame promised to hire 3000 new cops and put them "back on the beat." He promised to hire "Envirmaids" to "enforce the city's anti-pollution program and keep the streets clean." He promised expanded methadone-treatment programs. He promised to keep the City University "tuition-free." He promised on May 30, the week before the Democratic primary, not only to save the thirty-five-cent fare "but to reduce it." He promised to build industrial parks and a new convention center. He promised to freeze rents. And he promised to remove expense items from the capital budget.

He broke every promise. On June 5, the day before the primary, his campaign took out a full-page advertisement in the *Daily News*. The ad ended with this summation:

> There's going to be a 10 billion dollar budget sitting on the next Mayor's desk, and he'd better know what to do with it—fast.
>
> Believe me, I won't have to wait five seconds to know what to do with it. And you won't have to wait either. For more police protection. Better transportation. Education. To help hospital services. To fill up a few thousand potholes.
>
> Vision and leadership are beautiful words. But a city in trouble needs one thing more. Competence. A Mayor who doesn't know where the money is coming from, where it's going, and who has to rely on other people to tell him can never be his own man.
>
> That won't happen with Abe Beame.

If these words were in a stock prospectus for a public corporation, the author would be convicted of stock fraud.

June 26, 1973: a watershed day in New York City history. It is the day of the Democratic primary run-off for mayor between Abe Beame and the South Bronx Congressman Herman Badillo. The victor will certainly be the next mayor. The Republican, Liberal, and Conservative candidates have no chance to win the general election in November. And the two political forces propelling the Beame candidacy—the real-estate industry and the clubhouse system—are determined to win.

There are differences between Beame and Badillo. Badillo, remote, proud, rigid, "difficult"—is committed to the poor, especially to New York City's million Hispanic citizens. (Like Lindsay, he is a snob about white lower-middle-class problems.) He is independent of the party bosses like Esposito and Cunningham. He will not use the public payroll to subsidize the clubhouse system with patronage jobs. He will resist higher rents and zoning bonanzas for developers. He is against using taxpayer money to build a convention center. His priorities are hospitals and schools. And he is Puerto Rican.

In the frenetic last few days, money, big money, has been pouring into Beame's campaign headquarters at the Barclay Hotel. Beame has raised $857,000 for the primary, and he will get another $800,000 for the general election. Charles Bassine, the chairman of Arlen Realty, has contributed $85,000; Harry Helmsley and his partner, Irving Schneider, each donated $5000; Irving Goldman of the Shubert Theatre organization gave $5000 and made a $25,000 loan. (Goldman was later to be indicted for bribery, perjury, and tax evasion.) Albert Schwartzberg, the nursing-home builder, gave $25,000. Landlord Samuel Rudin gave $5000. Banker Abraham Feinberg loaned $25,000 and contributed $5000 under the name of "Elsmere Associates," a family trust. Bill Shea gave the campaign $30,000 and three full-time political operatives from his law firm— Bernard Ruggieri, Kevin McGrath, and Peter Smith. Nursing-home operator and slumlord Charles Sigety kicked in $1250. Anthony Scotto's longshoremen's union turned over $7500. Real-estate developers Sigmund Sommer and Sheldon Solow each wrote checks for $5000. Arnold Kagan, a stockbroker, gave $25,000 that later turned out to have been laundered through a dummy corporation in Canada and a Lichtenstein trust. And in the final week David Rockefeller, no Democrat, has contributed $5000 to stop Badillo. In the last twenty-one days, $206,312 has rolled into Beame's treasury.

We spent the day of the run-off election driving around the city, listening to John Dean testify on the car radio, watching the vote being pulled, and learning how the Democratic machine can still win an election in New York City when it feels its survival is at stake.

In Harlem clubhouse captains were distributing a flyer that said: "BADILLO IS NOT BRADLEY. BRADLEY IS HONEST." (Thomas Bradley was the newly elected black mayor of Los Angeles.) (After the election, Manhattan Borough President Percy Sutton acknowledged that *he* had ordered the 150,000 flyers printed and distributed.) In the Parkchester housing development in the Bronx, teenagers were giving out leaflets that said Badillo was a partner in the law firm of Strook, Strook and Levan. This was damaging because the law firm was at that time representing Parkchester's owner, Harry Helmsley, in an unpopular plan to convert Parkchester into a condominium. Beame had made this allegation on June 16, and Alan Strook had immediately responded that Badillo did not share in the firm's fees and had resigned as a partner three years earlier. Beame had not raised the issue again. But there was no way, no time, to refute the literature on election day in Parkchester. And the cynicism of it was that Harry Helmsley was actually a financial contributor to Beame's campaign. The chairman of the committee that circulated the leaflet was Stanley Friedman; after the election Beame appointed him deputy mayor.

In the Jewish middle-class Flatbush section of Brooklyn, clubhouse workers were giving out copies of a purported newspaper called the *Brooklyn News*. This sheet contained inflammatory and false statements about Badillo, among others that he "wants Forest Hills type projects throughout the city except where he lives"—a reference to a low-income housing project which the city was building in Jewish middle-class Forest Hills, and the subject of passionate controversy at the time. It also contained an apparent reprint from the *Daily News* that implied that this paper—the one with the largest circulation in the country—endorsed Beame in the run-off. This was also false. The *Daily News* did not endorse anyone in the election, and the reprint was a fake. All this material was, moreover, unsigned, in violation of the state election law. A few days after the election, Sheldon Katz admitted responsibility for the literature. His is vice-president of CHIP, a landlord association that lobbies to end rent control, and the brother of the Flatbush city councilman, Leon Katz, who also happens to be a landlord.

Finally we visited the Bensonhurst, Canarsie, and Bay Ridge district of Brooklyn—conservative, ethnic, and regular. Here we found thousands of copies of yet another leaflet, written half in Italian, half in English. It was wholly anonymous. It had no identification, no committee, no address. Section 457 of the election law says that all campaign literature must contain the name of the "person or committee at whose instance or request such handbill, pamphlet, circular, post card, placard or letter is so printed, published, or distributed."

The anonymous appeal to fear and prejudice said:

ABE BEAME'S opponent is in favor of quotas in hiring and education.

ABE BEAME'S opponent is supported by the Black Panthers and Young Lords.

We traced the leaflet to the Ropp Press, at 4509 New Utrecht Avenue. The owner of the shop, Alan Silver, admitted he had printed the leaflet and delivered it to a Beame campaign storefront at 1722 Kings Highway. Later, campaign finance statements filed with the Board of Elections showed that Ropp Press received two payments for printing totaling $4841.75 during the week of the run-off. The treasurer of the Beame committee that made the payments was Joseph Slavin. Slavin is now a judge in Brooklyn.

At Beame's storefront headquarters at 1722 Kings Highway, we found Arthur Brasco in charge. Arthur Brasco is the brother of Meade Esposito's chauffeur and the cousin of Brooklyn Congressman Frank Brasco (since convicted of conspiring to take a bribe from a mobster). He told us that the particular piece of literature we asked about had been shipped into the "Italian districts" where kids were giving them out "for a few bucks."

Abe Beame, on this day, received 548,125 votes. Herman Badillo received 354,105 votes.

Abe Beame's life, his values, and his way of looking at the world were shaped by the two institutions that nourished his career: the Brooklyn Democratic organization and the civil service. They made him cautious, suspicious of new ideas, reactive, a believer in patronage to the party, a believer in the old ways of doing things.

He had been a methodical doorbell ringer in the Madison Club, a Democratic party stronghold in Brooklyn, and a civil servant since 1929. In 1946, Mayor O'Dwyer appointed him to be assistant budget director, a job he got through the Brooklyn organization, where by then he was an election captain for one block and knew all 900 voters on it. In 1952, Mayor Impellitteri asked the Brooklyn organization to suggest a budget director. The name that came back was Abe Beame.

From his first days in the budget bureau in 1946, Beame surrounded himself with four advisers, known among the clerks and budget examiners as "the four bishops" because they were all austere Irish Catholics: John Carty, William S. Shea, James Carroll, and

James Cavanagh. When Beame became the city's 104th mayor, he made James Cavanagh his first deputy; he named John Carty's son to run the Office of Neighborhood Services; and he appointed Jim Carroll's brother John to be Municipal Services Administrator.

The civil service mentality was once summed up perfectly by Mildred Perlman, a thirty-eight-year veteran whose job is to classify New York's 3600 civil-service job titles. She explained her philosophy to a *New York Times* reporter: "You start by saying 'no' to all requests. Then if you have to go to 'yes,' that's okay. But if you start with 'yes,' you can't go to 'no.' "

As for the clubhouse mentality, that was summed up for us by Meade Esposito, the boss of Brooklyn: "Yeah, I pick every fuckin' law secretary in Brooklyn Supreme Court. I say there's nothing a matter with that. If any guy I send over to a judge turns out to be a rotten apple, I tell the judge it's okay to fire him. Only I get to pick the replacement. I keep pickin' 'em until one guy works out. That way the party keeps the job. The judge is happy. And I get the credit."

When it came time for Mayor Beame to staff the government of New York City, he relied most heavily on the civil service and the political back rooms. But he was not smart. Governor Hugh Carey would give the back rooms the harmless second- and third-level jobs, and make quality appointments for the top jobs. But Beame appointed unqualified hacks for his own staff and as commissioners.

Beame made Irving Goldman the Commissioner for Cultural Affairs. He made Michael Lazar, a councilman from Queens, the Transportation Administrator. He made Paul Screvane, a former City Council president, chairman of Off-Track Betting. He made Moses Kove, an old DeSapio crony, the chairman of the Taxi and Limousine Commission. He made Queens district leader Ralph De-Marco deputy sanitation commissioner. He made Bronx district leader Gerald Esposito deputy commissioner of Marine and Aviation. He made Stanley Friedman, the cigar-smoking caricature Bronx hack, his Albany lobbyist and then deputy mayor. He made Sam Berman the lobbyist for OTB because he was the most effective captain in the Madison Club. Beame named Cyril Regan, an ex-cop, to be the $37,500-a-year vice-president of OTB, when his only apparent qualification was that he made two separate $25,000 loans to Beame's campaign. (OTB was the only city agency to increase the number of its employees during the crisis months between December 1974 and October 1975. While 4125 policemen and 1,549 fire fighters were dismissed or lost through attrition, OTB increased the size of its payroll by 115.)

Beame appointed Abe Goodman, whose benefactor and sponsor, or "rabbi," was Stanley Steingut, to be first deputy administratoɪ of the Economic Development Administration—at $41,541 a year. And he chose Arthur Levine, a former Bronx district leader, to be an EDA administrative manager, at $30,967. Salvatore Grieco was appointed executive director of the Council on Port Development, at $29,253; Grieco was an assemblyman from Brooklyn who had been ousted, a Democrat who had given his name to Richard Nixon's campaign committee in 1972.

So it is no miracle that jobs and businesses continued to flee New York during the Beame years. The people hired to attract and keep business in New York City were unqualified politicians with no expertise for the jobs they were given.

Even some of the civil-service veterans whom Beame appointed had unpublicized political connections. John O'Hagan, the Fire Commissioner, was sponsored by Steingut and Esposito. Ira Duchan, the Real Estate Commissioner, had good relations with the Queens organization. As Director of Labor Relations, Beame appointed John Burnell, a sixty-three-year-old incompetent, because Harry Van Arsdale asked him to. And as Budget Director he named the inept Melvin Lechner, because Lechner was a nephew of Beame's oldest friend, Bernard Greidinger.*

And as first deputy mayor, Beame named his bishop, James Cavanagh.

This is the team that would face the gravest crisis in New York City's history.

Beame lost his credibility during the first six months of the city's fiscal crisis—between November 1974 and May 1975. After that he could not lead, and could not govern, because no one be-

---

* Lechner's incompetence was so powerfully apparent that he became a semi-public joke during the city's fiscal crisis, and he was forced to quit as Budget Director in January 1976. In August he was awarded $57,360 in city pension-fund consulting contracts. The job was pure patronage since almost all of the pension-fund money was being invested in city bonds. And Controller Goldin, who opposed the contract, said that an established pension consulting company, Dreher, Rogers & Associates, had offered to perform the same services for less than one-fourth the fee.

lieved any number he uttered. He destroyed himself. He announced lay-offs that never happened. He could never find out what the three basic numbers were: the size of New York City's total deficit, the total number of full-time city employees, or the total number of lay-offs actually made at any point in time. He relied on Cavanagh, who first treated the crisis as a game and then overcompensated and switched to advocating default. Budget Director Lechner was a comical figure whom no one took seriously, not Governor Carey, the press, the bankers, or Beame himself. And week after week, with perverse loyalty, Beame refused to fire the 5000 to 7000 clubhouse hacks on the city payroll, choosing to lay off cops, and firemen, and nurses, and teachers, rather than the dreck from the backrooms.

Why didn't Beame function better? He could have used the fiscal crisis as a personal liberation to do what had to be done. He could have acted with integrity and independence: At the age of sixty-nine, he should have been beyond blackmail or reprisal.

But he didn't. For months Mayor Beame refused to take New York City's crisis seriously. He had cried wolf so many times that he could not believe the real monster had appeared. He refused to admit the debt, because he took all criticism personally—and Beame's ego is more tender than most politicians'. He reacted in almost Nixonesque ways; he became bitter, stubborn, resentful, determined to survive while repressing the cause of his problem, covering up his past mistakes with public relations.

Beame could not do what had to be done because he believed in the system, the same system that had created both him and the crisis. Like Mrs. Perlman, Beame was conditioned to say no first, and then wait, and delay, and hope the problems would solve themselves or go away. But New York's new problems, building up for almost fifteen years, could not be solved by the automatic no. The historical moment required a heroic leader—a young Al Smith, a La Guardia, a Lehman, a leader of imagination and political independence, a leader who was tough and smart and truthful, and who had a sense of justice and reality. This was not Abe Beame.

The tragedy was that Beame's abdication was the justification for the bankers' taking over. The bankers did not exactly seize power; there was a vacuum, and they rushed to fill it. Wriston and Rockefeller and Rohatyn used New York City's fiscal crisis as a cover to do what the bankers wanted—kill free tuition, freeze wages, raise the subway fare, end self-government in New York City. If Beame had been competent and credible, the usurpation of power could have been averted.

But it was difficult for reasonable people to oppose the creation of MAC, and later EFCB, because Beame was not functioning. His personal default of leadership allowed the permament government to arrange a coup that looked like salvation. The banks and investment houses and securities brokers acted out of self-interest. Beame did not.

On July 1, 1974, the Beame administration implemented its budget for the 1974–75 fiscal year. More than $700 million's worth of expense items like textbooks and salaries were smuggled into the capital budget. A new agency, the Reserve Stabilization Corporation, was created to borrow $520 million. Another $280 million was raised by borrowing from union pension funds and changing the dates of collection of sewer taxes. The budget was balanced by predicting a decrease in the number of welfare recipients—pure fantasy, given the rising rate of unemployment.

Then, in October, Controller Goldin warned that unless the city reduced its short-term borrowing, its real-estate tax would have to be increased by 45 per cent over the next six years. But at that point, Beame was at the peak of his authorirty. He had just purged Matthew Troy as Democratic leader of Queens and replaced him with Donald Manes. Newspapers were printing generally favorable assessments of his first nine months in office. So Beame mocked Goldin's math, and said: "There is absolutely no question about the city's ability to repay all of its debts on time."

On November 30, Goldin sent a letter to Beame saying that the deficit accumulating in shortfalls and spending overruns in the current year's expense budget was $650 million. The mayor was in Florida when this hit the front page of *The New York Times,* so Deputy Mayor Cavanagh put out a rejoinder that rejected Goldin's figures as "inaccurate." Beame had said three weeks earlier that the deficit was $430 million. Goldin, however, when asked by reporters, refused to designate a single specific area where he thought spending cuts could be made. In a public relations thrust, Beame's budget bureau said that the city had made dramatic gains in productivity, including the repair of 862,000 potholes and the collection of 9.95 tons of refuse for each sanitation-truck shift. The data seemed dubious to anyone who had to drive over the city's streets or who saw the garbage on the sidewalks of the Lower East Side.

By January 1975, the sense of crisis was strong, and Mayor Beame had announced, at various times, that 5000 city employees had been dismissed. But each time reporters checked, the number of layoffs was inflated. Beame was firing ghosts who had already resigned, or retired, or died, or were only part-time or seasonal employees. At the time, one of Beame's close advisers told us: "It's not Abe's fault. The commissioners and the budget bureau are sending him rubber numbers. How can he go out and check every name personally?"

By February 12,000 city employees were supposed to have been dismissed. But a check by *The New York Times* revealed that only 1700 real, full-time bodies had been let go. The city was switching people from one budget line to another, and counting each move as a layoff. Commissioners would add up all the unfilled budget lines in their agency and count them all as layoffs. Five months later, on July 23, Beame acknowledged that he could not tell, even then, exactly how many full-time city employees had actually been purged from the payroll. Budget Director Lechner said he thought it might be 13,500, but he could not be sure. It was probably about 6000.

Meanwhile the City Club of New York was saying that Beame had at least 5000 useless "clubhouse patronage" employees on the payroll at a cost of $100 million a year. But Beame said there were none who were not necessary. Joel Harnett, chairman of the City Club, claimed at least 5000 3-by-5 index cards with the names of all the city's patronage appointees could be found in the desk of Beame's assistant, Thomas Roche. But Roche said no such file existed. Most reporters knew, though, that the backroom dreck *was* buried in the Office of Neighborhood Services, in EPA, in the Taxi and Limousine Commission, in OTB, in the Transportation Administration, in the Economic Development Administration (where sixteen of the twenty highest-paid people got their jobs through politicians), and in the Parks Department.

By June default was a fearsome specter. The city's paper was unmarketable. Investors confidence was long gone. Beame kept insisting that the budget deficit was now only $641 million, when it was actually $3.3 billion. One night, continuing to dwell in his cocoon of fantasy, he attended the annual Catholic Interracial Council Dinner at the Americana Hotel, with 2000 people filling the grand ballroom, where he paid tribute to the guest of honor, former Mayor Wagner, calling him "one of the greatest Mayors the

city of New York ever had." Wagner then got up, looked at Abe
Beame, and said, "I'm sure *he's* going to be the best Mayor the city
ever had."

One night also in June, Peter Grace, president of W. R. Grace &
Co. and an old friend of the mayor's, came to see him. Grace was
also a member of the board of directors of Citibank. Grace came
armed with a long confidential report about the city's fiscal crisis
prepared for Citibank's directors.

Grace told the mayor precisely how grave the crisis was and
said that he *must* act decisively to admit a specific deficit, make a
plan to reduce it, and stick to it.

On Thursday, July 10, Beame invited the regular City Hall
reporters into his office to tell them the city's fiscal agony was
"reasonably behind us now. . . . I think we've gotten over the major
problem." He told the cluster of incredulous journalists that the
only problem the city ever had "was cash flow. . . . There wasn't
a crisis, only a problem."

Then why had the mayor called his budget a "crisis budget?"

"You got me on that," the mayor replied with a giggle. "We
couldn't think of a better word."

During July, members of the governor's staff and members of
MAC were telling reporters off the record that, based on their observations in closed meetings, they thought Beame was "cracking
up," that he was a "basket case," a "zombie." The money men from
Citibank, Chase, Morgan, and Lazard Frères began talking about a
method actually to remove Beame from office. But they eventually
realized that Beame's legal successor would be Council President
O'Dwyer, and O'Dwyer did not understand the most primitive economics and had almost no one's confidence as a substitute leader
for the city. So the bankers decided their strategy would be to take
Beame's bishop—James Cavanagh*—and then impose a management structure that would remove Beame from all control over the
city's finances. At the time, a member of MAC said to us: "We
were close to trying to remove Beame. We backed off because we
were afraid it would be perceived as anti-democratic. And because
O'Dwyer is so bad. This city has no elected leader worth a damn."

---

* On Friday, September 13, 1975, Kenneth Axelson, the sixty-three-year-old
vice-president of J. C. Penney, was appointed to replace Cavanagh as deputy
mayor in control of the budget. On Friday, November 15, Cavanagh was
forced to resign completely. He had worked with Beame for thirty-seven years.

By this point, July 1975, large forces, inexorable forces, were exerting the accumulated pressures of history.

The flow of jobs and capital to the Southwest, to the Sunbelt, had drained the economic strength of all the old cities of the Northeast. Years of Richard Nixon's anticity policies had cut New York off from a vital source of funds. The national problems of unemployment and inflation had hit New York especially hard; the city was suffering an inflationary rate of 15 per cent per year. The state government was broke and could not help. And the city, in the minds of Arthur Burns and William Simon, had to be punished. Burns and Simon saw New York City as a guinea pig, whose death in an ideological test tube would prove, scientifically, that liberalism is a failure. And even the vice-president of the nation, Nelson Rockefeller, was trying to plunge the knife in. Rockefeller was telling anyone who would listen that free tuition and the thirty-five-cent subway fare were luxuries the citizens of New York could no longer afford.

New York was defenseless, ganged up on, at the mercy of external policies and people. It was too late for Beame to do anything. The game was up. The years of mistakes and waste had placed the powerless city at the disposal of Burns and Simon, who thought, for a while, they would fatten their reputations by making New York an example of profligacy, of excess humanism, to the rest of the country. Beame, overwhelmed by history, could do nothing.

Finally, on Friday night, August 29, Governor Carey, Controller Goldin, state Comptroller Levitt, and Felix Rohatyn forced Beame to admit that New York City's deficit was, in fact, not $430 million as Beame had said in November, not $641 million as he had insisted in June, but *$3.3 billion*. The man who was elected on the slogan, "If you don't know the buck, you don't know the job," was no longer the real mayor of New York City.

A campaign ad for Beame had said: "A Mayor who doesn't know where the money is coming from, where it's going, and who has to rely on other people to tell him, can never be his own man. That won't happen with Abe Beame." This language would seem a good description of Beame's relationship to the new Emergency Financial Control Board imposed on the city in September 1975.

There is a temptation to feel sorry for Abe Beame. He has an impossible job. He's small. He's shy. He's inarticulate. He's old. It's not all his fault. He has suffered humiliation.

But we resist the temptation. Beame made conscious decisions, and like all of us he is responsible for his actions. His campaign promises had no relation to reality. He misled us, all those years, when he said that New York City's fiscal health was excellent. He refused to fire the clubhouse hacks and continued to service the backrooms all through the fiscal crisis. He faked layoffs. He falsely certified to investors that the city's revenues matched expenditures. These things cost New Yorkers their self-government.

Mayor Beame and Robert Tisch,
landlord and builder,
in the hallway outside
a Board of Estimate meeting
in City Hall.

Governor Carey,
brooding alone
in his office.

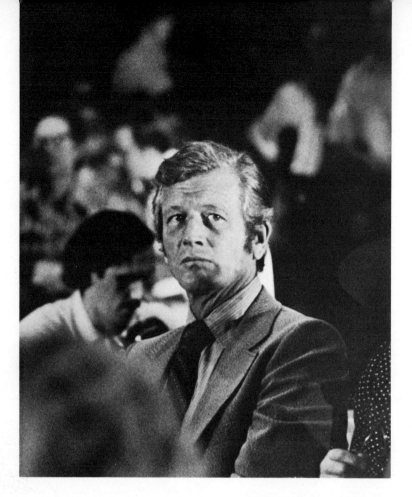

John Lindsay,
staring into space
at the 1972 Democratic
National Convention.

Nelson Rockefeller,
before giving testimony
to the Moreland Act Commission
investigating nursing-home abuses
during his terms as governor.

Patrick Cunningham,
boss
of the Bronx.

Donald Manes,
boss of Queens,
with Stanley Steingut,
Speaker of the State Assembly.

Thomas Cuite,
majority leader
of the City Council.

Meade Esposito,
boss of Brooklyn,
with Father Louis Gigante,
South Bronx city councilman.

City Councilman
Samuel Wright,
antipoverty
plantation boss
of Brownsville.

Attorney Roy Cohn
—indicted three times,
acquitted three times.

David Rockefeller,
chairman of
Chase Manhattan Bank.

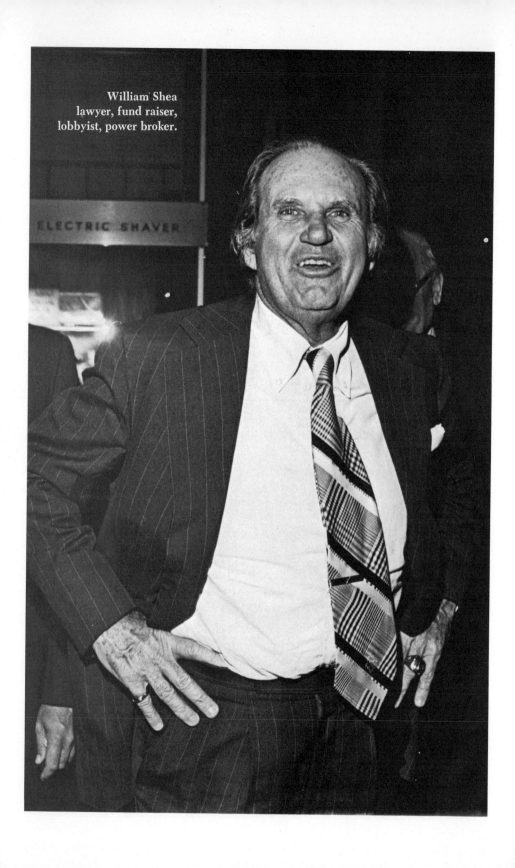

William Shea
lawyer, fund raiser,
lobbyist, power broker.

Jack Bigel,
pension-fund consultant
to the municipal labor unions.

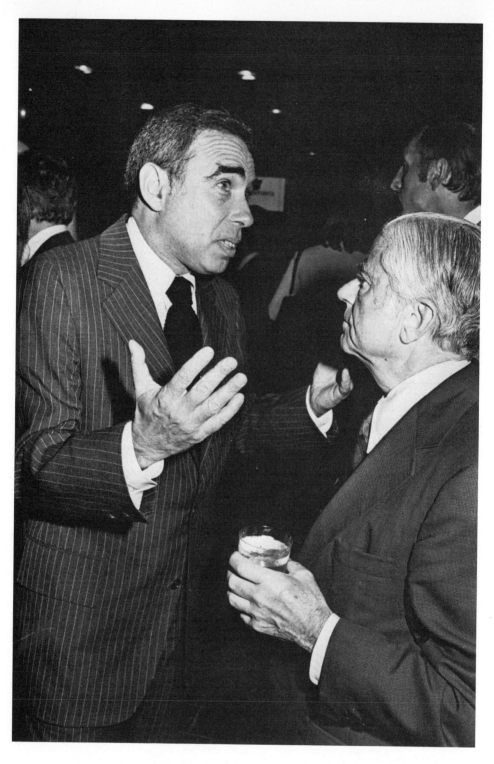

Felix Rohatyn (with Mayor Beame), chairman of MAC, member of EFCB, partner in Lazard Frères, and director of ITT.

Harold Fisher (with Governor Carey), lawyer, fund raiser, member
of MTA, and chairman of the Dime Savings Bank of Williamsburgh.

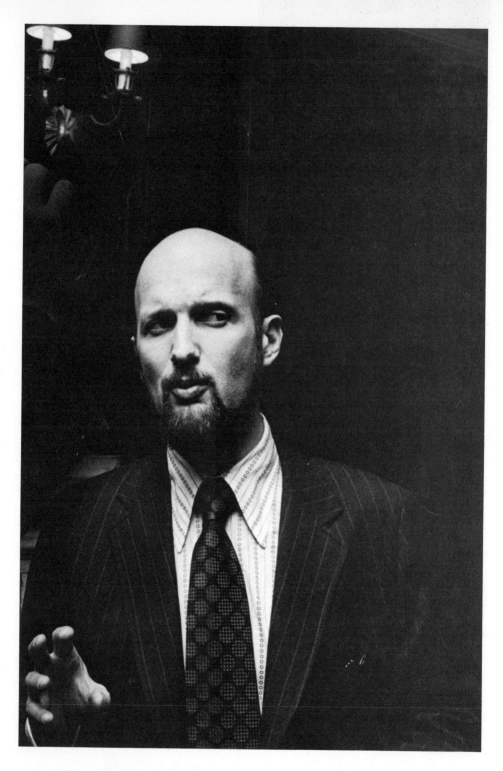

Stephen Berger,
executive director of the EFCB.

Bernard Bergman,
convicted
nursing-home
czar.

Samuel Lefrak,
builder, landlord, and contributor.

Charles Rosen,
leader of the successful
Co-op City rent strike.

THE BANKERS TAKE OVER

Power always thinks it has a great soul and vast views beyond the comprehension of the weak, and that it is doing God's service when it is violating all His Laws.

— JOHN ADAMS

In June 1975 the Municipal Assistance Corporation was created, and in September the Emergency Financial Control Board was put in place, and between them was a revolution in the governance of New York City.

Democracy has been a fragile membrane in New York. Boss Tweed, Robert Moses, and the Rockefellers always had more say than the rest of us. But throughout the history of the city and state, there had been occasional elected politicians of serious egalitarian views, and they served as a countervailing weight on the side of democracy: John Purroy Mitchell, mayor from 1914 to 1917; Fiorello La Guardia, mayor from 1933 to 1945; Governors Alfred E. Smith,

Franklin D. Roosevelt, and Herbert Lehman; Senators Robert Wagner and Robert Kennedy; and the gadfly Republican City Councilman Stanley Isaacs.

And throughout the history of New York, there had been moral catalysts for change who worked outside the structure of government. The journalist Jacob Riis, who described the immigrant poverty of the Lower East Side in the 1880s. The Reverend Charles Parkhurst, who preached against Tammany's Boss Croker in the 1890s. C. C. Burlingham, a lawyer, and Lincoln Steffens, a muckraker who inspired reform groups early in this century. And Rabbi Stephen Wise of the Free Synagogue, and John Haynes Holmes of the Community Church, who were activists for equality during the 1920s. And Judge Samuel Seabury, who harnessed his great legal mind to a sense of outrage, to conduct the investigations that ended the corrupt reign of Mayor James Walker in 1932. And then, for a time, during the late 1950s and early 1960s, two elderly private citizens—Eleanor Roosevelt and Herbert Lehman—were generally respected as custodians of democracy and honesty.

But in the summer of 1975, there was no citizen in New York City who could fill this role: No Steffens wrote, no Rabbi Wise spoke, no Seabury thought to say that self-government was threatened. In retrospect, perhaps this vacancy should have been recognized as a symptom of the city's decline, of what was missing from the chemistry of democracy.

The coup that looked like salvation transformed New York City's representative form of government. The theoretical repositories of the people's will—the mayor, the Board of Estimate, the elected legislators—lost much of their authority, which shifted decisively away from the elected mayor and the Board of Estimate, to the bankers and businessmen who dominated MAC and EFCB. Decision-making shifted from the semi-public forum of the Board of Estimate to an endless round of private meetings in boardrooms, summer homes, and law offices.

The concept, structure, and powers of the Municipal Assistance Corporation was worked out, according to most accounts, in a meeting held on May 26 (Memorial Day), 1975, at the Greenwich, Connecticut, home of Richard Shinn, president of the $33-billion Metropolitan Life Insurance Company. The participants included investment banker Felix Rohatyn, and several commercial bankers, including Frank Smeal, the municipal bond expert at Morgan Guaranty Trust. There is no transcript, no minutes are available of this informal meeting that changed the history of New York City.

The concept, structure, and powers of the EFCB were worked out, according to most accounts, over a breakfast of sausage, eggs, and pastry, on August 20, 1975, in the office of William Ellinghaus, the president of the New York Telephone Company and at that point chairman of MAC. Those attending this private breakfast meeting, besides Ellinghaus, included: commercial bankers William Butcher of Chase Manhattan; Walter Page of Morgan Guaranty Trust; and Edward Palmer of Citibank; Lazard's Felix Rohatyn; and Governor Hugh Carey, the only elected official in the room.*

Of the nine original members of MAC, five were picked by the governor, four by the mayor. MAC's responsibility was to convert $3 billion in short-term debt to long-term bonds. It was also empowered to audit New York City's budget for ten years, and had access to all the city's ledgers and records. It failed of its main original purpose—to market the city's bonds—and thus the creation of the EFCB was required after only three months. The much greater powers of the Control Board included: eliminating the debt, balancing the budget by 1978, the authority to review all city revenue and expenditure estimates and to monitor the budget, and authority to overrule municipal union contracts freely negotiated at the bargaining table.†

Of the nine original members of MAC, eight had banking or brokerage connections. The nine were:

• Felix Rohatyn: 47, a partner in the global investment banking firm of Lazard Frères, and a director of six corporations, including ITT, Engelhard Minerals, and Pfizer. He later became the chairman of MAC and at the same time a member of the Emergency Financial Control Board. As an investment banker, Rohatyn had arranged mergers or acquisitions for Gulf & Western and Loew's Corporation, had married Kinney to Warner Brothers and Lockheed to Textron, and had received underwriting fees for ten corporate take-overs by ITT. In 1970, he had been chairman of the special crisis com-

---

* The creation of both MAC and the EFCB were approved by the City Council and state legislature. Only one of forty-three council members voted against the creation of MAC—conservative Bronx Democrat Michael DeMarco, who said, "This bill will come back to haunt us." On September 5, Councilwoman Miriam Friedlander of the Lower East Side cast the lone negative vote against the creation of the EFCB. She said: "With each new plan we become a city more concerned with figures and less and less with people. . . ."

† On October 7, 1975, the Control Board rejected the contract which the city's 55,000-member teachers union had negotiated with the Board of Education, arguing that it was too costly. The contract had ended a five-day teachers' strike. The contract was finally approved in December of 1976.

mittee of the New York Stock Exchange to prevent bankruptcies by brokerage companies. Rohatyn's nickname, "Felix the Fixer," awarded him by the columnist Nicholas Von Hoffman, was given him when it was revealed that he had met privately several times with John Mitchell and Richard Kleindienst in 1971 and argued, successfully, that the Justice Department reverse itself and drop its antitrust suits against ITT. Later the Senate Judiciary Committee asked Rohatyn what he was doing, going over the head of the antitrust division and having private meetings about ITT with two attorney generals of the United States. "I was trying to make an economic case, sir, of hardship," Rohatyn told Senator Philip Hart, about a conglomerate with $12 billion in annual sales; 400,000 employees; and operations in ninety separate nations.

• Simon Rifkind: This brilliant corporate lawyer was born in Russia and came to New York at the age of nine as part of the great immigrant stream of 1910. A former federal judge, Rifkind was also a director of the Sterling National Bank.

• Robert Weaver: Lyndon Johnson's Secretary of Housing and Urban Development, a director of the Bowery Savings Bank and Metropolitan Life Insurance, he proved to be a passive, acquiescing member of the new governing agency.

• Donna Shalala: A professor of political science at Teachers College of Columbia, she emerged as the most independent-minded and skeptical member of MAC and the only original member without a personal banking or brokerage interest.

• Thomas Flynn: A partner (now retired) in Arthur Young and Company, the accounting firm; director of the Household Finance Corporation; trustee of the American Savings Bank, he was MAC's first chairman but was purged after five weeks. Flynn's fall offers an early example of Rohatyn's influence on MAC and his great gifts at palace-guard manipulation. Flynn annoyed Rohatyn at the July 14 meeting of the MAC board by warning the group that it should not usurp the democratic prerogatives of the elected city administration. Rohatyn made no direct response (although later during the meeting he chided Flynn about being indiscreet in his conversations with Mayor Beame's people, telling them of plans not approved by the MAC board or staff), but within a few days, he had used his unlimited access to Governor Carey to suggest that Flynn was a nice fellow but just not up to the tough task of being MAC's chairman. Rohatyn proposed the harder, blunter Ellinghaus as a substitute.

Rumors immediately began to circulate around town that Flynn was being eased out, and they were printed in the July 20 editions of the *Times* and *News*. But nobody had bothered to inform Flynn. Flynn told inquiring reporters on July 20: "I am still chairman. The stories come as a complete surprise to me. . . . I have been assured that there is no present change in the MAC board chairmanship being contemplated."

Flynn was allowed to twist slowly in the wind for forty-eight hours. On Tuesday, July 22, Governor Carey finally announced that Ellinghaus would replace him as chairman of MAC. From that point on the insiders respected—and slightly feared—Rohatyn.

• William Ellinghaus: In addition to being president of New York Telephone and chairman of MAC for six months, he was also a director of the Bankers Trust Corporation, a trustee of the Union Dime Savings Bank, chairman of the Regional Plan Association, a trustee of the New York Racing Association, and a director of J. C. Penney. Ellinghaus was a powerful force until January 1976, when he was named vice-chairman and director of the national American Telephone and Telegraph, possible apprenticeship for the board chairmanship held by John D. deButts. After that he was still influential, but his attention was divided.

• John Coleman: senior partner in Adler, Coleman & Company, a stock brokerage house; former board chairman of the New York Stock Exchange, and for many years a significant influence, behind the scenes, in the New York Archdiocese of the Roman Catholic Church. Coleman, seventy-three years old, was not in the best of health and did not become a full participant in the new structures of government. In January of 1977, Coleman would be replaced by his son, Thomas, also a partner in the brokerage firm of Adler, Coleman & Company.

• Francis Barry: the likeable president of Circle Line Sightseeing Boats; president of Campbell & Gardiner, a brokerage firm; chairman of the city's Council on Port Promotion and Development; and a valued fund raiser for the Bronx Democratic organization. He hardly spoke at MAC meetings.

• George Gould: chairman of Donaldson, Lufkin, Jenerette Securities, who in June 1976 had become president of the Madison Fund, a closed-end investment trust; in a disclosure statement filed in August, he listed: "working interests in some twenty oil and gas wells"; an "unsecured note" with Citibank; a "revolving letter of credit" with Citibank; and common stock in sixty-three companies.

Later, when Rifkind and Ellinghaus resigned from MAC, two new members were appointed: Richard Netzer, dean of the Graduate School of Public Administration at NYU; and George Brooker, principal stockholder of Webb & Brooker, a real-estate management and consultant company. Brooker, who is black, is also a trustee of the New York Bank for Savings and a director of the Real Estate Board of New York.

The members of New York City's Emergency Finance Control Board included Governor Carey, Mayor Beame, state Comptroller Levitt, city Controller Goldin, and three business members—Rohatyn, Ellinghaus, and David Margolis, the $364,000-a-year president of Colt Industries. Margolis is a former assistant to the president of ITT, where he met Rohatyn, and he says that Rohatyn was "instrumental" in getting him onto the Control Board.

Not on any of the public boards, but powerful factors in private, were the top executives of the three largest commercial banks—Citibank, Chase, and Morgan; and the chief officers of investment banking houses like Salomon Brothers and Lehman Brothers, and of securities brokerage houses like Merrill Lynch. And Metropolitan Life's Richard Shinn, who helped Rohatyn devise this new super structure and is chairman of the Mayor's Management Advisory Board, acts as a bridge to the commercial bankers and the more conservative elements of the business community. (Shinn is also a director of Chase Manhattan.)

The most striking deficiency of this whole structure is that it is so unrepresentative. The memberships were negotiated and screened by bankers, whose primary concern was the bond market. At an early point, the labor lawyer and mediator Theodore Kheel, a man of moderate liberal views, was blackballed from membership on MAC by the bankers, because of his years of perfectly sound criticism of the Port Authority. There is no labor-union representative on either board; Jack Bigel attends EFCB meetings with booming voice but no vote. There is no Hispanic representative on either board. The blacks who are present do not speak for, and are not in contact with, the propertyless black masses of New York City. There is no participant who clearly identifies with the point of view of the small homeowner, who has mortgage payments to make, and is worried about his job at the plant, and how he is ever going to finance three kids through college. There is no resident of either Brooklyn or Queens, the city's most populous boroughs, where most of the city's ethnic lower middle class eke out an alienated existence. There is no neighborhood activist on either new agency, no one who feels the importance of neighborhoods to the fabric of the city and to the psychology of its people. There is no one on either board who is an advocate for the city's badly organized 1.5 million tenants living under rent control. There is no one so poor as to need the use of a day-care center, or a municipal hospital. These new decision-makers are psychologically removed from the way ordinary people live in New York.

New York City's sovereignty, home rule, was lost, not to a pluralistic coalition government, which might have been acceptable under the emergency circumstances of possible default and unremitting federal hostility, but to a group dominated by one economic interest, one economic class, with scarce comprehension of common life in the city beyond Manhattan.

The banks, and those with banking connections, were parties at interest. Even after they had dumped city paper, the banks together held $1.2 billion of New York's paper debt and an additional $1.1 billion in MAC securities. They held billions more in the securities of other wounded cities. They were not about to consider a twenty-five-year or thirty-year debt repayment plan to save New York (although this is exactly what they were considering for the shaky loans they had made to foreign governments). They were not about even to place such an idea on an agenda they controlled.

At the time, a few voices were heard in dissent, raising questions about constitutionality, about democratic process, about priorities. Notable among the dissenters were New York members of Congress, Bella Abzug, Edward Koch, and Herman Badillo. But they were merely elected officials—and thus were patronized as outsiders in the crisis rush to judgment.

It is difficult now to reconstruct the exact decision-making process as it evolved during the summer and fall of 1975. It was meant to be secret. Much of the basic conceptual and strategic work was done ad hoc, on Long Island, where Carey owned a summer home on Shelter Island and Rohatyn rented a summer residence twenty minutes away in Wainscott. Having more information about a subject than anyone else is one form of power, and Rohatyn knew more and had more ideas than anyone else about how to finance a rescue of New York City. So Rohatyn and Carey were at the center of the wheel.

Separate spokes extended out to the banks; to Jack Bigel and the municipal labor unions; to Warren Anderson, the fair-minded but conservative Republican leader in the state Senate; to sympathetic reporters and editors whom Rohatyn briefed privately; and to the hostile forces in Washington—Treasury Secretary William Simon, and Arthur Burns, chairman of the Federal Reserve Board. The mayor of New York was kept informed as a diplomatic courtesy. The only person Rohatyn seemed to consult at all was his legendary seventy-seven-year-old mentor, André Meyer, chairman of Lazard Frères and one of the international finance masters of merger, acquisition, and arbitrage.

The formal meetings of MAC—there would be eleven in one thirty-one-day period—were closed to the media and to the general public. But minutes were taken, and after the participants had an opportunity to edit or modify any indiscretions, they were approved and are now available for inspection in bound volumes in the MAC offices on the 45th floor of the World Trade Center.

The minutes of one MAC board meeting are especially instructive to a student of the new power arrangements, that of Thursday, July 17, 1975, held at 345 Park Avenue, where Simon Rifkind has his law office. The minutes show that the entire leadership of the banking and bond-underwriting community were invited to this meeting: David Rockefeller, chairman of Chase, and his 39-year-old executive vice-president and bond expert Thomas Labrecque; Ellmore Patterson, the chairman of Morgan, and his bond advisor, Frank Smeal; William Spencer, president of Citibank and vice-regent of the boss banker, Walter Wriston; Donald Regan, chairman of the nation's biggest brokerage house, Merrill Lynch, and William Salomon of Salomon Brothers.

While these bankers met with MAC directors and staff, including the new executive director, Herbert Elish, three people were waiting, impatiently, uncomfortably, in a reception room in another part of Rifkind's law office. Waiting their turn, like petitioners, were Mayor Beame, Deputy Mayor Cavanagh, and Controller Goldin. Governor Carey sent his budget director, but did not attend himself, because at this point, for the political appearance of things, he did not want to be perceived as a responsible participant in the high-risk situation. Carey's undercover phase was to end a month later, when the bankers, who respected his intelligence and political adroitness, insisted he become a full, open participant, to help restore "investor confidence."

At the July 17 MAC meeting the bankers applied their muscle. According to the official minutes:

Mr. Rockefeller, acting as spokesman for the group ... said that there exists a perception on the part of the investors that the city is continuing on a "business as usual" basis. He said that the investors do not feel that the state is helping to develop a total plan, but rather is approaching the problem on a piecemeal basis. There is a crying need for a credible fiscal plan in order to support any further financing. ... He stated that in the judgment of the underwriters there are two basic requirements that are needed. First, there should be an immediate, dramatic, credible, highly visible program of fiscal control supported and backed by the governor, the state legislature, and the city administration. In addition, he said that a visible monitoring program by the corporation is also required.

The minutes show that Ellmore Patterson then emphasized that it was "vitally important that the corporation [MAC] take the leadership with the full backing of the legislature."

Rohatyn asked the assembled group whether "any action by the Mayor at this time would have a positive effect." The minutes read at this point, "They all expressed an opinion that any such action would be viewed as having no credibility."

So here were David Rockefeller, William Ellinghaus, William Spencer and the rest saying there was nothing—no act, no gesture—that the elected mayor of the city, sitting then just outside the room, could do; that he was totally irrelevant.

The bankers left, and then Beame, Cavanagh, and Goldin joined the meeting. At this point Beame did not have it in him to stand up to the demands of the bankers. For a few weeks he had blamed the banks for all of New York's troubles, just as at various other times he had blamed Lindsay, Goldin, the media, the state, and the president. He never made a coherent analysis in his own mind of what went wrong and when, although to his credit he never tried to make the welfare population a scapegoat. And just as Beame was essentially a party hack rather than a party boss, he was, in self-image and temperament, a bank employee rather than an important elected official who could talk to bankers as social equals. (Beame, had, in fact, worked for American Bank and Trust for three years, after he lost the campaign for mayor in 1965.) So he was not about to look David Rockefeller in the eye and tell him his historic and moral obligation to the city he had helped to bankrupt.

After Beame came into the room, Thomas Flynn began to summarize what the bankers had said a few minutes before. Beame said he agreed that "dramatic action should be taken." According to the minutes, "Mayor Beame said he was willing to consider a wage freeze and across-the-board service cuts." This, remember, was just seven days after Beame had invited the regular City Hall reporters into his office to tell them that the fiscal crisis was "behind us."

But a wage freeze for the city's workers and service cuts for the city's residents was not enough. Rohatyn, then, for the first time, raised the idea of ending free tuition at the City University and put on the table an increase in the transit fare. He said, according to the minutes: "An over-kill was required, if for no other reason than the shock impact. . . . The possibility of revenue increases such as fare increases and tuition increases should be examined. . . . It was apparent from what the banking community had said that the city's way of life is disliked nation-wide."

Rohatyn had graduated from Middlebury College in Vermont, but Beame had graduated from City College. The minutes read: "Mayor Beame pointed out that a doubling of fees at the City University would only produce $34 million . . . and that 71 per cent of the students come from families with an income of less than $14,000."

Everything the commercial bankers and Rohatyn discussed at this meeting happened within a year. The austerity agenda was set by the unelected men of privilege and property: a wage freeze for city workers, service cuts, more layoffs, a higher transit fare, and the end of free tuition at the City University of New York.

The minutes show no discussion of alternative ways of bringing the budget closer to balance, ways that would not fall so disproportionately upon poor and middle-class families. MAC never discussed the possibility of asking the banks, which had made pushers' profits all those years while New York became addicted to borrowing, to forgive the interest or accept a restructuring of the debt (a stretch-out of the debt payments to twenty-five or thirty years, say). No one argued that Beame must fire all the clubhouse hacks on the city payroll. No one suggested breaking the twenty-year leases that the Lindsay administration had given, without competitive bidding, to a few favored landlords. There was no mention of the unpaid real-estate taxes which landlords like Irving Maidman and Sol Goldman owed the city. No one suggested raising the taxes on Consolidated Edison, a monopoly that had nowhere to move and had been bailed out by the state with a $500-million sale and leaseback deal in 1974. No one urged de-politicizing the Tax Commission so that reduced real-estate assessments for "hardship" were no longer awarded to Prudential Insurance, Con Edison, Chemical Bank, Rockefeller Center, and New York Telephone. No one asked for an audit of all the Medicaid mills that were ripping off millions of dollars every year.

Yes, the pressures for symbolic, gross economies originated with Ford, Simon, Rockefeller and Burns in Washington. Yes, the senators and congressmen of the Sunbelt did not care much about New York City. Yes, most of the economic indices showed that New York City was anemic: Unemployment was high, retail sales were down, housing starts were down, the city was still hemorrahging jobs and capital. And yes, a wage freeze and some layoffs were necessary.

But "across-the-board service cuts" were not. Thoughtful, selective, pinpointed layoffs could have preserved the life-support services of fire, health, and police. The thirty-five-cent subway fare and free tuition could have been saved—if there had been just two or three informed advocates for alternative ways to increase revenues (for instance, collecting unpaid taxes) or to reduce expenditures (for instance, stretching out debt-service payments to the banks, which were 17 per cent of New York's total budget). And if equivalent sacrifices had been made by the banks and bond underwriters, the budget reductions that so deeply affected ordinary New Yorkers might have seemed fair.

But the great financial institutions would make no sacrifice during the crisis at all. They gave up nothing, not one per cent on their interest. They designed and controlled the new machinery of government, and their only function was to maximize profits. David Rockefeller has given a thousand high-minded speeches about the social responsibility of banks, about how Chase was "a good corporate citizen." But on July 17, 1975, all he cared about was his bank's bond portfolio, his bank's balance sheet, his bank's real-estate investment trusts.

Rohatyn's "over-kill," and the "service cuts" insisted upon at this meeting by bankers who did not know the city or have need of its services, in a few months had devastating consequences upon other people's lives. People bled to death in the emergency room of Lincoln Hospital in the Bronx for want of plasma, a nurse, an empty bed. Wood-frame houses burned to the ground because eight firehouses were closed. Twenty-eight day-care centers closed, displacing 1800 children of working parents. A new school—I.S. 390 in Crown Heights—was 80 per cent completed, but construction stopped. Eleven eye clinics treating 10,000 children closed down. Coney Island Hospital closed four of its seven operating rooms. Garbage collection on the Lower East Side dropped from six times a week to three. The Child Health Station on DeKalb Avenue, in the Fort Greene neighborhood of Brooklyn, shut its doors. The 70th police precinct in Brooklyn lost one-quarter of its force. Honest cops, cops young enough to run up four flights of stairs and catch a mugger or a purse snatcher, were the ones to lose their jobs. And because the budget cuts were simplisticly conceived to be made across the board, they ensured the layoffs of unskilled hospital workers, day-care counselors, school para-professionals—the last hired, the lowest paid.

The minutes indicate that the MAC meeting of July 17 ended with a short seminar on open government:

> **Some discussion took place regarding what should be said to the press upon adjournment of the meeting. Mr. Rohatyn strongly expressed his view that there should be no expression of optimism in the light of the gravity of the situation. Mr. Goldmark [state Budget Director Peter Goldmark] felt that the two points that should be made with the press would be a recognition on the part of all parties of the gravity of the situation and that everyone is going to work for a satisfactory solution. He advised that there should be no attempt to answer questions from the press.**

Let us examine two specific decisions made by the city's newly appointed managers—to raise the transit fare to fifty cents, and to eliminate free tuition at the City University.

Formally, the decision to raise the fare on busses and subways by 43 per cent, without even a public hearing, was made by the eleven appointed members of the Metropolitan Transportation Authority in August 1975. These loyal captains of the permanent government included: chairman David Yunich; Eben Pyne; Harold Fisher; and Donald Elliott.

But the MTA was merely the visible vehicle, and scapegoat, for a decision reached at an even higher and less accountable level. The Four Horsemen of Hostility—Ford, Rockefeller, Simon, and Burns—were certainly pressuring the city very hard to raise the fare. Walter Wriston and David Rockefeller also advocated an increase. And, as we have seen, at the July 17 MAC meeting Rohatyn had suggested it. By the next day, the MAC staff and state

Budget Director Goldmark had prepared a lengthy memorandum reporting that a 5-cent fare increase would produce $54 million in new revenue; a 10-cent increase would yield $102 million; and a 15-cent increase would generate $147 million. Within three weeks the decision was officially made by the MTA that a fifteen-cent fare increase would go into effect on September 1.

Immediately, many of the elected leaders of New York City objected—and demonstrated their futility by holding rallies, press conferences, and making speeches. A press conference at Grand Central Station was called by twelve legislators to demand passage of a "broad-based regional payroll tax" to raise the revenue necessary to freeze the fare at 35 cents. Wanderirng around Grand Central, trying to get interviewed by television news crews, Congresswoman Abzug, Congressman Koch, Borough President Abrams, Assemblyman Oliver Kopell, and state Senator Franz Leichter resembled frustrated student protestors of the 1960s trying to get attention for a cause, more than elected lawmakers in a democracy.

On August 19, City Councilman Henry Stern, the only elected Liberal Party legislator in the city, had summarized the reasons against raising the fare in a generally ignored press release:

> Even if the MTA were committed to a policy of soaking the poor and making transit pay for itself at the fare box, this increase would be unproductive, because it will simply lead to reduced use. The only people who should applaud this increase are the taxi industry, because only they will gain from it. . . .
>
> This 43 per cent increase is an imposition on the working poor and middle class. It will lead to increased traffic congestion and air pollution, it will weaken the central business district, and discourage shopping, theatres, and social visiting. . . . The MTA policy seems to be simply the futile pursuit of spiraling expenditures. . . .
>
> Another factor to consider is the relative lack of success of the MTA's cost-cutting efforts. There is an air of futility and unreality that surrounds the Authority in these matters. The MTA was created, in part, to avoid waste and bureaucracy said to characterize city agencies. Yet it has grown in size and expenditures, and is now immune from the constraints which necessity has imposed on city agencies.

It rather quickly became apparent that the disenfranchised critics were right. Ridership declined and the taxi industry flourished. Midtown retail merchants complained that business was off.

The MTA's bloated budget and bureaucracy remained uncut. And after a year, the fare increase had produced "about $50 million in revenue," according to MAC's executive director Herbert Elish, not the $147 million projected in the staff memorandum of July 18, 1975. Elish acknowledged to us that raising the fare to 50 cents, "with hindsight, on balance, was probably a mistake."

In August 1976 we interviewed Donna Shalala, a member of MAC. She candidly agreed that the decision to increase the fare by 15 cents "was a mistake," and she characterized the decision-making process as "irrational and uninformed."

> There was tremendous pressure [Ms. Shalala recalled] to get the Mayor to do something. The people on MAC who knew the [money] market, told us that a symbolic act for investors was necessary. They thought raising the fare was the symbolic act that was necessary, and something we could get the Mayor to do. . . .
>
> The process wasn't that rational. There was possibly a half hour of discussion about raising the fare, that's all. There was never a set of staff papers prepared, so we could study it. We did no background work. We had no hard facts. That's the horror of it. We were just throwing together a list of things that might be cut. There was no conspiracy to screw the people. Beame had his budget director, Melvin Lechner, in the meetings. It was just something decided in a half hour. . . .
>
> We were told this decision would open up the market. Now we know there was nothing, nothing, we could have done to open the market. I should have stuck to my guns and opposed the fare increase. I'm sorry we misled the public that the money markets would open.

When pressed on who was at the center of the decision-making process, Ms. Shalala responded, "Even though I'm a member of MAC, I was only on the fringes of things. There were a lot of private meetings going on all the time, with Carey, Rohatyn, Ellinghaus, various bankers, and Shinn. You have to remember it was a crisis, and things were happening very fast, and Felix can be very intimidating. But I can't really say for sure who is most responsible. I'm not even clear on how it came to be a fifteen-cent increase, rather than five cents or ten cents."

When we asked Rohatyn about the paternity of the fifty-cent fare, he replied: "It was mostly Beame, as I recall." When we asked Beame, through his public-relations adviser Howard Rubenstein, the mayor's recollection in August 1976 was: "It was Washington's idea."*

Free tuition for public higher education is an almost sacred tradition in New York. The Free Academy was created by a referendum of the voters in 1847. One hundred and twenty-nine years later the City University consisted of 275,000 students, twenty-one colleges (including eight two-year community colleges) and a graduate center. It includes the apparently inevitable excesses of high faculty salaries, mansions for college presidents, luxuries for a few bureaucrats, a proliferation of administrators, middle management, and consultants, generous welfare and pension benefits, and an over-ambitious construction program. But the quality of education is superior (in contrast, say, to the low quality of health care in municipal hospitals). And free higher education for the "worthy poor" had been a visa into the middle class for the Irish, the Jews, the Italians, and every other immigrant group that came to "the land of opportunity."

The City College (now University) produced Jonas Salk, the man who developed the vaccine against polio. Nobel Laureates had come from City: Julius Axelrod, Arthur Kornberg, Robert Hofstadter, and Kenneth Arrow. CCNY educated Felix Frankfurter, Upton Sinclair, Senator Robert Wagner, and Lewis Mumford. And Ira Gershwin, and Bernard Malamud, and Zero Mostel, and Paul Goodman, and Bernard Baruch, and E. Y. Harburg, and Irving Howe. And hundreds of thousands of other productive citizens who would otherwise never have had a college education. Moreover, the two authors of this book could never have afforded to pay tuition if Hunter College had not been free in 1956 when we entered the freshman class.

Since before the Civil War, free tuition at New York's colleges has meant upward mobility, an essential part of the dream among the working class that their children might have a better life than

---

* On November 19, 1976, state Comptroller Arthur Levitt released an audit that disclosed that MTA had concealed $58 million that should have been used to keep mass transit fares down. The $58 million was earned as interest on the investment of tolls from the Triborough Bridge and Tunnel Authority, an MTA subsidiary. The Levitt audit said: "The MTA has not used these TBTA surplus funds for fare maintenance or operating equipments as appears to be required by law."

their parents. The City University was the pure incarnation of the Jeffersonian ideal of an aristocracy of "virtue and talents," rather than "an artificial aristocracy, founded on wealth and birth." The City University system has also been one of the strongest reasons for middle-class families to stay in New York; as the president of one municipal college put it, "Free tuition is one of the best incentives for the middle class to live in New York. It is the single greatest financial attraction to middle-class taxpayers."

In July 1974, when Hugh Carey was running in the Democratic primary for governor, the CUNY students wanted their usual guarantee that free tuition would be preserved. Carey wrote a letter to Jay Hershenson, head of the City University Student Senate: "I have long supported free tuition at the City University of New York. I will do all in my power, whether I become Governor or not, to preserve free tuition at the City University."

But up-state and suburban Republicans in the state legislature, and most of New York City's bankers, have long resented CUNY's free tuition. Walter Wriston, in private, has been known to become irrational in his fury against free higher education, as well as against another of his pet peeves, bilingual education. And early in the fiscal crisis, in May 1975, Vice-President Rockefeller proposed the termination of free tuition at a White House meeting with Mayor Beame, Governor Carey, and President Ford. Rockefeller's attack— delivered in front of the president and widely reported—on a policy in his home state, where he was deferred to as an expert, was the first wounding blow struck against free tuition. The second, although the public could not know it at the time, was inflicted by Rohatyn at the private MAC board meeting on July 17. Rohatyn's words were taken as a signal that Governor Carey would not fight to save New York's free tuition.

The next critical public assault upon free tuition came on Tuesday, September 16, when State Education Commissioner Ewald Nyquist released the text of a letter he had written to Alfred Giardino, chairman of the Board of Higher Education. Nyquist's letter urged the imposition of yearly tuition of $650 on freshmen and sophomores and $800 on juniors and seniors—the same fees as those charged at the State University of New York. Nyquist's letter claimed that because of various state and federal subsidies, only those students whose families earned more than $20,000 of net taxable income would actually have to pay the tuition money out of their own pockets. Carey had been governor for only eight months when his own education commissioner thus advocated tuition. When he was asked to comment, Carey said: "I have not changed my position that applying tuition at the City University would solve very little. The numbers involved will not solve the city's fiscal problems. The Emergency Financial Control Board is not going to assume any decision-making powers over any aspects of city life. Mr. Beame has to make recommendations on matters within city jurisdiction. And if there should be a change in the tuition situation at the City University of New York, the initiative must come from that quarter." More appearances.

A survey by *The New York Times* made in September 1975 showed eight of the ten members of the Board of Higher Education steadfastly opposed to imposing tuition. Five of the eight eventually resigned in protest rather than be party to any change of policy.

By January 1976, the pressure to do away with free tuition was mounting in private from Washington and Wall Street. And the issue was becoming a political football between Beame and Carey. Again—the appearance of things. Who would bear the blame for annuling the last best hope of the dispossessed in New York City? In his "State of the City" address on January 22, Beame said: "The primary responsibility for higher education rests with the state.... The City cannot continue to finance the City University. We are exploring ways to achieve the necessary transition over the next few years." Beame did not say he would fight to save free tuition. And Carey was no longer making any promises. Two members of the BHE, Harold Jacobs and Dr. Gurstin Goldin, the psychiatrist brother of Controller Harrison Goldin, were already, in fact, maneuvering behind the scenes to prepare the transition to tuition.

On March 24, Stephen Berger, whom Governor Carey had appointed executive director of the Control Board two weeks before, came to lunch at the *Daily News* to meet with the paper's top editors and writers. Berger's self-image is that of a brutally frank tough guy. He had worked for the politically inspired Scott Commission, created in 1971 by Nelson Rockefeller to do a hatchet job on the Lindsay administration. Berger loved it and was very good at it, and Rockefeller still speaks admiringly of the job Berger did.

Earlier in his career, Berger had been a highly regarded campaign mechanic and technician for liberals who usually happened, like Rockefeller, to be millionaires, such as Congressmen Jonathan Bingham and Richard Ottinger. But by 1975, Berger was Hugh Carey's Commissioner for Social Services. In that position, Berger began a crusade against the "16,000 ineligible children" who he said were in city day-care centers. He did not begin any equivalent crusade against the day-care landlords who were getting paid inflated rents by the city on twenty-year leases.

So Stephen Berger, a graduate of Brandeis University, probably did not really mind being the hit man against free tuition when he came for lunch with the editors and writers of the *Daily News*. Berger was his usual factual, articulate, candid self. He said it, flatly, clearly: Free tuition must end. Berger, at least, did not calculate much about the appearance of things. The next morning, the *News* quoted him as saying: "You can't expect to have tuition in the state colleges, and expect the legislature to approve aid for the city system without some sort of a tuition program."

The crunch came in April. There was, by then, a $70-million deficit in the BHE's budget. The city was broke, and the state legislature was opposed to any state aid. In a desperate effort to stave off tuition, the BHE had voted to restrict admissions and to consolidate four of CUNY's branches. Franklin Williams quit the BHE on April 5, saying the board's new admissions policy was "racist" and would segregate the university into white senior colleges, and black and Hispanic community colleges. Henrik Dullea, an aide to Carey, was pressuring board members to vote for tuition. So was T. Edward Hollander, the deputy state education commissioner. When a reporter asked Dullea whether he had been "twisting arms" in behalf of tuition, Dullea replied, in bureaucratic off-English, "We've talked to a lot of people about all the issues confronting the university, but we haven't made any specific calls on tuition. I won't deny tuition has been discussed, because it's one of the principal options that have to be confronted."

By the end of April there were four firm votes in favor of tuition on the ten-member BHE: Harold Jacobs; Dr. Gurstin Goldin; James Murphy, the executive vice-president of the New York State Bankers Association; and Armand D'Angelo, who had been appointed by Carey in October at the urging of Robert Wagner, in whose administration D'Angelo had served from 1957 to 1965 without distinction. (In fact, D'Angelo had been marginally tainted by scandal during the Wagner administration. A 1961 report by the State Commission of Investigation charged D'Angelo, then the city's water commissioner, with "impropriety" in his dealings with Sydney Baron, Carmine DeSapio's PR man. And at the bribery trial, James Marcus testified that D'Angelo was friendly with the man who bribed him, the Mafia boss Tony "Ducks" Corallo.) On April 27, the board asked for a face-to-face meeting with Governor Carey, so that Carey could directly request the imposition of tuition. Several wavering members said they might vote for tuition if the governor was at least willing to accept the ultimate responsibility for the decision and not have it reside with an appointed board. They also wanted a commitment from Carey on the exact dollar amount of aid which the state would provide CUNY if tuition were imposed. Carey refused to attend the meeting. BHE member Rita Hauser said, "Mr. Carey's representatives have offered every possible kind of number [of state aid to CUNY] but they never commit the Governor. And if we ask them frontally—'Does the Governor want tuition?'—they back off." Again, the politician's concern with the appearance of things, not their actuality.

Also on April 27, Carey named Francis Kilcoyne, the former president of Brooklyn College, to take Franklin Williams's seat on the BHE.

In the middle of May Carey finally went public and said he reluctantly favored that City University students be charged tuition. Tuition, Carey said, would raise $135.5 million in operating revenues. The way the tuition formula was structured, those hardest hit would be part-time students who had to work, and students from families whose gross annual income is above $10,000. The poorest students would receive assistance and reimbursement grants from state and federal programs.

In the end, the victims of tuition would be lower-middle-class students and, perhaps, women in hard-pressed families that had to choose one child to send to college and chose the brothers. By September the combination of tuition and fewer admissions had cut CUNY's population by 38,000 students. And almost 1000 untenured faculty were dismissed. Some of the luxuries, managerial sinecures, and departmental duplication were uncut, according to the usual ass-backward priorities of the bureaucrats who controlled the budget axe.

On May 25, five members of the Board of Higher Education resigned rather than vote for tuition. They were led by the BHE's chairman, Alfred Giardino, who had graduated from Brooklyn College in 1934 and was the first member of his family ever to attend college. Vincent Fitzpatrick, Sandra Lopez de Bird, and Rita Hauser also quit. And so did Francis Kilcoyne, whom Carey had appointed only the month before.

On May 28, Mayor Beame promoted his old close friend the businessman and clubhouse Democrat Harold Jacobs to the chairmanship of the BHE, and appointed three new members, all quietly felt out in advance, as to their views on tuition: Albert Maniscalco, former Staten Island borough president and director of the Community National Bank & Trust Company; Nicholas Figueroa, a lawyer; and Loretta Conway, a lawyer active in the Fordham University Alumni Association. (The private colleges favored tuition at CUNY.) The appointments were made without the official screening-panel interviews. Howard Squadron, a member of the mayor's screening panel, said Beame circumvented the screening process "because our members have considered it our function to be sure that candidates are committed to free tuition. . . . I think the Mayor is making a terrible mistake."

The struggle was over. For longer than a century, from the Land Grant College Act of 1862 to the GI Bill of Rights, our national policy had been to expand access to higher education. But in New York City, one month before the national bicentennial, this policy was reversed. An economic barrier rose against higher education.

The City University was closed and broke when the Board of Higher Education met at its headquarters, at 535 East 80th Street in Manhattan, at 7:30 P.M. on June 1. Six members had quit rather than violate their consciences: Giardino, Williams, Hauser, Fitzpatrick, Lopez de Bird, and Kilcoyne. The climactic meeting was dull and passionless, according to the participants. The three new members asked almost no questions, though they had less than seventy-two hours to become familiar with the complex issues. The meeting lasted a little more than two hours. The vote was seven to one. Voting "yes," for tuition, were the new chairman, Harold Jacobs; the three instant appointees—Maniscalco, Figueroa, and Conway; Carey's appointee, Armand D'Angelo; Dr. Gurstin Goldin, the brother of the controller; and James Murphy, the banker. The formal resolution to impose tuition was offered by D'Angelo. The solitary "no" vote was cast by Vinia Quinones, an administrator at Arthur Logan Memorial Hospital in Harlem and the only black member remaining on the board. Two months later, Beame, the first graduate of the City University ever to become mayor of New York, refused to reappoint Quinones to the BHE.

In June Congresswoman Elizabeth Holtzman of Brooklyn delivered the commencement address to the graduating class of Queens College. Holtzman, one of the independent and intelligent elected leaders in the city, spoke an honest epitaph for New York's

129 years of free higher education. She told the Queens College senior class, "Tuition is being imposed at CUNY not because there is no other way to raise enough money for New York's survival, but because the city's managers want to appease a hostile federal government and an envious country . . . not to mention some bankers who graduated from Princeton or Fordham."

THE CLUBHOUSE SYSTEM

To grasp the essence of the clubhouse system, to feel its power, to understand its values, come with us to the annual dinner of the Kings County Democrats. See the long black limos, and the Brooklyn cars with license plates that display the owners' initials, double-parked outside the Waldorf-Astoria on Park Avenue. See five judges sitting at Bill Shea's table. Watch the judges approach Carmine DeSapio's table and pay respect. See the landlord with his arm around the deputy commissioner of real estate.

Come with us to the May 16, 1974, annual dinner of the Brooklyn Democracy. At table 23 is Congressman Frank Brasco, who will go to federal prison for conspiring to accept a bribe from a Mafia trucker. At table 16 is Congressman Bertram Podell, who will go to federal prison for taking a $41,350 bribe to influence the Civil Aeronautic Board's decision on an airline route. At table 92 is Eugene Hollander, who will plead guilty to stealing $1.1 million in Medicaid funds from four nursing homes he owns. At table 55 is Queens County leader Matthew Troy, who will plead guilty to income-tax evasion on money taken from the estates of his law clients. And at table 50 is Carmine DeSapio. DeSapio has served almost two years in prison for bribery. Manhattan public administrator Thomas Fitzgerald, who will be indicted with his friend, sits at table 53.

Irving Goldman, the city's Cultural Affairs Commissioner, is found at table 4. He will be indicted on charges of income-tax evasion, mail fraud, and conspiracy in a plot to cheat a subway vending-machine company of $200,000, and of offering bribes to Transit Authority officials to get the company's contract renewed. Congressman Mario Biaggi is also at table 4. A year ago he was caught lying to the voters about his refusal to testify fully before a federal grand jury.

Joe Pape is at table 14. Pape, a former party district leader in Manhattan and a business associate of Stanley Steingut, will be named in an eighty-count indictment claiming he falsified records of the Computer Specifics Corporation to conceal bribes paid to a Board of Education official. Speaker Stanley Steingut himself is at table 47, and his son, Councilman Robert, is at table 18. Their indictment for a scheme to get a $2500 contribution for Robert's campaign in exchange for getting the contributor an honorary position with the city will be dismissed on a jurisdictional technicality.

State Assemblyman Harvey Strelzin is at table 108. In 1957 Strelzin was forced to resign as chairman of the city's Board of Assessors after it was disclosed that he was a partner in a garbage-disposal business with a mobster named Anthony Ricci. Milton Kessler, also seated at table 108, was until March 1972 both the managing agent for a Crown Heights slum building that had been cited with 130 violations and an aide to Councilman Howard Golden. When Kessler's activities were exposed by *New York Post* reporter Joe Kahn, Kessler quit his job with Golden (but remained the agent for the slum building). When Kahn was working on his story, Kessler had said to him, "It's none of your business. All the other reporters know about it, and they aren't writing anything, so you better forget it."

Twenty-two city marshals have bought tickets to this dinner, including Kenneth Brand (table 101), who earned $181,000 in 1973; Herbert Klein (table 312), who earned $163,000; and Alex Chapin (table 101), who made $189,000. Frank Vaccaro, seated at table 110, will become a judge and then be suspended from the bench by the Commission on Judicial Conduct for accepting gifts from a lawyer who appeared before him. Roy Cohn is at table 35. He has been indicted and acquitted three times.

District leader George Meissner is at table 23; he is a convicted slumlord. And with him is Bernard Deutsch, who will be convicted of stock fraud. Irving Polk, seated at table 308, is president of Esposito's political club and a city pothole inspector who gets $666 a month for his work—a task notorious for requiring no work. Judge Jerome Steinberg is at table 116. In January of 1977, Steinberg will be indicted for perjury and contempt for lying to a grand jury probing his alleged "participation in a money-lending scheme" involving more than $250,000.

Frankie Folan, at table 88, contributed $13,125 to Beame's mayoralty campaign and a few months later became Democratic Party district leader in Bay Ridge. He was later caught selling 2500 tickets on a charter flight that never existed.

Seated at table 37 are Arthur Vare, Stanley Kreitman, and Saul Kagan, all directors of the American Bank and Trust Company. Mayor Beame once was a director of the bank himself, and the bank's president, Abraham Feinberg, was Beame's most important campaign fund raiser in 1973. On September 15, 1976, the charter for the American Bank and Trust Company will be taken away, and State Banking Superintendent John Heimann will accuse the bank of "practices in violation of law" and of being in an "unsafe and unsound condition." The Federal Reserve Bank will discover that one-third of the American Bank and Trust Company's $152 million loan portfolio is "sub-standard, doubtful, or lost."

Larry Gurino, at table 74, is a part-owner of the Queens Terrace Catering Corporation, which was denied a liquor license by the State Liquor Authority because Gurino had "business connections with various individuals who have close connections with organized crime." Among Gurino's partners in the ownership of the catering company were the son and the nephew of former Mafia boss Joseph Columbo. Gurino's brother John has at various times held six day-care-center leases from the city. These day-care centers received $590,000 in construction loans from the pension fund of Local 355, an independent trucking union which was started by the convicted labor racketeer Johnny Dio.

Builder and bank director Vincent Caristo is at table 104. In 1961, Caristo was banned from submitting construction bids to the Board of Education because of past rigged bids, a ban that was upheld by the courts but rescinded in April 1962. And now the Caristo Construction Company is the single biggest recipient of construction contracts from the Board of Education. (In 1969 it was disclosed that the file dealing with the decision to reinstate the Caristo company was missing from Board of Education archives.)

Sidney Lipkins, chairman of Broadway Maintenance Corporation, is at table 43. In 1961, the State Investigation Commission accused his company of "extensive irregularities" and "excessive profits" in its contracts with the city to service traffic lights and parking meters, and in 1976 Broadway Maintenance will once again be accused, in an audit by Controller Goldin, of over-billing the bankrupt city by $195,000.

Fortune Pope is seated at table 59. Pope is president of Colonial Sand & Stone Company and owner of *Il Progresso*, New York City's Italian-language newspaper. In 1961, Pope was fined $25,000 and received a suspended prison sentence after pleading guilty to filing false proxy statements with the American Stock Exchange. A few years later, he caused the dismissal of a city purchase commissioner after it was disclosed that he had made too much profit selling the city rock salt from the Dominican Republic.

Builder Fred DeMatteis, a registered Republican, is at table 9. His giant construction company had been accused of pouring weak cement on a Nassau County project—until DeMatteis hired away the diligent engineer who discovered his shoddy work. And builders Donald and Fred Trump (father and son), at table 10, have been accused by the Justice Department of violating the Fair Housing Act by discriminating against blacks in their rental policies. The Trump family owns and rents 14,000 apartments. The Trumps, and their lawyer, Roy Cohn, eventually signed a consent decree.

Louis Friedman, at table 81, was removed from the State Supreme Court in 1963 for abusing his office and obstructing an investigation into an ambulance-chasing racket. Norman Levy, at table 73, was once chairman of the City Tax Commission, but he was convicted of fixing parking tickets, a conviction that will later be reversed. Dr. Mario Tagliagambe is at table 211. The Waterfront Commission would secretly film Dr. Tags, as he is known, entering an organized-crime clubhouse on the Lower East Side. Joseph Parisi, at table 30, clerk of Brooklyn Supreme Court, is under indictment for illegally using union pension funds.

George Kerner, at table 38, and Frank Gilligan, at table 39, are law secretaries in Brooklyn Supreme Court. Gilligan has been the treasurer for twenty-five years of the Kings County Democratic organization. On June 18, 1976, Gilligan and Kerner will plead guilty to stealing the receipts of this dinner and of three previous Brooklyn dinners, thefts totaling $100,000 in party funds.

The guest speaker at this embezzled 1974 Waldorf-Astoria dinner is Abraham D. Beame, who was sworn in as mayor of New York City only four months ago. Beame is speaking with uncommon passion to the 2000 assembled guests—Podell, Brasco, Troy, Hollander, DeSapio, Goldman, Pope, Lipkins, Kessler, Gilligan, and all the other honorable men and women of the Brooklyn Democracy. The new mayor is saying:

> We are sometimes accused of running a strong county organization. Critics call it a machine. But Brooklyn has demonstrated that effective party organization need not be synonymous with smoke-filled rooms. Rather, it is a vital force in the American party system. . . . I have been a member of the Brooklyn Democratic organization the last forty years. I've always been proud of my membership, and my pride has increased. No one, no one need apologize for being part of this kind of party organization.

Our favorite insight into the mentality of a machine politician was given us inadvertently one night in September 1974. We ran into Brooklyn district leader and City Councilman Howard Golden one night during a Democratic primary for a congressional seat. We asked the recklessly extroverted Golden why he and his political club were working so hard to re-elect Bertram Podell, when Podell was under indictment for bribery.

"We're for Bert only because we have inside information that he's guilty and will be convicted," Golden explained in a confidential whisper.

We confessed we did not follow his reasoning.

"Schmuck," the councilman said. "If we help Podell win the primary and *then* he is convicted, that way we get to pick his replacement, and stop that kid Steve Solarz. We want to save this seat in Congress for our guy, Leonard Silverman."

Now Leonard Silverman, chairman of the state Assembly's Insurance Committee, happens to be even more mindless than is normal for Brooklyn hacks. He was briefly notorious in June 1976 when he sponsored a bill to raise the annual salaries for members of the legislature to $44,600, and to allow both parties' legislative leaders to collect $65,600 for their six months' work a year. The *Daily News* observed, "On the basis of performance, Silverman and colleagues should be down on their knees begging the public's forgiveness, instead of brazenly attempting to gouge the taxpayers further."

But the logic of I'm-for-him-because-I-know-he-is-corrupt remains the terminal absurdity of the clubhouse ethos. Howard Golden, philosopher of the Brooklyn Democracy, has since risen to become Brooklyn borough president. He has the potential of becoming an unconscious Plunkett.

In his definitive early history of Tammany, M. R. Werner quoted from an article that appeared in the *North American Review* of October 1866: "We have undertaken to write something about the government of the City of New York, and yet we have fallen into a discourse on stealing. The reason is, that, after having spent several weeks investigating our subject, we find we have been employed in nothing else but discovering in how many ways, and under what a variety of names and pretexts, immature and greedy men steal from that fruitful and ill-fenced orchard, the city treasury."

By the time of his death in 1878, William Marcy (Boss) Tweed, the leader of Tammany, had stolen at least $30 million from the ill-fenced orchard. The Tweed courthouse still stands just north of City Hall, at 52 Chambers Street, as a gray monument to Tweed's imagination. The courthouse, which was originally supposed to cost $250,000, ended up costing the taxpayers $13 million. A bill for three tables and forty chairs was $179,729, and Andrew Garvey, the "prince of plasterers," billed the city for "repairs" before the courthouse was completed. Tweed named the prizefighter Jim "Maneater" Cusick the court clerk, upon his release from Sing Sing Prison, and made Pudding Long, who could neither read nor write, the courthouse interpreter. In a final act of creative generosity, he placed three dead men on the courthouse payroll.

Since Tweed's day, political bosses all over the country have occasionally been portrayed as charming rogues, colorful Robin Hoods, who distribute turkey baskets to the immigrant poor at Christmastime. A mixture of nostalgia, amnesia, and romanticism has begun to sugarcoat the reputations of Hague of Jersey City, Pendergast of Kansas City, Curley of Boston, and Jimmy Walker of New York. Daniel Patrick Moynihan and others have rationalized that at least the clubhouse Democrats represented the working class, while reformers have represented the middle class. And, starting about a decade ago, a new conventional wisdom began to emerge among sociologists, journalists, and "urbanists," that the era of big-city political machines was over—except for Mayor Daley's in Chicago—and that television had changed everything, that the tube had replaced the old precinct captain in the voter's trust and loyalty.

It is our contention that the romanticization of the party boss is naive, that the theory of the vanishing machine is not supported by the evidence, and that the premise of the theory is based on an out-dated stereotype of the party boss and an overly narrow definition of the clubhouse system.

Some observers introduce as evidence of the machine's demise in New York City the defeat of organization-backed candidates for the Democratic Senate nominations in 1974 and 1976. And it is true that both Lee Alexander in 1974 and Paul O'Dwyer in 1976 lost state-wide primaries. But the Democratic machine in New York doesn't care that much about a Senate primary: Senators don't control leases on contracts; no patronage, no favors for clubhouse hangers-on are at stake. What the machine does care about is who is mayor and who are surrogate judges. And the machine continues to win primaries to nominate men for those positions, because that is where it invests its money and manpower.

As for the party structure, resilient as ever, it has adapted to modern times and become more modern itself, more subtle and, at its highest levels, more like a corporation than a gang of pirates. This is true all over America. Except for Daley in Chicago and Frank Rizzo in Philadelphia, there are few stereotypical boss personalities in the tradition of Tweed, Hague, or Curley. The more successful backroom type, as we find it in New York City, is the publicity-shy, affable private manipulator with a couple of corporate directorships—like Bill Shea, or Harold Fisher, or Eugene Keogh. In fact, the Democratic machine should be viewed as a corporate enterprise that is run to produce a steady profit for its Class A shareholders. Some of its well-publicized leaders, like Meade Esposito or Matthew Troy, may cultivate an earthy image of *macho* populism, but it is only an assumed persona. The clubhouse system is, today, what it was more than seventy years ago when Lincoln Steffens described it as "government of the people, by the rascals, for the rich." The only difference is that it is now much more sophisticated.

The New York Democratic machine, which was thought moribund when Lindsay was re-elected in 1969, now controls the whole machinery of the city government through Abe Beame, from pothole inspectors on up. It controls the courthouses in Brooklyn, Queens, the Bronx, and Staten Island, with more than 200 judgeships and several thousand courthouse patronage jobs. In the Bronx alone, six party district leaders have jobs as clerks on judicial budget lines.

The machine controls the patronage-rich Surrogates Court in every county except Manhattan. Each year the Surrogates award at their discretion millions of dollars in legal fees and guardianships for probate estates to lawyers from the clubhouses. In Brooklyn, judges we have interviewed have even seen a typed list of approved lawyers that the party headquarters delivers to the Surrogate. In addition, the Surrogates give out thousands of dollars in agate-type legal advertising to small, community newspapers—that is, to those weeklies that are willing to puff the clubhouse pols and ignore the local reformers.

Through Assembly Speaker Steingut, the machine controls $6 million's worth of jobs in the state Assembly—plus about $1 million in "lulus" (cash in lieu of unitemized expenses) for those lawmakers who vote the way they are instructed. The machine also controls the City Council payroll through majority leader Tom Cuite and the public administrator's offices in four boroughs.

And through Ramon Velez and Sam Wright, both district leaders and both city councilmen, the machine controls the multimillion antipoverty empires in Brownsville and the South Bronx.

Despite the fiscal crisis, despite the criminal indictments of Patrick Cunningham, Matthew Troy, Alan Hochberg, Robert Groh, seven judges, and three city councilmen, the clubhouse system is still strong because it is based on an infrastructure of institutions. Personalities are transient, but institutions are permanent. The machine's power rests upon the county organizations: banks; law firms; insurance companies; unions and union pension funds (especially Local 1814 of the ILA, run by Anthony Scotto). Its power rests upon antipoverty corporations; community newspapers subsidized by the Surrogates Court; and the agencies of government itself. These institutions are unaffected, even when a strong personality like Troy goes to prison. The only consequence is that the power and the profits shift to a different law firm, a different insurance company.

The Democratic clubhouse system, in this one-party city, bears its share of the historic responsibility for the city's fall. It is not as responsible as the great banks, or Nelson Rockefeller, or the managers of the national economy, or the anonymous, shadow government of public authorities—but it is responsible enough.

The clubhouse system made Abraham Beame the mayor of New York. It is responsible for rotten judges on the bench. Through its subservience to the real-estate developers and savings banks it has played a negative role in the decay of neighborhoods all over the city.* It has done favors for corrupt businessmen like Bernard Bergman and Eugene Hollander—at the taxpayers' expense. It has used the phrase "merit system" as a racial codeword to win votes, and then ignored merit and filled the city government with unqualified club members, in jobs that pay a lot for very little work. And it has put up for public office serfs who are not free to vote the way they think.

There was a great moment in the City Council ten years ago, when Dominick Corso of Brooklyn got so frustrated in a debate with a reformer that he blurted out an existential truth: "You think it takes guts to stand up for what is right?" he asked. "That doesn't take guts. What takes guts is to stand up for what you know is wrong, day after day, year after year. That takes guts!" Despite this confession, Corso went on to his reward for services rendered, and is now a Civil Court judge in Brooklyn.

The party apparatus not only fills the legislature and City Council with rubberstamps and future felons but aggressively tries to purge lawmakers, no matter how able, who exhibit independent judgment. For example, in September 1976, four hard-working, community-oriented members of the state legislature were punished with primary fights by the regular organization: Frank Barbero, Major Owens, and Joe Ferris in Brooklyn, and Vincent Marchiselli in the northeast Bronx, whose challenger was a realtor. All four incumbents, however, won their primaries.

The various forms of legal graft we have discussed, which have cost the taxpayers so many millions of dollars, are dependent upon the complicity of the clubhouse system. Stanley Steingut and Anthony Scotto put in a good word for Christopher Boomis to get his no-bid contract and tax abatement. Pat Cunningham and all the Bronx councilmen pushed for the public funds to renovate Yankee Stadium. Steingut did many favors for convicted nursing-home czar Bernard Bergman, including arranging a private meeting with Mayor Beame, and intervening in Bergman's behalf with state health offi-

* For the full account of what happened to Columbia Street, for example, read Denis Hamill, "Nobody Gets Indicted for Killing a Neighborhood," in the *Village Voice*, September 20, 1976. Hamill explains how politicians like Abe Stark and Tom Cuite were instrumental in the decline of a once-thriving shopping area in South Brooklyn.

cials, and in return he received campaign donations and insurance premiums. The beneficiaries of the padded, no-bid, twenty-year day-care leases included clubhouse politicians like Sam Wright, Leonard Simon, clients of Shea's law firm, and friends of Donald Manes. Cunningham was in the middle of the Bronx Terminal Market rip-off, as the high-priced lawyer for the landlord. Bunny Lindenbaum's clients got the highest proportion of reduced real estate tax assessments from the City Tax Commission. Democratic Party lawyers like Joseph Slavin (now a judge), Kevin McGrath of Bill Shea's firm, and Mario Biaggi were the ones chosen to be closing attorneys on mortgages from the city employee pension fund.

Because they are Democrats, and because they need the votes of New Yorkers, the clubhouse politicians say the words of economic liberalism, when they are required to speak on issues. But in practice —and this is perhaps the key to seeing the machine for what it really is—in practice the clubhouse Democrats usually vote in the interest of the banks and property owners. In his wonderful book *Boss*, about Richard Daley's Chicago, Mike Royko made this same point again and again: the Chicago Democratic machine fronts for, and favors, the real-estate developers, insurance companies, construction unions, banks, and city contractors, rather than the neighborhoods and families who vote for the Chicago Democratic machine.

And in *The Power Broker*, Robert Caro explains how clubhouse politicians supported all of the public works of Robert Moses, including his costly blunders, like slum clearance and the World's Fair. Moses used his control over bonds, legal fees, public-relations retainers, and, especially, insurance premiums, to purchase their support. And he had it. Despite the destruction of wonderful neighborhoods, and the waste of millions of dollars, the pols went along with him. One of the reasons, Caro shows, was that three of the five Democratic county leaders had insurance companies that derived profits from the patronage of Moses's Triborough Authority.

A recent example of collusion between the clubhouses and special interests occurred in June 1970, when New York's City Council voted on a complicated piece of legislation that permitted landlords to charge higher rents to about one million families. This first revision of the rent-control law, then twenty-seven years old, raised rents for some families by 15 per cent, and for others by 8 per cent. The bill also included a provision for the computerized calculation of rents, which proved to be an administrative nightmare and failure. At the last minute an amendment that would have protected low-income families from rent increases was deleted from the draft bill; it contained no protection for tenants against harassment by landlords, no machinery to compel landlords to provide heat and hot water, to repair violations of the housing code, or to pay their unpaid real-estate taxes before being allowed to increase rents. The bill had nothing for tenants.

The rent bill needed twenty-five votes to pass in the Council. After a nasty marathon meeting that adjourned at 3:30 A.M. the final version of the bill was approved 27–10. The three Republicans on the Council voted for the bill, which was no surprise, and two Liberal Party members as well, which was. And the remaining twenty-two votes were provided by clubhouse Democrats.

The rent-increase legislation had been sponsored by the Queens clubhouse Councilman Donald Manes (who has since risen to become, simultaneously, Queens county leader and borough president). Reform Democrats, led by Theodore Weiss, tried and failed three times to liberalize the bill through amendments.

Voting consistently against the interest of tenants were the two clubhouse councilmen from Staten Island, Edward Curry and Robert Lindsay; the last unreconstructed Tammany Democrat from Manhattan, Saul Sharison, who represented the rapidly decaying Lower East Side; and the late David Friedland, of Washington Heights, another regular. Every clubhouse Democrat from Cunningham's disciplined Bronx machine, voted with the landlords: Michael DeMarco, Aileen Ryan, Mario Merola, Bertram Gelfand, Muriel Stromberg, and Barry Salman. So did every clubhouse councilman from Queens: Manes, Matthew Troy, Edward Sadowsky, Mike Lazar, Tom Manton, and Walter Ward. Queens's one reform Democrat, Arthur Katzman, voted against it. Similarly, six of the seven regulars from Esposito's Brooklyn organization stood with the real-estate industry: Majority Leader Tom Cuite (who is a licensed real-estate broker); Rudy DiBlasi; Monroe Cohen; Leonard Scholnick; Ted Silverman; and Willie Thompson (who owned buildings in Bedford Stuyvesant, and is now a judge, as are DiBlasi and Scholnick).

Five years later, in the spring of 1975, the City Council debated another rent bill, this one allowing landlords to raise rents by $2 per room per month for 900,000 tenants living in rent-controlled apartments, to cover the rising costs of fuel. According to the bill, landlords would be allowed to do this without an audit of their financial records by any city agency to determine the actual margins of profit on their buildings. There was no allowance for the effect of escalating inflation upon tenants. And again no remedy for harassment or tax arrears by property owners.

On April 28, the Council's General Welfare Committee convened to vote on what was known as the fuel pass-along bill. Majority Leader Cuite had worked out a subtle deal to have the committee approve the bill by getting its one Republican, Jack Muratori, to support it—so long as his was the seventh vote, and not the decisive *sixth* vote, so that responsibility would appear to rest with the Democrats.

But there was a surprise. Freshman Councilman Luis Olmedo from the Williamsburg-Bushwick area of Brooklyn voted no, the roll call was tied 4–4, and Harlem Councilman Fred Samuel was explaining why he too would vote against the rent increase. As Samuel was speaking Cuite's aides began whispering to Councilman Ted Silverman, and Silverman jumped up to make a sudden motion to lay the matter aside—a quick maneuver to save the bill from formal defeat—and the lay-over motion passed, 6 to 3, with two abstentions. (In 1974, Silverman had voted against an equal rights bill for homosexuals, two weeks after he had voted *for* the same bill in committee.)

The next day the agenda called for the full Council to convene at 1:30 P.M. But for six hours the councilmen milled around City Hall corridors while Cuite, Mayor Beame (in Albany that day, and working by remote control), and the Democratic county leaders tried to line up six votes on the committee and twenty-nine votes in the full Council to pass the bill. One by one reluctant councilmen were escorted into Cuite's office for "private talks." Three wavering members received personal phone calls from the mayor. Esposito called Councilmen Robert Steingut and Sam Horwitz and asked them to vote for the rent bill. Then he called young Luis Olmedo and told him that if he voted no, he would face an expensive primary for renomination, and if he voted yes, funds could be found in the budget for a senior citizens center in his district, which Olmedo had been trying to get for a year. Donald Manes phoned Councilman Eugene Mastropieri, who had voted against the bill in committee. But the numbers did not add up, and at 7:30, the full Council meeting finally began, with the rent hike off the agenda.

On Friday, May 9, the bill that Beame and the landlords wanted was finally passed by the General Welfare Committee 8–3. Remember, Beame had gotten more than $600,000 in contributions from landlords in 1973. Mastropieri voted yes, after voting no two weeks before. Samuel from Harlem voted yes, even though he had been in the midst of explaining his no vote two weeks before. (As a reward, he became the one Manhattan councilman invited to private budget meetings with the mayor.) The other clubhouse Democrats who voted for the rent increase were Aileen Ryan, Ted Silverman, Robert Steingut, Anthony Geata, Stephen Kaufman, and the Republican, Muratori. The pro-tenant votes were cast by Olmedo, Tom Manton, and, as ever, Ted Weiss.

A half hour later, Cuite had the full Council considering the bill. About seventy-five tenants, from the Metropolitan Council on Housing, were in the balcony, cheering and booing, when the roll call began. Mastropieri of Queens voted yes, and the balcony chanted "Shame, shame, shame." They began the chant again when Robert Steingut of Brooklyn voted yes. In explaining his yes vote, Ted Silverman said, "It may not be right, but at least we're trying to do something." The tenants cheered as the usual Manhattan heroes of the Council voted no: Weiss, Greitzer, Wagner Jr., Stern, Burden, Friedlander. And cheered again when Katzman and Manton of Queens voted no. Olmedo said, "When oil was cheap, landlords did not give heat to my people in Williamsburg and Bushwick." He voted no.

But the $2 per-room per-month rent increase passed, 30 to 13. Five months later, Councilman Howard Golden from Brooklyn, who had voted in favor of it, announced that he was preparing legislation to repeal the new law. He said that landlords were cheating on the law by submitting fraudulent claims. But Golden's repeal bill never got out of committee.

There are other examples of clubhouse Democrats siding with special economic interests and against the larger public interest.

• For two years Manhattan Councilman Carter Burden has been trying to pass a bill that would abolish private, profit-making methadone-maintenance clinics, and strictly regulate the non-profit ones. The owners of the profit-making clinics make windfall medicaid profits—Dr. Allen Hausknect, in testimony before Burden's City Council health committee, admitted making $100,000 in one year, in one clinic. A city health department report disclosed "serious violations" at many of the clinics—charging for services never performed, inadequate medical attention, excessive dosages of methadone, and a lack of job or psychiatric counseling for the addicts, or any serious rehabilitative services.

When he was running for mayor, Abe Beame held a press conference outside a notorious methadone clinic—the Ithaca, on East 84th Street—and promised strict regulation of such clinics after he was elected. But Burden's bill has never gotten out of the Council's health committee, for Beame and Majority Leader Cuite are against it. And very quietly, so are some of the city's giant private hospitals, like Beth Israel, which controls thirty-eight methadone-maintenance clinics, and is not eager to see stricter regulation.

• On June 26, 1976, the state Senate passed a bill that mandated an audit and review by the EFCB of all 171 day-care center leases. By then almost everyone had agreed that they were scandalous. The idea behind the bill was to allow the EFCB to renegotiate, or cancel, any lease that was exorbitant, and Franz Leichter, who had co-sponsored it, predicted it would "save the city $10 million a year." But three days later, the bill, opposed only by the handful of day-care landlords and lawyers, was killed in the Assembly by Speaker Stanley Steingut. State Senator Major Owens, another co-sponsor, told us, "Our bill wasn't supposed to pass the Senate. When it did, Beame called Senator Conkin at 2 A.M. to complain about it. Then he phoned Steingut, and Steingut ordered the bill killed in committee on the last day of the session. It was a typical example of how the system works in Albany."

• For years the Citizens Union, the Legal Aid Society, and the Bar Association have been trying to abolish the system of using city marshals. The marshals are technically part of the city's Civil Court, although they are appointed by the mayor, on the recommendation of political party leaders, for six-year terms. There are no qualifications for the job, and no civil service test is required. They are under no day-to-day scrutiny by any judicial, executive, or legislative authority. The marshals are private entrepreneurs working with the authority—gun and badge—of government. Marshals execute evictions for landlords. They garnishee salaries and welfare checks for creditors. They collect judgments for banks, loan companies, credit companies. They repossess merchandise for department stores. They pull out gas and electric meters for utilities. They are the scavengers of the system. A Citizens Union pamphlet on the marshal system is called "A Puddle of Patronage."

Now the interesting thing is that the marshals receive no salary, but take 5 per cent off the top of all judgments they collect. Last year 14 of New York's 73 marshals grossed more than $100,000. They make such large incomes by refusing to collect the small claims of individual citizens and by working only for large institutions like Household Finance, Brooklyn Union Gas, landlords like Goldman and DiLorenzo, and stores like Korvette's. In theory, they are supposed impartially to execute the mandate of the Civil Court, including the Small Claims Court. But in September 1976, the Public Interest Research Group's three-year analysis of the Small Claims Court showed that more than 40 per cent of the individual claimants who actually won judgments were unable to collect their money because the city marshals would not exert themselves on their behalf against the landlords, or TV repair shops, or department stores.

A Legal Services lawyer told us this story of how the marshals can affect the lives of powerless people: The lawyer's client—a Puerto Rican dishwasher—owed a department store $200. The dishwasher offered to pay installments of $10 a week. The marshal illegally demanded a $75 down payment before accepting the installment arrangement. The dishwasher had to borrow $75 from a loan company to satisfy the marshal. Two weeks later, the dishwasher's child fell out of a tenement window. There was a doctor's bill. So he borrowed another $300 from the loan company. The marshal, suspecting he would not get paid, then went directly to the dishwasher's employer to garnishee his small salary. The employer, not wanting any trouble or extra paperwork, fired the dishwasher.

In 1975, an all-out effort to abolish the marshals was made in the state legislature, organized by Stephen Shestakofsky, the legislative representative of the Citizens Union. City Investigations Commissioner Nicholas Scoppetta wrote a strong letter to several legislators supporting the bill to outlaw marshals and replace them with salaried, less political people. The *New York Post* published an editorial urging abolition. And the abolition bill, sponsored by Republican Roy Goodman, passed the state Senate on May 7, 46 to 10.

Then it came under the jurisdiction of Stanley Steingut, the Democratic Speaker of the Assembly. In the past, bills relating to marshals had been assigned to the Judiciary Committee, but Steingut did not fully trust the membership of that committee—too many free-thinkers—so he ignored tradition and sent the bill to the Committee on Cities, chaired by Anthony DiFalco, a loyal clubhouse man and the son of the powerful Surrogate Judge Samuel DiFalco. (Josh Friedman of the *New York Post*, the only Albany reporter who paid any notice to this legislation, wrote a story pointing out a certain conflict of interest: Two district leaders in DiFalco's Lower

East Side Assembly district happened to be city marshals themselves. The honorable DiFalco quickly called Friedman to say there were actually *three* Democratic district leaders in his area who were marshals.) In committee, a Steingut acolyte from Brooklyn, Assemblyman Howard Lasher, helped DiFalco defend the marshals, and the Committee on Cities voted not to let the bill come to the floor for a vote, a necessary strategy, since no assemblyman would have wanted to get caught in public having to choose between good government and Stanley Steingut.

And there are the two cases we described in detail in chapter 4, where we told how Speaker Steingut, Assemblyman Cincotta, and other clubhouse Democrats refused to support a mortgage pool to end redlining by savings banks. Until there was intense lobbying from the savings banks, Steingut had been telling urban liberals and members of the Black Caucus that he favored the mortgage-pool concept; then he told them he had made a deal with the Republicans. And we told the story of how Arlen Realty and the Museum of Modern Art got a tax-exemption deal to build a $40-million luxury high-rise condominium, how on June 28, 1976, the deal was voted down in the Assembly, 72 to 53, how then the party bosses like Manes, Cunningham, and Esposito, along with other power brokers like William Paley and various Rockefeller viceroys, got on the phone to the legislators, and how thirty-three assemblymen changed their minds. As with the fuel pass-along rent increase, the politicians knew what was right on the merits, but they could not stand up to pressure; they believed they owed their elective offices not to the people, but to the political machine.

One reason for all this economic illiberalism might just be that so many elders of the clubhouse system have vested banking and real-estate interests that are a source of personal income.

Council Majority Leader Tom Cuite, a registered real-estate broker, is also vice-president of the Brooklyn Federal Savings and Loan Association. Alfred Lama, the former Brooklyn Assemblyman and still a quiet power, is a director of the Central State Bank, and a partner in Lama & Vassalotti, an architectural firm that does a lot of business on state-funded housing developments.

Counterfeit common man Meade Esposito is in the banking and insurance business. He owns a large interest in Grand Brokerage, is a director of a mortgage company called Mortgage Affiliates, and was a vice-president of the Kings Lafayette Bank—until former federal prosecutor Robert Morgenthau accused him of arranging an unsecured $225,000 loan for a company Anthony Scotto had an interest in, right after Scotto moved his union's pension fund account into Esposito's bank. Esposito was also on the payroll of the American Bank and Trust Company before it collapsed in September 1976.

Stanley Steingut is a director of the City Title Insurance Company, and of Modular Cities, which owns a tract of land on Staten Island.

Eugene Keogh, important power broker, was a congressman from Brooklyn for twenty years. He is a director of the East River Savings Bank; a director with Meade Esposito of Mortgage Affiliates; a partner in the stock brokerage firm of Hardy & Company; and a director of City Title Insurance with Steingut.

James Mangano, Brooklyn district leader for thirty-four years, was chief clerk of Brooklyn Supreme Court, where he controlled about 500 patronage jobs, until his retirement in 1976. Mangano is still a director of the Atlantic Liberty Savings & Loan Association. The chairman of the bank is George Clark, Sr., the father of the Republican county leader of Brooklyn.

Bill Shea, the clubhouse fund raiser and thinker, is a trustee of the Metropolitan Savings Bank; his law firm represents hundreds of clients ranging from the Catholic Archdiocese to landlord Harry Helmsley, to several banks, to Yonkers Raceway and Madison Square Garden, where Shea's partner Milton Gould is on the board of directors. Shea is also a director of four corporations. He is counsel to, and a director of, the Colonial Sand & Stone; chairman of the General Battery Corporation, which pays him $82,000 a year, plus expenses; a director of the Fidelity (insurance) Corporation and of Diamond International (with annual sales of $610 million). Shea is also a registered lobbyist for the American Stock Exchange and the Securities Industry Association. Lawyer Harold Fisher also has banking and insurance directorships. He is the chairman of the Dime Savings Bank of Williamsburgh. And he is a director of the American Plan Corporation, the holding company for American Fidelity Fire Insurance, and American Consumer Insurance.

Our focus on Democrats should not suggest that the Republicans are disinterested full-time servants of the public good. We are focusing this chapter on Democrats because they hold elected power in New York City. But clubhouse Republican politicians have a similar personal interest in real estate and banking. Vincent Albano, the Republican county leader in Manhattan, is chairman of the Century National Bank and receives an average of $25,000 a year in "consulting fees" from the National Kinney Corporation. George Clark, the Republican county leader in Brooklyn, is the vice-president of

George L. Clark Realtors, Inc. State Senator John Marchi, the Republican Party candidate for mayor in 1969 and 1973, is not only a lawyer but also a licensed real-estate broker. State Senator William Conklin is a director of the Bay Ridge Savings and Loan Association.

The selection of judges and court personnel in New York is, as it is in most cities, under the control of the clubhouse system. And of all the failing, unworkable institutions in New York City, there is none closer to total breakdown than the courts.

The Kerner Commission told us exactly what was wrong with America's cities. The McKay Commission did an excellent job documenting what went wrong at Attica. The Knapp Commission told us all we needed to know about police corruption. So we have a shelf full of documents that prove the New York City court system is a failure. The social cost of politicized, slothful, mediocre, and possibly venal judiciary can be substantial. It can undercut respect for the rule of law. It can lead to favoritism and unequal justice in cases involving landlords, insurance companies, and others with political influence. It can demoralize the legal profession. And it can contribute to the city-killing tide of street crime, by giving lenient treatment to narcotics dealers and mobsters in the junk trade.

In October 1972, the New York State Legislative Committee on Crime published an analysis of 1762 dispositions of organized crime cases in state courts in New York City between 1960 and 1969. The report observed that 44.7 per cent of all the indictments against Mafiosi were dismissed by state judges, while only 11.5 per cent of the indictments against all other defendants were dismissed.

During 1971 and 1972, one Brooklyn Supreme Court justice alone—Joseph Corso—dismissed criminal indictments against five different Mafia defendants, and all five indictments were later *unanimously* reinstated by the Appellate Division. Perhaps it is pertinent to add that before reaching the State Supreme Court bench, Joseph Corso had been chairman of the Assembly Ethics Committee.

In June 1973, the Economic Development Council released a study of productivity among judges. The study disclosed that Supreme Court justices handling criminal cases in Manhattan were on the bench an average of 3 hours and 21 minutes a day. And, the *Daily News* reported about a secret Bar Association document that accused five State Supreme Court justices of misconduct ranging from "improper" relations with lawyers, to laziness, to "screaming at lawyers and witnesses from the bench," to the imposition of "unduly harsh sentences." At the same time the State Investigation Commission concluded that the judiciary of New York City had "failed to fulfill its obligation to properly discipline judges. . . . The present practice of allowing the judiciary to police itself has not worked. In certain cases where serious allegations were made involving corruption, ulterior motives for decisions, and the failure to accord litigants basic rights, the responsible persons in the judicial system either took little action . . . or, at best, investigated them in the most cursory and unprofessional manner."

Five months later, the State Select Committee on Crime released a study that documented how fifteen different Manhattan Supreme Court justices had granted sixty-seven illegal discharges in narcotics cases. An illegal sentence under the state's old penal law was a conditional or unconditional discharge to anyone convicted of a narcotics felony. The report pointed out that of the sixty-seven defendants who were freed illegally, "41 were re-arrested, some within weeks, for crimes which often increased in magnitude and violence." The committee attributed 20 of the illegal sentences to Justice Harry Frank, 16 to Justice Gerald Culkin, and eight to former Justice Mitchell Schweitzer, who was forced off the bench in 1971, accused of conspiracy and of having private business activities inconsistent with his duties as a judge.

The same legislative committee, a few months earlier, had discovered nineteen illegal felony discharges in Queens drug cases; of the nineteen, eight were granted by one judge, Albert Bosch.

But one need not depend on lawyerlike reports to know the court system does not work. Just sit for a week in a chaotic courtroom, where justice comes to look like a meatgrinder gone berserk.

You will see arraignment proceedings in which bails are set in forty-second conferences at the bench. You will see judges with unmistakable prejudices against blacks and Hispanics. Judges too stupid to follow subtle legal argument. Judges who coerce guilty pleas and civil settlements, who malinger and manipulate the calendars, who will do anything to escape the mental labor of conducting a jury trial. You will see judges who are rambling and incoherent from too many martinis at lunch. Judges who are abusive, insulting, and sarcastic.

You will see judges who open court at 11 A.M., break for lunch at 1 P.M., and reconvene court at 2:30 P.M. for 45 minutes, and then leave to catch the last two races at Belmont Racetrack. One Friday at 4:30 P.M., in the summer of 1975, we were present when a rape defendant jumped bail in Manhattan Supreme Court, and court attendants urgently needed a judge to sign a bench warrant. *One* jurist out of the twenty-five who were supposed to be working at the time was actually in the building—Justice Peter McQuillan. He signed the bench warrant.

You will see judges bend the law to favor the clients of clubhouse lawyers. You will see judges in the landlord-and-tenant parts go out to lunch with the landlord's lawyer.

To be fair, you will also see perhaps thirty superb judges*—out of about 350 members of the bench. These thirty judges have a strong sense of justice and integrity, are impartial, hard-working, wise in the law, and independent. And some of them do come out of political clubs. But the considered generalization stands: The overwhelming majority of judges are unqualified for the job. They were chosen because of their influence with a district leader, or a relative's cash donation to the political party, and not for the brilliance of their legal minds. In Brooklyn, Queens, or the Bronx, a defeated candidate for Assembly has a better chance for judicial nomination than a law school dean. Merit is an alien factor—an accidental bonus—in the selection of judges.

And beyond the daily, grinding absence of justice for the average defendant, the average crime victim, and the average lawyer, there is another consequence of clubhouse control over the courthouse: corruption. As we complete this book in the autumn of 1976, seven judges in New York City are under criminal indictment, and awaiting trial.

The method for selecting State Supreme Court justices in New York is cynical and manipulative. In 1932, the Association of the Bar said in a report recommending the merit appointment of justices of the State Supreme Court: "The elective system . . . has merely permitted the electorate to vote for candidates selected by leaders or bosses of the various political parties, with no control by the electorate over the choice of candidates so selected, with the result that the elective system usually has resulted in the dominant party in every locality merely ratifying by election the candidate of such party so selected."

Today the Democratic and Republican Party leaders will meet in

---

* Among the fine judges in New York are Milton Mollen, Peter McQuillan, Samuel Silverman, Ernst Rosenberger, Irwin Brownstein, James Leff, Leonard Sandler, Richard Brown, Mary Johnson Lowe, Mel Glass, Leon Polsky, and Israel Rubin.

private to choose judges in bi-partisan deals that make elections a farce. Judicial delegates, usually party functionaries or patronage jobholders, run in party primaries, and then vote as instructed in judicial nominating conventions. The public never has a chance to vote directly for a judicial candidate in a primary, and then in the general election it usually can only rubberstamp a candidate who already has the nomination of both parties.

Of the last 150 State Supreme Court justices "elected" in New York, 126 ran with such a pre-arranged endorsement of both major political parties. And ten of these bi-partisan brokered judges were found to be "unqualified" or "not approved" by the Association of the Bar, although the public, by then, could do nothing to prevent the knighting of these incompetents.

In 1968, the Bar Association found four judges with cross-party nominations to be unqualified: Isidore Dollinger, the Bronx district attorney; Criminal Court Judge Manuel Gomez; Bronx State Senator Ivan Warner; and Paul Fino, the Bronx Republican Party boss.

In 1971, Frederick Hammer, endorsed by all four political parties, was "not approved" by the Bar Association, "because of his lack of judicial temperament."

In 1972, the Bar Association rejected Leonard Scholnick and Edward Lentol for the State Supreme Court in Brooklyn. Scholnick was a city councilman, and Lentol a state senator.

In 1973, the Bar Association found "not qualified" two bi-partisan Supreme Court nominees in Queen county—Ann Dufficy and Joan Marie Durante. The Association said Mrs. Dufficy was rejected because of a "lack of experience and professional ability."

In 1975, the Bar Association disapproved Irwin Silbowitz, a two-party nominee for Bronx Supreme Court, because he "lacked qualifications." Silbowitz had been "not qualified" before—he ran successfully for the Civil Court in 1972 with the backing of the Cunningham machine.

Here are a few examples of how the bi-partisan backroom manipulation of the judiciary has worked. In 1970, there were six vacancies for Supreme Court in Brooklyn. Instead of having an election, Democratic boss Meade Esposito, a former bail bondsman, sat down with several Republican district leaders and made a deal for cross endorsements of five Democrats and one Republican. The Republican Party gave their line on the ballot to five Democrats: Frank Composto, John Monteleone, Abraham Kalina, Irving Kartell, and Charles Rubin, a party fund raiser. In exchange, the Democrats gave their line on the ballot to a Republican—Joseph Soviero.

On May 17, 1971, when Matthew Troy was the Democratic boss in Queens, and the late Sidney Hein was the Republican boss, the two men met in a diner on Queens Boulevard and, in Troy's words, "divided up the county for the next couple of years." An agreement was made on the division of spoils, to avoid elections. "The Package," as Troy called it, was actually written up, and Troy carried the folded copy in his wallet for several years. He showed it to us one night, and later he allowed Richard Reeves to quote most of it in the March 5, 1973, issue of *New York* magazine. The Troy-Hein pact read in part:

> Five new Supreme Court judgeships. Repubs to get three—Dems to get two (plus Dems to get replacement for Tony Livoti)—all on a bi-partisanship basis. . . . If legislators go to Civil Court vacancies, then the special election for legis. vacancy will have no Repub. opponent. . . . Repubs agree to give bi-partisan endorsement to Boro Pres . . . District Attorney and Surrogate. . . . Repubs and Dems will split (half-each) Counsel to Public Administrator replacement for Lou Laurino. . . . Repub to permit MJT [Troy himself] to appoint reapportionment head, once Repub seats are protected. . . . MJT to receive bi-partisan Councilman endorsement in 1973.

It all came to pass, and the registered voters of Queens County had no voice in any of it.

In 1973 Troy worked out another package with the Republicans to share eight Supreme Court judgeships with cross-party endorsements. Troy's Democrats endorsed two infamously inept Republicans—Harold Hyman, counsel to the county clerk; and Bar Association reject Joan Marie Durante, the daughter of the county clerk, John Durante. And the Republicans gave their line on the voting machine to six Democrats: Seymour Boyers, Kenneth Browne, Edwin Kasoff, Leonard Finz, George Balbach, and Bar Association reject Ann Dufficy.

The same year, the Democrats in the First Judicial Department (Manhattan and the Bronx) made a deal with the Republicans to carve up four Supreme Court judgeships. The Democrats endorsed one Republican, Irving Kirschenbaum, the former GOP party treasurer in Manhattan. And the Republicans endorsed three Democrats: Joseph Marro, a former state senator; Alexander Chananau, a Bronx assemblyman of no distinction; and Alfred Callahan, a Civil Court judge of poor reputation. Once again, the voters were given no choice.

And then in 1976, the patronage-rich fourteen-year job of Surrogate of Brooklyn came vacant and was up for election. So the Democratic party boss, Meade Esposito, and the Republican party boss, George Clark, both decided to support the same candidate, Bernard Bloom. It was a marriage made in hack heaven. Bloom was a Democratic party district leader in Flatbush, and for years had held a seldom-show, $27,000-a-year state job as director of servicemen's voting. Bloom, an outspoken defender of clubhouses and patronage who called reformers "garbage," wasn't much of a lawyer and had no judicial experience, but it didn't matter. He had the endorsement of both the Democratic and the Republican organizations. When a lawyer of our acquaintance asked Clark why he had given his party's endorsement to a Democrat, Clark explained that Bloom had promised the Republicans 20 per cent of the patronage. We can't elect a Republican in Kings County, so why not take him? The reformers will give us zero patronage, and Bloom has promised us a regular slice.

Bloom, opposed by every good-government group, had a Democratic primary challenge from a respected attorney, Daniel Eisenberg. So to divide the "reform-Jewish vote" Esposito contrived the entry of a lower court judge, Abraham Schulman, into the race, and Schulman siphoned off enough votes to allow Bloom to win, and to go on to win the general election with dual party endorsement. This machine trick of covertly helping spoiler candidates is a tactic that the resourceful Esposito has used before. In 1973, he encouraged one Ruth Lerner to enter the race for Brooklyn borough president. The lady took enough "reform-Jewish votes" away from Stephen Solarz so that the clubhouse-backed Sebastian Leone won. She was then compensated with a $31,758-a-year job in the Beame administration.

The South Bronx and Brownsville are the two most deprived, squalid neighborhoods in New York. Since the mid-1960s, billions of dollars of city, state, and especially federal funds have been shoveled into these two slums under the auspices of worthy programs.

Critics, some called neo-conservatives, now argue that the social programs of Lyndon Johnson's Great Society and the War on Poverty were failures because "money was thrown at problems" and nothing changed for the better. In the South Bronx and in Brownsville money was not thrown at problems. Money was thrown at politicians. The ordinary people on Fox Street and Sutter Avenue never, never benefited from federal demonstration grants, model-cities funds, community corporations, manpower programs. The South Bronx is worse off today than ever. Brownsville is worse off today than ever. Unemployment is worse. Crime is worse. Housing is worse. Education is worse.

In the South Bronx and Brownsville, the rulers of the clubhouse system formed alliances with local plantation barons. The white political establishment—Cunningham in the Bronx, Esposito in Brooklyn—settled on Ramon Velez in the South Bronx and Samuel Wright in Brownsville and said, in effect: You are our boys. You run the slums. We'll help keep you in power. You can distribute all the antipoverty money, but you must support our candidates and deliver the plantations' votes to us.

Velez and Wright are both Democratic Party district leaders. In judicial nominating conventions they support the white machine's candidates for judgeships. They are both members of the City Council, and there they both vote the way the party leadership wants them to vote, even when it is not in the best interest of their own constituents. (For example, in May 1975, both men voted in favor of the fuel pass-along rent increase, a bill that hurt slum-dwellers more than anyone else, and gave them no housing improvement for their higher payments to landlords.) In return, the clubhouse system reciprocates. The machine protects their anti-poverty empires, especially in the courts. The machine lets them control the Community Development Agency, the municipal agency that is supposed to administer and monitor antipoverty funds in New York City.

The commissioner of CDA is Manny Parron, who got his job through Velez and is his close friend. The deputy commissioner is Robert Couze, a member of Wright's political club and the chairman of a fund-raising dinner held for Wright in the summer of 1976. Both Velez and Wright gained control of the antipoverty corporations in their districts in 1967 and 1968. In neither district has there been a community poverty election since 1970, although the law requires one at least every five years. The interface of the machine and the plantation somehow ensured that Velez and Wright stayed in power without risking the consent of the governed.

At various points, civil service professionals in the CDA have tried to stop the money going to programs controlled by Velez and

Wright, because of irregularities. But each time they were overruled by administrators who got their jobs through Velez or Wright.

Ramon Velez is forty-three years old, short, fat, loud, violent. He travels behind a wall of goons who have guns. Seeing him with his entourage on Jackson Avenue, the main slum thoroughfare in the South Bronx brings to mind Batista of Cuba, or Trujillo of the Dominican Republic—a gangster grown into a dictator. Being district leader and city councilman gives Velez his legitimacy, but not his power. His power comes from the twenty different antipoverty, community, and ethnic groups that he runs or controls through subordinates who are in his employ in some other agency. Velez is president of the Hunts Point Multi-Services Corporation and the Hunts Point Community Corporation; vice-president of the policy committee of the South Bronx Model Cities Program; chairman of the community board of the Ruiz Belvis Medical Center in the South Bronx; chairman of the board of the city-wide Puerto Rican Community Development Project and the city-wide Puerto Rican Day Parade Committee; chairman of the community advisory board of Lincoln Hospital. Altogether, he controls about $60 million a year of the taxpayers' money and about 1500 jobs in these various government-funded agencies.

There is almost no racket or rip-off that Velez has not attempted with taxpayers' money. In 1970, the Puerto Rican Community Development Project took out—but did not pay—$240,000 in withholding taxes. The Puerto Rican Day Parade Committee was given hundreds of thousands of dollars to distribute free summer lunches to poor children; when they were caught dumping the lunches, the State Education Department canceled the contract. Employees of agencies that Velez controls have testified that they have been cocerced into buying tickets to his political dinners under threat of losing their jobs. More than half of the contributions to his 1976 campaign for Congress came from employees of antipoverty agencies he controls. The unsalaried treasurer of the Puerto Rican Day Parade Committee, Roberto Napoleon, has accused him of misappropriating about $100,000 from the committee.

In 1970, the U.S. Department of Health Education and Welfare issued a 100-page audit of the Hunts Point Multi-Service Corporation. The feds found more than $1 million missing or unaccounted for, apparent double billing, $21,000 paid out for unsubstantiated consulting services. They also found that games had been played with the payroll taxes. Soon thereafter, HEW cut off all funding to the corporation, but no one was prosecuted. Accountants from several other agencies have been mystified by the absence of records and ledgers for Hunts Point and suspect there have been hundreds of ghosts, or fake employees, carried on the payroll over the years.

As for the Hunts Point Community Corporation, Velez installed a close associate, Robert Munoz, as its executive director, and on December 5, 1975, Munoz was convicted of conspiracy to use explosives and conspiracy to extort. What Munoz was doing was telling contractors that he would burn down, or blow up, their construction sites unless he was given control over hundreds of no-show jobs on the contractors' payrolls. He was running a basic arson-and-extortion racket on the very people who were trying to build up and create jobs in the South Bronx.

On February 27, 1976, Munoz was given a remarkably lenient suspended eighteen-month sentence from Federal Judge Constance Baker Motley, and today he remains on the public payroll as executive director of another antipoverty agency controlled by Ramon Velez.

The facts about Velez—precise, comprehensible, accurate facts— began to emerge during the summer of 1976. These facts did not come from the Bronx district attorney, or the city's Board of Ethics, or the City Council. They came from a street-smart thirty-five-year-old television reporter named Steve Bauman, who earlier had helped to expose other scandals and frauds in New York City. Bauman was working for WNEW-TV's low-budget news department, which had only three camera crews and eight reporters. In a series of nightly reports, some with dramatic and inventive film, Bauman did the government's work. Bauman showed pictures of people who were paid with public funds to work for antipoverty groups actually doing political work for Velez at the Bronx Board of Elections, trying to disqualify the nominating petitions of Herman Badillo, whom Velez challenged for Congress in 1976. He interviewed Roberto Napoleon, the treasurer of the Parade Committee, who showed him unexplained checks and unreconciled accounts controlled by Velez. (Napoleon's records also showed that the Parade Committee had made out a check for $25,000 to the city's Department of Parks as a deposit against damages for the use of Randall's Island Stadium and grounds for some event they sponsored. The Parks Commissioner at the time, Ed Weisl, told Bauman that since there had been $10,000 in damages, he had wanted to deduct that amount from the $25,000 but that he had been "ordered" by then Deputy

Mayor James Cavanagh to send the full $25,000 back to Velez because Mayor Beame "wants it that way."*)

The most dramatic film Bauman shot concerned the summer lunch programs. Velez was getting $312,000 from the State Education Department to feed malnourished children, but Bauman's film crews caught the lunches being dumped in vacant lots. Then they went to the places that were being paid to provide this squandered food. Some of the locations turned out to be nonexistent. One address, which had received $13,000, was a closed auto-parts store. Another location, where both breakfasts and suppers were supposed to be served, had served neither for a month.

Velez's response to all this was consistent: He accused Bauman of taking a $50,000 bribe from his political opponent, Herman Badillo, to say all these malicious things about the great Ramon Velez, "who feeds poor people." And Bauman also had his life threatened. An ominous telephone-caller said he was from a Puerto Rican left-wing terrorist group, but Bauman thought it more likely he was someone associated with Velez trying to scare him.

Samuel D. Wright is less extroverted than Ramon Velez. He tries to avoid publicity, speaks infrequently and inarticulately at the City Council, and is more effective operating in private than working the streets. But his path to power was similar, and so was the way he spent the public's money.

Sam Wright's pyramid of power began with school board 23 in Brownsville. He was chairman of the board for three years, and now controls it through loyal subordinates. School board 23 has an annual budget of $25 million. Wright also controls the Brownsville Community Development Corporation, with an annual budget of $2.5 million; the Oceanhill Community Council; the Brownsville Neighborhood Manpower Center; the District 17 school board (whose chairman is a member of Wright's powerful United Political Club); five day-care centers (including one named after himself); an adult

---

* Bauman found a receipt that showed that the $25,000 deposit check was picked up by one Hermes Caraballo on September 25, 1975. Caraballo is Ramon Velez's chauffeur. The $25,000 was then deposited in Brooklyn, where, according to Bauman, it went to pay for a house in Puerto Rico that was being raffled off by the Parade Committee. The raffle was won by the janitor of the Hunts Point Multi-Service Center, but a year later the janitor had not yet taken title to it.

home, soon to open; and three summer lunch contracts for 49,000 lunches a day, worth $750,000.

Wright doesn't even really live on his Brownsville plantation. He has a new house, with a swimming pool and a $40,000 mortgage from Bankers Trust, in Old Westbury, which is on Long Island, and he merely maintains a voting address in Brownsville.

In 1972, while Wright was chairman of school board 23, 162 people on the school board payroll were also members of Wright's United Political Club. Also, 32 businesses that received contracts from the school board had officers who were either members of Wright's club or financial contributors to it (purchasers of tickets to the club's dinners, or advertisements in the club's journal).

Until August 1976, Robert Story was one of Wright's most valued political operatives in Brownsville. Wright got Story a job, at $19,950 a year, as acting director of the publicly funded Brownsville Community Development Corporation, and also got him on the community planning board, where he was chairman of a drug-abuse subcommittee. And from July 1970 to June 1973, Story was on the payroll of school board 23. He could be observed at school board meetings shouting down and intimidating parents who disagreed with Wright's point of view. Then, in December 1975, Story pleaded guilty in federal court to selling heroin to an undercover agent, and he is now serving a five-year sentence in the federal prison in Atlanta. For nineteen months, between Story's arrest and the start of his prison term, he remained on the payroll of the Community Development Corporation.

When Wright first gained control of the school board in 1970, his rivals were characterized as violent militants by *The New York Times*, the United Federation of Teachers, and by Eugene Gold, the Brooklyn district attorney, who announced he was impaneling a grand jury to investigate the violence of the anti-Wright faction only. This image of Wright as the stable, responsible, nonviolent alternative in Brownsville had been promoted by the publicist Howard Rubenstein, who for three years was paid $17,000 a year by school board 23 (he stopped working for it in 1975). Rubenstein told us he arranged several meetings with *The New York Times's* editorial board for Wright.

Yet this image of Wright's doesn't jibe with what we know of another unsavory character in his retinue: Jimmy Lee Smith. We interviewed three people who told us they were beaten up by Smith at a local school board meeting after they tried to speak in opposition to Wright. One of Jimmy Lee Smith's punching bags was a woman in her forties, and another victim, who has filed assault charges in Brooklyn Criminal Court and had been beaten with brass knuckles, is a cripple. Many Brownsville parents are now afraid to speak out, or even attend, school board 23 meetings.

In February 1973, when Wright was still chairman of school board 23, he signed a "letter of intent" to purchase $410,000 worth of reading materials from a company called Behaviorial Research Laboratories (BRL) for use in district 23 schools. He signed the letter unilaterally, without competitive bidding and without the knowledge or approval of the full school board, while he was in California to speak at a conference organized by BRL—a speech for which he received a $5,500 fee from BRL's public relations company. (The main speaker at the closing banquet of the conference, California's Senator John Tunney, received only $300.) Moreover, BRL paid the air fare, hotel bills, and meal expenses for Wright; his wife; several members of the school board loyal to Wright, and their families; and several school board staff employees. The full $410,000 contract with BRL was never voted on by the school board membership at a public meeting, as required by law. Is it overly skeptical to believe that all this largesse might have been an inducement for the BRL contract?*

State Comptroller Levitt's office has audited the financial records of a dozen community school boards in New York City, but never of district 23. However, an audit of district 23 conducted by the central Board of Education disclosed massive irregularities while Wright was chairman, including overexpenditures, paid vouchers for mysterious trips to Las Vegas and the Caribbean, and missing accounting ledgers and financial records. Under the Freedom of Information Act, we requested *all* relevant and available material on school board 23 from the central Board of Education, in the summer of 1976, and got back more than 2000 pages of audits, memos, financial records, and correspondence. From this massive amount of material we pieced together the saga of one James Elsbery.

In 1973, Elsbery had four contracts with the Brownsville school board, worth more than $300,000, to evaluate educational programs. He also had consultant contracts with school district 12 in the Bronx, and an examination of his work showed almost identical, word-for-word language in the reports he submitted to the two school boards.

---

* See Jack Newfield, "Sam Wright: Why Brownsville Looks Like Beirut," *Village Voice*, September 13, 1976.

One of Elsbery's evaluations for district 23 was of Camporific, an upstate educational summer camp. In August 1973, Elsbery wrote a negative evaluation of Camporific, concluding it was not adequately educating the children. Then Camporific hired him as a consultant to draft its proposal for re-funding to Wright's school board. In May 1974, Elsbery had changed his mind and, in his role as consultant to school board 23, gave his new employer a favorable evaluation, recommending that the contract with Camporific be "recycled."

Elsbery next submitted a bill for $18,700 to the central Board of Education for reimbursement of expenses: membership in the Princeton Club, several trips to Europe, and many visits to Chicago. It eventually came to light that Elsbery was a full-time employee of the education department of the state of Illinois while he was being paid hourly consultant rates by the Brownsville school board.

Given this turn of events, the Board of Education stopped payment on $150,000 Elsbery claimed was owed one of his companies. The Board's accountants concluded after study, that Elsbery owed the taxpayers $66,201.15. Sam Wright, who as we have said is not comfortable speaking in public, made a rare appearance before the full Board of Education in August to urge that his friend Elsbery be paid the $150,000 as an "illegal but equitable claim." The Board refused.

The district 23 documents we obtained under the Freedom of Information Act also tell the story of a man named William Carr, who is a member of Wright's political club. From 1970 to 1975, he was, inevitably, an employee of the Brownsville school board and over four years was paid $127,000 in overtime alone. But Carr had submitted overtime vouchers for exactly the same number of hours he was paid to work under normal circumstances, and when he was caught at this little racket by the Board of Education, his only punishment was that he had to pay back less than one-third of the public money he had swindled. Recently, at Wright's direction, he was given a promotion to a $20,000-a-year job on the district 23 payroll, as director of para-professionals.*

The documents also indicate that one Larry Cushner, who shares a law office with Wright, has been paid $120,000 in legal fees over six years by public agencies controlled by Wright. And that Jules

---

* On January 5, 1977, Carr was indicted by Brooklyn District Attorney Eugene Gold for defrauding the city of $70,000 over four years, by billing the Board of Education for overtime he never worked.

Zeibel, the former president of Wright's political club, owns nine buildings in Brownsville (with a partner) where space is leased on generous terms to the antipoverty agencies controlled by Wright.

While Wright and his followers have been growing rich for six years on public funds meant for education, the reading scores in the Brownsville public schools remain among the lowest in the nation. And while the money vanishes into legal fees, rents, phony expenses, phony overtime, and consultant contracts, the city's budget crisis has compelled district 23 to fire 49 teachers during the last six months.

Another harmful factor working on the quality of education in Brownsville is Wright's warm alliance with UFT leader Albert Shanker. Having gotten campaign funds for school board elections from the UFT, in exchange Wright apparently gave over the schools to UFT influence. The best, most respected black principal in Brownsville was Carlos Edwards: Student reading scores had gone up more in his school than in any other, and he was widely respected by the community. But Edwards was fired because Shanker regarded him as a militant, and Shanker has also reportedly instigated the firing of several excellent black teachers.

Wright has needed favorable court decisions from Brooklyn clubhouse judges to acquire and retain his power, for the courts are a critical element in the machine's control over the plantation. In the first Brownsville antipoverty election in 1970, Wright's faction lost. So Supreme Court Justice Harold McLaughlin, whose son is a city marshal, ordered a re-run. But Wright lost that one too, and his lawyer, Joseph Slavin, made the necessary motions to get a third election. Slavin was then also the lawyer for the Brooklyn party organization, and has since become a judge himself. Meanwhile, in the 1970 school board election, Brooklyn judges disqualified eight of the nine anti-Wright candidates, and that is how Wright finally gained control over district 23 and its considerable public funds.

In 1975, there was another school board election in district 23. One of Wright's candidates, the Reverend Charles Lott, filed petitions claiming to live at an address outside the school district; in addition he was not even registered to vote at that address. Brooklyn Supreme Court Justice Charles Rubin, a former party fund raiser, ruled that these were unintentional errors and allowed Lott to remain on the ballot, even though he had clearly violated the only two legal requirements that exist for candidates for the school board.

In 1976, Wright supported one Elmer Hamilton as candidate for the state Assembly from Brownsville's 54th A.D. Hamilton's Democratic primary petitions were challenged, however, on the grounds that he actually lived in Georgia. Justice Gerald Held ruled that Hamilton did indeed live in Georgia, but that the committee on vacancies could substitute another candidate on the ballot—this despite the fact that the overwhelming majority of case law on the subject indicates that a candidate with a false residence is simply disqualified. (Only one case out of the last fifty in New York offers a precedent for allowing such a substitution.) Wright's club substituted another person named Hamilton, Charles Hamilton, a former chairman of the district 23 school board. But the second Hamilton lost the election to Thomas Boyland.

This, then is the clubhouse system. Corrupt politicians—like Matthew Troy, Carmine DeSapio, Frank Brasco, Frank Gilligan, Alan Hochberg, and Bert Podell. Corrupt entrepreneurs—like Bernard Bergman and Eugene Hollander. Intellectual serfs—like City Councilmen Eugene Mastropieri and Dominick Corso—who are not free to vote their own beliefs. Terminal cynics—like Howard Golden. Unqualified, incompetent judges—like Irwin Silbowitz, Harold McLaughlin, Joseph Corso, and Joan Durante. Lawyers with shady reputations—like Roy Cohn. Businessmen who have been caught cheating or breaking the rules—like Vincent Caristo, Sidney Lipkins, and Fortune Pope. And plantation barons—like Ramon Velez and Sam Wright.

This clubhouse system is presided over by the lowest common denominator, Mayor Abraham Beame. Let us recall again his words spoken to that boisterous and embezzled Brooklyn organization dinner in May 1974: "We are sometimes accused of running a strong county organization. Critics call it a machine. But Brooklyn has demonstrated that effective party organization need not be synonymous with smoke-filled rooms. Rather, it is a vital force in the American party system. . . . I have been a member of the Brooklyn Democratic organization for the last forty years. I've always been proud of my membership, and my pride has increased. No one, no one, need apologize for being part of this kind of party organization."

LABOR
PAINS

New York City's unions have been the big losers in the new power game that has been played since the city's fiscal crisis began. The public employee unions have been the most visible casualties, but almost every segment of organized labor is weaker today than at any time since the end of the 1940s.

In the winter of 1975–76 unemployment in the city's giant construction locals averaged 60–70 per cent, and for the first time in memory, highly skilled workers were applying for "traveling cards" to work in states like Louisiana and Texas or on the Alaskan pipeline. Some locals even had trouble meeting the payments on medical bills for members and families from their seriously depleted welfare funds. The powerful Communications Workers of America failed to stop the Bell system's New York Telephone from imposing a charge for information service, and this meant layoffs for hundreds of operators. (Thousands more are scheduled for the slag heap before 1980 as Bell pushes ahead with its Draconian automation program. Nationally, 50,000 operators will be displaced in less than four years.)

Under the dual impact of permanent recession and continuing loss of jobs, powerful labor leaders saw their memberships and treasuries shrink, and they knew that their political power—national as well as local—was ebbing away with the decline in bodies and dollars. This will, of course, hasten the transition to a new generation of leaders and, perhaps, a new style of leadership in New York City's unions.

Perhaps the biggest loser is Harry Van Arsdale, who for decades was the city's top labor power broker. Although superficially his power stemmed from his presidency of the New York Central Labor Council, his real power base has always been the numerically small but politically and financially potent building trades. Van Arsdale controls New York's skilled electricians who wire new buildings and keep the city's heavy electrical equipment running; his son Thomas is the nominal head of the union, Local 3 of the International Brotherhood of Electrical Workers. And, after years of bloody organizing wars, Van Arsdale also heads New York's 30,000 taxi drivers, who belong to a special "federal local" union, affiliated directly to the AFL-CIO in Washington. Both of these unions have fallen on bad days. Local 3, while not so badly hit as some other construction unions, has plummeted with the rest of the industry, and as for the taxi industry, it is coming apart at the seams. Most of the large fleets whose drivers Van Arsdale controlled grew up during Prohibition when bootleggers used them to deliver their goods. When Repeal was passed, the thugs who owned the fleets found they still had a lucrative business potential. By seeing to it that the number of cabs allowed on the streets was restricted, they retained a stranglehold on the only profitable element of New York's transportation business. This state of affairs persisted until the last years of the Lindsay administration, when blacks and Puerto Ricans effectively took control of the cab business in their own neighborhoods after white drivers refused to service the ghetto areas—so that today a fleet of "gypsy" cabs equal in size to the fleet that carries the official licenced medallions, plies the city's streets. The fleet owners had no stomach for the all-out war that would have resulted from any effort to drive the "gypsies" off the streets, and they began selling off their medallions to individual drivers. Employment for Van Arsdale's union members, and the health and retirement funds they produced are rapidly disappearing.

Perhaps the high point of Van Arsdale's power came in 1970, when he virtually stole the endorsement of organized labor in that year's gubernatorial election for Nelson Rockefeller. The incident is expressive of the state of democracy within America's most "liberal" labor bastion.

As we have earlier noted, Nelson Rockefeller "bought" large segments of the traditionally Democratic labor movement—not with his own sumptuous purse but with great gobs of gravy from the public treasury, especially his massive building projects and lavish pension settlements. In 1970, his Democratic opponent was Arthur Goldberg, a lifelong labor lawyer and former general counsel of the AFL-CIO, a former Secretary of Labor, a former Supreme Court justice. Goldberg turned out to be one of the most boring, inept candidates in American political history, but there was little doubt that he was also one of the most prominent members of the labor movement ever to have run for office anywhere in the nation. He deserved labor's support in New York, and everyone expected him to get it.

Trouble started as soon as the State Federation convened at the Concord Hotel in the Catskills late in September. Ray Corbett, head of the tiny Sheet Metal Workers union and permanent factotum of the State Fed, refused to give Goldberg's forces a list of the delegates accredited to the convention. Without it, there could be no valid rollcall votes. While Corbett stalled, Van Arsdale was rushing busloads of his electrical workers from New York City to the convention site. On the night of the vote, a reporter from the Buffalo *Courier-Express* wrote that a box of delegate badges, "slightly smaller than a shoe box," suddenly materialized and the badges were distributed to the newcomers. There were only 1303 delegates registered for the convention, but reporters who were present said that at least 2500 bodies packed the convention floor.

As soon as Nelson Rockefeller was nominated, Victor Gotbaum, a Goldberg partisan, demanded a rollcall vote. But Corbett called for a standing vote instead and ruled that Rockefeller—clearly the favorite of the newly arrived "delegates"—had won. Gotbaum continued to scream for a rollcall from the floor, but Corbett had Gotbaum's microphone turned off and then quickly recognized a Rockefeller delegate who called for adjournment. Without further ado the convention was adjourned and the lights in the hall were turned out. At this point, outraged delegates began scaling large glass ashtrays at the dais. Lights were visible only around the CBS-TV film crew; they silhouetted Gotbaum and Van Arsdale as the following conversation took place.

"What are you getting so excited about?" Van Arsdale asked.

"You stole it from us, Harry!" the hulking Gotbaum answered.

Despite the ensuing public outcry, the labor vote stayed stolen for Rockefeller. The governor spent the rest of the campaign claiming that he had "the backing of organized labor," effectively undercutting one of the few strong issues that the bumbling Goldberg might have used to win.

No single labor leader in New York City can be expected to exercise the degree of power until recently held by Van Arsdale. Albert Shanker, the man who Woody Allen said was most likely to instigate a nuclear World War III, was everybody's bet as Van Arsdale's eventual successor, but Shanker has become a surprising loser in the new arrangements of power since the onset of the fiscal crisis.

Shanker has a visceral understanding of how to accumulate power. We remember seeing him late at night in a small print shop on the Lower East Side in the late 1950s, editing proofs of the then fledgling teachers union paper. In those days, Shanker was a quiet, efficient bureaucrat who stood in the shadow of David Selden, his close friend, the dynamic leader of the teachers' efforts to win recognition from a hidebound oligarchy that ruled the city's schools from the fortress headquarters of the Board of Education at 110 Livingston Street. After the teachers' organization drive took fire, Selden ascended to the presidency of the national union, the American Federation of Teachers, in Washington, and left the crucial New York local, the United Federation of Teachers, in the hands of his trusted aide. Shanker quickly consolidated his power by dealing with the volatile and complex issue of race in New York City's schools as if nothing more were involved than bread-and-butter trade-union issues. He protected inept and insensitive teachers from parents' demands for change by strictly enforcing seniority regulations in the contract. His union members were frightened by the parents' growing demands to be involved in educational decision-making, by the racially charged atmosphere in the schools and the demands for more black teachers and administrators, by the growing debate over how New York's inadequate educational resources would be allocated between teachers' salaries and educational programs. Instead of building an effective coalition with the parents, Shanker consistently took the narrow view that the educational system would improve as teachers' salaries and fringe benefits were improved, period.

The incredible insensitivity with which Lindsay's administration introduced "decentralization" into New York's school system played right into Shanker's hands. Three trial districts for decentralization were chosen, not one of them in a white area. As a result, the flare-ups that occurred during the disastrous school strike of 1968 were easily portrayed as conflicts between "radical" blacks and embattled white professionals. It became a political strike over the issue of who would control the schools, and Lindsay dealt Shanker all the winning cards.

Since then, Shanker has been able to beat back any challenges to his leadership of the UFT. He has built alliances with corrupt political machines in the ghettoes, like Sam Wright's in Brownsville, which try to control the popularly elected, decentralized school boards and their juicy patronage pies. Shanker can now pick up the phone and have a "militant" black teacher fired in Brownsville or a dozen other localities whenever he chooses. He has convinced his membership that its security lies in politics, and, through alliances with the building trades and other right-wing elements in state labor, he has become a king-maker in New York politics. (At the same time, Shanker has used his New York power base to axe his old friend Selden and succeed him as president of the AFT. Until recently, Shanker appeared to be the "great white hope" of labor's right wing to succeed George Meany as president of the AFL-CIO. If nothing else, he is a man of limitless ambition.)

But despite Shanker's considerable local and national political power, the UFT and Shanker himself have fared poorly since the onset of the fiscal crisis.

As Stephanie Harrington reported in the November 17, 1976, *Village Voice*, 13,000 out of 56,000 full-time teachers have been laid-off, as well as 600 out of 3000 paraprofessionals, 3000 out of 8000 aides, and 1000 of 2000 school guards. The firings and vacant positions in the schools have resulted in up to 45 students in a class, the disappearance of guidance teachers, of music, art and library. New York City's schools are in even greater chaos than they were during the troubled years of the 1960s.

Of all areas of city life, the schools have been among the hardest hit in the layoffs for a variety of reasons. First, the parent constituency remains unorganized. As middle-class whites withdrew from the city's public-education system, the schools became yet another minority service that elicits little consideration from New York's new decision-makers. More and more they are seen on a par with the municipal hospitals, which also serve a predominantly minority population. Secondly, considerable savings can be made by laying off well-paid teachers, rather than larger numbers of other civil servants, so this naturally is particularly appealing to the politicians. Teacher salaries and benefits have been a key component in the rising costs of local government all over the nation, and there is also a clear desire among the corporate decision-makers to hamstring the teachers where they have been most successful. Finally, and ironically, Shanker is universally feared and hated, even by his political allies, and they have seized this opportunity to savage him and perhaps pull his fangs. Some people have that kind of effect on others.

But the real challenge to Shanker's power comes from another source entirely. The National Education Association, a sleeping giant which has undergone a fundamental transformation from a conservative professional association to a combative trade union for teachers, has mounted a full-scale organizing drive in New York with the hope of destroying the AFT on its home ground and winning back almost 100,000 organized teachers in New York State. Shanker is fighting for his life and the odds seem to be shifting against him.

Van Arsdale and Shanker typify the traditional "business unionism" of the old AFL, which has predominated over the "social unionists" of the CIO since the merger of organized labor in the early 1950s. But if these right-wing "bread and butter" unionists have now fallen on bad days, their traditional enemies in the "progressive" unions have hardly fared better. The entire labor movement is drifting without goals or direction, and many of the old rallying cries are obsolete. The unions seem to be suffering from a potentially fatal lack of ideas and leadership at a time when the hammer blows of change are falling with brutal regularity.

Typical of this drift are the public-employee unions, nationwide still the fastest growing segment of organized labor despite massive layoffs. Until quite recently the business press was always warning that the public-employee unions represented a radical new force in the house of labor, the modern equivalent of the CIO in the 1930s. Victor Gotbaum, head of New York City's polyglot District Council 37 of the American Federation of State, County and Municipal Employees, was the paradigm of the kind of sophisticated, hungry public-employee leadership which the editorial writers feared. But when we interviewed Gotbaum recently and asked what his program was for the new period of stringency facing public workers, he gave us a one-word answer: "Survive." Gotbaum's primary concern now is to avoid another wave of layoffs as New York City falls further and further behind in its impossible attempts to balance its budget in three short years while still avoiding the complete collapse of public services.

Yet in the wake of the fiscal compromises worked out by MAC and the EFCB, Gotbaum is in the unenviable position of being not only New York City's major labor leader but its biggest creditor as well. And public-employee pension funds are likely to go on being the city's fiscal crutch for at least a decade. To protect his billions in city paper, Gotbaum will continue to be asked to sacrifice his members. He walks a narrow line: a misstep in one direction means endangering the pensions; a wrong step in the other direction means new layoffs. In the event, Gotbaum has become frozen, a captive of the business elite running New York City and now effectively running his union.

Gotbaum recognizes his position—and he hates it. The constant tensions show in his craggy face, and he seems physically diminished, the husky body hunched lower, the roaring voice now an exhausted grumble. He admits that he did not foresee the crisis, that he never knew the banks were destroying the city's credit until he was told about it by a high-placed friend in Albany—six months after the fact. He is uncomfortable with the phalanx of fiscal experts with whom he now bargains ("I've got fiscal advisers up the ass," he told us), but at the same time he has no alternative approaches, no analysis of the larger crisis besetting the national economy. A young staff aide of his told us, "It's pitiful. There isn't anyone around Victor with any ideas. There's no one to counter what the banks tell him. He just stumbles from one crisis to the next."

What troubles Gotbaum most is the inherent impotence of public-employee unionism. He recognizes that the power to strike, the only ultimately meaningful power that any union possesses, is worthless in the current situation. His workers struck the city hospitals—and no one cared. Gotbaum's members serve the poor of the city, and the power brokers couldn't care less if the poor are victimized. Only half jokingly, he told us that about the only group of workers in his union who could inconvenience the rich are the sewer laborers. "Maybe we should just open up all the treatment plants and let all that shit float around the city for a few weeks," he growled.

More than anything else, Gotbaum really believes that New York "is dying." Felix Rohatyn has put together a coalition of midtown real-estate speculators and right-wing union leaders that advocated the construction of a $1.1-billion superhighway on Manhattan's West Side and a convention center which would require a permanent subsidy from the city treasury. Under changes in the Federal Highway Act, the funds for the highway could, on the other hand, be transferred to mass transit construction, benefiting the many city workers who use the subways as opposed to the three per cent of travelers, mostly Wall Street executives, who would use the new highway. Gotbaum endorses the construction plans for the superhighway and the convention center: "I guess that makes me a reactionary too. We need these symbols of movement to show that New York is still alive."

Unless he moves to Washington as the next president of his international union, which is likely, Victor Gotbaum will be New York's most important union leader for at least another decade. The other public-employee unions are small and their leaders are inept or aging. John DeLury, head of the Sanitationmen, which is loosely affiliated to the Teamsters, has always exercised power far greater than the size of his membership would warrant, because of his well-oiled political apparatus, but Gotbaum has long since eclipsed him in the scope of his political operation, and DeLury is reported to be ailing and on the verge of retirement. The Transport Workers Union, the leading public-employee union while the inimitable Michael Quill was alive, is now isolated and poorly directed. (Blacks and Hispanics make up three-quarters of the membership but have been excluded from leadership in a bitter internal civil war with Quill's remaining heirs. But this situation can't continue much longer.) The other uniformed services, police and fire, have been riven by factionalism and opportunism; they will be forced to accept the patterns established by Gotbaum whether they like it or not, and cannot much longer be the tail that wags the dog in municipal bargaining.

From the members' point of view, the best thing that could happen would be for most of these small fiefdoms to merge into Gotbaum's District Council 37. But this is unlikely, given the lush salaries and other benefits enjoyed by the legion of union officials that has proliferated under the current fragmented system. The only conclusion we can make is that city workers face a bleak future. After generations of being at the bottom of the employment ladder, they began radically to alter their situation in the late 1960s and early 1970s. But that progress has now been frozen, and it will take a drastic shift in the entire structure of the national economy before any thaw sets in.

This might be a good place to say a word about pensions, a subject that has generated a great deal of controversy in the public debate over New York City's indebtedness. Traditionally, ample pensions were one of the few attractions of public employment. The other significant benefit was security. The civil service didn't expand or contract with the sudden gyrations of the general economy, and once you had gotten a job, you were likely to keep it. Governments didn't suddenly go out of business. When you reached the end of your productive years, the pension was waiting. As his part of the tradeoff, the public worker was expected to forego high wages and decent working conditions—until the sudden upsurge of public unionism in the 1960s, that is.

For the elected officials who ran the system, at least, it was an ideal arrangement. The average worker lived only two or three years after his retirement at sixty-five, so pensions were no great drain on the public treasury and there were no sudden wage raises and attendant tax increases to deal with. Government was subsidized by its workers. Then, the rules changed. The increasing demand for government services required an expanded work force. The new workers were not the docile civil servants of the past. Very shortly, they attempted to "catch up" for the lost benefits of a generation.

At the same time, the public perception of government workers remained hostile. Civil servants didn't create things, they delivered services, and therefore they were "unproductive." Everybody wants policemen and firemen to appear when called, they want their garbage picked up, they want dozens of other necessities—sewers, schools, hospitals—to function well. But the people who perform these jobs are largely invisible, and their salary demands are, by definition, "excessive" since we pay for them directly with our tax dollars. When auto workers strike Ford, no one really gets upset. But when hospital workers walk out, the general public is alarmed— and outraged. After all, we all may *need* a hospital, but we may only *want* a new car. Public employees are therefore often perceived as public enemies.

As public employees achieved parity with, and in some areas actually surpassed, their counterparts in the private sector, attention focused on their lavish pension schemes. For New Yorkers in the early 1970s, it soon became apparent that the rivalry between Nelson Rockefeller and John Lindsay as to who could give away more of the public's money had created a monster that was costing the city $1 billion a year. Here are just some of the abuses:

• Retirement at half pay after twenty years' service had spread rapidly from the police and firemen to sanitation, correction, and transit workers. Other groups were demanding the same benefit. State legislators, the source of all these goodies, had also extended the twenty-year retirement scheme to themselves, undoubtedly because of the "arduous" nature of the work they put in as part-time playboys in Albany. Length of service before retirement has been under general attack. A New York City teacher, for instance, can retire at full pension at 55 with only 25 years of service.

• In an open bid to buy the support of the uniformed services in the 1969 election, Lindsay had granted dollar-a-day annuity payments to the police, fire, correction, and sanitationmen and all their officers. These amounted to "supplementary pensions" on top of regular pension and Social Security payments. This "sweetener" cost the city $16.7 million a year. In 1976, the New York Public Interest Research Group charged that these payments were "illegal" under the state constitution and brought suit to force the unions that were managing the money to return it to the city treasury. This suit remains unsettled as we write.

• The time span on which pensions were computed was constantly reduced until a worker's earnings in his final year became the common basis for pension payments, as opposed to average earnings over the last five years of employment. To add insult to injury, overtime pay was included in this final year's salary, the *Daily News* revealed, and supervisors, themselves the beneficiaries of this system, were allowing retirees to work excessive amounts of overtime to drive up their pension base.

While all of these things were going on, the true cost of public-employee pensions was systematically hidden from the public. This was accomplished by allowing the costs to be computed on the basis of outdated mortality tables, some dating back to 1918. Even though this outrageous gimmick reduced city pension contributions in the present, it left a vast gap to be made up by future taxpayers. As a matter of fact, the pensions were systematically underfunded by at least $1 billion a year. This underfunding also resulted from an incredibly poor investment return provided by the banks and professional money managers in charge of the funds. When the stock and bond markets were near their all-time peaks, New York City pension funds earned as little as 1 per cent a year.

Then, in the midst of the fiscal crisis, the pension funds were forced to accept most of the burden of forestalling bankruptcy by investing in MAC securities. By the end of 1976, the pension funds were holders of $3.8 billion in city debt, a little less than 40 per cent of their total assets. (A federal law had to be passed to allow the unions to invest more than 10 per cent of their pension assets in any one security.) Everyone recognized that unless some kind of federal insurance were provided for the MAC securities, the funds were on extremely thin ice.

A great deal of attention has been focused on the public pension mess in New York City, but it should be noted that the mess is endemic throughout urban America. For instance, a recent survey of forty-four cities in Pennsylvania showed that more than three-quarters of them lacked adequately funded pension accounts. Nor is New York the most generous employer, by far. The State of Louisiana provides pensions equal to 75 per cent of take-home pay plus $300 for its retirees. And many public pension plans include automatic cost-of-living increases, something New York's does not.

Congressman Les Aspin has revealed that U.S. military retirement plans are easily the most lavish of all. As he wrote in the December 1976 issue of *Harper's* magazine, "The average officer retiring this year is a forty-six-year-old lieutenant colonel receiving a pension of $15,400 a year; his opposite number in the enlisted ranks is a forty-one-year-old Army platoon sergeant getting $6,400 a year. These retirees continue to enjoy, among other benefits, subsidized medical care, military commissaries with cheaper food, and free aircraft flights." Aspin observes that military pensions absorb 8.5 per cent of America's military budget ($8.4 billion in 1976), and warns that by the year 2000, we will be paying $34 billion a year in military pensions. Total federal pension commitments amount to $300 billion, a "secret debt" half the size of the official $600-billion national debt.

These massive federal, state, and local pension obligations raise a basic question of equity. While public employees frequently retire on salaries higher than those earned while working, 70 per cent of all U.S. citizens 65 and older are forced to live on Social Security and savings. Only half of the current work force is covered by any pension plan at all, and most of those are inadequate by any standard. And these computations don't even begin to consider the pension plans, such as the Teamsters', which have been systematically looted by corrupt union officials and employers, often in collusion with the mob.

The time has clearly come to ask how we shall provide a decent retirement income for *all* Americans, instead of perpetuating the vicious two-tiered system we have now, which creates a tiny privileged elite while the rest must subsist at the margin of starvation. The current system simply doesn't work—in New York or anyplace else.

The Labor Day boast of politicians and labor leaders that New York City is a "union town" has a hollow ring. Among white-collar workers, who are a larger and larger majority of the labor force, union organization is almost nonexistent outside the civil service. Repeated efforts to sign up the clerks, typists, and general office workers who move thousands of tons of paper each day in the teeming office towers of midtown and Wall Street have foundered on the inverse class consciousness of a generation that considers it a privilege to wear clean clothes to work. It is ironic that college and school teachers have flocked to organize while bank tellers and computer clerks disdain a union card. Part of the problem involves the high proportion of young women in these latter jobs. Despite increased feminist consciousness, these women still see marriage and raising a family as their primary route of escape from the low wages and drudgery of their jobs—although the lower-middle-class family is less and less able to survive unless both parents work full time. The unions had hoped that the increasing proportion of young blacks and Hispanics in this work force might infuse some militancy into the white-collar group, but so far this seems not to have been the case, perhaps because these workers have little reason to feel any identity with organized labor; they know about their parents' experiences in factory jobs, where more often than not the union was as much an enemy as the employer was.

Despite the false image projected by the press and by the employers, New York remains what it has always been—a sweatshop city. Average wage figures in New York are misleading, because of the minority of relatively high-paid construction, printing, and uniformed civil service jobs. Most unskilled and semiskilled workers

struggle at jobs that pay far less than the minimum budget of
$10,266 prescribed by the Bureau of Labor Statistics in late 1975
for a "lower than intermediate" standard of living for a family of
four in New York City. Moonlighting is common, and is one significant reason why young workers find it so impossible to gain even
entry-level jobs in the shrinking economy. Inflation rapidly consumes
whatever benefits legitimate unions manage to win. This problem
is hardly limited to New York, however; for several years now,
the real wages of American workers—and their standard of living—
have been falling steadily. The average worker today makes less
than he did in real terms in 1971.

This general trend is exacerbated in New York City by
two special problems. The first is the recrudesence of gangster-
dominated locals, either "independent" or affiliated with the can-
cerous Teamsters Union, which dominate many marginal industries
in the city. Despite recurrent declarations of war against these
racket unions by the AFL-CIO Central Labor Council, little has
been done to curb their growth since the late 1950s. Larger, legitimate unions in the same industries ignore their parasitic neighbors,
refusing to commit the money and manpower necessary for an
all-out drive against corruption. Government at all levels has ignored
this problem since Robert Kennedy left the Justice Department.
Since this outrage affects minority workers almost exclusively, even
the press ignores the hegemony of the mob over a large segment of
low-wage workers. Very few papers any longer cover labor as a
regular beat, and then only when major strikes or negotiations are
in progress. But the mob's thumb is on the scale every time a house-
wife buys a pound of meat or a bag of fruit; they add a few cents
to the cost of every garment purchased, every manufactured item
that any American buys. Racket unions are the dirty little secret of
our economic life, and they will remain so until another Kennedy or
Kefauver comes along who believes that the Constitution doesn't
become "inoperative" at the factory door.

The second problem is the slow rot that has infected New York's
largest industry and the union that controls it—the International
Ladies' Garment Workers Union, AFL-CIO. The ILGWU has a
special niche in American labor history. Plays, movies, and dozens
of books have been written about it. It is the only American union
that had its own political party—the Liberal Party.

No one can deny the seminal influence of the ILG on American
labor. For decades its only peer in the fight for better wages and
working conditions was the United Mine Workers.

But the bright myth of the progressive ILG has a dark underside that is rarely examined. After a bitter struggle between Socialists and Communists for control of the union in the mid-1920s when pitched battles raged on the streets of the garment center, the victorious Socialists instituted an authoritarian regime that banned opposition caucuses in the union and concentrated power in the hands of a few hereditary bureaucrats. (ILG locals are famous for being passed from father to son or son-in-law. Dubinsky created Local 23A as a wedding present for his son-in-law, Shelley Appleton. As Herbert Hill, national labor secretary of the NAACP, says: "They call it a union, but in fact it's just a large family business.")

And long after any threat of a Stalinist takeover had disappeared, the rigid controls on democratic opposition within the union continued. Until the early 1970s, no member who was not a delegate to the national convention and a paid member of the union staff could run for either of the two highest international offices, president and general secretary treasurer. This reduced competition for the leading posts to perhaps 200 members in a 450,000-member union. Only 300 members could run for a post on the General Executive Board. Power was, and is, restricted to a small club that excludes the working rank-and-file.

Right after World War II, two profound changes began to take place within the garment industry. The Jewish and Italian immigrants who had made up most of the work force in New York's garment shops were replaced by blacks and Puerto Ricans. And the manufacturers began to leave New York in search of low-wage havens in the South or in gangster-protected runaway shops in northern Pennsylvania. New garment products, especially leisure wear and bathing suits, developed mini-industries near their resort markets, primarily in California. The union had a basic choice to make. It had a huge treasury (it still does; union assets in 1976 were $147 million), and it could have followed the runaways and organized the nonunion shops or enforced a boycott of their products in the big Eastern cities. Instead it chose what at the time seemed an easier alternative. It began to cut wages and working conditions in New York and its neighboring states to make local manufacture "competitive." It also began making loans to garment manufacturers from the union treasury. This in turn led to "soft enforcement" of union contracts in favored shops.

This is how the NAACP's Hill explains the union's waning militancy. "They were never old-fashioned racists; they never said 'nigger.' But in fact they were afraid of these new workers, they had nothing in common with them. They had more in common with the bosses in the industry, many of whom were former members of the union who had scraped together enough capital to open a shop. The union and the bosses sat down and negotiated sweetheart contracts over the heads of the workers, and they even refused to show the workers the contract."

When the workers began setting up caucuses to seek power within the ILG, or even when they protested speed-up and declining piece rates, the union identified these "trouble-makers" to the bosses and had them fired. Hill tells of hundreds of meetings with minority workers over the years. "It was like being a member of the Resistance in occupied Paris. These workers lived in terror of being exposed by the union, because they would never be allowed to work in the industry again." As a result of these conditions, he says, garment workers as a whole were reduced to a "condition of poverty." *The Wall Street Journal* recently reported, "Average hourly earnings of apparel workers are still only two-thirds of the average for all manufacturing employees, and the union's $100-a-month pension after twenty years is among the lowest in the nation." In a union whose membership is 80 per cent women and 90 per cent black and Hispanic, there is only one woman on the General Executive Board; she is also the only black.

In weighing these charges, it is interesting to contrast the newly merged Amalgamated Clothing and Textile Workers Union with the ILG. The Amalgamated is the dominant union in men's clothing, and it faces many of the same problems found throughout the garment industry in general. It has had a markedly different history from the ILG and is not only one of the most democratic of American trade unions, but the most innovative and crusading. The Amalgamated never crushed the Communists; it allowed them democratic rights even during their most destructive phase. When in the 1930s the ILG flirted only momentarily with the CIO and then scampered back to the AFL, the Amalgamated became a bastion of the CIO, and Sidney Hillman, its long-term president, became a major architect of labor's crucial activities during World War II. In the years thereafter the union fought the runaway shops and never gave up the difficult, demanding task of organizing the anti-union clothing factories in the South. (It was an Amalgamated local in Georgia that gave Jimmy Carter his first crucial labor support in his second, and successful, attempt at winning the governorship.) It waged a $6-million national boycott against the Southwest border sweatshops of the Farah pants company, and it conducted the first mass organizing drive among Chicano workers. Last year, the union merged with the always embattled Textile Workers Union in order to mount a massive new effort to bring union wages and benefits to the infamously anti-union textile industry. As the first stage, they launched a $1-million boycott against the $1.4 billion J. P. Stevens textile empire, which has consistently broken the law and kept unions out of its plants. And through all of this it has successfully maintained wages and working conditions in its organized shops in New York City. (The Amalgamated, by the way, was one of the most outspoken opponents of the war in Vietnam, while the ILG stayed in the trenches with George Meany and his septuagenarian band of Cold War bitter-enders in the right wing of the AFL-CIO. There is no record that the white, male leadership of the ILG polled the black, Puerto Rican, and Chicano mothers who make up the membership, and whose sons provided such a high proportion of the cannon fodder in Southeast Asia, on their views about continuing the struggle.)

The Amalgamated has continued to grow, surpassing the ILG, while the latter has lost 75,000 members in only eight years. Both unions face an increasing challenge from foreign imports. One out of four garments sold in the United States in 1975 was imported, compared with one in twenty only a decade ago. Much of this competition comes from the police states of ILG's beloved "free world" like South Korea, Taiwan, and Haiti, but there is also a flow of men's garments from sweatshops in Eastern Europe, especially Rumania and Hungary. The large banks and multinational corporations are financing this flood of imports—and exportation of American jobs. It will demand a drastically altered stance on the part of the entire labor movement if national policies favoring these forces are to be overturned.

There are some slight glimmerings that the ILG may be awakening to the need for a change in internal structure and external policy. Sol C. Chaikin, the first American-born president in the union's history, has recently taken the helm. (Chaikin also received a chauffeur-driven limousine and $52,000 salary with the job.) There are rumblings that he is easing out some of the *alte cockers* who were cronies of Dubinsky and Stulberg and who have been getting fat salaries for running dying locals. He has hired a handful of new organizers, and plans to add more. But *The Wall Street Journal* recently reported on a pep rally for employers led by Chaikin in New York at which he preached the need to increase assembly-line pressures in order to improve the workers' ability to compete with Southern and foreign competitors.

The crucial question is how far Chaikin is willing to go in allowing the rank-and-file to compete for union office. As Hill has pointed out, the irony of the ILG is that its "hysterical anti-communism actually recreated the model of Stalinist totalitarianism within the union in the name of a free labor movement." Chaikin and the restless minority members of the ILG must effectively break with that ossified past and establish a transition to full democratic participation for the membership without rending the union apart. A healthier course would probably be to merge the ILG into the new ACTWU, but this seems unlikely. Very few labor leaders can be found today who will sacrifice their limousines in the name of class solidarity.

In a very real sense, the economics of the Northeast region will determine the fate of organized labor not only in New York City but throughout the country. Union organization in the South still faces a long and bitter struggle, forty years after the CIO began the first mass unionization drives in Dixie. Today less than 18 per cent of the American work force is organized, and the unionized workers are still concentrated in the heavy-industry states of Pennsylvania, New York, Ohio, Michigan, New Jersey, Illinois, Indiana, and Wisconsin. Unless labor hangs on to jobs and members in these states, it will wither into impotence.

To succeed, labor must rise to a number of fundamental challenges. The first is to create a new leadership that can replace the "country club" pork-choppers who control so many large unions. This process began when the Mineworkers overthrew the murderous Tony Boyle and his henchmen. Now tough young reformers like Ed Sadlowski have dug in for the long fight to win back the Steelworkers. Other insurgents at the local and district level are succeeding by the hundreds, although the victories go largely unreported in the press. Many of the old progressive unions, like the United Auto Workers, the International Union of Electrical and Radio and Machine Workers, and the Machinists, are undergoing evolution from within. Younger unions, like the Oil, Chemical and Atomic Workers, seem to have healthy internal democratic structures and are in the forefront of the crucial struggle for the worker's health and safety. But the building trades, with their obdurate resistance to integration, remain a bastion of the status quo. Recent attempts to reform New York's scandal-tainted District Council 9 of the Painters Union have been stamped out. Many of the building-trade baronies make the ILG look like a model of democracy. And the same can be said for the Longshoremen, the Seamen's unions, and, of course, Shanker's AFT.

In New York City, the question of black ascendancy haunts the left as well as the right of the labor movement. In the Hospital Workers union and in District 65, a generation of white radicals who worked openly and valiantly to improve the lot of black workers is approaching the point where it must turn its cherished institutions over to the workers it liberated. It will be a difficult parting. Many militant black workers have grown old waiting for their benefactors to retire. In unions like the Transport Workers, the struggle will be bitter, but black hegemony is inevitable. In others, the new black leaders may lack the tactical skills or ideological fervor that allowed some marginal unions to persevere, but this is a risk of democracy well worth taking.

The ideological crisis facing labor in American cities is far more serious than racial turmoil alone. When Samuel Gompers was asked what labor wanted, he could answer simply, "More." It was a formula that worked for half a century as America became the world's dominant power. Now every American must learn to live with "less," and the crucial question is how the "less" will be apportioned. Living standards of the lower and middle classes are already being sacrificed to maintain the hierarchy of privilege that grew up when social tensions were minimized because everyone—no matter how poor—was doing at least "a little bit better" than the preceding generation. That time has ended. The banks, and the clever manipulators like Felix Rohatyn and Stephen Berger who do their bidding in the councils of government, have decided that New York's workers and its millions of average citizens will bear the principal burdens in the bleak new age. The banks have moved quickly to secure their radically decreased investment in New York City by gaining sequestered tax revenues to back MAC securities. They have accelerated their disinvestment in New York's housing and neighborhoods. No matter how much others lose, the banks will win under these rules. After all, they invented the game.

If the unions, and New York City itself, really want to "survive," then the game itself must be changed. Banks are not immune to democratic control. The simple fact is that no social force, except perhaps the ill-fated prairie Populists of the late nineteenth century, has ever even tried to bring them to heel. Banking giants like Citibank and Chase can be required to invest specific percentages of their assets in social spending. State-chartered savings banks can be forced to invest in viable city mortgages. Their rates of profit can be regulated. They can be forced to pay full federal and state taxes.

A successful publicly owned bank can be established, as it was in North Dakota. We have no illusions that these reforms will be easy. Right now, the banks, the giant insurance companies, and other financial powers own the New York State legislature and control the majority of votes in both houses of Congress. This stranglehold can be broken by concerted political action, and political action can be helped significantly by tough prosecution of laws, already on the books, against fraud and collusion. Labor lacks not an alternative program, but the will to break with its comfortable past and get on with the tough, bitter job of making America a political *and* economic democracy. We think that one is impossible without the other.

THE
POLITICAL
ECONOMY
OF ORGANIZED
CRIME

First it was the Irish gangsters, coming out of the Five Points and the Bowery, stealing and stabbing, killing and bribing their way into what America called respectability. They were followed by the Jews, by Arnold Rothstein and Herman Rosenthal, by Lepke Buchalter, and Gurrah Shapiro and the other boys from Brownsville who organized murder along the lines of the American corporation. And it was the Italians who perfected it, creating the Mafia as the first multi-national corporation, with help from Meyer Lansky and a lot of lawyers and respectable people in a lot of high places. Now, in this town, it is the turn of the blacks, the Puerto Ricans, and the Cubans.

— PETE HAMILL, 1974

The gangster is the man of the city, with the city's language and knowledge, with its queer and dishonest skills and its terrible daring, carrying his life in his hands, like a placard, like a club.... For the gangster there is only the city; he must inhabit it in order to personify it; not the real city, but that dangerous and sad city of the imagination which is so much more important, which is the modern world.

— ROBERT WARSHOW
The Gangster as Tragic Hero, 1948

Most people get their image of the gangster from the movies. They get it from Edward G. Robinson, James Cagney, George Raft, Richard Widmark, Humphrey Bogart, John Garfield, and Marlon Brando playing public enemies and syndicate bosses. This film fantasy of what a gangster is really like exerts its power over even the originals. A friend of ours grew up with the Brooklyn gangster Joe Gallo. He remembers the young Gallo going to the movies to see Richard Widmark playing Tommy Udo in *Kiss of Death* "at least ten times." Gallo, an aspiring hoodlum, began to imitate Widmark's slang, body language, and style of dress. Years later, when Hollywood was preparing to make another gangster movie and Gallo was by then a chic Mafia symbol, an actor asked Gallo if he could hang out with him, to observe and learn some *macho* mannerisms, those Gallo had originally borrowed from another actor.

This story suggests some of the difficulty in separating myth from reality, legend and lore from fact, in attempting a serious, sober perspective on organized crime. The problem is complicated by the fact that relatively little reliable material on organized crime is available that is untainted by hype or melodrama.*

The actual power of organized crime in New York City has gen-

---

* Law enforcement agencies have a near monopoly on the raw data about organized crime. But prosecutors have the incentive of publicity and funding, which occasionally incites them to self-serving exaggerations, especially when estimating the "street value" of confiscated narcotics. Probably the best sources of dependable information about the mob are the bound volumes of the Kefauver and the McClellan Senate committee hearings of the 1950s. More recently, a valuable resource has been the work of scholars like Harold Lasswell and Thomas Schelling. Several books have offered realistic insights into organized crime, including: *The Valachi Papers* by Peter Maas; *The Fall and Rise of Jimmy Hoffa* by Walter Sheridan; *Black Mafia* by Francis A. J. Ianni; *The Crime Confederation* by Ralph Salerno; *Lansky* and *The Silent Syndicate* by Hank Messick; *The Politics of Heroin in Southeast Asia* by Alfred McCoy; and *The Grim Reapers* by Ed Reid. There has also been excellent journalism by Nicholas Pileggi, Jeff Gerth, Jim Drinkhall, Tom Renner, and by *Wall Street Journal* reporters Stanley Penn and Jonathan Kwitny.

erally been underestimated by historians, economists, political scientists, and other academics.* But it has also been fantasized about and exaggerated by some reporters and other media faddists trying to cash in on the Godfather market. Also, the values and life-styles of gangsters have occasionally been severely romanticized. They are not immigrant populists, or street-corner philosophers with benevolent dignity, or tragic, half-ethical Godfathers who draw some moral line at pushing white powder.

Low-level Mafia men walk out of restaurants on Mulberry Street without paying the bill—because they are so cheap. Most mobsters would rather stick an icepick in someone's ear than work. Powerful mob bosses like Carmine Galente are as bestial as the most vicious elevator mugger you will ever read about. Talk to the federal agents who knew Carmine Persico, the Snake. Talk to now broke and broken former boxing champions who were owned by Frankie Carbo, and then were tossed aside like pieces of contaminated meat when their eyesight was damaged. Talk to Herman Goldfarb, who worked undercover for seventeen months in the garment center, infiltrating the mob. Talk to respected prosecutors like Joe Hynes and Thomas Puccio. Read the trial record of Louis Cirillio, a heroin dealer who had one million dollars buried in his Bronx backyard. Read the transcripts of the tapes made secretly by the Brooklyn district attorney inside Paul Vario's junkyard trailer in Canarsie. These men, and these pieces of evidence, will tell you that Mafiosi are not Bogarts and Brandos. They are mean, greedy, small-minded men. "Mutts," as Joe Hynes likes to call them.

It is instructive to recall this dialogue from tapes released by the FBI in New Jersey after a long period of electronic surveillance of the Mafia there. The colloquy is between one Angelo DeCarlo (called Ray) and Tony "Boy" Boiardo:

TONY: How about the time we hit the little Jew?

RAY: As little as they are, they struggle.

TONY: The Boot hit him with a hammer. The guy goes down and he comes up. So I got a crowbar this big, Ray. Eight shots in the head. What do you think he finally did to me? He spit at me and said [obscenity].

* In *Governing New York City*, Sayre and Kaufman devote only 2 out of 699 pages to a discussion of organized crime.

We hold the view that organized crime is a separate permanent government in New York City. It is dangerous, corrupting, and virtually all-powerful in specialized areas like the waterfront, the garment center, and the private carting industry. It holds, through the threat of force, cartel franchises on illegal services like narcotics, loansharking, gambling, pornography, and prostitution. Its dominant role in the international heroin traffic makes the mob one of the central villains of this book. But, ultimately, organized crime has less economic and political power than the biggest banks, insurance companies, corporations, and utilities. For example, the mob's leading loanshark, Fat Tony Salerno, is reported to have about $80 million out on the street in loans at any given time, but that—though Salerno charges 156 per cent annual interest and has the muscular helpers to make default quite risky—should be measured against Citibank, with *$56 billion* in assets, and the Metropolitan Life Insurance Company, with *$33 billion* in assets.

There is also a problem of definition. Organized crime, to us, is not limited to Italians who shoot other Italians. There is a level at which corrupt businessmen and lawyers and politicians, crooked union leaders, and traditional gangsters meet and become indistinguishable, where businessmen begin to act like racketeers, and racketeers begin to act like businessmen. In this gray area crime and capitalism converge and become almost identical in their values, methods, and influence. This is where Bebe Rebozo, Frank Fitzsimmons, C. Arnholt Smith, Richard Nixon, Adrian Khashoggi, Bernard Bergman, Meyer Lansky, Robert Vesco, Sidney Korshak, Richard Kleindienst, Roy Cohn, Michele Sindona, Robert Dorsey, and other power brokers operate in a twilight realm.* Bernard Bergman's stealing of $2.5 million from Medicaid perhaps should be considered as a form of organized crime. And what is Gulf Oil chairman Bob Dorsey's disbursing of millions of dollars of corporate funds in secret payments to domestic politicians and foreign governments? The bilking of various Teamster Union pension funds has certainly been crime that is planned and systematic. And so was C. Arnholt Smith's complex bank frauds in San Diego. And what of the hundreds of burglaries committed by FBI agents?

So our definition for the purposes of this book must remain

---

* The most original and sophisticated account of this twilight world can be found in the four-part series on lawyer, "fixer," "mob intermediary," and labor consultant Sidney Korshak, written by Seymour Hersh and Jeff Gerth, and published by *The New York Times*, June 27–30, 1976.

somewhat open-ended. Unlike a bank or a public authority, organized crime has no one definition that is universally acceptable.

Organized crime's domination of New York City's politics and judges began during Prohibition, when bootlegging was the source of illegal wealth. It reached a peak during the 1940s and 1950s, when Frank Costello, Thomas Luchese, and Joe Adonis cemented the alliance for mutual profit between the clubhouses and the underworld. But today the influence of organized crime upon the governance of the city seems diminished.

Under Frank Costello's Mafia reign, Tammany district leaders were asked to resign at gunpoint. Costello had the power to make a man a judge with one phone call. Costello is even credited with arranging Tammany's backing for William O'Dwyer in the 1945 election for mayor. O'Dwyer did come to Costello's apartment for a meeting in 1942, and the graft and corruption that flourished under O'Dwyer represented a golden era for the mob.

The man who interrupted the mob's hold on New York politics was Senator Estes Kefauver, whose televised committee hearings during 1950 and 1951 exposed the Mafia's deep, systemic influence on the Democratic Party in New York and other major cities. The mob's withdrawal from politics continued when the sophisticated Costello was replaced by more primitive, Old World Mafia bosses like Vito Genovese and Carlo Gambino, men with little appreciation of the value of political power.

Since the Costello period, organized crime's influence on New York City's government has been more *ad hoc,* more personalistic. Individual mobsters have had access to individual politicians and judges. City Commissioner James Marcus and Brooklyn Congressman Frank Brasco went to prison for corruption involving Mafia leaders. State Supreme Court Justice Andrew Tyler is under indictment for allegedly lying to a grand jury about his meeting with "Spanish Raymond," a convicted gambler who is believed to be the mob's biggest policy banker in Harlem. But these seem to have been particular circumstances, not the structured graft of the 1930–1950 era. The waterfront union leader Anthony Scotto has been repeatedly accused of ties to the mob, but the evidence seems ambiguous. And some judges appear to display generosity toward organized-crime defendants. Supreme Court Justice Joseph Corso has dismissed five separate indictments against Mafia members, indictments that were all subsequently reinstated by appellate courts. Supreme Court Justice Dominic Rinaldi has twice personally gone to police stations to release alleged Mafioso Santo Patti, who had twenty prior gambling arrests, rather than wait for Patti to be arraigned before another judge the next morning. Police records show that Justice Rinaldi did this on April 18, 1969, and again on June 15, 1970. But no crime has ever been proven against Corso or Rinaldi. The secret connections between Mafia dons and politicians and judges are raw meat for gossip and television drama. But the element of legal proof seems lacking, although we would not be surprised if it were discovered tomorrow by an enterprising prosecutor.

The gossip and drama, however, may be distractions from the real, concrete, and devastating impact organized crime does have, in many areas, upon New York City and its people.

The juice of a plant is destroying New York. The cultivation, processing, importation, distribution, and sale of heroin is probably the most organized crime in all history. What the fine white powder has done to America as a whole is beyond mathematical calculation. It has created an army of muggers who cause more than half of all the violent crime in our large cities. It is responsible for the overloading of our courts and prisons. It has cost billions and billions of dollars in public funds to combat, treat, and prevent the plague of crime and addiction. The federal government estimates that 15,000 deaths—murders and overdoses—last year were related to heroin use. Heroin corrupted the police departments of many big cities during the 1960s, including New York.* And there is no possible way to measure the personal pain of the addicted, and the fear of the nonaddicted, caused by *Papaver somniferum,* the beautiful opium poppy.

Heroin is New York's tumor. Heroin is causing the crime that is chasing the white middle class to the suburbs, thereby eating away the city's revenue base. Street crime equals organized crime because of heroin.

---

* A good summary of police corruption and narcotics can be found in the Knapp Commission Report, pp. 91–112. For a longer account, read *Serpico,* by Peter Maas (New York, 1972).

The Police Department says that heroin is a $1-billion-a-year industry in New York City. The number of addicts is estimated at 150,000–300,000, and is now increasing again, after leveling off between 1972 and 1974.

The Mafia is the ITT of heroin. One needs computers, processing laboratories powered by electric generators, and private planes with radar to transport heroin from Asia, Turkey, Mexico, and France to the Pit in Harlem, and to all the young men without veins in their arms. And despite the mythology to the contrary, the traditional Italian Mafia has always been in the heroin business. Court records show that important Mafia members and associates have been indicted, tried, and convicted in narcotics cases for twenty years. Among those who have gone to prison for violations of the narcotics laws have been: Vito Genovese, Carmine Galante, Carmine Trumunti, Joseph DiPalermo, Angelo Melo, Virgin Aessi, Vincent Papa, John Ormento, Louis Cirillio, and Frank Cotroni, one of the leaders of the Montreal syndicate that smuggles heroin into the United States.

Thomas Puccio, the executive assistant United States Attorney for the Eastern District of New York (Brooklyn, Queens, and Long Island), set up the narcotics unit in his office and has supervised the prosecution of more than a dozen major narcotics cases. He told us: "The Mafia has the cash to bankroll the heroin traffic. They use the cash from policy banks as the front money to start an international shipment of 25 kilos coming to New York. Italian Mafia people may deal through a Cuban or Latin, who has the direct contact with the overseas supplier, but I would say that the Mafia causes the heroin importation to happen, because they are the financiers of the traffic.

"I've worked for the Justice Department since 1969, and there has never been a time when organized crime wasn't involved in the heroin business. I have never seen any evidence to support the newspaper publicity that Gambino kept them out of it. Heroin is just too lucrative for those guys to stay out of it."

What has happened, it seems, is that blacks and Latins have taken over a piece of the narcotics market at certain levels and on certain routes of distribution. Spanish-speaking Latins obviously find it easier than Italians do to deal with Mexican cocaine suppliers. Most law-enforcement authorities regard the Latin and black gangs as simply a part of the organic structure of organized crime, and as examples of the historic continuum of ethnic succession in crime.

In December 1975, the New York Police Department released the names of the thirteen biggest narcotics importers, financiers, and dealers in the city: The list consisted of five blacks, four Latins, and four Italians. But with a new Turkish crop of white heroin now being harvested, and with the rise to power within the Mafia of the convicted heroin dealer Carmine Galante, the Italians will continue to control a share of the trade and be the capitalists of junk. Also, Galante has exceptional contacts with Montreal gangsters for smuggling heroin from the north; soon there might even be a movie called "The Canadian Connection."

The traditional Mafia still has international distribution networks, and access to the modern laboratories in France that process Turkish and Asian opium. European underworld chemists can provide up to 90-per-cent-pure heroin. Special Narcotics Prosecutor Sterling Johnson has said that, "In the heroin business, the Mexicans are the short-order cooks. The French are the chefs."

Heroin is far from being the only contribution organized crime is making to the problematic fate of the city. New York's district attorneys and Police Commissioner estimate organized crime's gross annual income from illegal gambling at between $1.75 million and $2 billion. What is so hurtful to the city is that none of this revenue is taxed. The experts all agree that sports betting and the numbers game—the ghetto lottery—are the biggest sources of income for the mob, and this money is used to finance other rackets like narcotics, loansharking, pornography, and the infiltration of legitimate businesses and unions. Mafioso-turned-government-witness Vincent Teresa told a Congressional committee in July 1971: "If you could crush gambling, you could put the mob out of business."

A useful insight into the city's biggest illegal gambling operation was afforded by the eight-week trial of Jimmy Napoli and eight associates during the summer of 1976 before Federal Judge Jacob Mishler. Tapes made by the FBI and played during the trial told of bets being placed at the HiWay Lounge on Metropolitan Avenue in Brooklyn. The tapes also indicated that cops from the Public Morals Division were being paid off to protect Napoli's phone banks, runners, and comptrollers. FBI agents testified that Napoli and his employees took between $120 million and $150 million a year in bets, mostly on horse racing, that between 1969 and 1975, Napoli personally took home more than $1 million a year, and that he lived in a $150,000 Manhattan townhouse. Napoli also paid (in addition to his bribes to police) the salaries of about twenty assistants; the three closest to him (including his son) each took home about $500,000 a year in untaxed illicit income.

Napoli was convicted, and in October 1976 he was sentenced to five years in prison by Judge Mishler.

Several years earlier, the final report of the Knapp Commission in December 1972 had made two important points about organized bookmaking and the numbers racket in New York City. Organized "pads" created by gamblers to pay off plainclothes police, the report said,

serve as an important breeding ground for large-scale corruption in other areas of the Department. . . . Policemen, especially those in plain-clothes units, were found to shake down gambling operations through-out the City on a regular, highly systematic basis. . . . But perhaps the most important effect of corruption in the so-called gambling control units [of the Police Department] is the incredible damage their per-formance wreaks on public confidence in the law and the police. Youngsters raised in New York ghettoes, where gambling abounds, regard the law as a joke when all their lives they have seen police officers coming and going from gambling establishments and taking payments from gamblers.

In dozens of areas of city life racketeers have infiltrated, or completely taken over, legitimate businesses and unions. Wherever this happens, the cost of extortion, padded payrolls, bribes, shake-downs, or kickbacks, is inevitably passed along to the consumer. The extra cost of private garbage collection, of linen supply, of construction, of vending machines or jukeboxes, of labor "con-sultants," of truckers, of security, of liquor licenses, of cargo thefts at airports and on the waterfront—all of it is paid by each of us in higher prices. This is the mob surcharge exacted unwittingly from virtually every citizen of New York City.

A few years ago, for example, Moe Steinman, the former vice-president of labor relations for the Daitch-Shopwell supermarket chain, which has shops throughout the city, pleaded guilty to a bribery and kickback scheme that involved union racketeers in the meat business. At Steinman's sentencing, Manhattan Assistant Dis-trict Attorney Frank Snitow said that the racket cost New York City housewives 1 to 3 cents for each pound of meat they bought at several supermarket chains. "The sole victim has been the con-sumer," he said.

In April 1975, the New York-New Jersey Waterfront Commission, a watchdog agency, accused the major airlines of concealing vast amounts in cargo thefts at Newark, Kennedy, and La Guardia airports. Its report said that in 1973 all airlines combined had reported a total of only $805,118 in cargo thefts, but that in reality there had been "close to $16 million" in cargo thefts at the three metropolitan airports. The conclusion was gloomy:

The incontrovertible fact is that the airlines are helpless to deal with the problem of organized crime at the airports. The dominant air freight trucking union, for example, remains under the control of criminal elements. The problem of cargo security is simply a facet of the larger problem of organized crime; and conditions at the airports cannot improve until a government body, vested with sufficient powers to break the grip of organized crime over the airports, intervenes to regulate the airports.

The airlines intentionally underreported the cargo heists by $15 million in one year to avoid such regulation and to keep labor peace with Harry Davidoff's Teamster Local 295, which is the union involved in air freight trucking. The airlines chose rather to pass the cost of the mob's thefts along to their own innocent customers.*

The oral history of New York has always maintained that the mob controlled the private carting industry. In 1972, the Brooklyn district attorney, Eugene Gold, and the head of his rackets bureau, Joe Hynes, set out to test the thesis by buying a used garbage truck for $3800 and setting up their own undercover private carting company.

The undercover project lasted for sixteen months. According to Hynes, the detective who ran the business knocked on doors, distributed flyers, and even took newspaper ads offering restaurants, supermarkets, and shopkeepers prices *30 per cent* below all other competitors, but still only got 19 clients out of 2000 directly solicited. The reason was that the small businessmen in the Coney Island and Bay Ridge sections of Brooklyn were afraid to change their carter. Those who tried to were threatened with bombing and arson, and others who attempted to remove their own trash found it returned to their doorstep the next morning, with a menacing note attached.

* The original scoop on the airport ripoffs was by Nicholas Pileggi in "New Hustles on the Waterfront," in *New York,* May 21, 1973. As usual, Pileggi was two years ahead of the government in recognizing a problem—one that is still unattended and unremedied. Local 295 still runs the airports.

The undercover cops found that honest shopkeepers and restaurant owners had to pay for carting even on days they were closed; that they had to pay large, sudden rate hikes; and that they had one carter assigned to them by the borough-wide Trade Waste Association "for life." This Trade Waste Association was controlled by hoodlums from three different Mafia families, and they cooperated with each other no matter what gang wars raged elsewhere. Hynes recalled for us how the association assigned "territories" to cartmen, and that the cartmen had to pay exorbitant dues to the association to keep their routes. In Brooklyn it eventually became apparent that the Trade Waste Association was a mob monopoly when the undercover company was denied membership in the association.

In March 1974, the Brooklyn DA's office announced the indictment of fifty-four private carting companies and the officers of the Trade Waste Association for conspiracy, restraint of trade, and perjury before the grand jury. In November 1975, the carting companies and two association officials pleaded guilty, and Brooklyn Supreme Court Justice Milton Mollen ordered that the association be dissolved. The grand jury that heard the evidence and voted the indictments also released a presentment proposing that the city take over the entire $300-million-a-year private refuse collection business as "the only way to break organized crime's stranglehold on the private carting industry." The grand jury observed that shopkeepers and retail businessmen in Brooklyn were paying private carters twice as much per cubic yard as they should be, and that this inflated rate became the mob surcharge that the "mom and pop" storekeepers of Brooklyn had to pay.

But the Beame administration ignored the grand jury's proposal, and the city has not even taken away the convicted companies' carting licenses. The city's silly Consumer Affairs Commissioner, Elinor Guggenheimer, who has the authority to revoke, was quoted in the December 11, 1975, *New York Times* as saying: "We have no evidence now that the [carting] industry is ridden with crime."

And so, despite sixteen months of hazardous undercover work, despite indictments and convictions, nothing has changed, and organized crime continues to run the private carting industry in Brooklyn.

In the spring of 1973, two much larger and much more ambitious undercover operations were set up in Manhattan, and these concerned not garbage but one of New York City's central industries—the garment industry. One was a coat company, given the code

name of Operation Detroit, which was financed by the federal Law
Enforcement Assistance Administration (LEAA), and the other was
an undercover trucking company, known as Operation Cleveland
and financed by the New York City Police Department. The two
projects together led to 34 indictments and 21 convictions (several
cases are still pending); mobsters and union officers have been
convicted of extortion, illegal receipt of money by a union official,
bribery of an IRS agent, conspiracy, and tax evasion. (However,
because of inept federal prosecutors, Matty Ianiello and four other
defendants were acquitted in November 1976.)

We spent about twenty hours interviewing the principals in the
undercover trucking company, at the conclusion of the investigation.
The principal undercover agent was Herman Goldfarb, a dapper
fast-talking civilian ex-convict with a 159 I.Q. and an adding-
machine brain; also involved were Lieutenant David Durk, who
helped expose police corruption with Frank Serpico, and three
members of Durk's squad, including a blonde policewoman who
posed as the secretary of the company. (Goldfarb has been awarded
the highest honor the Police Department can confer on a private
citizen, and has been given a new identity and relocated outside
of New York by the Department of Justice.) The story they told us
was educational:

On March 28, 1973, Gerro Trucking started business at 1441
Broadway under new management, for it had been purchased by
the Police Department for $60,000. Hidden cameras and micro-
phones were installed in the third-floor offices; four legitimate
drivers and three undercover agents carrying hidden microphones
were employed. Goldfarb ran the company while secretly reporting
back to a task force consisting of the FBI, the organized crime strike
force, the IRS, and the Police Department. Every day, as he met
with street-level gangsters, crooked union business agents, and
Mafia bosses, Goldfarb wore a Nagra tape recorder and a Kel
transmitter concealed in his crotch. Although he was Jewish, Goldfarb was trusted by the Mafia bosses because of his ability to earn
money and think up legitimate business ventures, and also because
of his prison record for grand larceny and forgery.

As soon as Gerro Trucking opened for business in the garment
district, mobsters started coming through the front door with their
hands out. Over seventeen months, Goldfarb paid out $20,000 of
the Police Department's money in bribes and "commissions." For
organized crime siphons millions of dollars annually out of the ten

square blocks of dress houses, cutting rooms, trimming rooms, clothes racks, and triple-parked trucks which New York knows as the garment district. The garment industry is a declining, under-capitalized, seasonal business, regulated by no agency except organized crime. The mob controls dress houses, union locals, building cleaning services, private carters, even parking places. (If a businessman doesn't pay the mob, his trucks get sand in their gas tanks and slashed tires.) And most significantly, the mob has a monopoly on trucking—the lifeline of the fragile industry.

The tapes make it clear that a businessman cannot fire his trucker, even if the trucker suddenly wants to charge him twenty cents more for hauling each dress. Every garment-center businessman needs a trucker to move his "goods," and every trucker belongs to a mob-dominated association. So, the businessman must pay, and pass the cost along to the retail customer. This has been going on ever since Johnny Dio took over garment-center trucking in 1935.

The mob has bookmakers all over the garment industry, in delis, in cafeterias, on street corners. If a manufacturer falls into debt to his bookmaker, he quickly gets a visit from a mob loanshark. If the manufacturer can't pay the "Vig" (the interest) to the loanshark to pay off his gambling debts, then the mob moves in as an undisclosed partner in his company, and starts placing its own people on the payroll in phantom jobs. Moreover, union "consultants" will take payoffs not to unionize a shop or a trimming room. This is called "controlling labor costs."

The cost of all this untaxed tribute to the mob is passed along to the general public in the retail price of dresses, coats, and other apparel. The August 1975 issue of the trade publication *Chain Store Age* quoted a "retail executive" as estimating that the cost of corruption adds "an easy five per cent" to the pricetag of every garment. The same article quoted a second apparel-industry figure as saying that the mob surcharge "could be as much as ten per cent of the retail price tag."

The 2000 undercover tapes recorded by Goldfarb showed, for example, that he had to pay an extra ten per cent "commission" to the trucking association in order to join it and have labor peace. And that he paid $10,000 in cash to one official when he sold Gerro Trucking at the end of the investigation. Goldfarb also had to hire a mob "enforcer" named Larry Paladino for $200 a week, for which price Paladino became Gerro's expeditor—he was known to have "respect" on the street. Paladino made sure Gerro had no union problems, made sure Gerro's trucks had curb space, and allowed his name to be used at Kennedy Airport, where it guaranteed friendly cooperation from Teamster Local 295. The weekly payments also insured that no rival trucking company raided Gerro's accounts, or "jumped" its routes.

In a mob-dominated subculture like the garment center, the psychology is that everyone pays, so why not me? It is the conditioning of history, reinforced by the fear of violence—a beating, a fire. The corruption is so ingrained that it is easy for the average businessman not to notice it, really, and view it as merely another tax or licensing fee.

During Operation Cleveland, Lieutenant Durk asked a well-known garment-center manufacturer, whose company grosses $110 million a year, to help in the investigation. The manufacturer took off his shirt and showed Durk the ugly scar tracks on his back, inflicted by gangsters in the 1930s. He explained that he was now, thank God, successful enough to hire an accountant who knew how to write off all the "commissions" and "labor costs" as deductions on his corporate income tax.

While the mob still can be found, then, in many of New York's major industries or areas of activity, the illegal services that organized crime sells—gambling, heroin, cash at high interest—find most of their consumers in the city's slums. The poor, as ever, suffer most from organized crime. The junkies, craving their daily high, will rob, mug, and slash other poor people for the price of their $5 bag. Welfare checks sometimes go directly to pay loansharks, because slum dwellers are so often denied credit by "legitimate" sources. In 1970, the late State Senator John Hughes, chairman of the Joint Legislative Committee on Crime, said: "The flow of money from the ghetto to organized crime is so great that there can be little meaningful economic improvement in New York City's ghettoes until it is stopped."

In September 1972, a pioneering study, "The Impact of Organized Crime on an Inner City Community" by Harold Lasswell and Jeremiah McKenna, was released by the Policy Sciences Center in Manhattan. The study analyzed the economic consequences of organized crime upon the Brooklyn ghetto of Bedford Stuyvesant, one of the city's six main slum neighborhoods. It covered the geographic area of the 77th and 79th police precincts, in which 280,000 people reside.

Lasswell and McKenna concluded,

> Organized crime was the single most powerful force in the community. It grossed more revenue from its gambling and narcotics operations than the federal government collected in income taxes; it was the single largest employer of community residents; it had effectively nullified whatever counterattack had been mounted against it by government; and no present program, public or private, appears capable of controlling or reducing its major illegal operations. . . .

> This analysis demonstrates the important position of organized crime in the social process of Bedford Stuyvesant. The policy and narcotics operations are continuous and stable, so that increased income for the community will result in the transfer of a larger amount of community wealth to organized crime; a larger demand for narcotics; and further deterioration of the whole area.

One of the most interesting data sections of the report was the research on the disposition of persons arrested in the course of various police raids on policy banks that controlled the numbers gambling. Lasswell and McKenna found that out of 356 persons arrested, 198 had their cases dismissed by judges; 63 were acquitted; 77 were fined (the average was $113); five were convicted and sentenced to jail (the average term was 17 days); 12 had their sentences suspended; and only one of the 356 received a sentence of more than a year in prison. Their conclusion was that the best thing for the economy of the ghetto, and the best thing for the integrity and productivity of the Police Department, would be the legalization of gambling, particularly of numbers betting.

McKenna is now at work on a new study of organized crime in New York City, in collaboration with the urban historian Johnathan Rubinstein, who wrote *City Police*. We interviewed McKenna in October 1976 about his latest findings. "Based on the data I've seen so far," he said, "I would say that organized crime is taking more money out of Bedford Stuyvesant and other slum areas than ever before. Although there is less police enforcement in gambling, when policy banks are raided, more cash is found now than five years ago. We're also discovering that more people are betting a dollar on the number, rather than a dime or a quarter. In 1970, the total policy play in Bedford Stuyvesant was $36 million a year.

Now it's a lot more. And, of course, the money the mob makes from illegal gambling goes right back into heroin."

Organized criminals violate law and decency in many more ways than those we have recounted here—from laundering money in order to legalize criminal wealth, to shooting each other in public places. But the illegal rackets described here have been the most direct means by which organized crime has become a factor in New York City's pain.

ARROGANT
POWER

On November 9, 1965, an electric relay device malfunctioned in Queenston, Ontario, and northeastern United States and eastern Canada were plunged into darkness by a cascading power failure. The effects of this Great Blackout touched everyone in the region, sometimes tragically but generally without serious effect. (A study published a few years later showed that the birth rate in the area had taken a mysterious jump nine months after the Blackout; perhaps this suggested what television-watching has done to our mating habits.)

New York City was different, however. In one wrenching moment, the metropolis simply stopped functioning. At the height of the evening rush hours powerless subways coughed and expired in airless tunnels far below the city streets. Packed elevators lurched to a halt twenty stories above the ground. Streams of homebound autos turned into churning rivers of metal as traffic lights blinked out. Tenants huddled in apartment-house lobbies before starting the exhausting climb to their apartments twenty and thirty stories above. Tons of foodstuffs slowly spoiled in refrigerators and supermarket freezers.

Some hospitals were lucky enough to have auxiliary power, but others did not, and nurses flitted from patient to frightened patient in true Florence Nightingale fashion—candles aloft. In many ghetto neighborhoods, trash baskets were ignited to provide at least momentary protection from muggers and rats.

There was a lighter side to the crisis. Movies and theaters were closed, but Broadway was far from deserted and midtown restaurants thrived under candlelight as a Blitz mentality infected secretaries from Brooklyn and junior executives from Larchmont stranded together.

Few who experienced that night in New York can't recall it vividly after more than a decade. They remember that it was warm for November, how frustrating it was to be unable to get information about loved ones (the phone system collapsed for several hours under the sudden overwhelming demand for circuits), the sense of fear and impotence because the machines on which New York depends could no longer do their bidding at the flick of a switch. In those long hours of darkness, New Yorkers came to realize as they never had before just *how* dependent they were on the invisible electric network running beneath their streets.

Or rather, how dependent they were on the Consolidated Edison Company. A subsequent study of the Blackout by the Federal Power Commission demonstrated that Con Ed lacked the automatic load-shedding devices that could cut off customers selectively and avoid a total blackout (these were standard for other utility systems). The engineer in charge of the company's power control center had ten minutes between the beginning of the breakdown and the total collapse of the system, but he lacked instructions on cutting ties with the other systems in the region that had already blacked out. Far more serious was the fact that Con Ed lacked auxiliary generators and had to rely on slow-starting steam turbines for reserve power. Boston's subways continued to run through the entire blackout period, but New York's were disabled for fourteen hours.

In the years since 1965, blackouts—although never so cosmic—have become commonplace to New Yorkers. There was no connection between these localized equipment failures and the gigantic 1965 breakdown, which was a combination of freak technical failures and bad judgment that is unlikely to recur. But Con Ed used the 1965 trauma as a convenient bogeyman for several years when seeking rate increases or new plant approvals. New Yorkers became more and more familiar with "brownouts," or voltage reductions, invoked every summer by the utility.

Con Ed, the nation's second largest utility, which supplies electricity to three million customers in New York City and Westchester County as well as natural gas to 1.2 million consumers, and the steam that heats the spires of midtown Manhattan, was rapidly falling apart after generations of corruption, bad management and almost nonexistent "regulation" by state officials. In response to a growing chorus of criticism from small consumers, the New York business community, and city government, the company and the state Public Service Commission gave essentially the same answer: The problems could be solved only by money, and consumers would have to pay a whopping bill to put the old girl back together again. In the intervening years they *have* paid (New Yorkers consistently pay the highest electric rates in the nation, and the average bill tripled in the decade 1965–75), and although service has taken a sharp turn for the better—partially because many consumers simply can't afford to use as much electricity as before—most Con Ed customers are still wondering whether the price has been worth it.

By 1967 the company's board of trustees was convinced that a new image, if not a new policy, was necessary to allay public anger. Charles Eble, chairman of the board and chief executive officer, the quintessence of Con Ed's "up from the ranks" management (he started as an office boy forty years earlier and worked his way up through the accounting department without benefit of higher education) announced his retirement, and the search for a successor began.

The choice fell upon Charles Franklin Luce, an austere lawyer-bureaucrat who once worked as a meter reader in his native Wisconsin and subsequently rose, through political connections with Senators Henry Jackson and Warren Magnuson in his adopted state of Washington, to become administrator of the giant Bonneville Power Administration, one of the nation's largest public power agencies, and then Assistant Secretary of the Interior in the Johnson administration. (In a 1970 profile of Luce, Susan Brownmiller wrote that he had been hired by two Con Ed board members representing Citibank, "the heavy bank in Con Ed's financial relationships." This description best fits Richard S. Perkins, now retired but at the same time chairman of the executive committee of the bank and its holding company, and Frederick M. Eaton, a partner in the prestigious law firm of Shearman and Sterling, which represents both the bank and the utility. Both men are still Con Ed board members.)

Luce's introduction to his new employer was harsh but revelatory. Only four months after he assumed his new job, Con Ed and Mayor Lindsay's new city administration were rocked by the disclosure of an attempt to shake down the company for granting an important construction permit. The conspirators included a city commissioner, the former behind-the-scenes leader of the state Democratic Party, a major contractor, a bizarre double agent, and assorted Mafiosi. Before the dust had settled the public had been given a rare view of the inside workings of the giant utility, and it disclosed that business-as-usual at Con Ed was a network of political deals and payoffs between contractors and top corporate officials which resulted in untold millions of dollars in padded construction costs systematically passed along to consumers in the company's rate base. New Yorkers are still paying the bill for those decades of corruption.

A brief history of the Marcus scandal is important to a basic understanding of the milieu in which privately owned utilities operate in a major city. The conspirators have long since served their time; only one, Carmine DeSapio, has re-emerged into the limelight. But Con Ed remains immersed in the political life of the city and the state, a major generator of profit and power, a permanent member of the permanent government.

James Marcus, a charming ne'er-do-well who had married into the Lodge family and used his ties with the first family of Republicanism to ingratiate himself with the GOP mayoral candidate John Lindsay, seems to have had an irrepressible attraction for other people's money and for stocks with a propensity to sink—a fatal combination. John Lindsay had a similar attraction for impressive but flimsy resumés. He made Marcus his Commissioner of Water Supply, Gas and Electricity.

Somewhere along the way, Marcus had acquired a not-so-silent partner named Herbert Itkin, one of the legion of bright hungry young lawyers in New York and every other big city who see their diplomas as licenses to steal. Itkin would have thrived at the court of the Borgias but managed to do well enough in America of the 1960s, working simultaneously for the CIA, FBI, various DAs, and his own account at the same time. When Itkin met Marcus, he thought he had finally found El Dorado.

Itkin was already deeply immersed in the dank netherworld where mobsters, larcenous "legitimate" businessmen, and corrupt union officials hunt together to share the benefits of pension-fund mortgages, government contracts, and deals within deals. He quickly introduced his friend "the Commissioner" to some of these acquaintances and the two were already negotiating their first corrupt deal on the day Marcus was sworn into office. That afternoon, Marcus and Itkin met with Tony "Ducks" Corallo, a top Mafioso, to learn how much a favored contractor (Henry Fried of S. T. Grand Co.) would kick back for being granted an "emergency" noncompetitive contract to clean one of the city's aging water reservoirs. It is instructive that as Marcus joined Corallo at a restaurant, he later testified, his predecessor as Water Commissioner (in the previous Wagner administration), Armand D'Angelo, was just leaving the great man and heartily shook Marcus's hand and wished him well. A changing-of-the-guard ceremony.

It is impossible to tell exactly how much Marcus-Itkin reaped from their hegemony over this one small section of the city bureaucracy. (Itkin claims he personally made $120,000 in one year.) What is clear is that all other deals were seen as merely an appetizer for the main course: Con Ed.

Con Ed is "regulated" by the state Public Service Commission, which establishes utility rates and sometimes presses the giant companies under its purview to improve service. But on a day-to-day basis, Con Ed performs most of its functions within New York City and enters the jurisdiction of several city departments concerning such matters as street repairs, air pollution, taxation, etc. City decisions are rarely decisive for the company, although there are enough legally binding relationships between the two to make it desirable that Con Ed remain on friendly terms with leading public and party officials.

Charles Eble, Luce's predecessor as chairman, explained the relationship to a writer for *Fortune:* "Over the years I struck up friendships with many politicians. It was not something that I set out objectively to do at the beginning. But, as time passed, I found that many of my friends had moved into positions of authority in government. I could talk to them. It was as simple as that."

Well, not quite that simple. What Eble failed to mention was that many of these friendships were undoubtedly struck at the numerous political dinners he attended to further the fortunes of various individuals and both parties, dinners for which the utility never failed to buy a table at about $1000 a throw. While this excessive largesse has now ceased, officials of the utility are still to be found as paying guests at important political functions, and a staff of county coordinators and PR men make it a point to jump when elected officials bring them some constituent complaint about the shortcomings of the company. Con Ed is also extremely charitable with its rate-payers' money, passing out free baseball tickets and donating to the favorite causes of the powerful without regard to race, religion, national origin, or expense.

What Marcus-Itkin had in mind was somewhat more direct. New York City has the best and most extensive system of water supply in the world, with millions of acres of land outside the city in the Catskill Mountains watershed. This massive aqueduct system alone is as large as some of the world's smaller nations. For many years, it had been an abiding dream of Con Ed to build a large pumped storage plant on Storm King mountain above the major tunnel carrying water to the city. Marcus, protector of the city's water supply, would have to supervise the construction carefully. In 1967, the price tag on this job was $200 million—enough to set the mouths of Marcus-Itkin and their legion of co-conspirators watering.

Before tackling Con Ed on this "big one," however, they cut their teeth on something smaller. Con Ed also had a high-tension transmission line built on some of the aqueduct lands. Now, in the midst of the "power shortage" that had resulted from inducing consumers to buy more appliances than Con Ed could comfortably service, the company decided to break with tradition and expand modestly its ability to buy power from other utilities with surpluses to sell. They also planned to build a number of new plants upstate in the future. Increased transmission capability was the key to these projects.

As an aside, it should be noted that monopoly electric companies can remain profitable only by constantly building more and more expensive plants since their rate base is determined on a "cost-plus" basis, i.e., the more they spend, the more the regulators allow them to collect from consumers. Companies therefore try to produce by themselves every kilowatt that they sell, and religiously avoid buying surplus power from one another, although that would be much cheaper for their customers. Con Ed had lagged behind other firms in this regard and had purposely kept its transmission capacity to an absolute minimum over the years.

In 1958, the company had turned down a chance to buy cheap hydropower (1.5 million kilowatts every hour) from Niagara Falls. In 1964, they rejected a similar offer from the Churchill Falls power project across the border in Canada. Together these water-powered sources would have supplied half of Con Ed's peak load needs. Instead they plunged into the incredibly expensive construction of nuclear plants and polluting, oil-fired plants to maximize expenses—and profits.

Marcus would have to give his permission for the new transmission line. Instead of demanding a direct bribe from the company, the conspirators were told that they should work through the utility's independent contractors. The logic was that in return for getting the permission to build, the grateful company would reward the contractor who had had the initiative to "take care" of the sticky palms at the Department of Water Supply by granting to that contractor the lucrative construction contract for the high-line, on a noncompetitive and highly lucrative basis.

Henry Fried, the beneficiary of the reservoir contract, decided that he would be the one to help his old friends at Con Ed. It subsequently came to light that he already had Con Ed's vice-president for construction on his own payroll at $1000 a month ($2500 at Christmas) and, along with a number of other contractors for the utility, maintained good relations by distributing smoked turkeys and cases of whiskey to various key Con Ed employees at the festive season.

Fried had become wary of the ability of Marcus-Itkin to carry off so complex a deal, and he decided that the suavity of a master fixer, not the blunt-edged style of their earlier Mafia intermediaries, was needed. He introduced Itkin to Carmine DeSapio.

DeSapio, who had been the dominant figure in Democratic politics in both the city and the state throughout the 1950s, had backed Robert Wagner in successful bids for the mayoralty in 1953 and 1957 and was an architect of Averell Harriman's victory in the gubernatorial race in 1954. He subsequently became Harriman's Secretary of State, a position from which he nominated Henry Fried as an unpaid Commissioner of Corrections. (Had he been prescient, Fried would undoubtedly have done much more to improve life in the state's prisons than he apparently did.) As we have seen, DeSapio's fall from formal power came in 1961, when Wagner suddenly dumped the "bosses" and ran successfully against his own record on a "reform" ticket, and when the liberal Village Independent Democrats unseated DeSapio as district leader in the Greenwich Village fiefdom he had controlled for so long. But although "out of politics," DeSapio was still considered the man to see in certain circles.

His counsel to Marcus was simple: Do nothing on the transmission line contract until Con Ed was desperate and confused. Then he would make the proper representations to the proper people showing he had had the ability to "deliver," and the deal would be struck. As it turned out, this was exactly the correct strategy. The only problem was that Marcus was neither a good bureaucrat nor a strong personality. Although he was being bled white to cover loans on a bad stock investment and desperately needed money, he wavered under the pressure being applied by Con Ed. In a bungled attempt to delay sending the utility a letter of commitment on the project, he alerted honest city officials that a new franchise for the line should be negotiated, since Con Ed was actually increasing its transmission capacity ninefold without increasing its rental payments to the city treasury.

The collapse of the conspiracy soon after is a tangled tale with an ironic twist. Both Marcus and Itkin came under separate investigations for misappropriating monies a businessman had entrusted to them for private business investment. Itkin had long since been "turned" by the FBI and in a desperate attempt to stay out of prison was telling everything he knew about everybody. At the end, he threw in the hapless Marcus, who had already resigned after disclosure of his stock mess. Marcus spilled everything, including the reservoir deal, which led to Fried's indictment. When Fried was removed from Con Ed's list of accepted bidders, he attempted to blackmail the company into continuing his services, and blurted out the details of his dealings with Con Ed officials to a member of the company's brass. This led to the forced retirement of Gerald Hadden, the vice-president for construction, and the demotion of Max Ulrich from vice-president for public relations to director of Brooklyn operations. (Within the company, the Ulrich move was actually seen by some as a promotion.)

Marcus ultimately served eleven months of a fifteen-month sentence in a minimum-security federal prison. DeSapio was sentenced to two years. Corallo received three years, to run concurrently with an earlier sentence. Fried got two years, and so did Daniel Motta, involved in the early stages of the plot.

Itkin's federal friends kept him out of jail, but he has emerged since in a characteristically convoluted child-custody case, and his most recent utterance to the press was that he was spending his days waiting for the Mafia finally to mark "paid in full" to his indiscretion at having kissed—and then told and told and told.

A crucial question emerges from this tangled skein. Where were the "regulators"? The New York State Public Service Commission is mandated to audit the books of utilities in order to protect the public from overcharges, yet it never questioned the company's unorthodox contracting procedures. Luce himself ordered competitive bidding as a result of the scandal, but the beneficial impact of that order remains doubtful.*

If this system of kickbacks and bid-rigging was common on Con Ed's smaller contracts, what had gone on in the building of hundreds of millions of dollars' worth of generating plants—by the same group of contractors? The simple answer is that we will probably never know. But we pay dearly for that ignorance with each new electric bill.

Even more urgently we must ask whether the system of public regulation of natural monopolies such as the utilities, or even unnatural monopolies like the giant oil companies or defense contractors, can ever truly protect the best interests of the public. Monopolies are inherently inefficient; there are no market forces to punish either greed or poor judgment. Con Ed has no incentive to keep its costs low if its profits rise along with those costs.

Regulators, such as the Public Service Commission, live in a world dominated by the regulated. They require highly specialized skills, skills that can often be acquired only in the service of the utilities. There is no moral judgment automatically implied in noting that the last two chairmen of the Public Service Commission

---

* As Walter Goodman points out in *A Percentage of the Take* (New York, 1971), a study of the Marcus scandal:

"As it happens, Henry Fried was master of another method of beating the nuisance of competitive bidding—an arrangement among contractors to rig their bids for paving and trenching contracts with Con Edison, with the Brooklyn Union Gas Company, and with the Empire City Subway Company, a subsidiary of the New York Telephone Company. In October 1969, Fried was sentenced to four months in jail and fined $25,000 for his role in this accommodation; Mackay Construction was fined $50,000; and S. T. Grand was fined $10,000.

"Henry Fried's fellow conspirators, a list of the city's contractor nobility, included: Vincent P. Di Napoli, chairman of Tully and Di Napoli; Francis Jordan, board chairman of Poirier and McLane; Alfred Korsen, vice-president of Slattery Contracting; Theodore Galucci, Jr., president of Samuel Galucci and Sons; Joseph J. Haggerty, Sr., board chairman of Sicilian Asphalt Paving; Samuel Aviron, superintendent of Lipsett, Inc.; Robert Crimmins, president of Thomas Crimmins Contracting; Arthur Cipolla, vice-president of Yonkers Contracting; Robert E. Lee, secretary of DeLee General Contracting; and Ernest Muccini, Sr., president of Oakhill Contracting. Two other companies were in on the bid-rigging: Gull Contracting of Queens and Casper Hellock of the Bronx. The price-fixing companies are still handling the bulk of Con Edison's $30 million a year worth of trenching, paving and foundation work. Explains Chairman Luce, 'These firms are among the largest in the city and there simply are not enough other qualified contractors staffed and equipped to do the job.'"

had both served as consultants to the utilities they ultimately came to supervise. (Joseph Swidler had been a consultant for Con Ed, and Alfred Kahn did a major pricing survey for AT&T.) The conflicts are inherent in the system.

From its very inception, the electric power industry has been deeply enmeshed in politics—an inevitability where vast fortunes could be made in the exploitation of a new technology, as it rapidly progressed from being an interesting novelty to being a basic necessity of life. A fundamental understanding of how and why the industry developed as it did and of the imperatives of the technology it pioneered is necessary to see how Con Ed has grown and the reasons why it, and its counterparts across the nation, face such a questionable and costly future.

It was probably inevitable that the first large-scale applications of electric power should have been tried in New York City. Thomas Edison established his company in a four-story brownstone at 65 Fifth Avenue in 1881. Then, as now, New York was the financial capital of the nation, and electricity has always required massive capital to build the gigantic generating plants and distribution networks that have been the hallmark of its spread. Electricity remains the largest industrial investment in the history of the nation.

Two men, Thomas Edison and Samuel Insull, can be fairly credited with developing the modern power company, although neither actually created any of the technical components of the electric generating system. Edison, however, was the first to understand that electricity could be sold as a commercial product. Insull, his young British secretary, made an even more fundamental contribution: He "invented" the electric monopoly corporation.

Until Edison established his central-station generating plant at Pearl Street in the heart of New York's financial district in 1882, the nascent electric industry confined itself to selling the electric components necessary to establish individual, limited-purpose generating plants to supply street lighting in downtown neighborhoods of a few blocks, or to drive single-purpose motors such as elevators or pumps in large office buildings. J. P. Morgan and Henry Villard, already famous as "robber barons" in the nation's monopolized rail industry, controlled the development of this new industry.

Edison was the first to grasp the logic of creating a generating network that would provide a pre-existing system, or electrical infrastructure, into which individual customers could be wired without the cost of each establishing his own generating plant. He put together the components of such a system—generators, switches, underground cable, et cetera—and patented it. In essence this gave him ownership of an entire new industry. The only flaw in his system was that it used low-voltage direct current (D.C.) and therefore could be used only over a fairly limited distance—about a one-mile radius from the central generating station. This meant that hundreds of generating stations would have to be built to serve a city the size of New York, but since Edison owned the patents he was perfectly willing to see hundreds of small companies spring up as his licensees to meet the power needs of the metropolis. In fact, dozens of companies were formed in New York and Brooklyn, and these were ultimately merged, under the financial pressures of the Great Depression, into today's Consolidated Edison Company.

Samuel Insull immediately began barnstorming the nation selling the Edison system to municipalities, the most logical customers for the new technology. The irony in this was that Insull ultimately would spend much of his later life fighting to destroy the municipally owned electric systems he helped to spawn and attempting to replace them with privately owned electric companies.

The Edison system, as was so common in the early days of technological innovation in America, soon had unwanted competition. George Westinghouse had overcome the limitations of direct current by developing alternating current (A.C.), which made it possible to produce electricity at much higher voltage for transmission over much longer distances. This current could then be reduced or "stepped down" by the use of transformers to make it usable in low-voltage appliances such as light bulbs.

The rivalry between the two systems became bitter, and if the technical merits didn't win the day with municipal buyers across the country, bribery often took its place. Technology ultimately had little to do with the outcome of the struggle, however. The Thomson-Huston Company, controlled by J. P. Morgan, stole many of Westinghouse's patents and ultimately bought out both competitors. In 1889, Edison received $1.75 million for his patent rights, and distributed about $1 million to his early associates, including Insull, who received $75,000. Thomson-Huston then emerged as the General Electric Company. Westinghouse left nothing except his name to the only other competing company, Westinghouse Electric, and the two are still the only makers of heavy electrical equipment—as well as the predominant forces in the nuclear power industry—to this day.

(One gruesome reminder of the Edison-Westinghouse rivalry persists to the present. Edison had attacked alternating current as the "killing current" because of its high voltage, and in 1888 he managed to induce the legislature of New York and its governor to adopt the "electric chair," using A.C., as its legal means of execution.)

Insull emerged from the wreckage of Edison Electric to become president of the fledgling Chicago Edison Company, later to become the mammoth Commonwealth Edison. Still only twenty-nine years old, Insull devoted the next thirty years of his life to fulfilling Thomas Edison's dream: the creation of a single national monopoly over the electric power industry. He almost succeeded. By the time the Depression destroyed his vast electrical empire in 1932, he was president of eleven power companies, chairman of sixty-five others and a director of eighty-five more.

The construction of this empire was no easy task. Despite their intense rivalry, Edison and Westinghouse had failed to convert the country to central station generation, and the spread of electricity into homes and offices was very slow to progress until the boom of the 1920s. Large companies still preferred to build individual power plants for each building or factory they owned. The largest users of electric were the traction companies that ran the street railways or trolley cars that dominated urban transit by the turn of the century. Most traction companies had their own single-purpose generating plants, larger than anything ever constructed by Edison or Westinghouse.

In his masterful history of the American power industry, *The Electric War,* from which much of the foregoing information has been drawn, Sheldon Novick notes: "We are so used to the monopolies held by the electric power companies that we forget how recent they are and how bitterly they were opposed by the progressives and reformers of their early days. The power company which has a monopoly of power supply was an invention, not an inevitable development, and by and large it was Samuel Insull's invention."

When he took the helm at Chicago Edison, Insull immediately began absorbing the competing companies in the Chicago area with the assistance of General Electric. In 1907, the city of Chicago designated him as power supplier for the streetcar companies, which doubled his sales at a single stroke.

Insull not only created the model for the consolidation of electric-power generation in the hands of one regional company but developed and tirelessly proselytized the ideology of monopoly. Much of his case rested on the technology of electric production. Insull's argument is still the foundation for the industry's rationale for high rates and for most forms of government regulation of electrical utilities. The basic point he emphasized was that electricity, unlike competing fuels such as natural gas, cannot be stored. This means that since demand for electricity varies with the time of day, generating capacity has to be built to meet maximum demand but might stand idle for significant parts of the day or even week. A power company can use its generation more efficiently to supply all possible demands around the daily cycle than can a number of single-purpose generators that might, for instance, operate only during the rush hours for streetcars, or during the production day for a factory. Since power plants are expensive to build, and bigger plants are more efficient than small, he argued, there is a significant saving in providing one system to meet all demands. (Despite this efficiency, power companies consistently overbuild. Con Ed last year, for instance, had installed capacity to generate 75 billion kilowatts but actually sold only 32 billion—less than half.)

As long as there was no way to store electricity, Insull's argument made economic sense. What he carefully ignored, however, was that a way *had* been found to store electricity. In 1881, Lord Kelvin had traveled from Paris to Glasgow with "a box of electricity," the original storage battery, invented by a Frenchman named Fauré. If electricity could be stored on a large scale—that is, produced at a steady rate around the clock and then released during peak demand periods—there would be no need for either massive generating complexes or monopoly control. It is hardly an accident that the storage battery and other means of electrical storage have been ignored over the years by the utilities or that Insull's basic case for monopoly went unchallenged until the advent of the environmental movement in the mid-60s with its emphasis on decentralized, alternate power sources such as wind, solar, and thermal power.

Insull didn't content himself with making a successful case for monopoly. He recognized two other areas crucial for the survival of private power companies: regulation and perpetual growth. He had carefully observed the ferment occasioned by the growth of the railroad monopolies and recognized, long before the public or reformers, that only two alternatives could emerge to deal with the utilities' unlimited powers to establish rates and terms of service: some form of public regulation, like the railroad commissions which had grown up in almost every state, or public ownership and socialism. As early as 1898, when he launched his crusade for monopoly utilities, he combined it with a call for state regulation. As Novick notes: "Insull, therefore, became the first public advocate of regulation of the power companies, at a time when they were not even recognized as utilities in need of regulation.... In 1898, as in modern days, regulation was seen as a means of preserving the private ownership of power companies."

Soon the reformers were echoing Insull's arguments for regulation, and, despite Socialist demands for outright public ownership and the persistence of numerous municipal electric companies, state regulation became the dominant form of public control over monopoly utilities. Many states simply added the electric companies to the responsibilities of the railroad commissions, although today every state has a separate public utilities commission.

This early history has had a profound effect in shaping the pattern of regulation. The fundamental court decisions relating to railroads became the basis of the commissions' attempts to control utility prices, especially the basic regulatory law which required that the companies be allowed a "fair rate of return" on investment. In effect, this "cost-plus" mechanism of rate determination, which has subsequently been epitomized by the Pentagon in its relationship with defense contractors, was the driving force behind the industry. A monopoly company's rates were based on how much money it needed not only to provide existing service but to attract new investment funds for additional plant construction. This meant that a company would make more money if it spent more money, a fantastic incentive for waste which persists into the present.

Utility commissions never felt it was their place to tell the industry how or when to spend money for new plants. They were relegated to the bookkeeping tasks of determining that the company had spent the money and deciding how the cost of that spending was to be allocated to different classes of customers. If consumers rebelled over rising rates, the regulators and the elected officials who appointed them simply pointed to the companies' balance sheets to show that the new rates were justified by expenses. Again, it wasn't until environmentalists in the late 1960s questioned the doctrine of perpetual growth and pointed to the pollution and destruction that constant growth was causing, that state commissions even began to compare real demand with the companies' construction plans.

The only difficulty in this self-perpetuating cycle of expansion from the companies' point of view, of course, was the need for a constantly expanding market: Someone had to buy all the new electricity that could be produced by the new plants. This was no problem while vast numbers of homes were without electricity, although the companies dumped the expensive task of bringing electricity to isolated farm homes and the poverty-stricken areas of the South onto the government, in the Rural Electrification Administration and the Tennessee Valley Authority. But once America had been electrified, stagnation could be avoided only by creating new, and unperceived, demands for power. Thus the industry supported the development of electric appliances from the washing machine to the electric toothbrush. Most importantly, it stimulated the conversion of home heating from coal and gas to electricity by offering incentives to builders to install its products in new homes and subsidizing homeowners for converting their existing heating systems to electricity. The utilities spent billions to make the "All-Electric Home" the new American dream. Today that dream has turned into a nightmare.

For instance, tens of thousands of New York-area homeowners discovered the true economics of electricity only after the 1973 oil crisis. Con Ed, having already terrified the state government with tales of its impending bankruptcy, managed to win a fuel-pass-along clause from the compliant Public Service Commission. (Like most regulatory ripoffs, this one spread rapidly from state to state because no commission wanted to be left holding the bag when angry consumers asked, "But how come they don't do this in ———?" The pack instinct for survival is as great among regulators as it is among wolves, perhaps even greater.) Suddenly, homeowners found that their electric bills were greater than their mortgage bills, and all of Con Ed's customers found that electric rates were rising twice as fast as everything else combined during the worst peace time inflation in the history of the country.

One of the reasons why electric heat is so expensive is that it is incredibly inefficient. Utilities today make electricity much the same way that Thomas Alva Edison did when he opened the Pearl Street plant in 1882. Fuel—oil, coal, natural gas or uranium—

creates heat which turns water into steam. The steam is released, as it is from the spout of a boiling teakettle, and directed at high pressure to turn a rotary turbine. The shaft of the turbine rotates a giant magnet within a coil of copper wire—a dynamo—and electricity flows through the wires and into the distribution system.

Most of the heat used to make electricity is wasted, i.e., is not converted into electricity. The waste heat gets pumped into the air or into a neighboring body of water, where of course it doesn't belong and where it does generally harmful things such as ruin our lungs, kill fish, alter the weather. Even after the electricity is produced, however, about ten per cent of it gets used up in transmission to the point of use. In the case of electric heating, it is then used to heat wires: The heat comes from the friction caused by the resistance of the wire to the passage of the current. About 27 per cent of the original fuel is converted into useful electricity in our home radiators. A well-maintained gas furnace, in contrast, is 60–70 per cent efficient. (European furnaces are more efficient than American furnaces because they have flues that keep down fuel consumption, but the flue has been forbidden here by the collusion of the electric and gas industries.)

As Novick again points out: "All other things being equal, two or three times as much fuel must therefore be burned to provide electric space heating as would be needed for gas or oil heat. This means, roughly, three times as much pollution and three times the rapid depletion of natural resources." And for those once-proud possessors of all-electric homes, three times the cost.

Now let's resume the story of that controversial transmission line, because it leads inexorably to the next stage of Con Ed's crisis.

For four years the issue was dead; neither Con Ed nor the Lindsay administration wanted to summon up the Marcus scandal. In early 1971, however, a new contract was brought quietly before New York City's Board of Estimate and a new controversy was born. Con Ed agreed to pay the city for an enlarged franchise, but this time it was dealing with a far more enlightened cast of participants. Bronx Borough President Robert Abrams led a one-man crusade against any new contract unless Con Ed agreed to carry low-cost public power generated by the Power Authority of the State of New York over the proposed 345-kilovolt line. Abrams even questioned whether the transmission line shouldn't be twice the proposed size, equal to the 700-kv. lines then in operation in the Northwest. Con Ed balked, and for good reason.

Abrams had reopened the public power debate, which had blown hot and cold for thirty-five years ever since Mayor Fiorello La Guardia had proposed that New York buy up Depression-plagued electric companies and operate its own public electric system. For many years the city had actually owned the beginnings of a power network—the electric plants that ran the subways. These had originally been acquired when the private subway lines, the IRT and BMT, went bankrupt. In 1959, during one of the city's perennial cash squeezes, Robert Wagner had sold the plants to Con Ed. They were old, inefficient, and highly polluting, but the chairman of Con Ed's board told a stockholders' meeting that the purchase had been made to remove "a temptation for the city to expand its own power system in other fields."

E. F. Hutton, the brokerage house, concurred with the decision, stating: "Considering that it finally stilled the threat of public power, purchase was by far the wisest course." These reports of the death of public power were premature, to say the least.

As a matter of fact, the public power issue had re-emerged briefly in 1968 when a consultant hired by the Lindsay administration had written a scathing report on Con Ed operations and suggested that the city might find it necessary to "nationalize" the company and run it as a municipal power system. This report, uncovered by Lucy Komisar and discussed at length in *New York* magazine, had been buried by Lindsay staffers. When confronted by Komisar, Deputy Mayor Timothy Costello said: "Public power is not something that can be instituted lightly. A city power system would require a huge investment of capital funds. The city has no means of distribution." Costello noted that the city was negotiating with Con Ed to use its distribution system in return for granting the company a right-of-way over a municipal aqueduct. "They have been resisting," he told Komisar.

Lindsay offered a different view of the report, which had been written by C. Gerard Davidson, like Luce a former Assistant Secretary of the Interior and, ironically, Luce's former boss as general counsel at the Bonneville Power Administration. (Recalling Luce, Davidson told Komisar: "He was very competent, but you never had the feeling about Chuck that he was ever dedicated to the philosophy of public power.") Lindsay shied away from the idea of public ownership but said the city *might* intervene to gain low-cost power from PASNY or public agencies in Canada, or buy the power itself and resell it to Con Edison. This possibility was never pursued, however, and Davidson angrily charged that Lindsay had been influenced by his close personal ties to Luce. (Chairman Luce, who seemed genuinely appalled by the more tawdry side of his predecessors' political methods, quickly proved to be a master of political log-rolling of a more sophisticated sort. In 1968, he was already chairman of Lindsay's Business Advisory Committee.)

When Abrams demanded that the contract terms reportedly under negotiation in 1968 be implemented in 1971, Lindsay staffers said the plan was "unworkable"—and proceeded to make the same arguments in opposition that Luce had announced three years before. Let's pursue those arguments for a moment because they show how even the state's massive public power agency has been converted for the use of the private power companies.

The State Power Authority has a long and interesting history. It was inaugurated in the late 1920s under the governorship of Franklin Delano Roosevelt and subsequently served as the model for the creation of TVA. Its fortunes flourished under Democratic governors and waned under Republicans. Since its basic source of power was the waters of the St. Lawrence, an international river, it was subject to federal as well as state law, and New Yorkers were protected in the use of the power by clear provisions in the statutes of both levels of government. Under these statutes, the output of the St. Lawrence River generators was to be allocated first to municipal power systems, and half of the power was irrevocably reserved for this purpose. Localities in the state's depressed North Country used the cheap power to attract industry, but since transmission technology was in its infancy, that is where the St. Lawrence power stayed. (The huge aluminum smelter complex at Massena was built specifically to benefit from the cheap power.)

Under Governor Harriman's administration, large expansions in the PASNY system were undertaken. As fate would have it, however, the new power became operable under his successor, Nelson Rockefeller, a man with an instinctive commitment to using public investment for private profit. Rockefeller simply took this new public power and sold it on long-term contracts to upstate private utilities. The irony of this was that several public power systems, including two on Long Island, were unable to benefit from their "preference" for the new public power because private utilities like Con Ed and Long Island Lighting refused to "wheel" or transmit the public power through their transmission systems.

This battle over "wheeling" rights, the basic method used by the private companies to quarantine public power, raged for decades in Congress. And it was why Abrams demanded that the Con Ed contract be based on a willingness to use its ties with other utilities to bring power to the city. (Electricity from different sources is as indistinguishable as one gallon of water from another once it enters a transmission network.)

The company's answer, and subsequently the city government's answer, was that no power was available since it had all been sold by Rockefeller. Abrams rejoined that these sales were specifically barred by both federal and state law and that the city could break the existing contracts and bump the illegal users. This would not mean that lights would blink out upstate, however, since PASNY had also begun building nuclear plants, and the million-kilowatt Fitzpatrick plant at Nine Mile Point was due to open soon. This power could be used to make up the difference. (The Fitzpatrick power had been committed already to upstate companies, but since no one was using it, it could easily be re-allocated.) The city therefore could benefit from a minimum of one million kilowatts (about 12 per cent of Con Ed's capacity) of cheap hydropower and at the same time reducing Con Ed's need to borrow for expensive new generating plants. This transfer would substantially reduce the average consumer's electric bill and end Con Ed's perpetual growth cycle.

The debate went on throughout the spring and summer of 1971. The contract was scheduled twice for a final vote and twice postponed. Finally, in the dog days of August, Abrams announced a victory. The city had agreed to sue for its fair share of PASNY power and Con Ed had agreed to deliver the new power over its transmission network. Like so many consumer victories, this one proved to be illusory. The city simply refused to implement its part of the bargain, and as subsequent court decisions ruled, Abrams, although a major elected city official, could not bring suit on behalf of the city. (Lindsay, then contemplating a run for the presidency and keeping his options open for other statewide offices, had the added incentive for inaction of not wanting a protracted legal battle that seemed to pit the city's interests against the desire for unlimited industrial growth upstate. While this wasn't the actual case, Lindsay had learned one lesson as mayor, and that was that the appearance frequently becomes the reality in political dogfights.) A compromise of sorts was struck when the state legislature in 1972 mandated PASNY to build two new plants to service New York City, but this solution was outrun by events, in the form of the Mideast oil crisis in 1973 and the controversial Con Ed flirtation with bankruptcy in 1974.

While high rates and lousy service were undoubtedly the major irritants in Con Ed's relations with its customers, air pollution ran a close third. Because of Con Ed's desire to produce all of the power it sold as near as possible to the center of its service area (the only exception being its complex of nuclear plants twenty-five miles north of the city line), the company accounted for half of the city's sulfur dioxide pollution by burning vast amounts of oil each day. Subsequently, by burning "sweet" (lower sulfur content) but more expensive oil, the company was able to cut this pollution in half, and naturally, this additional cost was borne by the consumers. But Con Ed remained heavily reliant on oil.

The Arab oil boycott in 1973 and the subsequent escalation in oil prices hit the utility, or rather its customers, very hard. Once the extent of the crisis was clear, Con Ed got busy and made sure that its increased prices were passed along to customers, already reeling under the highest electric bills in the nation. Finally, the Con Ed consumers struck back: Many stopped paying their bills on time. At the same time, electric consumption also began to fall (actual consumption in 1974 and 1975 was two billion kilowatt-hours less than the record year of 1973 and still lags several hundred million kilowatt-hours behind 1971 consumption.) As a result, Con Ed experienced a cash squeeze.

In what can only be called a brilliant political power-play, Chairman Luce proceeded to seize opportunity from the jaws of adversity. On March 31, 1974, a front-page story appeared in *The New York Times* hinting that Con Ed was on the verge of bankruptcy. It was the first of a three-part series by David Andleman, and by the time Andleman had finished recounting the dire prophecies of Luce and other company officials, Wall Street analysts, and PSC Chairman Joseph Swidler, most New Yorkers were surprised that their lights were still burning.

Three days after the *Times* series concluded, Luce was in Albany for a public meeting with Governor Malcolm Wilson. The "solution" he proposed for the crisis was surprising in the light of Con Ed's past history, but quite in keeping with government bailouts of troubled corporations, which have become commonplace in this age of corporate welfare. Luce urged that the state, through the Power Authority, purchase two plants under construction for $500 million. The plants would ultimately be run by Con Ed and the power they produced would become part of its baseload generating system but would be completed and owned by PASNY. This would see the company through its cash-flow crisis and ultimately provide some relief for consumers.

As Judith Bender revealed in *Newsday,* the "emergency" meeting was simply the culmination of a bailout campaign that Luce had been conducting since January. He had decided to turn up the flame in order to force the governor, currently running for reelection, and a legislature that was in no mood for seeming to aggrandize the most hated utility in the state to capitulate.

Luce got the furor he expected. What the public didn't get was the careful analysis by the press and public regulators that would have thrown cold water on the whole thing. As David Kusnet, an energy specialist and consumer advocate, wrote in the December 7, 1974, issue of *The Nation:* ". . . consumers would have been ready to pull out their electric cords, turn off the lights, and vote out every seat-warmer in Albany if their daily newspapers had told the full story of the Con Ed bailout."

On April 23, Luce played his hole card. The company's board of trustees voted to suspend the utility's 45-cent quarterly dividend. The action sent a tremor through the nation's financial markets and Con Ed's stock plummeted from a high of $18 to $6 in a few weeks. Con Ed was front-page news everywhere. Editorialists jumped into the fray; typical of the unquestioning support they gave the company's tale of woe is the following specimen from the May 10 *New York Times:* "There are abundant grounds on which to fault Con Edison, but legislators will be making no useful contribution to protection of the company's hapless customers in this city and Westchester County if they adjourn without authorizing the issuance of self-liquidating bonds for purchase of the two plants. Such a default would merely invite a collapse as devastating in its way as that of the Penn Central."

The legislature got the message, and on May 16 it passed a bailout bill authorizing $500 million to be paid to Con Ed for the unfinished plants and an additional $300 million to cover the costs of completing construction. (Subsequent studies have shown that the actual total cost of this undertaking may rise to more than $500 million.)

But what was the real story? Well, for one thing, Con Ed was making money while it was threatening bankruptcy in May. When *this* information surfaced months later, only the *Times* reported it— on an inside page. And it wasn't until the September issue of *Fortune* that anyone bothered to report that the missed dividend payment amounted to only $28 million, an amount the utility could have scraped together in its petty cash accounts or taken from a $130-million line of credit it had with New York banks at the time. If the company was feeling a genuine pinch, why not just halve the dividend ($14 million) instead of throwing the financial markets into a tailspin? This question was asked by angry executives at other utilities whose stocks felt a serious spillover from the Con Ed "collapse."

Even more interesting was the irrational behavior of the state legislature. With Con Ed's stock plummeting, the state could have purchased the *entire company* outright for little more than the $500 million it paid for the two uncompleted plants. The issue was actually raised at the time, but New York state legislators are not known for their "socialistic" or foresighted tendencies. The simple reality was that in the midst of the carefully orchestrated bankruptcy campaign, no one dared ask some very fundamental questions.

Con Ed's recovery after the bailout has been nothing short of astounding. Token 5- or 10-per cent pay cuts issued to corporate executives during the crisis were quietly restored the following October. The dividend was restored to 20 cents per quarter in the second half of 1974, rose to 30 cents quarterly in 1975, and was further increased to 40 cents in the first quarter of 1976. In January 1977, the dividend was again increased by 25 per cent to 50 cents per share—its highest rate in history.

Yet even in the light of this "miraculous" recovery and a radically altered economic climate, the bailout has gone on like clockwork. With New York State itself teetering on the edge of bankruptcy, Governor Carey rejected pleas from Abrams and then Representative Bella Abzug to rescind it. The legislature has been silent on the issue, apparently unwilling to sift the ashes of its earlier mistake in public. (Some apologists argue that since PASNY is an independent agency, its borrowing $800 million in the credit market has no relation to the plight of the city and state in those same markets. This is nonsense. The PASNY borrowing simply means that there will be $800 million less seeking an investment vehicle and helps to assure that the nation's financiers can continue to do without the credit demands of New York city and state, two of their biggest previous customers.)

The largest question remaining is why Charles Luce opened the door to public power, and brought Con Ed's greatest nightmare to life? The answer is simple: He didn't. As we have already suggested, PASNY was coming to the New York market as a result of the protracted transmission-line controversy, and it was scheduled to build two new plants for the city by 1980. Luce saw a way to make the inevitable serve his company's purposes. By selling the two existing plants, Luce not only removed Con Ed from the capital markets at a time when costs for borrowers were soaring, but also forestalled the building of additional capacity in the New York region by PASNY that would have cramped Con Ed's long-range plans. Con Ed gave the game away when it entered into a long-term contract with six other private companies in the state to build seventeen additional plants, mostly nuclear, at a conservatively estimated $3.5 billion during the 1980s. The contract was announced at exactly the same time that Luce was in Albany pleading bankruptcy—another crucial fact ignored by the New York press.

In addition, technical reports by PASNY auditors show that the two plants that were sold will require $130 million more in repairs than first estimated, for such reasons as "inadequate storage practices, lack of cleanliness during assembly, and unsatisfactory construction processes." It also turns out that one of the plants, a nuclear reactor known as Indian Point 3, was built near a geological fault and its safety devices are being challenged by environmentalists, which may mean years of delay before final operation. Mr. Luce sold New York State two of the most expensive "lemons" in history.

In September 1976, PASNY power began flowing to New York City and Westchester governmental agencies. The city alone expects to reduce its electric bill by $25 million a year because of PASNY's lower rates. But in the "heads I win, tails you lose," world of Con Ed, the PSC has already granted the utility a "transfer adjustment" that will increase the bills of consumers and small businesses by $57 million to make up the revenue it is losing by no longer having these government agencies as captive customers. A similar situation arose when Con Ed launched its highly successful "Save a Watt" campaign. Consumers cut their consumption but subsequently found themselves paying more per kilowatt hour to sustain Con Ed's guaranteed minimum rate of profit, which is now officially 13½ per cent.

How does such a universally despised utility manage, year after year, to work its will on a hostile public? Part of the answer emerges from a look at Con Ed's board of directors, a sort of snapshot of the permanent government in action.

• William S. Beinecke is the chairman of the board and chief executive officer of Sperry and Hutchinson Company, a conglomerate best known for its "green stamps" but also a major supplier of business services and interior furnishings. Beinecke is also Felix Rohatyn's partner in a real-estate venture in the Bronx called Lambert Houses. (The third partner is Jane Englehardt, the widow of the owner óf Englehardt Minerals of South Africa, an infamous employer of black indentured labor. Mrs. Englehardt is best known, at least in certain circles, for her stable of thoroughbreds.) Beinecke is also a director of Manufacturers Hanover and of Bigelow-Sanford, the giant carpet company. He is a trustee of the Pingry School and Yale University.

• Edmund Virgil Conway is chairman of the board and president of Seamen's Bank for Savings. He is a board member of J. P. Stevens, the giant Southern anti-union textile concern that is currently the object of a nationwide boycott by the Amalgamated Clothing and Textile Workers Union. He is also on the boards of National Securities and Research, Atlantic Mutual Insurance, and Centennial Insurance. Conway, a longtime critic of New York City's social spending, is on the boards of the city's Chamber of Commerce and Industry, Economic Development Council, and Citizens Budget Commission, a business front group. Mayor Beame appointed him to the Mayor's Management Advisory Board. He is also a trustee of Colgate University.

• Frederick M. Eaton, as previously noted, is partner in Shearman and Sterling, a law firm that does work for Con Ed and Citibank. He is also on the board of New York Life Insurance, a provider of mortgages to landlords in the city's direct-lease day-care scandal. Like almost every other member of the permanent government he keeps his fingers in the city's cultural and philanthropic life as a board member of the American Museum of Natural History and the Columbia-Presbyterian Medical Center.

• Mrs. Andrew Heiskell is better known as Marian Sulzberger, one of the heirs to America's most powerful publishing empire. She is director of special activities at *The New York Times;* her present husband is chairman of the board at *Time.* She is New York's reigning lady bountiful, serving simultaneously as chairman of the board of the Community Service Society; co-chairman (with the mayor) of the city's Council on the Environment; and board member of Rockefeller University, New York Botanical Garden, and the Polytechnic Institute of New York (formerly Brooklyn Poly). She is also a member of the advisory councils for the National Parks, Historical Sites, Buildings and Monuments Committee and for the Dartmouth Medical School; a board member of the Inter-American Press Association, the National Planning Association, and the drug-manufacturing company Merck.

• Grayson L. Kirk is president emeritus of Columbia University— and will always be remembered for his activities there during the famous "Columbia bust" of 1968, when policemen invaded the campus and severely beat student protestors. Kirk has always had close ties with the financial community and serves as a board member of Nation-Wide Securities, Franklin Publications, Dividend Shares, Monthly Income Shares, and the Greenwich Savings Bank. He also serves on the board of International Business Machines (IBM), which did $7.2 million's worth of business with Con Ed in 1973.

• William W. Lapsley was briefly president of Con Ed until he was replaced by Arthur Hauspurg in 1975. Prior to joining Con Ed in 1969, he had spent thirty-two years in the U.S. Army, retiring with the rank of major general—an unspectacular achievement. He also served as program manager for Kaiser Jeep Corporation on Taiwan.

• Hobart D. Lewis is chairman and chief executive of the *Reader's Digest.* He is also a member of the international advisory committee of Morgan Guaranty Trust, a director of the Boys' Clubs of America, a trustee of the Northern Westchester Hospital, former chairman of the U.S. Advisory Commission on Information, and a member-at-large of the Board of Governors of the American Red Cross.

• Charles F. Luce sits on a number of boards, befitting his rank as Con Ed's chief executive. At least two of them appear to be conflicts of interest. Luce is a board member of U.A.L. Inc., and United Airlines. These are the source of the turbine generators used by the company. He also sits on the board of Metropolitan Life Insurance, which did $10.2 million's worth of business with Con Ed in 1973. He is a trustee of Columbia University; the Conference Board, a major business forecasting group; GAB Business Services Inc.; the New York Chamber of Commerce and Industry; the Economic Development Council; the National Association for Mental Health; the Fresh Air Fund (which sends poor kids away from the Con-Ed-polluted streets of New York each summer); and the New York Botanical Garden.

• Milton C. Mumfort is a director and former chairman of the board of Lever Brothers. He is also a director of Atco Industries, Crown Zellerbach, Equitable Life Assurance, Thomas J. Lipton, the Presbyterian Hospital, the Stamford Hospital, and Educational Facilities Laboratories.

• Peter S. Paine is chairman of the executive committee of Great Northern Nekoosa, a giant paper manufacturer. He is on the boards of the Continental Corporation, Continental Insurance, and Irving Trust, and is chairman of the Essex County-Champlain National Bank. He is also a board member of the Vincent Astor Foundation, the Juilliard School of Music, and the Bodman Foundation.

• Richard S. Perkins is Con Ed's friend at Citibank, former chairman of the executive committee of both the bank and its holding company. He is also a director of Allied Chemical, Hospital Corporation of America, International Telephone and Telegraph (ITT), New York Life Insurance, Southern Pacific, the Carnegie Institution of Washington, the Metropolitan Museum of Art, and the Vincent Astor Foundation.

• Luis Quero-Chiesa, the board's token Puerto Rican, is senior vice-president of Roy Blumenthal International Associates, a public relations and advertising firm. He is also on the boards of Blue Cross and Blue Shield of Greater New York, Inter-American University, the New York Philharmonic, the Academy of Arts and Sciences of Puerto Rico, and the city's Committee on Cultural Affairs.

• William S. Renchard is chairman of the executive committee of Chemical Bank and a director of the bank's holding company. He also sits on the board of the oil firm Amerada Hess, which received $53 million from Con Ed in 1973, as well as Armstrong Rubber, Baker Industries, Borden, New York Life Insurance, C.I. Realty Investors, Cleveland-Cliffs Iron, and the International Executive Service Corps. He is chairman of the Citizens Budget Commission and president and director of the Manhattan Eye, Ear, and Throat Hospital.

• Lawrence A. Wein is senior partner in the law firm of Wein, Lane & Malkin. He is also a director of Borden, Brandeis University, the Federation of Jewish Philanthropies of New York, and the Lincoln Center for the Performing Arts.

• Ralph A. Weller is chairman of the board and chief executive officer of Otis Elevator. He is a board member of United Technologies Corporation, Charter New York, the Harlem Savings Bank, Penn Mutual Life Insurance, the National Multiple Sclerosis Society, the Phelps-Stokes Fund, and the New York Building Congress, a contractors' group. He is one of the executive board of the Boy Scouts of Greater New York.

• Franklin H. Williams is the board's token black. An attorney, he is president of the Phelps-Stokes Fund. He is also a director of Chemical Bank and of its holding company, U.R.S. Inc., Lincoln University, the New York state advisory committee to the U.S. Civil Rights Commission, and the New York City Center of Music and Drama.

As the maverick state assemblyman Andrew Stein has revealed, these men and women are amply rewarded for lending their names and influence to the people who run Con Ed. Compensation for board members works out at about $8.22 per *minute*. Since each member also serves on a number of committees, Con Ed gives them between $7000 and $15,000 each year for tasks which rarely take more than thirty hours of their time.

Charles Luce had his salary increased to $200,000 plus stock options in 1975.

This lucrative joyride may be headed for a nasty smashup. For the first time, the business community itself has taken the lead in fighting Con Ed's most recent request for a $248-million rate hike. Thousands of small and medium-sized businesses finally recognize that Con Ed is bleeding them white. When several breweries left New York City recently, they pointed to rising electricity costs as a major component in their decisions. The final irony is that Con Ed may have to be taken over by the state so that other businesses may survive.

THE MIDDLE-CLASS REBELS

The weather was ominous. As huge banks of black, rain-laden clouds blotted out the rays of a sinking summer sun, thousands of people, many of them elderly couples trundling aluminum beach chairs, emerged from the red brick towers of Co-op City and made their way to a huge field known as the Greenway which serves this giant housing development as a natural amphitheater. As they filed along the dirt paths that had been worn in the grass, they glanced at the lowering clouds. Several called encouragement to the others: "Don't worry, Charlie won't let it rain—not tonight."

It didn't rain, and a little after eight o'clock the tenants of Co-op City began the "victory" rally for which they had waited through thirteen long and bitter months of the largest rent strike ever brought in the United States. Several of the tenants' leaders—hard-working middle-aged and middle-class people who had been threatened with the loss of their homes, massive court-ordered fines, and jail sentences—spelled out some of the details of the settlement they had just won from the New York State government. Then Charles Rosen, a slim, chain-smoking, electrically charged thirty-

three-year-old who was leader of the strike, stepped to the microphone set up on the grassy knoll overlooking the Greenway. He
explained that he had just gone from being a "crazy radical" to
being the head of a housing corporation with assets of almost $500
million. He paused for a moment, while television cameras whirred
and flashbulbs popped, and then he shouted: "We beat the bastards!" The crowd went wild.

It was an unexpected victory by an unlikely group of revolu-
tionaries. The people of Co-op City—bus drivers, construction
workers, office clerks, housewives—had taken on the might of a
determined state government, New York City's financial community,
the courts, the political machines, and a generally hostile media.
They demanded nothing less than control of their community and
the quality of their lives. They created their own leaders, had few
outside allies, hammered out their tactics as they went along. They
risked everything they had.

There are few real success stories in urban America today. Traditional centers of resistance like the unions, ethnic groups, the
churches, and popularly elected leaders have proven to be inept and
powerless at confronting today's economic crises. In the face of a
series of numbing defeats, the Co-op City story deserves to be carefully studied by those who would save our cities. It points the way
to effective resistance and, perhaps, survival.

Co-op City is America's largest single housing development. It
looms on New York City's northern border between the Bronx and
Westchester County like some urban Stonehenge, with thirty-five
massive housing towers surrounded by six clusters of townhouses,
three internal shopping centers, and its own educational park—a
city within a city.

At the groundbreaking ceremonies in 1968, Robert Moses had
called Co-op City the cornerstone of his plans for a "slumless" New
York. He envisioned other developments, on the same scale, that
would be constructed on vacant land and would allow whole deteriorated neighborhoods to be relocated en masse, with the slums
left behind razed for new developments; thus would a new, well-
housed city emerge from the rubble of the old. But more than anything Co-op City represented an attempt to deal with "white flight,"
with the accelerating outflow of white, middle-class taxpayers from
declining inner-city neighborhoods to the suburbs, a flight that had
begun soon after World War II and threatened the viability of
central cities all over America. Many saw Co-op City, and similar
projects then being planned for outlying sections in Brooklyn and

Queens, as the "last hope" for a socially balanced New York. If these projects failed to keep middle-income populations within the municipality's geographic and fiscal boundaries, then the city would become home only to impoverished blacks and other minorities, and to the elderly white poor, who together were denied access to suburban housing. The very rich would also remain, but in carefully guarded enclaves on Manhattan's East Side or in suburbs-within-the-city like Riverdale in the Bronx and Douglaston in Queens. This kind of bipolar city was the nightmare of city planners and politicians. Its tax base would disappear at the same time that greater and greater demands were placed on public services by the unemployed poor. It was a prescription for breakdown and chaos.

Preserving the middle class had been the watchword of city politics from the mid-1950s. In 1955, the state legislature had adopted the Mitchell-Lama middle-income housing program to substitute public initiative for the refusal of the private housing market to produce new housing for most of New York state's urban population. But the program had gotten off to a slow start, and even with Governor Rockefeller's constant creation of new housing agencies and financing gimmicks, it failed dismally to meet the real needs for housing construction.

The idea behind Mitchell-Lama was simple enough: If private enterprise refused to do the job on its own, then the state must subsidize the housing industry's profits. The state would therefore use its preferential borrowing power in the financial markets to provide low-cost mortgage money. The cities in turn would severely limit real-estate taxes on this new construction. In many cases, the city would also use its urban-renewal powers to reduce the initial land costs for developers. Ninety per cent (later increased to 95 per cent) of project costs would be borne by the public. In return, developers were expected to limit their profits to 7½ per cent—although federal tax loopholes and depreciation actually increased the true profit substantially. But even these inducements proved inadequate to seduce the necessary response from private investors in the "go-go" 1960s, and much of the housing was ultimately created by "nonprofit" developers like the United Housing Foundation, a housing conglomerate formed by the liberal needle-trades unions and "good government" housing types.

Concerned that the state alone would never meet New York City's needs, the city demanded its own parallel Mitchell-Lama program, an action that left it eventually holding the bag on $1.3 billion a year in housing debt. Together, both programs today house about 300,000 residents in more than 100,000 apartments. This is about five per cent of New York City's actual housing stock.

From the start, the Mitchell-Lama program was plagued by scandal. It became a cesspool of legal graft. MacNeil Mitchell, one of the original sponsors, was a Republican state senator from Manhattan's Silk Stocking district. His private law firm got a large share of the legal work on the major projects. Alfred Lama, the architect and wheelhorse Democratic assemblyman from the Brooklyn machine, got numerous architectural contracts for the housing program bearing his name. City Title, the bipartisan title insurance firm run by Assembly Speaker Stanley Steingut, Rockefeller protégé Alton Marshall, Brooklyn ex-Congressman Eugene Keogh, and upstate Republican assemblyman Willis Stephens, reaped the proceeds of title insurance on $50 million in Mitchell-Lama projects in a single eighteen-month period.

In January 1966, the State Investigation Commission held hearings on Mitchell-Lama ripoffs. A state auditor, Leo Silverman, testified that Fred Trump, a major builder, had overestimated construction costs on a Brooklyn project by $6,650,000, thus reaping a windfall profit of $598,000. Trump was also accused of having charged the state $1,228,000 more for the project land than he had paid for it. Abraham Kazan, head of the United Housing Foundation, testified that he had been forced to surrender half of the forty-acre project to Trump after the politically well-connected builder had held up final approval for the project for three years at the Board of Estimate.

Omnipresent wheeler-dealer Bunny Lindenbaum admitted under oath that he had been working on Trump's project while a member of the City Planning Commission, but declared, "Any work I did for Mr. Trump had nothing to do with the city." Lindenbaum at the time of his testimony was suing the state for a $520,000 legal fee he earned for evicting tenants from the site, but documents were introduced showing that the work had actually been done by the city corporation counsel's office and a private relocation firm that had been paid $382,419 for removing 1000 families.

Lindenbaum wasn't the only hustler with his hooks in the project. MacNeil Mitchell received $128,000 for legal services involved in selling cooperative apartments in the project, and Trump was also cited for renting construction equipment at excessive rates from another company he controlled.

When Jacob Grumet, one of the four Commission members, asked, "Is there any way to prevent a man who does business like that from getting another contract with the state?" Silverman answered, "I don't think so, under our present laws."

It was the tenants in the Mitchell-Lama housing who bore the costs of this corruption, and suffered the effects of poor construction on many of the program's sites. At Lindsay Park in Brooklyn, the ceilings began to collapse. At Jamie Towers in the Bronx, gaping holes appeared in the walls. In other projects, poorly insulated steam lines shifted and broke underground, the plumbing constantly backed up, the heating systems malfunctioned. When tenants complained about these atrocities, they quickly found that when the city or state "signed off" on the job, the contractors were absolved of repair costs. Tenant leaders we interviewed complained of the "indecent haste" with which state and city officials had okayed faulty construction jobs, and suggested that the chummy relationship with the builders might be explained by the fact that a number of men "graduated" from public employment to jobs with the very housing companies they had been supervising.

Yet for most tenants, the Mitchell-Lama program until quite recently represented a modest success. The problems were offset by reasonable rents and generally pleasant and well-maintained surroundings. Paternalistic management, which especially characterized UHF developments, was bearable, even reassuring to middle-income families who saw other communities elsewhere undergoing wrenching change. There were special benefits for tenants in cooperative developments (more than half the program) since they could subtract pro-rated tax and mortgage interest payments from their federal and state taxes. For the numerous Mitchell-Lama tenants who were approaching retirement, the prospect of a stable, affordable rental was particularly pleasant. Many of these people had fled from neighborhoods undergoing rapid racial change and had experienced the pathology of poverty at first hand. Now they took a quiet pride in the fact that they lived in "integrated" communities with middle-class blacks and Hispanics who shared their fears and aspirations.

Inflationary pressures generated by the Vietnam war bit deeply into the Mitchell-Lama program. As the number of units being built accelerated, so did the costs of labor and materials as well as the cost of mortgage money—the largest component of any rent check. Builders had little incentive to resist these increases, since the city and state guaranteed them a fixed profit and were always willing to enlarge the mortgage as a project moved ahead. The mortgage at Co-op City, for instance, went from $236 million when the apartments were first offered for sale in 1965 to $390 million when the first tenants moved in five years later, an increase of more than 50 per cent.

State and city housing administrators attempted to deal with these escalating costs by postponing permanent mortgages and financing their housing costs in the short-term market. The city's Board of Estimate, under strong tenant pressures, began to raise the amount of tax abatement allowed the projects. Soon many were receiving the maximum tax reductions legally allowed. These steps were only temporary palliatives. Rents continued to soar. (The state, from a much stronger borrowing position, finally decided not to gamble with mortgage rates and opted to put most of its projects on permanent mortgages after a few years. The city assumed that the war would end quickly and mortgage rates would fall. It was wrong on both counts, and short-term rates paid by city Mitchell-Lama tenants are 50 per cent higher than the long-term rates paid in many state projects. This has led to massive mortgage delinquencies in city projects encompassing 49,000 apartments.)

By the early 1970s, the entire program was in a full-fledged crisis. Sporadic rent strikes broke out as tenants demanded government assistance in the face of annual rent increases. The largest of these strikes took place at Rochdale Village, a large UHF cooperative in Queens. But the strike was poorly organized, and the leadership was factionalized. Less than a quarter of the tenants actually participated, and the strike was finally broken by threats of eviction. The housing bureaucrats had won a temporary "victory," but it is exactly these kinds of victories that lead to the loss of wars. Continued confrontations were inevitable so long as no long-term solution to the problem of unlimited rent increases was offered to the tenants. In 1975 the battleground moved to Co-op City, where almost 20 per cent of all Mitchell-Lama tenants lived. For both tenants and government, it was a fight to the finish.

Investigators are still trying to unravel the tangled financial past of Co-op City. But it isn't easy. Appropriately, it was built on a swamp. Much of the land under the project was originally owned by the scandal-scarred Teamster Union pension funds. A racetrack had originally been scheduled for the site, and when this scheme failed, William Zeckendorf, one of the most flamboyant real-estate speculators in New York history, erected his most spectacular failure—a $13-million amusement park called Freedomland. Zeckendorf's empire came crashing down in 1965 when the firm he headed, Webb & Knapp, was forced to declare bankruptcy, and most of the Freedomland site was again recycled to the Teamsters, who proceeded to sell 300 acres to the United Housing Foundation for the astounding sum of $16 million. Those familiar with the early days of the project claim that Robert Moses was the godfather of this deal.

As Charles Rosen tells it, "Even the geology of this project was crooked. UHF bought every inch that was under water or filled in with garbage. The Teamsters held on to every piece of land with a rock foundation, including an 83-acre site which cuts Co-op City in half and the two gas stations that service the community."

As a result, Co-op City became something of a construction marvel. Fifty thousand piles had to be driven to shore up the swampy subsoil and a two-mile pipeline was constructed to Long Island Sound so that millions of gallons of sand could be pumped to the site to buttress its foundations. It was these extraordinary construction costs which officially forced the mortgage to almost double its anticipated size. At one point in the complicated legal exchanges that took place during the rent strike, the tenants charged that other irregularities during the construction period included the building of a summer home for UHF's construction superintendent, with materials from the site, the use of Co-op City materials in a private health center, and the use of its materials and labor to renovate a foreign embassy. Due to other developments, these charges were never argued in court, but the construction of Co-op City seems to have been highly "irregular," even by New York's notoriously flawed standards of normal construction practices.

Perhaps the strangest element of all was the construction of a $27-million power plant for the exclusive use of Co-op City. Abraham Kazan, the founder of UHF and an important pioneer in bringing cooperative housing to New York City, had always been at loggerheads with the Consolidated Edison Company over its exorbitant rates. He had successfully built his own "total energy" power plant at Rochdale Village, which burns natural gas to produce electricity as well as to heat and air-condition the buildings. During the 1965 "blackout," Rochdale Village was the only community in New York with lights, a threatening memory to Con Ed, which always made it a point to stamp out even the smallest hint of competition in its service area.

Kazan's nephew, Leon, was engaged to design a similar power plant for Co-op City. Con Ed saw the handwriting on the wall and made a deal with UHF to sell them power cheaper than they could produce it themselves. The exact details of this arrangement are obscure, but Co-op City ended up with the "Cadillac" power plant *and* the cheap Con Ed power, so the plant was completely unnecessary. If Kazan was bluffing Con Ed, it was one of the more expensive bluffs in city history. The power plant was used only once in six years to provide electricity. A tenant lawsuit begun in 1972 by Louis Nizer charged that it had been "designed and constructed in a defective and unsound manner." Rosen charges that the turbines originally ordered for Co-op City actually ended up in another UHF project in Brooklyn (which has since been bought by the Starrett Construction Company and has been renamed Starrett City).

Whatever the truth is behind these charges and countercharges, the tenants of Co-op City were left holding the bag. Con Ed established a special low rate structure for the development, Rate Structure 13, but subsequently doublecrossed the tenants and had these preferential rates set aside by the compliant state Public Service Commission. Electric costs in Co-op City rose 300 per cent in only a few years. In addition, Co-op City was granted low "commercial" rates for its natural-gas supplies, but this category, used almost exclusively by industry, was "interruptible" by the utility if supplies in the interstate pipelines were reduced. As a result of a producers' strike by the oil giants that own most of our natural-gas reserves, and the rerouting of gas supplies to unregulated intrastate users in the Sunbelt, Co-op City is now forced to rely on high-priced imported oil during the winter months. That adds $1.5 million to rents each year. And the residents continue to pay for a huge power plant that federal energy officials have called "worthless" and "a total redundancy."

The tenants are critical of almost every action taken by Community Services, Inc., UHF's wholly-owned subsidiary which became the general contractor and sales agent for the project (although it had a net worth of only $200,000 at the time of its designation). Instead of buying appliances direct from manufacturers, a common practice for such a huge job, they used an expensive separate buyer. Twenty thousand stoves and refrigerators were bought for the 15,372-apartment project. "We're still looking for 5000 missing stoves and missing refrigerators," says Rosen. When the tenants eventually assumed control of the project, they found that there was no inventory control system to administer the $53 million annual budget. "They ran this place like a corner candy store. There is no way to even begin to discover how much was stolen. We must assume that they run their other projects the same way. And the state, which received $1.08 million a year just to supervise the project, never said a word. The guy in charge of supervision for the state was a former UHF employee. The whole program is an incredible mess, and they just expected people to pay the costs of their incompetence and never ask questions," declares Rosen.

The tenants did raise questions when they saw their rents constantly escalate. When they bought their apartments in 1965, rents, called "carrying charges" in the cooperatives, were estimated at $23 a room per month. By 1970 carrying charges had risen to $31.46; on July 1, 1974, they rose again to $42.81. A $10-a-room increase meant $50–$60 more in rent payments each month for average families. Finally, rents were raised to $53.46 a room on July 1, 1975, retroactive to April 1. This was, in fact, only a 25 per cent first bite in an increase of 82 per cent projected by the management over the next five years. The tenants rebelled.

Co-op City was an extremely organized community from the day it was opened. Tenants had found themselves rushed into a community without sidewalks or schools. The project had been built next to one of New York City's largest garbage dumps, a continuing irritant even when the wind blew the smell away. Committees sprang up to deal with these and other problems. Soon there was an organization for every possible concern as well as dozens of fraternal, religious, and hobby clubs. The residents had brought their politics with them from previous neighborhoods, and the development soon had the largest Democratic machine club in Bronx County, as well as a fledgling group of Democratic reformers.

This organizational mania soon spilled over into the struggle to control the rents, and a series of broad-based people's parliaments sprang up and were given the generic title of steering committee. By early 1975, the residents had run through Steering Committees I and II and formed a Steering Committee III. Charles Rosen had been elected to the committee from his building, and he soon became its chairman.

Rosen belongs to a generation that was called the "red diaper babies." His parents were immigrant workers who became Communist activists in the Depression and passed their radical politics along to their children. Rosen spoke only Yiddish at home, and his mother transliterated his given name of Shockner into Charlie on his birth certificate, after long debate with a woman in the neighboring bed at the hospital. (His eloquent, if scatological, command of Yiddish has endeared him to the 60 per cent of Co-op City residents who are from Jewish working-class homes, many of whom are of his parents' generation.) He grew up with the kind of fear for "right wing deviation" that most teenagers reserve for bad breath, and shifted, with his older brother Jake, from the Communists to the Maoist Progressive Labor Party in the early 1960s. At Progressive Labor, Rosen was in charge of producing the group's voluminous printed materials, and he managed, by a quirk, to acquire a much-valued card in Local 6 of the Printers Union. He met and married his wife, Lynn, while both were PL activists, but the pressures of raising a family forced him to pick up his union card and move to the *New York Post* as a journeyman printer.

The Rosens, along with thousands of other young families, moved to Co-op City in search of stable rents and a decent, integrated environment in which to raise their children. Rosen's politics matured until he became an independent, unaffiliated socialist and "radical democrat" who believes in the right of every individual to exercise effective control over the forces that shape his or her life. When he confronted the UHF management, he found the kind of contemptuous, bureaucratic paternalism that he felt had destroyed the vitality of the labor movement and other mass insurgencies in American life. "They always spoke of 'our people'—'our people wouldn't do this,' and 'our people wouldn't do that,' and what they meant was 'these dumb Jewish workers whom we have always pushed around will do exactly what we tell them to.' They were the same Social Democratic whores I've hated all my life."

Rosen's lifelong involvement in radical politics had given him an uncanny sense of tactics and an awareness that his neighbors now had their backs against the wall. He knew they would fight, and he began in January 1975 to organize—floor by floor, building by building—for a long strike.

Two months before the rent increase was to take effect, the tenants engaged in a show of force and collected 85 per cent of Co-op City's rents and delivered them to the governor's Manhattan office. (Eight months before they had shown the same level of support in collecting rents giving them to UHF.) Then the rents were turned over to the housing company. The following month, June, they repeated the tactic of collecting rents themselves and deposited the money in a separate bank account. As a result, the UHF-appointed board of directors resigned and were replaced by a board of state employees from the Division of Housing. Steering Committee III was hauled into court and ordered to turn the money over to be held in escrow. Four hours after the money was turned over to the court it was given to the housing company.

At the same time, Steering Committee III was hit with an injunction by Supreme Court Justice Joseph Brust that barred it from "collecting, soliciting, handling, depositing or holding in any way all or any part of carrying charges and any other monies payable by tenant cooperators of Co-op City to plaintiff, Riverbay Corporation." It was further forbidden even to advocate a rent strike "by exhorting, urging, advising, instigating, authorizing or otherwise recommending or encouraging tenant cooperators to withhold all or any part of carrying charges or any other monies payable to plaintiff." Push had come to shove.

That same evening, June 20, 1975, Rosen called a meeting of the twenty-three steering committee members. Their attorney, Herb Freedman, explained that violating the judge's order and continuing the strike could mean fines and jail terms for the members. (Originally hired to represent the Steering Committee because he had had some contacts with the cooperative housing movement, Freedman was later elected to the Committee unanimously, in gratitude for his unstinting devotion to the strike.)

For many of them, going to jail would mean certain loss of their jobs. Rosen then passed out resignation forms. Fifteen members resigned on the spot. Rosen was stunned, but determined to carry on. He devised a stratagem to keep the state from discovering how badly split the strikers were: Those who had resigned would become a "rent stabilization" committee and would not undertake any activities that would make them liable to violate Brust's order. The rest would continue as the "strike" committee.

The strike committee represented an interesting cross-section of tenants. In addition to Rosen, they were:

• Esther Smith, the only black and the only woman to remain formally active in the committee. The director of an East Harlem day-care center, she had been chairlady of the Co-op City advisory council, a management-appointed residents' group that had originally opposed the steering committee.

• Al Abrams, a shoe salesman who had to work especially hard to meet the costs of raising one of his children, a young son with cerebral palsy. Abrams had preceded Rosen as chairman of the steering committee and had been a vice-chairman of the advisory council.

• Bernard Cylich, an electrician who had spent time in a concentration camp as a child. He also had been a member of the advisory committee and had opposed what he considered to be Rosen's "Maoist adventurism."

• Murray Lerner, a retired fur worker in his eighties. Lerner was chairman of the coordinating council of senior-citizen organizations in the development. He shouted down another member at a public meeting and won an active competition to become the first resident to break the injunction by advocating a continuation of the strike.

• Joel Dannenberg, a soft-spoken quietly pleasant man who worked for the state government as a senior bank examiner. More than anything else, Dannenberg was outraged by the Brust order's infringement of free speech. He would tearfully tell his neighbors, "I fought in Korea because I believed in what this country stood for—now I know I was wrong."

• Charlie Parness, a systems analyst active in community affairs, who was also outraged that his rights as an American citizen had been circumscribed by the court.

• Larry Dolnick, the vice-chairman of Steering Committee III. The production manager for a small manufacturer, he had been the only member of the steering committee to serve as a resident director of the UHF board. He became the group's "foreign minister," tirelessly organizing support for the strike at other Mitchell-Lama developments in the city and suburbs.

• Ben Cirlin, who drives a school bus for handicapped children. He resigned (but rejoined) the committee in three weeks. Along with Al Abrams, he handled the strike's incredible communications system, producing thousands of leaflets daily.

• Jules Honor, who works for a collection agency, at first resigned and then rejoined the committee one week before the other members were to go on trial, the most threatening period for the committee members. He shamefacedly told his friends, "I can't look at myself in the mirror."

These ten people developed a second-line leadership that could immediately replace them if they went to jail. This second group was carefully segregated from public involvement in the administration of the strike. (Eventually, *all* the members of the strike organization, including building captains and area marshals, had backup partners who could fill in if they were arrested.) The strike committee also ferreted away ten printing machines inside and outside Co-op City in case their equipment was seized.

In retrospect, all of this may seem a little melodramatic. But to most of Co-op City's tenants, winning the strike had become tantamount to family survival. They were, and are, trapped people. Soon after Co-op City opened, Rockefeller's administration had begun the destruction of rent control through vacancy decontrol. Vacant apartments were no longer available in attractive neighborhoods at rents that Co-op City tenants could afford. By the same token, the neighborhoods they had moved from were deteriorating. (Co-op City itself had sounded a premature death knell for several mid-Bronx communities, by luring so many stable tenants away all at once.) They couldn't go back and they couldn't go forward. Young families might make the leap to the suburbs, but the price of new homes was soaring and they could be mortgage-poor for decades to come. And the suburbs were out of the question for older families preparing for retirement or financing children in college.

State housing officials, and some higher members of the Carey administration, were determined to break the Co-op City strike. Lee Goodwin, Commissioner of the Department of Housing and Community Renewal and chairman of the Housing Finance Agency, a holdover from the Rockefeller administration and a surrogate for the Republicans in the legislature and in the financial community, considered the strike a threat to the fiscal security of the program and a personal affront. Her only goal was to break the strike and collect the mandated increase.

In July 1975, the rent checks were again collected by the steering committee and were submitted directly to HFA. They were then given to UHF but were sent back to the tenants because they didn't contain the mandated increases. The steering committee held on to the rejected funds. In August, they were ordered to be tried for contempt of court before Judge Alfred J. Callahan, who like his father before him was a minion of the Bronx County Democratic machine. Callahan became nervous, and sought negotiations. The tenants went to Borough President Abrams and he agreed to act as an "honest broker" and brought the contending parties together. Negotiations dragged on through late September, when Goodwin broke them off.

In the meantime, the state engaged Owen McGivern, a recently retired justice, to institute foreclosure proceedings on the project. If the foreclosure succeeded, a receiver would be appointed to run Co-op City with its $53 million annual budget and the disbursement of millions in legal fees. In October, a Bronx reform lawyer approached the state's Special Prosecutor, Maurice

Nadjari, with information that Judge Callahan had offered Bronx boss Pat Cunningham the power to name the receiver. (Another interesting fact was that McGivern's law firm, Donovan and Leisure, had submitted their fee schedule for the foreclosure action [$400,000] in May 1975, although the foreclosure itself did not begin until August.)

Early in October, the seven-week trial of the tenant leaders began. Five thousand Co-op City tenants filled the Bronx County courthouse and masses more appeared each day as the trial dragged on. Meanwhile the steering committee collected the rents, but it hid the money in various apartments and homes outside the development.* When the tenants were convicted of being in contempt of both Brust and Callahan, Steering Committee III received a fine of $250,000 and $5000 more for each day the rent checks were undelivered. In addition, each strike-committee member was fined $25,000 plus $5000 a day. Callahan hit the steering committee with a separate $50,000 fine plus $5000 for each day the money was withheld, and the individual defendants with a $10,000 fine and continuing fines of $1000 a day. Bank accounts were seized and safe deposit boxes were sealed. The court even managed to find a joint account which Ben Cirlin administered for his disabled mother. They seized it, too. In the search for assets, the court subpoenaed the defendants' spouses and threatened them with jail if they refused to testify (an action that is possible in a civil proceeding). Among them, the defendants had a total of twenty-two young children who now faced the possibility of having both parents jailed. All of the wives and Esther Smith's husband agreed among themselves to refuse to appear for any hearings about their spouses.

Soon thereafter the state staged a raid on the rent collections in the buildings, with officials bursting into Co-op City lobbies, along with city police, to snap pictures of the building captains and area marshals collecting rents. These strikers were in turn issued injunctions which, if violated, carried the possibility of jail sentences.

All this legal maneuvering had a comic side. As part of the

---

* The search for these secret hiding places was a comedy of errors. At one point, Rosen threatened publicly to deliver the rents to Governor Carey's summer retreat on Shelter Island. The state alerted the Coast Guard to be ready to board any boat that headed for the island. Rosen got wind of this and cancelled his armada. Despite other elaborate state efforts to find the money, it remained successfully hidden until after the strike was settled, when Rosen took TV newsmen on a tour of his caches and then in a rented truck delivered almost a ton of checks to the court.

foreclosure proceeding, the state had issued a massive subpoena that listed every tenant who hadn't paid his rents. The book became an honor roll, and tenants who had been mistakenly omitted hung signs from their windows proclaiming that they too had paid their rents to the steering committee, not to the state. It was discovered that Steven Kaufman, a young machine hack who lived in the development and had become a city councilman in 1973, had paid rent plus the full increase to the state, at the same time he had been vowing support for the strike and encouraging others to withhold their rents. Kaufman couldn't show his face in public for several weeks, and he is not expected to be re-elected in 1977.

The strike had dragged on for six long months when the authors of this book brought Charles Rosen together with a prominent and widely respected figure in Democratic politics who put him in touch with New York's Secretary of State, Mario Cuomo, a man with a deep commitment to saving neighborhoods who, before entering public life, had used his many negotiating skills to resolve two major housing crises in Queens. It had been Cuomo who saved many private homes in Corona that had arbitrarily been scheduled for demolition for a school site, and Mayor Lindsay had appointed him to work out a compromise over a proposed public housing project that was bitterly resisted by the middle-class residents of Forest Hills. Rosen and Cuomo quickly arrived at a memorandum of understanding in February 1976, but the strike dragged on for another seven months because of the resistance of Commissioner Goodwin and Republican legislators.

Inevitably, the economic struggle for fair rents became a political struggle for effective representation. The people had been betrayed by the Democratic machine: The receivership offer made to Cunningham was widely publicized, and Kaufman's cheap little betrayal was a constant topic of conversation. Machine judges were persecuting the rent-strike leaders. Then another bombshell burst. The local machine assemblyman, Alan Hochberg, approached Rosen with an "offer." At our urging, Rosen went to the Special State Prosecutor, Joe Hynes, and was wired with recording equipment before he agreed to meet with Hochberg again. Then, in a Yonkers diner, Hochberg offered Rosen a "no-show" job and financial support in any future race for public office if Rosen would simply not oppose Hochberg in the approaching Democratic primary. Hochberg claimed he needed to serve only one more term in the Assembly before being promoted to a judgeship. He was subsequently indicted and tried for corrupt use of authority and making unlawful payments. After a skillful prosecution by Robert Hill Schwartz, Hochberg was convicted on December 15, 1976.

The angry rent strikers merged with the fledgling reform Democrats in the Bronx and decimated the machine candidates in two separate primary elections in 1976. Ironically, their sweep of thirteen out of sixteen judicial delegates in September provided the additional strength needed by reformers in both Manhattan and the Bronx finally to break Patrick Cunningham's stranglehold on the courts. If the delicate reform alliance struck with certain ghetto politicians can be strengthened in future judicial conventions, court patronage—the remaining stronghold of the machines in these two counties—can be effectively destroyed.

On June 29, 1976, the memorandum of understanding between the tenants and the state was approved. It provided that the tenants would assume management of Co-op City for six months in return for delivering all monies collected during the rent strike and promising to meet all mortgage interest payments. For the first time, the "cooperators" would be issued the stock shares that had been previously held by the UHF management. They would for the first time democratically elect their own board of directors. No rent increases would be imposed during this time. Most importantly, they had embarked on the largest experiment with tenant management ever undertaken in the United States.

If real, grass-roots democracy in housing can be made to work in Co-op City, there is no reason why it can't be made to work throughout urban America.

Commissioner Goodwin resigned shortly after the Co-op City strike was settled, her power and political clout exhausted. At one point, Vice-President Nelson Rockefeller had urged Governor Carey to back her anti-strike position, and rumor has it that Rockefeller had also advised him to send the strikers to jail—an automatic Rockefeller reaction to strikes of all kinds. Carey was furious but kept his feelings to himself (as always), and did nothing to ruffle the feathers of the strategically placed Senate Republicans until the legislative session ended. Then he assented to the strike compromise.

Commissioner Goodwin's departure sweetened the tenants' victory, and they believed they would now get cooperation from the housing bureaucracy. But this was a mistake. Goodwin's successors (there have been two) were obstructionist at best and overtly hostile at worst. Whenever Rosen sought cooperation, the bureaucracy attempted to "hang tough," creating a series of mini-crises. The pettiness was astounding. For months, mail for the new Co-op City management was still sent to the ousted UHF at its Manhattan headquarters. (When Rosen told them he would not pay his bills until they learned to readdress his mail to the Bronx, the mail suddenly began arriving promptly at the Co-op City office.) The bureaucrats also refused to sanction routine actions of the new board that had been proforma in the past. Rosen dissolved the board and ousted the state representative until they came to their senses.

Despite these actions, the new directors have forged ahead with management reforms. Their first objective is to convert Co-op City's power plant from a liability to an asset. The local congressman, Jonathan Bingham, has won the support of New York City's entire congressional delegation for a feasibility study by the Federal Energy Research and Development Administration of upgrading the facility, and the plan under study involves fueling a full-capacity power plant with methane gas produced from garbage at the nearby Pelham dump. New York State is committed to develop just such a facility for Con Ed on Staten Island, and if the feds build the Co-op City facility instead, the state can save $42 million and the city will be relieved of the need to pay additional millions of dollars for shipping Bronx garbage to a Staten Island landfill. The tenants then would sell the power plant to the State Power Authority in return for a $6 million annual payment and electricity for the development at cost. This would reduce the current annual Co-op City deficit of $10 million by 60 per cent, and assure stable power costs from a pollution-free source for decades to come.

The new board of directors also has an ambitious plan to maximize income from existing and potential commercial tenants in Co-op City. They are trying to convert the roofs of eight large parking garages into commercial facilities such as tennis courts, swimming pools, restaurants, and health clubs for the recreation-starved North Bronx. They are also offering developers vacant land on the adjacent Hutchinson River for all-weather tennis courts and a marina. Space in the modernistic educational park, including an 1800-seat auditorium and a 200-seat planetarium and theater-in-the-round, would be offered for concerts, theatrical performances, and community events. "We offer an audience that includes not only the entire northeast Bronx but all of southern Westchester, as well as excellent modern facilities," says Rosen. "We're hopeful that everyone from the Metropolitan Opera to Broadway shows will recognize that they can substantially enlarge their audience by coming into the community at a time when cultural institutions locked into midtown Manhattan are dying."

"Sweetheart" leases with commercial tenants already on the site are a major target of this drive to increase revenue to offset operating costs. These leases were given for periods ranging from fifteen to forty-five years, with no provision for rising costs (especially electricity, which is currently supplied at prices way below what the development itself must pay).

The most exciting innovations have taken place in the day-to-day operation of the mammoth complex. Individual tenants in Co-op City are now involved at almost every level, including the negotiation of contracts with outside vendors and supervision of work done on the premises. They have proved once more that the only true "experts" on urban services are the people who use them.

Let's look at one small example. Laundry rooms in each of the thirty-five buildings had been owned and operated by the housing company. During the strike, they were closed and badly vandalized. Since tenants are forbidden to have individual washers and dryers in their apartments (to avoid wasting electricity), loss of the service was a serious hardship and restoring it was made a high priority by the strike committee. A committee of tenants was appointed to solve the problem. The decision was made to hire an outside contractor to maintain the facilities and repair the machines. The tenant committee examined a number of bids and set special requirements. One member of the committee, the bus driver Ben Cirlin, whom Rosen calls a "machine buff," went out and independently evaluated the available equipment in terms of power efficiency, reliability, etc. The committee then specified the brand of machine it wanted. The final contract assures that the project will receive a minimum payment of $520,000 a year from the private contractor, who now has full responsibility for maintaining not only the machinery but the upkeep of the laundry rooms themselves. "And we'll count the money as it comes out of the machines to make sure we get every penny we're entitled to," explains Rosen. The new contract will provide much more profit to the cooperative than the previous arrangement, and better service to the tenants.

The new management has already abolished more than $100,000 in unnecessary bureaucratic jobs and has adopted a policy of upgrading jobs and hiring new workers from among project residents wherever possible. The security force, for instance, has hired several residents who were young city cops laid off during the city budget cutbacks.

"People who live here are going to do a better job because they are working for themselves and their families. By the same token, we want every worker in the development, whether he lives here or not, to know that he will receive better jobs as he increases his skill. Nobody should begin shoveling shit and then retire thirty-five years later, still shoveling shit. That's what breaks workers' spirits and leads them to goof off or do a lousy job. We wrote upgrading into the union contract for the first time," Rosen states.

Among other reforms under way are:

• A computer system, designed by tenant volunteers who work in the industry, which will not only handle rent checks and other routine paperwork but allow the new management to make work assignments and control inventory. The previous management had spent $28,000 to design just such a system but had never installed it, renting a computer from UHF for issuing rent bills.

• The community newspaper, which had been subsidized by more than $100,000 annually under the old management, now makes money for the development and is completely self-sustaining.

• The board of directors is seeking to activate the single generator in the existing power plant to provide baseload power for as many as seven buildings of the complex, which could save $250,000 a year.

• Lawyers and accountants have been put on annual retainers rather than being allowed to charge by the hour for their services.

Individually each of these savings is small, but together they begin to mount toward the $1-million mark. And even the minority of antistrike tenants now seem to agree that service today is better than it was before the strike. Tenant management is working at Co-op City. The important question is can it continue to work on a permanent basis, and can similar reforms emerge elsewhere in the foundering Mitchell-Lama program?

Charles Rosen is leaving his full-time job as supervisor of the project's management (his salary was paid by tenant contributions) to return to his printer's job at the *Post*. He will, however, remain active on the committee. Despite strong urgings to run for elective office, he refuses: "We all took a pledge that no leader of the steering committee could run for public office while the strike was on. As far as I'm concerned, the strike isn't over until we have solved all of our problems; this is just a truce. We proved that the ability to be influential doesn't require being an elected public official; actually it's a detriment. The worst thing about the 'sixties was the ease with which the leaders created by the people, especially the blacks, were coopted by the system. They got high-paying jobs, they were elected to office, they lost touch with the very people they were supposed to represent. I'm not non-political or anti-political, but the important thing is that the people determine the policies and then tell the politicians what to do. That's what happened here. The system has to know that there are local leaders who can't be bought, or seduced. They have to know that real power resides with people who perform jobs in factories, or stores, or offices. That is the only way we're going to begin to keep everybody honest."

Rosen would like to see the Co-op City experience produce similar changes throughout Mitchell-Lama housing, but he warns that replication will be difficult. "I'm afraid that other projects will rush into strikes without organizing first. We did everything we could to avoid a strike for as long as possible. This gave us a chance to learn their game. The important thing was we demystified the bureaucrats' mumbo jumbo. We explained bonds and mortgages in terms that everyone could understand, a loan from their credit union or their Mastercharge card. Then we told them, 'Okay, now just add a few zeros.' The experts lose their false authority when you make everybody an expert. The important thing is that each housing company is special and no one wants to do the hard job of concretely evaluating each situation.

"In the long run, we may not win. We have taken on incredibly powerful forces in the private sector who are married to the bureaucracy. For instance, we proposed that all Mitchell-Lama projects do joint purchasing. This would save millions. It took fifteen weeks for the state to even reply to our request for a meeting to discuss it. Every management company out there was opposed, even though their developments would obviously benefit. If tenants make these kinds of proposals, what do they need professional managers for? There are some very powerful people with a stake in the existing inefficiencies; that's where their profits come from."

If the twenty-two-year history of Mitchell-Lama is any guide, Rosen's pessimism is well placed. Vast profits have been made by developers, builders, bankers, contractors, and managers, while the tenants have seen their rents rise and their amenities disappear. Now both the state and city programs have reached the breaking point: No new projects are being built and existing projects are incapable of meeting their operating and debt costs. If Co-op City and other housing developments like it go under, the real losers will be not only the tenants but the taxpayers of New York State, who will have to pick up the bill. The bureaucrats and the "experts" have failed. The tenants are the only force left that can make things work, and they have clearly earned the chance to try.

NEW YORK 13 CITY NEED NOT DIE

Can New York be saved? Is it too late? Are there specific government programs and policies that can still make a difference?

We want to think so. There is nothing inevitable about the life cycle of cities. No one is predicting the death of Paris, Amsterdam, or London, and they are much older than New York. Neighborhoods like SoHo—once filled with light industry, now a thriving residential and artistic haven—have been regenerated, so why not other communities in the city? Italian, working-class Belmont, in the Bronx, has preserved its vitality, so why not other neighborhoods?

To begin with, any agenda for the restoration of New York must start from a national vision. New York City by itself does not have the power, or the authority, to alleviate unemployment, print currency, control interest rates, tax its suburbs, or receive an equitable share of federal economic assistance. And federal programs are essential to any long-term solution to the economic predicament of New York.

America, as always, seems in jeopardy of becoming two nations:

a wealthy, growing, satisfied Sunbelt in the South and Southwest, and an impoverished, withering, bitter slum belt in the Northeast quadrant. New York's problems are also the problems of Philadelphia, Providence, Detroit, Cleveland, Newark, Utica, Bridgeport, Buffalo, Yonkers, Gary, Boston, Jersey City, and Pittsburgh.

The Sunbelt is prospering for reasons deeper than the mass production of air conditioners, and its sunny climate. The national government, beginning during the New Deal, devised a consciously compensatory policy of assisting underdeveloped areas of the nation. As a result of RFC, the Federal Housing Administration, the Federal Farm Mortgage Corporation, the Tennessee Valley Authority, the Electric Home and Farm Authority, millions of federal dollars were channeled into the depressed regions of the South and Southwest. It was an appropriate national policy at that time to give economic priority to the regions with the lowest living standards, the greatest hardship, the slowest growth rate.

Since the Depression of the 1930s, many national policies have nourished and encouraged the prosperity of the Sunbelt, at the expense of the Northeast. The Highway Trust Fund and national transportation policy subsidized Houston, Phoenix, and Los Angeles with interstate highways, but starved the New York subways and the Northeast rail corridor. Farm subsidy programs, like cotton price supports, helped speed the introduction of mechanized farming in the South. But this threw hundreds of thousands of unskilled agricultural laborers out of work and forced them to migrate to the alien cities of the North, where they applied for welfare. Moreover, as an article by Laurence Stern and Richard Harwood for *The Washington Post* on July 2, 1969, revealed, federal subsidies to the 10,000 richest farms in America exceeded all federal funds spent for housing the poor.

The geometric growth of the national defense budget has also been a significant factor in swelling the new economy of abundance in the Sunbelt. The fifteen states from Virginia to California contain 38 per cent of the nation's population but receive half of all the defense expenditures, including military installations and bases. The fifteen states from Maine to Minnesota hold 44 per cent of America's population, but have only 31 cents of each military dollar. New York State ranks twentieth in defense contract payrolls.

The Northeast slum belt also has to pay disproportionately high energy costs because of its climate and its need to import foreign oil, which costs $5 more per barrel than domestic oil. Five hundred kilowatts in New York City cost $3733 but only $1757 in

Houston and $1502 in Atlanta. Meanwhile, federal tax statutes have given tax subsidies and shelters to the oil and gas industry centered in Texas, Oklahoma, and Louisiana.

The Sunbelt has received dams, soil banks, agricultural extensions, land-grant colleges, and a favorable tariff policy. But Nixon and Ford allocated comparatively little for urban reconstruction.

Thus, for a generation, the federal government has been redistributing wealth and power, not from the rich to the poor, but from the Northeast to the Sunbelt. The first step toward reviving New York City has to be an end to this policy that discriminates so severely against the Northeast quadrant. For thirty years the national government has deliberately funded and favored the South and Southwest. This was a justified and successful investment strategy. But today this strategy is unfair and unnecessary. Now a period of compensatory development and legislation is required to save the entire Northeastern United States from urban death.

Here are our recommendations:

CREATE FULL EMPLOYMENT

The national unemployment rate is 7.9 per cent. That comes to 7,569,000 people out of work. In New York City, unemployment is 10 per cent; among blacks and Hispanics, 20 per cent.

The Bureau of the Census reports that the number of Americans living below the poverty level (an income of $5,469 for a family of four) increased from 23.3 million in 1974 to 25.8 million in 1975. In 1975, 4.3 million citizens were unemployed for so long that they exhausted all their unemployment benefits, compared with only two million the year before.

So the creation of productive jobs is probably the most important initiative the Carter administration can take to reduce poverty and assist the Northeast. Jobs reduce welfare. Workers pay taxes. The goal of what is called the Humphrey-Hawkins Full Employment Bill, as amended by the House Education and Labor Committee, is a maximum unemployment rate of 3 per cent within four years for all adults over the age of twenty—a goal to be accomplished through public employment programs, planning, and the stimulation of jobs in the private sector.

Having investigated and exposed some of the ripoffs in antipoverty corporations and Medicaid, we are painfully aware of the potential for waste and bureaucratic corruption in such a program. Strict management controls, constant auditing, and the exclusion of political influence would be imperative in making a public employment policy work. Eliminating the social porkbarrel must be part of any new federal effort to rescue our cities.

We are skeptical of bureaucracy. We are skeptical of centralization. We are skeptical of big federal programs. But the unavoidable fact is that only the national government has the money to create millions of jobs.

REFORM THE TAX STRUCTURE

Genuine tax reform would produce billions of dollars of additional federal revenues that could be used to restore housing and fund urban programs like day care and mass transit. A progressive tax system would also be the simplest way to equalize, at least somewhat, the maldistribution of wealth in America. The existing tax code is so distorted by exemptions, deductions, and shelters that Nelson Rockefeller admits he paid no federal income taxes for 1970.

Every year, Congressman Charles Vanick, a Democratic member of the House Ways and Means Committee, releases an analysis of corporate tax returns. His 1975 report showed that eight companies, with profits totaling $884 million, paid no federal income taxes at all for 1974, and that another eighteen companies, with $5.3 billion in profits, paid an effective tax rate of less than 10 per cent. (An individual who earns $12,000 a year pays about 15 per cent back in federal income taxes.) Vanick concluded that the biggest recipients of "undue tax favoritism" were the oil industry, the banks, and utilities. His report noted that commercial banks had been able to lower their effective tax rate from 38.3 per cent in 1961 to 11.7 per cent in 1974. A year later, his 1976 study disclosed that 148 corporations whose 1975 income tax returns were analyzed, paid an average tax rate of 21.3 per cent, although the statutory tax rate for corporations is 48 per cent.

An excellent summary of the necessary tax reforms is contained in the book *Tax Politics*, by Robert Brandon, Jonathan Rowe, and Thomas Stanton, all members of Ralph Nader's Tax Reform Research Group. The authors argue that all the existing exemptions should be replaced by direct subsidies or grants. They believe that such subsidies would be more and more difficult to legislate each year, if the voters correctly perceived them as direct appropriations of public monies to private enterprise.

The most glaring inequity in the income-tax laws is the preferential treatment of capital gains—gains from the sale at a profit of securities, real estate, or other investments—which are taxed at half the usual rate. Only one out of ten taxpayers is affluent enough to profit from capital gains. In 1974, the top one-tenth of 1 per cent of all taxpayers, those who earned more than $100,000, received 50 per cent of all benefits from capital gains. The total annual cost of this tax preference for the rich is estimated at $8.7 billion. It is indefensible to tax income earned by working at a higher rate than income derived from wealth.

Aside from the low tax rate on capital gains, the most flagrant tax inequity is the one that permits American multinational corporations to defer and evade paying taxes on their foreign earnings. Foreign taxes are taken as a dollar-for-dollar credit against federal taxes, although they are really just a cost of doing business.

Senator Edward Kennedy, the most egalitarian member of the Senate Finance Committee, has introduced legislation that would close enough tax loopholes so that the federal treasury could gain about $15 billion a year in new revenues. The author and tax-reform muckraker Philip Stern has estimated that the total amount of money lost through tax loopholes is $77 billion a year.

The first individual income tax levied by the federal government, in 1913, exempted the majority of working people and applied only to wealthy individuals. It was actually an equitable tax. But it didn't endure for long, since business interests soon ended this founding populist passion. All the recent crusades to make the tax code fairer have died in the velvet bowels of the Senate Finance Committee. The issues have been too technical for nonexperts to follow, so the privileged have made the campaign contributions, and hired the lobbyists to prevail. But tax reform remains a potentially winning issue—feasible, appealing to the self-interest of the majority, unifying the poor and the middle class against the banks, corporations, and the very rich.

FEDERALIZE WELFARE; CHANGE AID FORMULAS

For fiscal year 1976–77, New York City had an expense budget of $12.5 billion. Of that sum, 12.1 per cent went for welfare and 14.7 per cent for Medicaid. New York is not likely to become a viable economic organism until all, or most, of that dual burden is lifted by the federal government. Federalizing the cost of welfare, and a fiercely administered system of comprehensive national health insurance, would help to solve this problem for New York, and would benefit other deteriorating municipalities at the same time.

A federal assumption of welfare costs seems reasonable, since poverty is a national responsibility, and many of New York's poor arrived in this city as internal American migrants, life in other parts of the nation being unbearable. Many varieties of national health plans are up for consideration; while none is perfect, the Kennedy-Corman bill seems the best attainable version. Any system would have to be sensitive to the potential for waste, and to the need for quality care.

Another crucial thing a national administration can do to assist the Northeast quadrant would be to rewrite the formulas according to which federal dollars are distributed. Instead of basing federal grants and federal revenue-sharing on population, the government should base them on unemployment rates and cost-of-living statistics. This would concentrate federal aid on the communities and the people who need it most, and prevent better organized, middle-class and suburban constituencies from absorbing a disproportionate share.

CREATE A FEDERAL URBAN BANK

In 1975–76, debt service represented 16.9 per cent of New York City's expense budget, and in 1976–77, that figure rose to 17.6 per cent. (For 1977–78, the projected debt service, including MAC bonds, is 19.3 per cent.) Debt service today is the single largest expense for New York City, bigger than welfare, bigger than Medicaid.

The best way to alleviate this crushing burden would be to create a federal urban bank that could sell New York City securities, and other cities' paper debts, at lower interest rates than is now possible. The idea of such a bank, which was first circulated in a memo by union pension fund consultant Jack Bigel in February 1975, is based on the concept of using the power of the federal government to create a new market.

An urban bank would be a federal agency that would buy municipal debt at reasonable interest rates. It would issue its own bonds to the public in order to raise revenue, which, in turn, it would use to purchase municipal debt. New York City would be able to recall its outstanding debt, issued at interest rates as high as 9.4 per cent, and reissue it to the urban bank at a lower interest rate.

Since an urban bank would issue its own bonds at market interest rates to the general public, the bank and the federal government would be receiving *two* types of income to offset the cost of issuing the debt: the interest income from city debt issues, and the revenue from income taxes applicable to the interest on the debt issued by the bank to the public. It is even possible that an urban bank could make a profit.

In addition to providing fiscal relief to local governments, an urban bank could be a mechanism for tax reform. If fully implemented, it would remove municipal bonds as a tax shelter used by trust departments of banks, bond departments of brokerage houses, and a small number of rich people.

An urban bank, according to Bigel, would save New York City "a minimum of $210 million a year" and "would allow the city to borrow again for current needs."

Until about twenty years ago, New York City was the biggest blue-collar *and* white-collar employment center in America. Today that situation has radically changed. We have lost 600,000 jobs, mostly blue-collar, in just the last seven years. New York is now dangerously dependent on the paper economy of finance, multinational corporations, and media/advertising. In the past, the diversity of its economy always left it better able than many cities to deal with the cyclical economic wrenches characteristic of capitalism, so it suffered less than essentially one-industry cities like Detroit, Pittsburgh, or Gary at the bottom of recessions, and was always the first to begin the climb to recovery. Now it has come closer to being a one-industry city itself, and that industry looks to be the most troubled industry of late capitalism. The financial markets have been undergoing a permanent contraction/consolidation for several years and it seems clear that automation will continue to take a heavy toll among the work force in all aspects of this industry. Even if New York holds on to its position as the world's financial capital, fewer and fewer workers, requiring ever greater technical skills, will be needed to serve the sluggish arteries of capital.

At the same time, an entirely new picture of the city's economic future has been coming into focus. It is a harsh future of scarcity and conservation, not the mythical "post-industrial" society that was so effectively propagandized during the 1950s and 1960s. It should be apparent, even to those academics who have grown rich preaching the disappearance of manual labor and class struggle, that the

energy-short world of tomorrow is the reverse of the one they envisioned. It will be labor intensive, not energy intensive. We must
once again emphasize conservation and reuse of natural resources
and man-made structures, instead of constantly expanding the
"throwaway" habits that made everything—including our cities—
disposable. As population growth rates stabilize and then begin to
drop, we must develop the productive and intellectual capacities of
each individual—not only because it is the decent and liberal thing
to do, but also because we shall need their labor power to sustain
the quality of life. Decency is vindicated by necessity.

These new environmental realities give the lie to the latest pet
theory of corporate ideologues like Felix Rohatyn that the cities'
best economic bet is "planned shrinkage." While exact definitions
may differ, Rohatyn, Stephen Berger, Roger Starr, and other decision-makers apparently believe that services to the poor—hospitals,
transportation, fire, police, sanitation, and public education—should
be withdrawn, until life in poorer communities becomes so intoler-
able that the inhabitants will migrate out of New York City. (A
statewide variant on "planned shrinkage" is being promoted by
Governor Carey's Commerce Commissioner, John Dyson. He wants
to lower taxes on high-income individuals and corporations, abolish
environmental safeguards against polluters, force individual consumers to underwrite preferential utility rates for large industries,
and cut state spending on social services for the poor in order to
keep existing businesses and attract new ones to New York State.
Dyson's plan, parts of which have been implemented already,
parallels the economic "incentives" offered by many of the underdeveloped police states of the Third World.) Liberals have wasted
an extraordinary amount of time denouncing these plans as "inhu-
man" and "racist." While they are both, they contain an even greater
flaw: They won't work.

New York already has ample experience with the migration patterns of the poor to know that when life becomes unbearable on one
block, say, they will simply move to the next one over. They don't
go back where they came from because (1) in most cases, they
haven't the fare, and (2) the situation "back home" is just as bad as
it was when they fled to New York. Nor will New York's poor go
"where the jobs are," in Starr's words, because there is no such
place. By and large, the poor people we're talking about make up
what used to be called the unskilled labor force. Production lines
were the magnets which drew them from their homes, and production lines have (temporarily) gone out of style everywhere. Job

growth in other parts of America is for skilled workers. The auto industry used to be an excellent place for a hard worker with no skills to make a decent living, but today Detroit is a wasteland. Even the dismal profession of coal mining has been broadly mechanized. Textiles, furniture, even toys and novelties—all focuses for unskilled labor in the past—are experiencing mini-depressions because of competition from slave-states such as South Korea, Haiti, and, increasingly, Brazil.

No, the poor will remain in cities like New York no matter how much we "shrink" the already minimal government services they are now receiving. And the blight that follows them—redlining, housing abandonment, the collapse of health services, drug use, and crime—will engulf larger and larger sections of the city, until we abolish poverty by providing job training and decent jobs for the potential work force that constitutes most of the welfare poor.

This is our last and only hope. How can it be accomplished? By almost any standard, New York is well adapted to the new shape of our environmental future. Cities, by the very nature of their intensive development of land, are energy efficient. One eighty-family apartment house with one central-heating system is far more efficient than eighty private homes spread over dozens of acres. A subway car is at least 100 times more efficient than 100 private automobiles traversing the same distance. Large office buildings and multistoried industrial structures combine the same economies. Since it is most unlikely that anyone in the foreseeable future will make the breakthrough to a safe, cheap, reliable, and inexhaustible energy supply (the modern equivalent of the medieval alchemist's search for a formula that would turn stone into gold), we must begin immediately to use the resources we have with extreme care. This reality makes cities the wave of the future. If they didn't exist, we would have to invent them.

New York is still the heart of America's largest, and still richest, internal market, the industrial Northeast. The city must return to its basic activities of manufacturing, assembling, and shipping the products needed by that market. As the cost of shipping goods over long distances grows, the city's economic attractiveness grows with it. The key task is to create the economic infrastructure—railroads, new factories, and especially a modern port—that will enable us to exploit the energy-scarce future whose contours are so clearly visible. Industrial rebirth will provide tens of thousands of jobs at the skill-level possessed by those who live here. We may even once again find ourselves growing because of an influx of opportunity-seeking migrants. History has played stranger tricks on the Cassandras of the past.

REBUILD THE RAILROADS; RESTORE THE PORT

Incredible as it may seem, New York City is the only major American city without direct rail freight access. Freight cars destined for New York from the West must be routed north to Albany where they cross the Hudson and travel south, a ridiculously circuitous route. The Institute for Public Transportation (IPT) estimates that this raises the cost of each car-load by $198 and adds two to three days to an average trip. It adds $100 million a year to freight charges for New York, according to the Institute.

Until a few years ago, rail freight crossed the Hudson on an ancient wooden bridge at Poughkeepsie, and the additional cost to shippers was about half what it is today. When the bridge burned down, it was supposed to be replaced by new construction paid for with state transportation bond monies, but the financial crisis has kept the bonds from the market. Actually, there is no reason to use either the Poughkeepsie or the Albany route since an existing rail tunnel crosses the Hudson and enters New York directly, at 34th Street, right behind Penn Station. Railroad companies used to claim that this tunnel was too small for freight cars and could be used only for passenger cars—a charge that enabled them to extort extra payments for "lighter" cars, i.e. cars placed on barges and floated across the river. (This was a classic ripoff by the railroad robber barons, and gives a good idea of why the privately owned railroads went bankrupt.) But, as IPT director Robert Rickles has shown, the railroads artificially "shrank" the tunnel by raising its roadbed by three feet. While this effectively barred larger freight cars, the Hudson tunnel is still actually larger than the existing Detroit River and St. Clair river tunnels that provide freight service for Detroit.

Limited direct freight service for New York City could thus be resumed immediately, and larger piggyback trailers could soon be accommodated if the tunnel trackbed were lowered three feet to its original level. Rail freight destined for the city, Westchester County, Long Island, and the bedroom communities of Connecticut is currently unloaded in New Jersey and transferred to trucks. Yet severe traffic congestion costs New York businesses at least $100 million each year. Restoring rail service would reduce traffic congestion and pollution in New York City and its suburbs by 2000 trucks a day. It would also mean the equivalent of a $200-million tax cut for shippers and their customers. More importantly, it would permit the industrial development of hundreds of acres of vacant and un-utilized land adjacent to the rail lines, and the intense development of existing land in and above railyards. This is New York's richest development frontier.

The Carter administration is committed to upgrading the North-east rails generally, something its truck-oriented Republican pre-decessors carefully avoided. This will be a major shot in the arm for the entire region, and an especially hopeful sign for the Port of New York. In the last five years, the port has lost 20,000 jobs. Much of this loss has been because of a continuing revolution in ocean shipping—the containerization of cargo so that it moves from a truck bed or freight car directly into the hold of a ship without ex-tensive unpacking and repacking. New York has lagged behind other ports in establishing the new facilities needed for this tech-nology.

With improved rail links to dockside, however, and with the completion of at least two container ports (whose construction was arrested by the fiscal crisis), this trend could be reversed. A third container port should be constructed in the Hudson River at 34th Street, adjacent to the Penn Central yards now designated as a pos-sible site for a white-elephant convention center.

All of these projects should be undertaken by the Port Authority of New York and New Jersey, an immensely wealthy monstrosity that grew rich servicing the automobile instead of dealing with the development of the port and mass transit—its original mandate. The Port Authority is run by a handful of bankers and Wall Street lawyers who have used its resources for the pleasure of bondholders and banks, not for the people of the region. The Authority's defiance of governmental demands is one more example of the astounding power of the permanent government over the elected government. It is a mockery of democracy.

The best index of how much elected officials like Hugh Carey really want true economic development will be the stance they take toward the Port Authority. Today it is one of the few non-federal agencies capable of funding major public works to provide new jobs in the New York City area. In 1975, it had reserves of $267 million, which could generate at least $2 billion in new spending for the port and for long overdue mass-transit improvements. Instead, these reserves have been invested by the banks in federal debt and other financial obligations.

High on any construction agenda for the Port Authority should be the completion of a new rail tunnel under the harbor (actually begun and then abandoned in the 1920s) which would link Staten Island with Brooklyn. This would provide a direct route for rail freight and mass transit from Long Island to New Jersey and finally tie together the five boroughs in a coherent transit network. The facility could be built for $1 billion and would pay for itself in ten years. Since the Arab countries alone are expected to purchase $163 billion in American-made goods in the next five years, ocean shipping from a port like New York should experience a vast renaissance. But the Port Authority stands as the major obstacle to New York City's getting its fair share of this commerce.

REFORM THE BANKING SYSTEM; END REDLINING

The banks have been the central villain of this book. Frankly, this was not our original thesis. But the deeper we probed, the more interviews we conducted, the more we realized that behind almost every horror stood a banker.

The banks, through their participation in the panic selling of city securities, provoked the "crisis" of March 1975—and then profited from it. The savings banks redlined New York and siphoned its vast capital to other states and cities. The banks made excessive profits by charging the city extortionate rates of interest. They organized a credit boycott of New York in the spring of 1975. They threw their depositors' money away on phony "loans" to mask the inevitable default of the UDC.

Democratizing and limiting the extraordinary power of banks will obviously be a difficult task. But since Sisyphus is one of our political heroes, we believe the effort must be made. "The struggle itself . . . is enough to fill a human heart," Camus wrote. "One must imagine Sisyphus happy."

The first objective in reforming the banks should be greater disclosure, combined with stricter regulation. The two federal agencies that regulate banks are the Federal Reserve Board and the Office of Controller of the Currency. As long as Arthur Burns remains as chairman of the Federal Reserve, there is little hope that it will do anything except what it has done in the past—protect the banks from their mistakes and, whenever necessary, pass the costs of those mistakes along to the American taxpayer. Given the way Burns has manipulated economic policy to aggrandize the aims of corporate planners, the only hope is that his power can be weakened by a determined president and Congress and, in the best possible situation, that he can be forced from office. The Controller of the Currency is appointed by the president and can insist upon significant changes in disclosure regulations: disclosure of all loans, including loans made to bank directors, disclosure of municipal security holdings, and breakdown of domestic loan portfolios by basic industry.

It is urgent that Congress act as a second line of defense for the public, demanding important information from the banks and making it available to the press. The difficulty involved here was amply demonstrated in the fall of 1975 when, in the midst of a critical investigation of the banks' growing dependency on deposits by the oil-exporting nations, the Senate subcommittee on multinational corporations meekly surrendered to a combined offensive by the banks, the Federal Reserve, and the Treasury. A year passed before the details of this disgraceful episode became public.

As Alex Cockburn and James Ridgeway disclosed in the November 15, 1976, *Village Voice,* the bankers simply refused to tell the subcommittee either the extent of deposits they held from the OPEC nations, or the amounts of loans made by private banks to foreign nations. Since approximately half of these loans are insured by U.S. taxpayers, this is a particularly arrogant attitude. Congress naturally has the power to subpoena the records, but subcommittee chairman Frank Church pulled back from a direct confrontation. Instead, he floated one compromise after another to meet the banks' objections that disclosure was "bad business" and might lead the OPEC countries to put their money in Switzerland. Finally, browbeaten within his own committee by Charles Percy of Illinois and Stuart Symington of Missouri, Church agreed to allow the banks to submit the information through the Fed, in what would, in fact, be a meaningless form. The final indignity was that the deal had first to be approved by Chase Manhattan Bank's David Rockefeller.

Direct methods for dealing with the perfidy of redlining are available. The state legislature should enact a law that would mandate savings banks—and insurance companies—to invest at least 25 per cent of all their new mortgages in neighborhoods that are now denied credit. Also at least 75 per cent of all the mortgages given by the city and state employee pension funds should be within the city or the state.

The legislature should place a ceiling on interest rates. City and state governments, and public authorities, should end their policy of favoring banks by depositing public monies in non-interest-bearing accounts.

We cannot permit a savings bank to prosper on deposits from a neighborhood by investing that money in a shopping mall in Dallas or a sewer system in San Diego, to redline the community of its own depositors, and to close the local branch when the neighborhood begins to decay. We cannot forget that banks are creations of the chartering power of democratic government. We must compel banks to behave in the public interest, and in the interest of their depositors. If they do not, they should lose their charters and their right to make their money with our money.

GET TOUGH ON CRIME: CERTAINTY OF PUNISHMENT

In some ways crime may be New York's deepest and most intractable disease, because effective remedies seem so problematic. We know that crime is driving taxpaying families and businesses out of the city. We know that the crime rate is rising each year. A month does not go by without some hideous homicide in the city: an elderly woman beaten to death in her apartment for pennies, a young woman walking her dog stabbed to death in Central Park, a shopkeeper shot to death by a junkie in Brooklyn.

The fear of crime has become a prison for many citizens of the city. Many old people subsist on the food neighborhood children will buy for them, because they are afraid to venture out alone into the street. In the South Bronx, on the Lower East Side, in Times Square, hunting gangs of what former Bronx Police Commander Anthony Bouza memorably called "feral youth" terrorize people.

Liberals and radicals have often been reluctant to face the crime problem squarely. (In 1968, Eugene McCarthy equated any mention of crime with a covert appeal to racist voters, not realizing how concerned minorities were about their own safety.) In no other area is what we think we are supposed to think more at odds with what we do think, if we are honest about our experience and our real feelings.

We believe that in the short run, one effective remedy against violent street crime is swift punishment and significant penalties for those found guilty.

In the fall of 1976, a nineteen-year-old named Ronald Timmons was arrested in the Bronx after he was caught beating and robbing an elderly woman. He was released on $500 bail, because the judge did not have legal access to Timmons's confidential juvenile criminal record. This juvenile record included seventeen arrests, and an accusation of murdering a ninety-two-year-old man in 1972. Timmons immediately jumped bail. The confidentiality of juvenile records seems to us less important than the prospect of a murderous youth roaming the street. We also believe that 15-year-olds in Family Court should be fingerprinted and photographed, and treated as adult offenders.

Most penologists agree that certainty of punishment is probably the most likely deterrent to crime. But there is no certainty of punishment today. Most violent juveniles know that the first couple of times they are arrested, they will simply be recycled back onto the street by the Family Court. Also, the median lapse of time in New York between arrest and trial is six months; this should be reduced to sixty or ninety days.

We have to agree with Harvard Professor James Q. Wilson, who argues in his book *Thinking About Crime* that harsher penalties against persistent violent criminals might discourage the marginal criminal from predatory offenses. Wilson believes that some portion of the criminal population is not indifferent to the likely risks and rewards of his occupation, and if the mathematical odds on serving three years for a violent mugging increased, then the criminal would think twice.

Our belief in swift, sure punishment, however, does not mean we have any sympathy for the extreme remedies conservatives promote, like capital punishment, Rockefeller's drug law, or other notions based on *severity* rather than *certainty* of punishment. All we are saying is that liberals have been too slow to recognize that there is some value in prison terms for recidivist violent criminals. And that freedom from fear to walk the street is also a civil liberty that needs protection.

A fifteen-year-old who commits a homicide should be treated as an adult. A nineteen-year-old who is convicted of a second violent robbery should go to prison for four or five years. Many of the teenagers who commit violent crimes may be psychotic, in the sense that they have no feelings of guilt and may not know right from wrong. There are no existing facilities in which to treat such offenders adequately. Certainly the prisons and juvenile facilities offer scant programs geared to rehabilitation. But, nevertheless, we think that even without hope of rehabilitation, those guilty of violent crimes should be incarcerated, just to separate them from, and to protect, the rest of society.

All this said, prison reform and rehabilitation should be high-priority goals, and probably together are the best preventive method to combat violent crime. But our experience is that private organizations like the Fortune Society have been more successful in accomplishing individual rehabilitation than any of the agencies of government, especially in the realm of therapy and self-image.

History has chosen to remember its most brutal cultures by their prisons. Stalin by the Gulag; the Nazis by Auschwitz and the other concentration camps; the South Vietnamese under Ky and Thieu by the tiger cages; the Chilean junta by the prison ship *Esmeralda*. And America by Attica.

We have visited Attica, Clinton, Greenhaven, and the Tombs when it was open. There can be little question that these New York prisons, like so many others, cause rather than cure crime. Men come out of prison ten times more bitter and antisocial than they were on entering it. They meet potential crime partners and learn more subtle criminal skills in prison. Prison reform—including job and psychiatric counseling and conjugal visits—is imperative. So is removal of all the licensing provisions that now discriminate against and deny employment to ex-offenders in more than fifty different job classifications.

In the long run, the causes of crime remain unemployment, racism, lack of education, and drug addiction. But poverty is only a reason for crime, not an excuse. The enormity of the crime problem demands a simultaneous attempt at finding immediate, short-term remedies. Otherwise we are setting the stage for a demagogue to exploit and manipulate our fear.

Stricter, swifter criminal sanctions, especially against the hunting juvenile gangs, is a distasteful, simplistic solution whose time has come.

CREATE AN EFFICIENT TAX-COLLECTION SYSTEM

In November 1976, the director of the New York State Taxation and Finance Agency acknowledged that his department fails to collect $300 million each year in sales taxes and $353 million in income taxes. When all the state's potential revenues are calculated, the total tax loss in New York State may actually be as much as $1 billion annually. The city loses an additional $1 billion in taxes each year, as we have detailed. If a conscientious effort were made to collect these revenues, the fiscal situation would be radically altered —without the imposition of new taxes.

Other massive tax frauds have gone uncorrected for decades. It was recently revealed that the New York Telephone Company has avoided the payment of sales taxes on $1 billion in long-distance calls originating within the state. Life insurance companies keep vast tax-free reserves amounting to more than $2 billion annually by using ridiculously outdated mortality tables and understated rates of return on investment to cheat the state of at least $200 million a year and to maintain artificially high premium structures for their subscribers. Stiffer regulation could produce an additional $250 million a year for vital services like mass transit, schools, and housing.

Tax cheating on states and localities is endemic and universal throughout the country. The additional revenue from efficient enforcement of the tax code would be so great that not only could services be improved, but tax rates on lower-income families and property owners could actually be lowered across the board.

ABOLISH CERTAIN REAL-ESTATE TAX EXEMPTIONS

Because of tax exemptions, 40 per cent of New York City's property is untaxed. A decade ago it was only 33 per cent, and now the value of this tax-free real estate has risen from $15.6 billion to a current assessed value of $25 billion. Tax-exempt property includes land and buildings owned by religious organizations, universities, foundations, hospitals, charitable organizations, the state, the federal government, the Port Authority (including the World Trade Center), and foreign governments. If all the tax-free real estate were taxed, the city would gain more than $2 billion in revenue each year.

Our view is that at least a portion of the tax exemptions are unwarranted and should be withdrawn. For example, income-producing buildings owned by universities and hospitals are not taxed, although they receive city services like fire and police protection, and garbage collection. These properties should be taxed at the normal rate.

The definition of religious organization has been imaginatively applied, so that the properties owned by the Reverend Moon's Unification Church, by the Scientology church, and by other exotics, mystics, and swamis pay no taxes.

The Chrysler Building, owned by Cooper Union for the Advancement of Science and Art, valued at $22 million, pays no real-estate taxes. St. Patrick's Cathedral and its land are worth $25 million, but no taxes are collected. Apartment buildings owned by voluntary hospitals and used by their staffs are tax-exempt. State-owned buildings, valued at $44 million, pay no taxes. The property owned by Columbia University is valued at $44 million, and this wealthy and politically influential institution is tax exempt. The Boy Scouts and the YMCA also have tax exemptions.

Many of these tax exemptions were given in a better economic climate. New York City now cannot afford to have $25 billion of its most precious asset—real estate—off the tax rolls.

In February 1971, Richard Lewisohn, then the city's Finance Administrator, urged the state legislature to allow the city to tax the Port Authority on the basis of gross rents from leased property. Lewisohn said that on such a formula, the Port Authority would pay the city annual real-estate taxes of $66 million, instead of the ludicrous $2.6 million "in-lieu-of-taxes" payment the Port Authority made to the city in 1970. The bankers and brokers who control the surplus-rich Authority ignored Lewisohn's prophetic proposal.

At this point in New York City's history, we think every real-estate tax exemption should be reconsidered case by case. The Port Authority, state and federal governments, and affluent private institutions should be compelled to pay their fair share. The World Trade Center, the Rockefeller Foundation, and Columbia University can surely afford to pay real-estate taxes.

Experts estimate that the city might recover between $300 and $500 million a year if all the obviously unworthy, political, and frivolous tax exemptions were abolished.

MUNICIPALIZE CON EDISON

High utility rates are damaging the economies of all the states in the Northeast quadrant. The worst offender of all is the Consolidated Edison Company of New York. We have already described how the public regulation of privately owned monopoly utilities is an expensive charade from the consumers' point of view. The time has come, we think, to go to the root and institute a series of takeovers of utilities, starting with Con Ed.

As might be imagined, the legal mechanism for a public takeover is cumbersome, but far from impossible. (The small upstate city of Massena has recently rejected the giant Niagara Mohawk monopoly and set up its own public power system.) New York City and Westchester County would have to schedule simultaneous referendums at which time the people would be asked to vote for condemnation of Con Ed's properties. Such a vote is likely to pass. PASNY—the state regulatory agency—could then be instructed by state comptrollers have discovered waste, laxity, inefficiency, and various abuses in almost every agency of city government, from the concession contracts awarded to vendors by the Department of Marine and Aviation, to rental leases signed by community school boards. Moreover, as we have demonstrated, the taxpayers lose money through political favors like interest-free bank deposits, reduced real-estate tax assessment, patronage jobs, and city leases with private landlords.

In general, we believe, with Louis Brandeis, that sunlight and publicity are "the best disinfectant." We believe that merit, accountability, and disclosure are three principles that can help clean up a municipal government and party structure that thrives on legal graft.

Some of the specific reforms we have in mind to foster frugality and integrity in government include:

• Truly competitive bidding on all city contracts and leases above a nominal amount should be instituted. Disclosure of all equity partners in companies doing business with the city should be required.

• Members of the Board of Estimate should be disqualified from voting on projects involving anyone who has contributed more than $500 to their last campaign.

• No member of the state legislature should be allowed to represent a client before a state regulatory agency. This practice was an element in the nursing-home scandal, and the legislature has twice defeated efforts to abolish this conflict of interest.

• Lobbyists should be required publicly to disclose and itemize all their expenditures and all their contacts with members of the legislature.

• Party and legislative leaders like Pat Cunningham, Stanley Steingut, Vincent Albano, Meade Esposito, and John Calandra should be compelled to withdraw from their law firms, insurance companies, and banks that do business, even once removed or indirectly, with city and state government. Party leaders should be salaried; in the long run, this will probably save the taxpayers' money.

• Every level of government should hire more auditors. When the nursing-home scandal broke open in 1974, the State of New York had fewer than twenty auditors on the payroll, with responsibility for auditing for more than 2000 health-care facilities.

• There should be independent, professional selection committees for all engineering, architectural, and construction contracts let by the city.

• We need merit appointment, by independent screening panels, of all judges, including State Supreme Court justices, who were not even mentioned in Governor Carey's last "court reform" legislation.

• There should be a permanent state-wide prosecutor for all Medicaid related fraud. Joe Hynes, the special prosecutor for nursing homes, obtained 78 indictments of nursing-home owners, administrators, vendors, and public officials between January 1975 and December 1976. He identified $30 million in fraud he believes can be recovered. And his legal jurisdiction does not include private hospitals, Medicaid bills, methadone clinics, or health-related facilities.

The future is unknowable. With Antonio Gramsci, we are pessimists of the intelligence, and optimists of the will.

They have done their worst to us—the banks; Nelson Rockefeller; Lindsay, Beame, Nixon, Ford, and lesser politicians; the muggers; the Sunbelt; the permanent government. Our services have been cut. Cops and firemen are unemployed. People are dying for want of a bed or a night nurse in municipal hospitals. Our children are not learning, fifty to a classroom. The upward mobility that came with a free college education is gone. Democracy is diminished.

But we are still standing. We are still here. We are survivors.

These ideas, these remedies offered, will not become law easily or quickly. We cannot trust our leaders to do all this just because it is logical, or necessary, or promised.

The most important lesson we have learned, as political citizens, is this: Reform—change for the better—comes only when movements of common people rally around an idea and create new leaders from the bottom up. Movements of ordinary people, acting out of self-interest, can write law. The moral authority of exemplary action can change lives.

Leaders sell out. Leaders get tired. Leaders get killed. But movements of our countrymen stopped the Lower Manhattan Expressway, passed the Voting Rights Act of 1965, ended the Vietnam war.

From Rosa Parks starting the Montgomery bus boycott to Frank Serpico exposing police corruption, to Charlie Rosen leading the Co-op City rent strike, common people saying *Enough!* have transformed consciousness, and altered history.

INDEX